PRIVATE
FACES

PUBLIC
PLACES

*"I AM AT THAT STAGE
IN MY LIFE WHEN A
WOMAN LOOKS BACK
WONDERING AND PONDERING.
WHAT HAS IT ALL BEEN ABOUT?"*

In public, Abigail McCarthy was the wife of Senator Eugene McCarthy, the man who changed the face of American politics. But to those who know her, Abigail McCarthy is a brilliant, sensitive individual in her own right, a vital personality who gave much of herself to her husband, her children, her country.

Now she tells her story—the good and bad, the happiness and heartbreak. It is the story of a perfect marriage that ultimately failed; the story of a campaign that began with hope in New Hampshire and ended in shocked despair in Chicago; above all, the story of a woman who through both triumph and trial continued to grow rich in wisdom and spirit.

"One of the best books in years . . . written by a most rare creature, an utterly selfless person"

PRIVATE FACES
FACES
PUBLIC
PLACES

Abigail McCarthy

CURTIS BOOKS
NEW YORK, N.Y.

Contents

Private faces in public places
Are wiser and nicer
Than public faces in private places.

—W. H. AUDEN

Prologue

I am at that stage in my life when a woman looks back, wondering and pondering . . . What has it been about? For those of us whose lives have been defined by others—by wifehood and motherhood—there is no individual achievement to measure, only the experience of life itself. And that seems so incredibly full, complicated, and various as I look back. There are the dark things: hunger, cold, loss, fear, the deaths of those who loved and nurtured me, sickness and pain, fruitless childbirth, hopes unrealized and betrayal. There are many more bright things: love and abiding friendship, the mystery of children growing and changing, the joy of intense thought, the gift of books and teachers of many kinds, the human capacity for simple fun, the pleasure of shared comfort and warmth, the great multiplicity of the people of this earth with whom one can be in some kind of communion, the simple wonder of the colors, and the sounds of the parade of life.

And for me there was a background to these things in many beautiful places of this earth and in some of the most interesting cities built by man. I have found life unfailingly interesting; I believe it has meaning. A writer I respect wrote of me in 1968 at the end of my husband's primary campaigns, "Somehow you get the idea that she's far less interested in what happens to both of them personally, than what is happening in America." But I think you can only know what is happening in the larger world by examining what happens to yourself.

1 / Beginnings

Over the years the story of how I met Eugene McCarthy became a staple of my campaign talks at luncheons and coffee hours. It is hard now to sort out the real memory from the polished little vignette I worked out. The first time I told the story to an audience was during Gene's first campaign for Congress in 1948, a year of political upset.

The Business and Professional Women of St. Paul sponsored a voter information luncheon and, in an effort to get publicity, asked that the candidates be represented by their wives who would speak, with the candidates themselves as passive members of the audience. It was a frightening prospect. The Business and Professional Women were a formidable group for any person to address and some of their national board members were going to be present. Furthermore, the press promised to be there in full force because of the gimmicky nature of the program. And finally, 1948 was probably the first year of the "speaking wife" for Minnesotans, and Minnesotans were far ahead of the rest of the nation in accepting the fashion.

At this time we were living in a converted barracks on the St. Thomas campus in St. Paul. The barracks were heated by oil space heaters. The plumbing was sketchy and keeping clean, not to mention well-groomed, was a problem. I was expecting Mary, our second child, and busy with Ellen who had just had her first birthday. The other occupant of the hut, as it was called, was our rather large water spaniel, Peva. This was before the day of chic maternity wear and my campaign wardrobe was a challenge because of our slim resources and my expanding waistline. The thought of appearing before the well-dressed business women, with the governor's wife and the wife of the incumbent congressman, a charming woman with a brief stage career behind her, terrified me. The biggest problem of Gene's campaign, however, was the problem of exposure: how to reach the voters in a monopoly newspaper city like St. Paul in the pre-television era. A candidate challenging an incumbent could be completely obscured from the general public by a silent conspiracy of the publisher and the rest of the Establishment. The luncheon would be reported. Furthermore, to refuse to appear would be to risk offending an important segment of the women's vote.

Gene's campaign committee was an extremely informal group of personal friends and representatives of some of the tattered remnants of the Farmer-Labor party and the once-powerful Democratic party. There was Ray Devine of the Machinists Union, now chief engineer at the Shiely Gravel Works; Frank Foldesi, an insurance agent; Ted Mitau, a young political science professor at Macalester College in St. Paul. They eyed me dubiously, but agreed that the speech had to be made.

On the day of the luncheon, we left Ellen in the care of Mrs. Heinrich Rommen, wife of the German-refugee professor who lived in the other section of our hut, got into our 1937 Chevrolet and started out. On the way I rehearsed my speech for Gene, but I left out the anecdote I had decided to tell about our meeting. Gene always had a horror of revealing anything personal in public and even at that time refused to use the pronoun "I" in his speeches, preferring the more generic and indefinite "we," a verbal habit which was to confuse some of his young followers in 1968.

The photographer's session preceding the luncheon was traumatic. Marcelle Devitt, wife of the Republican representative and Gene's opponent, was beautiful and chic. Mrs. Luther Youngdahl, wife of the Republican governor, was every inch the correct club woman. Marcelle and I had known each other casually in North Dakota so we were able to make small talk about old acquaintances. She was, I thought at the time, surprisingly confidential about her feelings as a congressional wife. (I was to learn in later years that what bound congressional wives together was stronger than the politics that worked to separate them.) She told me that she would be glad if her husband lost, that trying to live on the $10,000 congressional salary was impossible. I was aghast. It seemed incredible to me, a professor's wife, that one could not live on that princely amount.

The program chairman of the Business and Professional Women had plumbed every picturesque possibility of the situation by seating each candidate's wife next to her husband's opponent. So I sat down for lunch with Ed Devitt. He was a thoroughly civilized companion and I found myself trying to allay his trepidations about his wife's speech, rather than worrying about my own.

A candidate's wife making a speech is, by the very nature of things, at a terrible disadvantage. Gertrude Raymond, wife of Jack Raymond, long-time Washington and international correspondent for the New York *Times*, told me recently that she could not remember a first lady about whom the gossip in Washington and the country had been kind or admiring. This observation is true of the wives of all other officeholders as well, even the wives of mayors in the smallest hamlets. It is only a very dull woman who is unaware of the speculative curiosity mixed with hostility with which her every platform appearance is greeted. She is terrified that what she says may in some way harm her husband and inhibited because she is not speaking for herself but for him. However, from my point of view, starting out as a political wife with a swollen waist line and the ill-fitting maternity clothes of the time, the alternative—the languid wave and brilliant smile—was worse. After ten years of teaching and a modest career as a part-time lecturer, I knew that if I said something, anything, I could at least attract attention. Then, too, I had already survived the encounter with the most critical and potentially hostile audiences in existence—adolescents in high school and the early years of college. Still, I would have been glad to do what Beryl Ann Bentsen, whose husband is now a senator from Texas, said that she did in that

1948 campaign—"Honey, Ah just stayed home and let the ladies enjoy Lloyd." But in Minnesota the ladies had decreed otherwise.

It is true that Minnesota liberals gave lip service admiration to Mrs. Franklin D. Roosevelt and all Minnesotans were rather proud of the articulate and able Martha Taft, who had been one of our own. We had also known a formidable and effective political woman in the Farmer-Labor era by the name of Anna Dickey Olson, but she was a political personality in her own right—not a wife. Therefore each of us at the luncheon table that day was trying to feel her way in a situation fraught with pitfalls.

Mrs. Youngdahl's speech was a nice mixture of reminiscence, biblical quotations, and wifely indignation. I remember her leaning out and looking down the table when she said, "The children and I cannot believe that it is of our daddy people are speaking when they say some of the things being said in this campaign." I do not recall what Mrs. Devitt said, but I do remember that she used her theater-trained voice to very good effect.

When it was my turn, I found my palms wet and my hands shaking; but I remembered to use the device a teacher learns for self-preservation—to pause, to wait, to look them in the eye before beginning to speak. That moment of hesitation gets attention; from then on it is up to you to hold it. It was my first campaign speech for Gene to a large, potentially hostile, certainly indifferent group and I think my campaign style evolved right there. I believed passionately in his probity and his idealism so my deep sincerity was inevitable. Then I sought to make the most of those qualifications which would mean a great deal to that particular audience. I stressed Gene's academic credentials. I stressed the need for youth in the leadership of the postwar period, of the returning veteran and the multiplication of new problems. The elaboration on Gene's particular academic qualifications in sociology and economics seemed to me very important, because in Minnesota, then as now, an educated man is a respected man.

Finally, I tried for the personal bond and the human touch that I knew as a person and as a woman I myself would want.

"I must tell you how I met Gene McCarthy," I said. "I met

him for the first time when he—and I know this audience will appreciate my feelings—got the job I wanted and he got it because he was a man. I was furious and I didn't plan to give him a very warm reception or much of a helping hand. But when I met him, I saw that he was a very handsome man, and within three weeks, I learned that he was a man of great capability and goodness as well. I decided he was the man for me and three weeks from now I hope that you will decide he is the man for you!"

And that's the way I've told the story ever since.

It wasn't really quite that way. It is of the way it really was that I want to remember now. I want to tell that story for our children and for all the people who have lived, as we have, through these times of great change, because in the remembering I have struggled with the questions of life and with experience in terms of one relationship: my marriage to Gene McCarthy. The relationships which preceded our meeting, those which flowered from it, and all the relationships through the years which were part of it or impinged upon it. Where are our roots? What abides? What changes? What is love? What is vocation? Why do we live? I do not have answers, but my experience reflects light on the questions.

I have to think hard to remember how it was in Mandan, North Dakota, that fall of 1936, even though Mandan is a town I love to remember. It is the place in which I was first on my own, Abigail Quigley, nobody's niece, nobody's daughter, just the new teacher in town. So it was the scene, I suppose, of my greatest adventure, the adventure of discovering just who and what I had become after twenty-one years of living. To casual tourists, Mandan, pop. 11,000, would seem just another rather raw and ugly western town in the foothills of the Missouri slope, but I remember it as a place of high, wide, blue skies and beckoning, undulating plains stretching without barrier to the horizon, a place of breezy western friendliness, and the place in which I first fell in love with students and teaching and the whole special world of school life.

The teaching job in Mandan was like a gift from heaven to me in that Depression year. It was almost impossible for an inexperienced teacher to get a teaching position in those days—one which really paid a salary, at least. Some of my contemporaries went out to teach in private academies for $25 a month and their board and room. Others took secretarial and clerical jobs at $65 a month rather than accept the overloaded roles assigned to teachers in the rural towns of the Midwest. The hope of getting into a city school system was a hope to be long deferred. After a long apprenticeship in small towns, one could hope eventually to make it into Minneapolis, St. Paul, or Duluth. I was the first inexperienced teacher that Mandan—a city by Dakota standards—had employed in years; and that the job opening existed at all was owing to a curious combination of circumstances.

Purely as a matter of accumulating credits, I had acquired a German major at the College of St. Catherine in St. Paul, second to my chosen major area of study—English literature. The German teacher in Mandan had suddenly, after years of trying and a week after school had started, been offered a position in California, the mecca of all schoolteachers in those days. Without so much as a by-your-leave and farewell to the school board, he had walked out the door and gotten on a train to California. Hence, Mandan suddenly had a vacancy for a teacher of German and English, an almost unheard of combination; and I, a recent college graduate still unemployed a week after school started in the fall of '36, was the only one who turned up on the lists of the teachers' agencies with those particular qualifications.

I had been sadly packing my bags after a summer of fruitless applications to return to the Twin Cities to begin graduate study at the University of Minnesota. Twenty-four hours after the telegram came from the Schummer's Teachers' Agency, I was on board the Northern Pacific train for Mandan. I had a job! I had a full-fledged teaching job, and I was going to get $100 a month! And, as a bonus from St. Jude, to whom I had made novena after novena, I was going West to a different state. I had a career and I had adventure as well. This is what Mandan meant to me and Mandan also came to mean the place where I met my husband.

My return to Mandan two years later, in the fall of 1938, the year Gene came to the faculty, was also something of a coincidence. Despite my happiness at Mandan, I kept being reminded that I was not getting experience in the field for which I was really qualified and that, if I hoped to go on to English graduate work and if I hoped to go on as a teacher, I would have to get experience in that field, not in German. So each summer I dutifully applied for other positions, purely English positions, and in the summer of 1938, I finally got one at Little Falls, Minnesota, best known as the boyhood home of Charles A. Lindbergh.

I was interviewed by the superintendent in Schummer's bleak

office and signed the contract for $5.00 more a month, of which the agency would get a percentage that would almost amount to my first month's salary. Still, it meant an increase because it would not cost me anywhere nearly as much to go back and forth from Wabasha, where my home was, to Little Falls, as it had cost to go to Mandan. I left the agency with a sense of oncoming depression and walked around the block to St. Olaf's Church to make a visit, as we Catholics used to say. As I sat in the dark church where banks of vigil lights glowed in the space before the side altars, I realized that I couldn't leave Mandan just yet. I went out to find a phone booth to tell the superintendent so.

I couldn't leave Mandan—not just then—because I loved it. From the moment the first train carrying me there left Bismarck, North Dakota's capital, and crossed the bridge over the Missouri, I had known I would. It was then a bleak town of small frame houses laid out on a grid of wide streets between the Northern Pacific tracks and the bare bluffs. But I remember the sunshine and friendliness of its welcome. Lucille Dahners, a Mandan girl who had graduated from St. Catherine's before me, had read in the paper that I was coming and was waiting on the platform to greet me and take me home with her. The Dahners family took me in and helped me search for permanent quarters. In the months that followed they made their house my second home and initiated me into the ways and lore of the town. In one of our long, rambling conversations about the pioneer days I found out that I was really part of their family. Mrs. Dahners' mother had come from Minnesota and turned out to have been my grandfather's cousin. In the frontier days families scattered all over the west and often lost track of each other in a generation.

The fast-moving history of the nineteenth century had broken over Mandan in wave after wave. The town is situated near the confluence of the Heart and the Missouri rivers at the foot of the Missouri slope, where the land begins to rise slowly toward the foothills of the Rockies far to the west. It had been a trading center for the peaceful tribes of the Dakota country—the Mandans, the Arikaras, and the Hidatsas. The curious tentlike earthen homes of the Mandans had been reconstructed south of the town on the original site of a village described by Lewis and Clark. Each summer a pitiful remnant of the Mandans danced for tourists on the platform of the Northern Pacific railroad and camped by the Heart in a huddle of old cars and tattered tents. Their children played about half-naked in the stench and dust under the trees where slaughtered dogs were hung to dry amid clouds of buzzing flies.

Custer had set out, they said, from Fort Abraham Lincoln near Mandan on May 17, 1876, for the Little Big Horn and his rendezvous with Sitting Bull. There was still open range to the west of town and I learned to ride there, western style, my first year. My new-found thirteen-year-old cousin Greg Dahners and I would ride out after school in the fading light of the fall afternoons until the town dropped out of sight behind us as we went over a rise and could pretend that we were living in the early days of the West. I used to think of the women who first rode out over that lonely land knowing that they were leaving their homes for good and might never come back. And I was glad when we turned back toward town and we could see the first lights coming on in the dusk.

Greg and Lucille's mother, Alice Dahners, used to tell me stories her mother had told her about the first homesteaders. When her mother was a little girl she had heard women screaming all night long in the jail after the first spring thaw. Their husbands had brought them into town in wagons from the sod huts where they had spent the terrible Dakota winter; they were on their way to the insane asylum in Jamestown.

Alice herself remembered when Mandan had been a cattle town before the railroad had brought in German-Russian farmers and artisans to settle the area. More than half the population of Mandan and the surrounding area was now of this stock. They were a people with a strange history. They had been brought from Germany to Russia by Catherine the Great and settled in the Ukraine to improve the farming there. They were allowed to keep their Roman Catholic religion and their language. In almost the same way and for the same reasons they had been brought to North Dakota by the railroads, which advertised for settlers in the parts of Europe they thought resembled the land they wanted settled. Dakota was wheat country and it was believed that peasants from the Ukraine would be ideal. Although they were commonly called Russian and called themselves so—and indeed they must have mixed with the Slavic population because many of them were squat, rather brown-skinned, and had high Slavic cheekbones—they were essentially German. It was for their sake that German was taught in the school and it was for them, really, that I had come to Mandan.

Compared to the Minnesota towns of the period, where everything seemed to have come to a dead stop, the mood of Mandan was relaxed and cheerful. Anyone whose family had taken a chance on North Dakota in the first place had a gambler's optimism in his bones. Then, too, the combination of drouth and dust storms, added to the long farm depression, had resulted in a number of federal relief programs in North Dakota. The bureaucracy of these agencies had brought some business and some bright young men to town. Agronomic scientists were working at the Department of Agriculture experimental station. In addition to the faculty of the senior and junior high schools and the two elementary schools, there was a second faculty at the state institution for juvenile offenders which was just outside town. The county government and some state agencies were there. All this made for a transient community of young marrieds and career people who gave their business to the small stores, restaurants, rooming houses, and hotels.

Residential Mandan was rather arbitrarily divided between the west end where the bankers, doctors, and owners of the town's businesses lived—there the houses were bigger and the streets shaded by elms—and the east end where the Russians lived—railroad and creamery workers and farmers who had come to town to go on relief. The streets there were bare or lined with a few cottonwoods. Across the tracks there was a little community of tar-papered houses near the Dead Heart, a slough left when the Heart River changed its course in the restless way of western rivers.

The room the Dahnerses found for me was in the comfortable house of Mrs. Peter Rippel, a hard-working Hungarian woman who protested at first that her house was not good enough for a teacher.

12   *Private Faces/Public Places*

It was her way of expressing pleasure at the recommendation. It was a house of shining cleanliness, but the Dahnerses insisted that its chief virtue was that it was warm—a matter of vital concern in a climate where it is often 40 degrees below zero. Her husband was a butcher with a downtown meat market. He was rough-voiced and rough-mannered. We always thought of the house as Mrs. Rippel's because he seemed a visitor and he eventually became one when, a few years later, he left and set up housekeeping with another woman, in the east end.

I was the youngest teacher on the faculty, the first inexperienced one to come to Mandan in many years, and something of a novelty. The students found me more inclined than the older teachers to listen and laugh in the after-school hours and many took to "helping" me then. For my part, I discovered the wonderful zaniness of thirteen- and fourteen-year-old boys and willingly spent hours with them.

I came from a teaching family and from my earliest years schools and students, books and learning, had been staples of family conversation. My grandmother's certificate authorizing her to teach "in any common school in Minnesota" was a cherished family memento. We were proud of the fact that my father, who had graduated from Minnesota's oldest teachers college in the 1890s, had become a county superintendent of schools in his twenties and thus met my mother who spent a year teaching in a one-room school at Indian River before she went on to the University of Minnesota to complete her college work. I had aunts who taught, and cousins, and they all liked teaching. My mother's foster sister, Mary Ellen O'Shea, used to tell about setting all the pillows up on her bed when she was a little girl and "teaching" them.

The real joy of teaching and its true purpose—the communication of enthusiasm, the passing on of values, the waking of curiosity and creativity—I learned from the example of my mother's sister, Abigail O'Leary, for whom I was named. She was the greatest single intellectual influence in our lives. After my mother died when I, the oldest, was nine, we were rich in care from substitute mothers—my grandmother, by great-aunt, my father's sisters—but it was Abbie who, more than any other, had faith in us and great expectations. In 1968 her influence on me was mentioned in an article in the New York *Post* and letters from her former students began to pour in—from a rabbi on the West Coast, from a nuclear physicist, from an advertising executive, all testifying to her influence on them. "Miss O'Leary was one of the great teachers of all time," said a New York speech writer, ". . . I owe her a debt of love."

Abbie taught English and creative writing and was adviser to the school magazine at Central High School in Minneapolis. In the twenty years she was there, her students were invariably winners in the national creative writing contests sponsored by the *Atlantic Monthly*, *Scholastic*, and other magazines. During those years Central changed from the high school for the affluent of Minneapolis to a school in a changing neighborhood beset with minority tensions. Abbie taught her boys and girls to use their backgrounds and their problems as the stuff of their writing. She battled anti-Semitism, ethnic snobbery, and finally racism by using literature to arouse empathy and a thirst for justice, and by her unshakable faith in her students' ability to achieve.

She was proud of her rapport with her Jewish students—"I think we Irish are the lost tribe," she used to say; and she considered every step forward by her Negro students a personal triumph. (In 1945, when she lay dying, roses came from one of her black writers fighting in the South Pacific.) We knew all about her students—their troubles and their prizes—and they knew all about us. What she loved she shared with us. So it never occurred to me that I was anything but lucky to be teaching—and I carried into it her conviction that every student could learn and that students were interesting and exciting people.

Mandan was a good place for a teacher to start. Professionalism was encouraged by the young principal, Mr. Neff, and was practiced by the veteran teachers, who, with few exceptions, loved teaching. Mr. Neff was a square-faced, sententious young man with a canny sense of the town's inner workings and his own self-interest, but he was genuinely interested in education. He was respectful of the teachers and believed in them, and the students and teachers in turn were interested in the school and in each other. He sponsored "professional meetings" at which we discussed new trends in teaching, motivation, and the problems of teaching young people of whom English was a second language. It was probably through his example that we were all most punctilious in referring to each other as Miss This or Mr. That. To those of us who were younger such professional behavior became an affectation we enjoyed. We made nicknames of our professional titles and for years afterward referred to each other half-facetiously as Miss J. and Miss S., and we delighted in the pun on my name, Miss Q.

Mr. Gould, the superintendent of schools, was a pleasant man, with sagging features and pale, protruding blue eyes, who did not bother much with the teachers. It did not seem strange to us that he took care of the plants in the school, making daily trips with a watering can to all three buildings in the compound comprised of high school, junior high school, and grade school. He liked to drive for the teams on football and basketball trips and wrote the school sports news for one of the local papers.

Mr. Gould left all the details of administration to his secretary, Lila Clark, a crisp young woman of equable if authoritarian temperament, whose only loyalty was to him. She had the keys to all supplies and, in effect, handled all monies, a circumstance particularly galling to teachers of supposed responsibility like department heads.

"When I went to the office today," Gene once wrote, "I found that Gould—more probably Lila—had decided to allocate the funds from the Gavel Club benefit to the age-old debt of years past. There goes the trip. What this place needs is an administration!"

Lila decided when our tests could be mimeographed and how many pages they could be. She doled out our pay checks in the hours convenient to her. Her serene and high-handed use of authority, derived as it might be from that of the superintendent, seemed to us to undermine our professional standing and to imply that we were, after all, not professional people but just job holders.

She was my first example of the power of the aide who, by assuming all burden of detail, makes her employer dependent, and by controlling access to him, gains a subtle power over his subordinates. (She was a small-town prototype of the Washington aide whose power of access extends to friends and family.) Despite all this, we liked her; camaraderie overrode principle in Mandan.

Both Mr. Gould and Mr. Neff fought a subterranean battle for their own professional futures and economic survival; they had little time to interest themselves in the economic slavery which really constituted classroom teaching for most of us in the thirties. Mandan was not unique in this respect. Our classes were overcrowded and we were overworked; I taught six classes without a break, was expected to act as counselor to my home-room students and to manage and finance an extracurricular activity besides. Discipline was a test of energy and will power, for the German-Russian boys were docile enough under a firm hand but not disposed to give in easily to a woman. In addition, the Depression had brought unemployed former graduates back to school to occupy their time by taking courses they had not had before—language, for example, typing, advanced math, or science. There were some great hulking young men in my classes, some reputedly twenty or twenty-one—my own age. But I loved the challenge. And I found it exciting to be part of a faculty, on a par with teachers much older.

Now, thirty-odd years later, I can still see those teachers and hear their voices. There was Miss Runey, a small round gray-haired woman, head of the English department, always sweetly pleasant but aloof from the rest of us. She had been part of the county administration at one time and was a friend of the superintendent and his wife. There were the Helens, as everyone called Miss Miller and Miss Taipale who shared an apartment, dressed alike, and had grown to look alike, both with dark, waving hair drawn back into a knot, Miss Taipale's a little lighter than Miss Miller's. Miss Miller acted as assistant principal and taught mathematics. Miss Taipale taught music, directed the orchestra and glee clubs, and ran the school library with the help of school girls paid by the National Youth Administration. Each constantly lamented how hard the other had to work.

Gertrude Gilbert, a tall, slightly stooped, graying Scandinavian from Minnesota, taught the business courses. She had a taste for nice clothes and an abiding interest in food; she was easily made happy by a well-made cake or pie at the restaurant we all frequented.

Gertrude had a surprising, quiet independence. When the Lutheran minister who was a member of the school board said that he would like to see her at choir practice, she said firmly that she was sorry but that her bridge foursome met on that night. (Playing cards was, of course, anathema to him.) When she served on the committee to select the most outstanding student for the annual DAR award, she insisted that it go to the highest ranking senior girl even though she was a Catholic. The local committee had previously guarded against that possibility by including vaguely defined criteria like "poise" and "patriotism" and seeing to it that the teachers who served as judges were, as they supposed, like themselves. "But Margaret is the most outstanding," said Gertrude. No revolutionary, she was just devoted to facts. "Did you ever hear such nonsense?" she demanded of us later.

There was Verena Hentges, kindly, slightly hypochondriac, peering through thick glasses at her Latin classes. There was Elwell, the bandleader, suggestive in conversation, fatuously sure that he was irresistible to the high school girls, but likable all the same. Mr. Mackin, called Bucky by the older teachers who had taught him, was a member of the town's elite. An English teacher, he tended to treat me as a competitor and alternated between a faintly malicious attitude and bouts of gay friendliness. The faculty sophisticate was Miss Schroeder, no longer quite young, but her beautiful clothes hung on an elegantly slim figure. She had heavy auburn hair waved from a center part, violet eyes and creamy skin, but slightly prominent upper teeth bespoke a certain kind of Irish heritage concealed by her name. She carried her head tilted back and sniffed often so that she seemed to disdain everyone and everything. On closer acquaintance she turned out to be wryly funny and warm. Her best friend was Helga Restvedt, a home economics teacher in Bismarck, with whom she often double-dated and who shared her interest in clothes and the minutiae of gracious living. They had little time for the rest of us.

My instant love was Irene Franks, who taught English and speech and drama. She was essentially kind with the well-disposed, completely unenvious attitude of the born teacher toward the young. She adopted me as a protégée and we were soon very good friends. I was unreserved in my admiration. She seemed to me all that I would like to be—small, feminine, poised, and ladylike. She had a style of her own, which I thought must be like an Englishwoman's. She wore her long blond hair in a soft chignon and affected semitailored suits and soft hats which she pulled this way and that way to frame her face. I was awed by the fact that she had actually traveled in Europe. She found me endlessly entertaining and I loved her for that. At Christmas time we moved together into a little apartment Mrs. Rippel had made on the third floor of her house. The rooms fit into the gables—a small living room with a studio couch, a chair, and a desk; a comfortable bedroom; a bath and a center hall with a kitchen table, a small cupboard, an electric plate, and a coffee pot. We brought our books; Irene had some pillows and vases. I hung my Van Gogh print and an etching of Stratford-on-Avon and we were at home.

I was soon made aware that there were social distinctions in Mandan, both in the town and in the faculty. Through Irene I was invited to join the faculty bridge club. No one could believe that I literally did not know how to play. When they discovered that it was actually true, the Helens and Irene coached me patiently, starting at the very beginning with what a trick was, what "follow suit" was, what bidding was. It was unthinkable that I should not join, once having been invited, or that my invitation should be rescinded. I tried hard to learn and tried to remember to practice between meetings, but it was traumatic to me to discover that there was something I was naturally stupid about, and I remained a burden to my polite partners for all of my three years of membership.

Early in the fall I received an invitation to a dance from the Mandan Dinner Club. "What's the Mandan Dinner Club?" I asked of the teachers assembled in the dressing room getting ready for the cold walk downtown at noon. There was a general silence. Irene squeezed my elbow in warning and answered lightly, "Oh, that's a little group here in town." Once we were outside walking toward the hotel for lunch, she asked if I had had an invitation. When I said I had, she explained that not all of the teachers received them. The dinner club was a group of young people from the few leading families of Mandan and some of the young professional people. They had formal dinner dances once a month, strictly by invitation, four people taking turns as hosts. If I had had an invitation, I must surely go—I would like the people there.

At Sunday dinner the Dahnerses seconded her opinion. It would make all the difference to my time in Mandan if I began going to the Dinner Club dances. Lucille Dahners would find me an escort. He turned out to be a young newcomer, an earnest dull functionary in the bank, with a permanently listening, worried expression as if he were afraid of not understanding what was being said, or were listening to a conversation in a language he did not know very well. I had gone to Bismarck and bought a black evening dress—something forbidden to me in my college years. Mrs. Rippel was blissful over her roomer's social debut. Irene, escorted to the dance by a well-established lawyer and bachelor about town, saw to it that I met everyone.

I soon found myself going out a good deal, sometimes dating the young business and professional men, sometimes other teachers. The former worried me. I liked having fun but they weren't very interesting to talk to. They had no serious concerns. And I was frightened by what I thought was the worldliness of former fraternity men. But they showed me the night clubs and one after-hours place in an east side basement where I found one of my high school students, Bill Froehlich, behind the bar. It was the very substance of the freedom I found in Mandan that he was not surprised to see me there at two o'clock in the morning, and I thought his nonchalant, "What'll you have, Miss Quigley?" very funny. It was, I understood very well, a family business venture to him and as for me, I was very far from small-town Minnesota and its mores.

But more to my liking was the little discussion group I met as a result of that first dance. There were a young agronomist and his wife, Lyle and Nell Weber, a young liberal doctor and his wife, Harry and Avanelle Wheeler, Milton Higgins, Irene's lawyer friend whom she was to marry in two years, and Colin and Marian Carey, the undisputed social leaders of the area's young marrieds. ("If you have any doubts," Gene wrote to me tongue-in-cheek, after we were engaged, "I think they will be allayed by knowing that Marian Carey thinks we are ideally suited to each other—so Milton and Irene told me.") We argued passionately and furiously about the Spanish Civil War and Roosevelt and quoted the recent *New Republic* or *Nation* or *Atlantic* or *Harper's* to each other. It was not very original but it was stimulating and satisfying.

So my life filled up, and by the second year I missed less and less my friends at home in Minnesota and looked forward to returning to Mandan. Irene left to teach elsewhere, but Marion Schroeder joined me in the apartment and I found a new close friend in Celeste Hanson, a small strong girl with a quiet humor. She had gone to St. Benedict's College in Minnesota and came to teach history and be dean of girls. Lucille Walsh, a breezy energetic North Dakotan from Carrington, came to teach kindergarten, moved into the Rippel house, and quickly adopted me in an older-sisterly way.

Mandan up to this time was typical of the pattern of public education as it evolved in this country. The public school was a Protestant school and the regular election of Protestant ministers to the school board guaranteed that fact. (It is ironic to think that the Catholic school system in this country would never have come into being if the children of Catholic immigrants had not been compelled to take part in the Bible services and hymn singing which gave a Protestant cast to public school life.) Although the states of the Northwest Territory and those of the West banned religion from the schools in their charters, the close supervision of textbooks and the seasonal celebrations by vigilantly Protestant school boards tended to maintain the Protestant flavor. But the struggle with the Protestant ascendancy was not confined to the Catholics. During the three years I was in Mandan some of my students from an obscure Pentecostal sect were in constant conflict with the physical education department because they refused to take showers since doing so meant undressing. (Those in my classes considered my social life sinful—it was well known that I went dancing and to the movies—and filled their German notebooks with pleas to me to repent and be saved.)

In Mandan I met my first political priest. He was a bald, round-headed German Benedictine, Father Hildebrand Eickhoff. He had a

Private Faces/Public Places

passion for improving the lot of his people and a great contempt for the "cheese-knifers," as he called the Protestants of the town establishment. Some years before my arrival in Mandan it had occurred to Father Hildebrand that when his children—the German-Russians and a few Irish—left the safe environs of St. Joseph's parochial school for the public high school they were delivered into the hands of the cheese-knifers who controlled the school board and thus the teachers who would mold their adolescent minds. The only Catholic teachers were ones with local family connections. The solution was simple. There were more Catholic German-Russians in town than anyone else. He urged some of his parishioners to run for the school board and recommended them as good candidates to the rest of his flock. And the majority ruled. The new school board selected my principal, William Neff, who had a master's degree from Notre Dame and proved to be a really fine educator. The board began to elect a few Catholic teachers to fill vacancies on the faculty as they occurred. It was tactfully done. The first selections were men with local connections and degrees from North Dakota state institutions. (My own election, Catholic college graduate though I was, was due to my German-English major.)

Recently an old friend said to me, "You know, in many ways Hildebrand was great almost in spite of himself. He looked at the situation, saw that it was inequitable and that it was possible to do something about it within the American system. And he knew that the social sciences and literature were where the action was going to be. And he was right."

One of Mr. Neff's first suggestions to me was that I might like to drop in and see Father Hildebrand some evening. "He reads a lot," he said, "and he likes to talk to the teachers." I thought this an intriguing idea because I had never known a priest socially. In the days of his prime, our pastor in Wabasha, Minnesota, where I was reared, had ministered to us in an aloof, irascible, and authoritarian way. I had had priests as professors in college, but they lectured to classes of a hundred at a time and turned us over to nuns for the discussion sections.

So I went to visit Father Hildebrand with lively curiosity. The square brick rectory sat between the church and the school in a yard almost bare of grass in those years of the great dust storms. I was aware of the housekeeper's surveillance as I walked self-consciously up the walk and was taken aback when she snatched open the door, stared at me with obvious disapproval, ushered me in without a word, and disappeared, leaving me standing in the dim hall. But Father Hildebrand emerged almost at once from the back of the house. He was dressed in the Benedictine habit he wore at home with its long scapular, hooded cowl, and black leather cincture. He gestured after the housekeeper with his cigar, tapped his forehead to indicate his low opinion of her mental stability, bared stubby brown teeth in a grin, said, "Jealous, you know," and beckoned me into his study. I was mildly shocked, but I accepted the statement in the matter-of-fact tone in which it was delivered. It was clear to me almost at once that Father Hildebrand, living happily and autocratically in his little Benedictine community of two assistants, had no problems with celibacy—that he simply had a rather obsessive but necessary housekeeper who was jealous of everyone—the assistants, visiting teachers, the janitor, anyone who took the time of the pastor. In her opinion he was a being who should not have been at the beck and call of ordinary people.

The study was a room I grew to know well. There was a worn sofa, a utilitarian mission-type desk, and an old cracked leather chair where Father habitually sat indulging his passion for reading. There were books everywhere, on the desk, on the sofa, in piles on the floor. Father Hildebrand ordered them directly from London—from Longmans Green and Sheed & Ward—and from Herder in Germany and in St. Louis. He devoured history and biography. He accepted Hilaire Belloc, G. K. Chesterton, Christopher Dawson, Carlton Hayes, Christopher Hollis, the Sheeds without question. He was fascinated by Fanfani and especially interested in the scholarship which was re-examining the Reformation and the Middle Ages, abolishing old myths, and discovering that nationalism and new economic systems had as much to do with the conflicts in those times as religion.

He loved to share what he was reading. He would read and paraphrase and jump from book to book, saying, "Listen to this, girl, listen to this!" And he always sent me home with books to read, insisting darkly that they hadn't taught me much in "that place." To him my alma mater, St. Catherine's—non-German and non-Benedictine—was not quite orthodox. St. Catherine's had been founded by the sister of the great Americanizing archbishop of the Midwest, John Ireland, in the same quarter century as Radcliffe and was in the mold of the "seven sisters" college. I think that Father Hildebrand thought that the professors—St. Joseph nuns with degrees from Oxford, the Sorbonne and the like as well as from the great American universities—our Phi Beta Kappa chapter, our accreditation, were all evidences of truckling to the cheese-knifers and their values.

In a sense he was right. The St. Catherine's I left in 1936 was a very fine liberal arts college that happened to be Catholic. Those of us who were graduated from St. Catherine's in the twilight years of Mother Antonia, its foundress, were unaware of how unusual our school was for its day. Mother Antonia was a woman of amazing energy and intellect, with a passion for excellence. When she was chosen to head the fledgling Catholic college, she was determined that it was going to be the very best college possible.

I was the beneficiary of what Mother Antonia had accomplished, but during my college years I, like my classmates, rather took it for granted. We did not realize how recent such a good education for women was, nor what boldness Mother Antonia's achievement required in the world of the Catholic Church. Through the first three decades of this century, a time when university education for women was still for the few, and thirty years before Catholic University allowed nuns to register at all (and then only on a separate campus), she sent her nuns to the world's best universities. When she wanted a young sister to study at Juilliard in New York and another to take her master's at the library school of Columbia University, she learned that the Archbishop of New York would not allow a convent in his archdiocese to harbor any nuns attending such godless institutions. She rented an apartment for them and told them to consider it their convent. (In this she reminded me of my own grandmother who calmly risked the excommunication threatened by her German pastor when she entered my mother in public high school to prepare for the university. When she wanted to go to confession, Grandma hitched the horse to the buggy and drove six miles to see the more lenient Irish pastor in the next town.)

We came out of St. Catherine's with an awakened interest in the arts and sciences of our time because of the strong liberal arts orientation of the college. We came out prepared for a world of specialization, prepared professionally to be journalists, writers, teachers, social workers, musicians, technicians, librarians. We wanted and expected to be part of our world. We believed in and had benefited from the New Deal; some of us were beneficiaries of the National Youth Administration. Dorothy Day's *Catholic Worker* was beginning to be circulated on the campus, but we were aware of the movement as a novel and attractively direct form of social work rather than as a movement of social criticism. When we thought of the terrible problems of our time in terms of Catholic solutions at all, we were apt to take the view of *Commonweal,* the liberal Catholic weekly, which was strongly against Franco and fascism and pro-Roosevelt.

Thus, educated to involvement and discussion, I was fascinated by Father Hildebrand's ideas and his theories of history. I loved thinking about the clutter of personages, of plot and counterplot, as he plucked them from his reading and transformed them to his satisfaction, even though I could not accept his corollaries for the 1930s: that Roosevelt was as cynical and devious as Wolsey and that Franco was the herald of a new Christian Europe. But I gave up arguing with him early because he found nothing congenial in the historical method I had learned from my college history professors: Sister Angèle coolly and elegantly dissecting Europe after 1914, and Sister Eucharista Galvin, whose doctorate from the University of Chicago had left her with an abiding faith in archaeological discoveries and research scholarship.

Father Hildebrand came out of a different tradition from that of the Sisters of St. Joseph, whose community was established to teach in modern times. He was a Benedictine of St. John's Abbey, the largest monastery of the oldest order of monks in the western world. Benedict founded it at Monte Cassino in 529, a community of lay monks living in what he called a lifelong school of worship and work. From the first abbey a chain of religious families for both men and women spread across the world. Each group was an extended family connected to other Benedictine houses only by adherence to the rule and spirit of the founder. There was no central authority or bureaucracy, so each Benedictine foundation could truly identify itself with the locality in which it was established and, at the same time, transplant the ideals and culture of European Christian civilization. Historians of the American frontier have noted with amazement that the growth of St. John's in Minnesota repeated much of what happened in Anglo-Saxon England and in medieval Central Europe. Only the names and dates were different.

Metten, from which St. John's was established, was founded in 792, during the reign of Charlemagne, on the Danube in Lower Bavaria where the Benedictines carried on missionary, cultural, and educational activities for a thousand years. In the early centuries the monastery endured successive waves of invasions from the east, converting and educating the invaders as they came. In the Napoleonic era, the monasteries of Europe were reduced to a handful of poverty-stricken houses, but within a generation the revival began. It began at Metten and it was a priest of Metten who brought Benedictinism to North America, first to St. Vincent's in Pennsylvania, then to St. John's which celebrated its centenary in 1956.

In the 1930s St. John's was linked to whatever was going on in the Christian world. Monasteries, no matter how remote, are in touch with their counterparts everywhere. Their brightest scholars are sent off to Rome or some other world center for advanced study; their missionaries go off to Asia or Mexico or the Caribbean, as well as to remote parishes in North Dakota, and come home again. Therefore St. John's had been touched by many trends and had begun to play a significant part in a few. At St. John's the liturgical movement took American form and became united with the social action movement, largely through the efforts of Father Virgil Michel, a remarkable monk from a remarkable midwestern family. These movements were, briefly, the first structured efforts to cope with the rediscovery of the Church as a whole people—not as a hierarchy with a ruling few and a passive many—and of Christianity as the religion of God come to earth to renew all things—not a religion of man going to heaven.

The college of St. John's University, Gene's school, which had grown from the monastery, was unique among Minnesota colleges in the way it became a second home for life for the men who attended it. Perhaps this was because a significant number of the students entered the monastery and were always there in a more unchanging way than alumni at other universities. And the Benedictine professors stayed there, grew old, and finally gave their names to headstones in the graveyard where the men of St. John's walked with their wives when they came back to visit. The graduates of St. John's thought of themselves as part of the Benedictine family.

It is not fair to idealize St. John's too much, however. Until the 1920s it was still a school for German pioneers, tending to the needs of the pioneer church—educating priests and giving high school and business educations to the sons and grandsons of a sturdy immigrant people. It turned out more hardy and convivial parish priests than scholars, more hardware merchants than college teachers, more ROTC graduates than conscientious objectors, a handful of judges and officeholders. Still, parish priests like Father Hildebrand had been made aware of major movements in the church and the world because St. John's did carry on the Benedictine tradition. In the 1930s the efforts of the monks to act on the implications of the Mystical Body—that we are all one in Christ—were opening educational and social vistas just at the time when world events were making apparent the interdependence of the family of man. Father Hildebrand espoused these ideals as far as he understood them. The boys and girls of Mandan were going to learn history and literature from people who had a world view, he insisted. He simplified the church edifice, the building of "the people of God," to something more suitable for a communal type of worship. Old Irish residents of Mandan told me sorrowfully of the wonderfully carved high white altar, the statues of angels and saints they had had before his coming. "I left them their idols there in the back of the church," grinned

Father Hildebrand. It was true that a few gilded figures and a sad Pietà stood out against the walls he had had painted a liturgical rose—a color the old parishioners described feelingly as "Russian pink."

He was benign about the drama experiments of one of the assistants, Father Othmar, with skin drawn so tight over his forehead and cheekbones that he had the look of a complacent death's head. Father Othmar had acquired at St. John's a belief in the educational, community-building powers of modern drama which revived the content and method of the medieval morality play. He staged plays with enormous casts in the Mandan community building. The local audiences were strictly movie-bred and were quite unsettled by one play called *Theatre of the World*, in which hordes of "unborn souls" completely shrouded in black bombazine crept up the aisles from the back of the auditorium, eerily wailing and lamenting.

Father Valerian, the other assistant, was big and workmanlike and usually involved in building projects which had something to do with social justice. Father Hildebrand himself looked forward to the establishment of co-operative housing projects and credit unions. His first step was to have Father Othmar oversee the building of an addition to the parish school with the help of parish labor. He then credited those who had laid bricks and nailed two-by-fours with contributions to the church in the amount of man-hours they had spent. He computed the time according to the highest union scale, with time-and-a-half for overtime. In the annual report that year, plasterers and depression-ruined farmers came out as bigger contributors than the town doctors, merchants, and undertakers.

It was Father Hildebrand who brought Gene to Mandan in the fall of 1938.

In the spring of that year Madge Runey had died of a worn-out heart. After a life time of teaching, church work and involvement in community affairs she seemed to be remembered by too few people during this last illness. Superintendent Gould and those of us from the faculty who felt moved to come to visit her in the hospital in Bismarck stood awkwardly by in her last hours while one old friend, her very aged father, and her minister sat with her. None of us from the English department knew Miss Runey very well, and we had been critical of her because she did not spend much time with the faculty and left school early each day. Her chairmanship of the department had meant only that she had a free period each day and no extracurricular activity.

The night she died, I realized that during my years in Mandan Miss Runey had been saving her little remaining strength. I thought miserably of her painful little trips to my classroom door to talk a little about her plans for retirement. She needed one more year to qualify for the benefits with which she could live for awhile without working. But, like so many teachers of the Depression years, she died working.

In a week or two the small gap in the faculty ranks closed. Soon after her death, applications for the vacancy on the English faculty poured in. Bucky Mackin, now senior among those of us who taught English, inherited the chairmanship temporarily. One day Mr. Neff called me to the office and threw three folders on the desk before me with a gesture of exasperation.

"Why don't you tell them at St. Catherine's to make some differentiation in their recommendations? How can an administrator make a sensible selection from those?" he asked. "See if you know them and tell me the truth about which one is best."

Mr. Neff had begun to look on St. Catherine's as a prime source of teachers. The college had a good reputation in Mandan because of the local girls who had gone there and I seemed to have upheld it. Mr. Neff had asked me to inform St. Catherine's of the first vacancy on the faculty which opened after my arrival. A recommendation had come for an experienced alumna. It had somehow not made clear that she had been unemployed for some years and we had all been somewhat taken aback when Miss Marcella Frank appeared. She was dried and wispy, wore pince-nez, and had the first frankly dyed hair I had ever seen in an associate. But she had turned out to be an interesting teacher, colorful enough to be popular with the brighter students, and St. Catherine's was unharmed. I took pride in my influence with Mr. Neff and in the fact St. Catherine's had become his favorite source of teachers. But when I looked at the folders Mr. Neff had thrown down on the desk, I could see his difficulty. Sister Helen Margaret, the placement director, aware of her girls' desperate need for jobs, had included only the very best recommendations. It was difficult to make a choice.

"But it's all true," I said. "They're all terribly intelligent and well-prepared and hard-working. They've each had a year's experience."

"All right, tell me what isn't said there."

I laughed. "Well, this one has little personality. It shows in her eyes, too—look at the picture. And this one would be very, very good and drive you crazy with anxious little problems. And this last one you will like, and so will the kids. And so will the other teachers." I was glad that I could say this honestly because I had already had a letter from a friend saying that Margaret Fahey needed the Mandan job as a respite from home cares. Mr. Neff said nothing more, but I had a letter from Margaret soon saying that she had heard that the board had agreed to her selection. It made me feel helpful and I was glad, too, that I was going to have a former classmate in Mandan. No matter how much I like the place where I am, I have always been homesick for one place or another. When I came back alone from my first trip east and turned up the highway along the Mississippi at La Crosse, there was a steamboat on the river and I cried with relief. I always think I will not see places again. Seeing people who knew them, too, and love them, helps.

It turns hot suddenly in North Dakota when spring finally comes. In those years of drouth the heat was very dry—you only realized it when you became aware that your skin was growing hot like the skin of a baking potato. It was a day like that, in 1938, and I was chatting with the few students who had hung around after school when Bucky Mackin stuck his head in the door and beckoned wildly. I followed him into the hall. "I've got the Bismarck job," he hissed. "I just told Neff. Go put in a bid to advise the *Courier* and to teach Runey's classes—quick, before Frank does."

It was the first I had heard about the Bismarck job—a teacher who was job-hunting kept his counsel in those days—and I was surprised at Bucky's concern for me, but I was off at once. Yes, agreed Mr. Neff reluctantly, I was to have the senior English classes and I was to advise the *Courier*. Miss Frank might be difficult. She was more experienced, but I had been there longer. Yes, I was probably entitled to be head of the department, too, if the board agreed. It seemed very wonderful to me. I was twenty-three. I was a full-fledged English teacher in a first-class school system. And I was going to advise a school publication. My Aunt Abbie would be very pleased.

When I was home for vacation, one day that summer I had a long distance call from Mandan. My whole family was electrified and I was sure that Mrs. Yost, Wabasha's afternoon telephone operator, was all attention. A long distance call across state lines was a very rare thing then. It was Mr. Neff. He sounded very far away. There was a man the board was very anxious to hire. He knew he had promised me the English job, but that would leave no vacancy for my friend, Miss Fahey, and he remembered that I had been concerned about her.

"But why?" I asked stubbornly and hopelessly. "Why do you have to hire the man? There wasn't any English vacancy left."

He didn't like being cornered. "It's complicated. The vacancies in other departments have complicated things." He said, "Of course, you can have the other English job if you feel so strongly about it."

"I do feel strongly. But I can't do that to Miss Fahey. I'll just teach German all my life."

He softened at that. What if Miss Fahey were to be told—? But he already knew my answer to that.

My sisters and brother were upset because I cried so hard and so long. When they learned that I hadn't lost my job, they couldn't understand why I had given the English classes to someone else. "Why should you, if you care so much?" asked my brother. But I think I really cried because Mr. Neff had let me down and I knew that he couldn't help doing it. My professional concerns would have seemed ludicrous to the school board—not worth a thought to Father Hildebrand. Men cannot afford to seem ridiculous. But Mr. Neff was a professional as well as a politician, and he knew that I had a right

Private Faces/Public Places

to want to do what I knew I could do well. Well, at least he had called.

So Gene McCarthy came to Mandan that fall.

There were several other new teachers in Mandan that September: a serious young man for the junior high school; the Protestant teacher to balance the senior high school English department—a very self-confident pretty Miss Johnson—and an unheard of innovation—a *male* principal for the Catholic school, who was a layman at that. The town buzzed. In a self-contained community like Mandan the coming of new teachers each year brought an infusion of excitement. It was a healthy thing for the school community, too, because it broke up old patterns and challenged leadership.

The leadership challenge was especially evident in Mandan that year. There was an implied threat to Mr. Neff in the arrival of Gene McCarthy as the new head of a department and of Raphael Thuente as the new head of the parochial school, by far the largest elementary and junior high school in town. Both men were St. John's graduates, with the obvious advantage of sharing associations and memories with the Benedictines at the rectory. Furthermore, they were eligible, attractive and young, and they would enter easily into the social life of the town.

At the first English department meeting of the term I sat in the back and watched the new chairman with critical attention. He seemed to slough off our serious concerns as unworthy of his full attention. I set about a course of petty harassment by scrupulously sending him notes asking his approval of my every choice of text or schedule change. During my first visit with Father Hildebrand that fall he was full of praise for the new head of the English department and complacent about his part in bringing him there. "He's a genius," he said, "a fine man from a good family. Lots of priests and nuns. Went through college in three years."

"So did I," I said defensively, but he ignored me.

"He's at Mass every morning," he continued. "Never misses devotions either."

"Why isn't he a priest?" I asked.

That daunted Father a little. He pulled on his cigar.

"I don't know. I don't know," he said.

It was something of a mystery to us both. In the days prior to World War II men who went to daily Mass other than during Lent were old men preparing for death or seminarians home on vacation. Clearly Father Hildebrand was puzzled. Something had gone wrong somewhere. Raph Thuente, now, was no problem. He was an ex-seminarian.

But Father Hildebrand brightened as he expatiated on his plans. Superintendent Gould would go eventually. He'd retire or the town would get sick of him. Neff would take his place and there would be McCarthy, ready for the principalship.

If this was the plan, it should have been reassuring to Mr. Neff but there was an implicit threat in the situation. Father Hildebrand was developing the instincts of a true political boss; he was not putting all his eggs in one basket and, if his first choice showed too much independence, he had a second and a third. I met Mr. Neff in the school hall one day. "What do you think of this McCarthy?" he asked. I wasn't at all sure what I thought except that he was too handsome to be true, but I didn't think that was relevant to the conversation. Mr. Neff offered his own assessment gloomily.

"I think he's a wolf in sheep's clothing," he said.

"Oh no," I said indignantly. I had already decided that Gene McCarthy was some sort of inaccessible saint with a mysterious purpose of his own.

"Not that kind of wolf," he replied.

I understood then and confided what Father Hildebrand had said about the eventual superintendency. He cheered up a bit and told me that he liked Miss Fahey very much, that I had certainly been right about her.

That was another of my troubles. Everybody liked Miss Fahey very much and I was trying hard not to be jealous. She roomed on Mrs. Rippel's second floor, and Miss Schroeder, who had decreed that we would wait a month before asking her to share breakfast with us, had succumbed to her obvious respectability and good humor after the first weekend.

The students liked her too. Her classroom was beginning to fill after school, but she was less apt to linger than I. And, worst of all, while I was dutifully attending a pep rally with the coach, she was invited to a party for the new teachers and came home full of Mr. McCarthy and Mr. Thuente. They were marvelous. They were *so* intelligent. They knew all about philosophy and theology. They had read everything—they quoted poetry and the literary magazines. I could see the handwriting on the wall. Mr. McCarthy would fall in love with Miss Fahey. They would get married and live properly and happily while I continued my stormy career, battling ahead professionally while managing to stay alive socially by sparring with amorous local escorts on the side.

My mood of depression was deepened by the fact that my dating situation was no longer quite as pleasant and as lighthearted as it had been. My most reliable escort was demanding that I become serious and was increasing surly about his competition. It was not the fashion to marry early in those pre-World War II days. "I am glad to hear about the new men in town," Irene Franks wrote me, "but be careful, Abbie. Don't get married before you have a chance to develop your gifts. There's time for that." Educated girls were career-minded, and, since marriage usually meant the end of a career, they were willing to put it off for some years unless they really fell in love. It did not seem strange at all to us that our thirtyish colleagues— Miss Haagenson, Miss Loomis, Miss Schroeder—were only beginning to be serious about their plans. So I was dismayed at the turn in my own life.

As I had suspected, Miss Fahey began to see Mr. Thuente and Mr. McCarthy in the evenings. When she began to see only Mr. Thuente, I took heart. They often came to the apartment for coffee after they had been out, or he would call for her on a Sunday evening. We engaged in long discussions which I was sure were duly reported to Mr. McCarthy and since many of Raph's contentions were quotes from Gene, I knew that I was really arguing with Mr. McCarthy himself. Then, too, Raph was as interested in the personality of Gene McCarthy as anyone has ever been, and I was a very attentive audience as he mulled over his friend's ideals and idiosyncrasies. Although I could see no reason why such a paragon would be interested in me, I nursed a secret hope that, by indirect means, he was at least aware of me. And he was. He told me the next year that he waited at each professional meeting for my "late arrival"—I was always late—then watched me secretly through the meeting.

It was the Mandan High School custom for each department to sponsor a school dance to raise money for the extracurricular activities connected with the department. Teachers as well as students welcomed these dances in the gym as interruptions in our routines and as economical ways to enjoy ourselves. There was always a pleasant stir of preparation. Committees proliferated. Girls talked about dresses. Refreshments were debated and solicited. Those students thought of as the most artistic surveyed the cavernous reaches of the gym for the dozenth time and conferred with the drama coach who might have an idea about decorations. Students who belonged to the DeMolay, that mysterious junior division of the Masons, surreptitiously used the Temple mimeograph to run off orange flyers. It was before the days of a self-conscious generation gap and the teachers and students all danced together happily.

We didn't question the need for the department-sponsored dances so it was disconcerting to find, at one of our first meetings, that our new head did. But I was more interested in another aspect of the event. If I maneuvered the right job, I could foresee a slight chance that Mr. McCarthy and I would be the last to leave the building— teachers were responsible for school property and had to lock up— and, naturally, he would have to offer to see me home, wouldn't he? To the surprise of Miss Frank, Miss Fahey, and Miss Johnson, I offered to take charge of the food committee, a chore usually relegated to the last and least of the teachers because it involved staying to the bitter end.

There were complications. The coach announced that he was coming to the party and that he would take me home as usual. I couldn't quite see how I was to make my secret wish come true without offending him, but on the night of the dance all the powers of chance seemed to be on my side. The older, very nubile girls looked forward to dancing with the young men teachers and the younger women teachers not so far from college dances were very much aware of the better dancers among the high school boys. The pretty Miss Johnson danced with one senior boy after another and, quite oblivious of her responsibility as a chaperone, paused beside me only long enough to confide prettily that she didn't know what to do—she just had to get to Bismarck after the dance; her aunt was expecting her. Did I think it would be all right if she asked that nice senior boy to drive her over?

"Well, I don't know," I said. "His parents might not like it. But Coach has been dying to ask you out. He'd jump at the chance to take you. Let me tell him."

It never occurred to Miss Johnson to doubt me. For weeks she had regaled us at lunch with her conquests among the football players who unanimously bemoaned the training regulations and the age difference that made it impossible for them to ask her for dates. Now she accepted my statement as nothing less than the expected truth.

I sought out the coach and said, "Miss Johnson's in a dilemma. She has to get to Bismarck right after the dance. She asked if I would ask you to take her. I'll have to wait here for the clean-up committee anyway so there'll be time."

He was wary. "And leave you here with McCarthy! We'll wait and you and I can drive her over together."

"Oh, silly, you know Mr. McCarthy is not my type," I said. "Besides, I'm afraid it will be too late. She said she was in a terrible hurry. Her aunt and uncle came especially to see her and they're so disappointed that she had to chaperone this dance. Anyway, I think she has sort of a crush on you. She probably doesn't want me to come along. Why don't you talk to her?"

He had normal human vanity and curiosity. He went. I got close enough to hear him say "I hear you need a ride to Bismarck" and to note Miss Johnson's seductive smile. I crossed my fingers and prayed.

No clean-up committee members in the high school's history ever had such enthusiastic help from a teacher or were dispatched so quickly into the night to join their various dates. I was desperately computing the time it took to drive to Bismarck and the time it took to walk to Mrs. Rippel's without any shortcuts. Finally I put on my coat and picked up Mrs. Rippel's salad bowl just as Gene turned out the last lights and joined me at the door.

"Anything else the authorities require?" he asked.

"Just to test the doors when we lock them," I said. The crucial moment had come. We were outside the door in the clear Dakota night. He indicated the bowl. "Can I carry that for you?"

He was going to walk me home! It had all worked out! Then, as we walked down the street together with the fall leaves skittering along the sidewalk, I began to feel ill. I had done a terrible thing. I had schemed and entrapped this man, who was completely unaware of my devious nature. He was too good for such things. If he did walk home with me, what would it mean? Just that he was too gentlemanly to let me walk alone!

We came to Third Street and the corner where our ways would normally part. I snatched the bowl.

"Thank you so much," I said breathlessly. "I'll take it now. This is my corner."

He protested, but I was already halfway across the street calling "Goodnight, see you Monday" in a false, cheery voice, hoping that he might follow me at the same time that I was making it impossible for him to do so. I was miserably unhappy.

It seemed only a fitting aftermath when the coach came thundering up to the apartment later, having learned from Miss Johnson that I had suggested the ride. I compounded all my sins by saying that we had finished early and that I had come home alone, to wait for him —a rather loose version of the truth. He wanted to believe it, but he was puzzled. "You mean he let you?" he asked. "What kind of guy is this McCarthy anyway?" It was a question many people in Mandan were asking by then.

Soon after that something happened to make me decide to end my dating days forever and to retire into a nunlike devotion to my career. My escort to the Dinner Club dance drank too much and decided to make an issue of his periodic suggestions that we become engaged. When we left the dance he drove wildly into the hills beyond town and parked on a bluff overlooking the Missouri, insisting that he was going to keep me out all night and ruin my reputation. Then I would have to marry him. When I tired of scolding, arguing, pleading, I was suddenly seized with fury.

"Take me home, take me home at once," I said, "or *I will kick out your windshield.*" (A man's car was a precious possession in those days.)

"We're staying here," he said blurrily.

I aimed the heel of my evening slipper at the windshield and kicked with all my might. It was shatterproof but my spike heel went neatly through and cracks rayed out crazily from the hole.

"My God," he gasped, sober at once. "My God, you *are* a violent woman."

"We knew you were equal to it, darling," said Miss Schroeder dryly when I stormed into the apartment later. She and Miss Fahey and Mr. Thuente were having a post-dance snack. I took perverse satisfaction in telling them about the windshield and observing Mr. Thuente's shocked fascination. Let him go home and tell that to McCarthy, I thought. Let that Perfection know what kind of person I am. I don't care. Let him know how terrible I am.

I started refusing to go out, and when Advent came and I could decently do so without being obvious, I started going to church more often.

On December 5 of the next year Gene reminded me that it was the anniversary of the day I had, as he put it, run away from him in the dark after Rosary. It was true. I was afraid that he would think I had gone to church hoping to see him—as, of course, I had.

We finally began to talk to each other, and then to know each other a little on the train trip home at Christmas time. This ride together was not a matter of accident but the scheming was on Gene's part, not mine. He said of the teachers who wanted to drive with him the following year that they seemed to have forgotten his sudden tendency to incurable car-sickness which made it necessary for him to take the same train that I was taking at the last minute.

The train left Mandan in late morning. We had lunch together and talked all the way across the prairies of eastern Dakota and western Minnesota. When he left the train at St. Cloud, I think we were both sure we were in love. Gene wrote me a Christmas card when he got home and was reduced, he said, laughing in reminiscence, to his last card and envelope by destroying those on which he had experimented with closing and signatures (E.J., Eugene, Gene). Then when he had no answering card—I think I did not get it until after Christmas—he worried because he had mailed it in the west-bound box on the Watkins station platform and thought that it might have been lost in the transfers necessary to bring it east to Wabasha— or that I had purposely or, worse, indifferently ignored it. Mailing the card made him feel free, he said, as if he had made a confession of a kind.

Companions on a train trip are like the only inhabitants of a world. In some ways on that journey we grew to know each other as no one else knew either of us. When I admitted that I thought him aloof and disparaging of the teachers and students with whom I was so vitally involved, Gene had made a confession of another kind. He said that he struggled with a deep disinclination to accept life— a state he later described as being neither "hot or cold" toward it, "an inertia of years." He marked it as beginning with an incident when he was twelve and after a heavy rain had come upon a baby sparrow thrown from its nest to the sidewalk. He stepped on it and watched the life go from it. That was all there was to life, he thought, that faint flicker.

During that Christmas vacation Gene struggled with a poem in which he compared me to the wild rose which grows everywhere in Minnesota, along the country roads and the railroad tracks, thrusting its way out of the gravel or the cinders, "born of life, affirming life, guarded by thorns, but a rose." A long time later he showed it to me. The lines had begun to blur on the much-folded and creased piece of paper he had carried about with him. I have it still.

After vacation Gene asked me to go to a movie. This caused a wave of excitement among the Rippel roomers to whom our new rap-prochement was a surprise. "I never!" exclaimed the irrepressible Lu-cille Walsh. "The guy is human after all." But we never saw the movie. After the first five minutes Gene said, "You aren't really in-terested in this silly thing, are you?" And I, who still like to know how even the most puerile television script ends, said, "No, of course not." He thought I must be impatient with the entertainment he had chosen. I was afraid he would think me hopelessly low-brow if I said I would like to stay.

"What's the matter?" asked Joe Reis, the high school student who worked as an usher. "You seen it before?"

On another night we went skating together. It was bitterly cold and the rink—a boarded and flooded vacant lot in south Mandan—was deserted. Naked trees and lonely houses, each with a single lit window, bordered it. There was one floodlight high on a pole. We skated in and out of its pale light, veering together for brief colloquies which sent our words in short puffs of mist into the freezing night air, and then, too cold to stay still, stroked away again over the rough ice.

"It was such a tentative coming together," Gene said later.

A month after that Christmas vacation in 1938, Gene asked me to marry him. ("I looked at the calendar today to make sure of the dates when I will see you again," he wrote me a year later, "and came across February 3 circled in red.") We sat together in the little attic living room with the fierce Dakota wind lashing branches against the roof so close to us and solemnly pledged our lives to each other. I had never expected to be so happy. We talked a little vaguely of marriage in two years and made plans that were half dreams. In those bleak Depression years we all thought of our system as having failed us and schemes to renew it were everywhere in the air. Gene believed in renewal through the rural life movement and I was ready to assent to whatever he thought right. We would live on a farm—but, of course, a farm like none either of us had ever known, a farm which would become the center of a community of writers and scholars.

It was a very happy spring. Always given to sporadic bouts of piety, I became a steady attendant at daily Mass partly to please Gene. "It must be love if it gets you up early," sniffed Miss Schroeder. Gene bought a car, a second-hand 1937 blue Chevrolet. The car enlarged our world, allowing us to roam and explore the prairies and hills together. A snapshot taken at the time shows the two of us beside the car, looking very much like the hero and heroine of a 1930s' movie. Gene has the conventional good looks, the black wavy hair parted on the side, the handsome smiling face; he has on the large casual overcoat and carelessly worn muffler of the decade. He looks shyly pleased. I am wearing a coat I remember well—black wool with puffed sleeves and a stand-up Persian lamb collar. My hair is upswept in a roll on either side and crowned with an oversized pillbox fashionably aslant. The car is mud-splashed and behind the car is a tangle of bare trees and vines. The picture must have been taken beside the Dead Heart River; in Dakota trees grow thick only in the river bottoms. It is a sunny picture except that my hands are tightly clasped as if something precious might escape.

As the weather grew warmer we became inseparable and our pleasure in each other was reflected in the people we knew. "Oh, you lucky, lucky Miss Quigley," laughed a high school girl as I flew past her down the front steps of the school, intent on joining Gene for the walk to lunch. We became favorite chaperones for the homeroom picnics which multiplied every spring and I sat happily with the girls watching Gene play softball with the boys. Afterward around the fire we sat studiously apart, aware of each other in every nerve and gleefully conscious of the students' sharp interest. We had informal suppers and Sunday dinners, too, with the Higginses, the Dahnerses, the Webers, warmed by their pleasure in our happiness and their indulgence of our absorption with each other.

There was a somewhat less happy interlude at Easter when I went home with Gene to Watkins. He had told me about his family, each one, and I was ready to endow them with all the extraordinary qualities I found in him. From Gene, who described him with a sort of amused respect, I knew that his father was a cattle buyer and superintended the family farm, that he was quick-tempered, irascible but sentimentally warmhearted. I had no clear picture of his mother— her note of invitation had been painstakingly correct—but Gene seemed very close to her, and I thought of her as classically devout and home-loving. There was Mildred, his older sister who had been away from home for a long time, now married and living in Panama. That seemed a romantic circumstance to me and I warmed to the idea of Mildred; Gene said I sometimes reminded him of her. There was Marian, also a teacher, who would be home for the vacation and Austin, his younger brother, who was at medical school and would not be there.

Mentally I pictured the family as revolving around Gene. And I, as belonging to him, would become part of its center—a fond conceit but understandable considering my state of mind in those days. I had always been at home with older people, having grown up in an extended family of grandmothers, great-aunts, aunts, uncles, and cousins, and I looked forward to being accepted by Gene's father and mother. The acceptance was to come eventually but not just then, and in ways I did not then foresee.

The McCarthy house was a two-story frame on Watkins' second street, a house with a small screened porch across the front and two windows like eyes above; its replicas line thousands of midwestern streets. Gene's father had built it with the help of Gene's grandfather, a carpenter when he was not playing his violin. Gene's grandfather was known to the family and all the relatives as Carty-Pa; he and his strong-willed wife, Carty-Ma, had moved into the house before Gene's father and mother could get married and come home to it. Inside, the house seemed a little cramped in all its dimensions. The stairs ran up from the living room; three of the bedrooms were just big enough for a double bed and a dresser, the fourth for a daybed and sewing machine.

In those days of foreclosures and unemployment, it was something for a house to have survived, well-roofed and warm, as a family home and a haven for the children who had gone out to make a living in a world devoid of warm welcomes. That was how I saw it then and I tried eagerly that vacation to enter into its life.

Carty-Ma's redoubtable spirit seemed to fill the house she had dominated until she died at the age of ninety-seven. Her sayings were quoted and her ways were still followed. She was a legend among her kin. Many years later, when Gene nominated Adlai Stevenson, a Montana cousin of his father's wrote, "Eugene, you're every bit like your grandmother—she could say the whole Litany of the Saints without a prayerbook." The gaiety of Mildred, called Mid, still lived in the house, and Austin, clearly the apple of his parents' and sister's eyes, was present in his likes, dislikes, the memories of his boyhood. Gene's mother, a neatly and stockily built woman in her early sixties, was sweet and welcoming. Her features were strong and very like Gene's except that her face was broad and she had the dark ivory cast of complexion from her south German ancestors, not Gene's Irish fairness. Her almond eyes were the brown of shiny buttons and sometimes made me uneasy with their steady regard. Her voice had a musical timbre—she had, I think, sung in the choir in her youth—and she interspersed her steady conversation with inquiring little hums. She seemed to find her worth in doing things for us all, especially in feeding us, and she was constantly jumping up from the table to bring us something else, some pickles or another kind of jelly. It was only later that I learned she still clung to the hope that Gene would one day be a priest; his going so far as to bring a girl home was a threat she was not ready to face. She showed no interest in our talk of life in Mandan, but plied me a little hungrily with questions about St. Catherine's and St. Paul and the people I knew there. Only once during those few days did she show anything but approval.

"Doesn't Abbie remind you of Mid?" Gene asked one dinnertime when he was amused at my recounting of some St. Paul story.

His mother stopped dead still and regarded me with an opaque look.

"No," she said.

Marian I liked at once. She was Gene's senior by five years and she was stocky like her mother but blue-eyed and placid. At home she took on the mildly clucking personality of the older sister who had spent long years minding younger brothers and being teased by them. She laughed easily and helplessly and seemed unreserved in her friendliness. But in order to ease the strain of my visit, I learned later, she had invited home her closest friend, Harriet Hauge, already an intimate in the house and a great favorite with Gene's father. Harriet was Marian's age, skinny rather than slim, and aggressively cheerful and helpful. She called Mr. McCarthy by his first name, bantered with him constantly, and courted his admiration of her long blond hair which she usually wore in a braid around her head, but which she brushed out often wherever she happened to be. He chaffed with her as one could imagine he had with waitresses and boardinghouse keepers near slaughterhouses and railroad stations in his nights of exile in a world of men. The image I had cherished of Gene's father vanished, and I knew he would never look on me with the same favor he felt for Harriet. He did, however, enjoy talking with me about North Dakota. He had made many trips through the cattle lands in the western part of the state. He admired success and he would dwell on the owners of the biggest spreads, their houses, their foremen and cowhands, and the expansiveness of their hospitality. He was delighted to find that a rancher in the Turtle Mountains, one whom he particularly admired, was a connection of mine through my cousins the Dahners. For years thereafter whenever we met after an absence he would open a conversation with me by inquiring about that rancher, as a prelude to his own reminiscences.

He called Mrs. McCarthy "Mom" and his attitude toward her was laced through with a condescending teasing which passed for rough affection. He seemed to look on any show of tenderness or emotional dependence as weakness. When Gene, half-shamed by his teasing, left me behind once during the visit, his father snorted with approval. His appraisal of his fellow men was almost universally sour and he had the habit of limning them unforgettably with biting, homely witticisms. He belonged to that generation of men for whom the Depression was the last defeat—who had struggled out of bitterly hard-working childhoods into moderate success in the early part of the century only to have their world changed radically by the First World War. Farm failures and the decline of the small towns were accompanied by changing business mores. A man's word was no longer his bond; bills were no longer settled when the crops came in; barter disappeared and a subconscious conviction of helplessness grew with the realization that the wellsprings of commerce were far away and beyond control. My own father, stubbornly practicing personal journalism, accepting cabbages and potatoes as payment for subscriptions and advertisements, selling real estate and insurance for commissions guaranteed verbally, gradually lost his newspaper and all but the appearance of his other businesses; he took refuge in a mild alcoholism and an equally mild conviction that a mysterious "they" had ever sought to ruin him. Gene told me that his father refused to acknowledge that he had lost his job as a commission man for a South St. Paul firm, continuing to ride the cattle trains as usual and to make regular trips to the stockyard district. Years later over coffee in our kitchen, he used to say to me that he didn't understand the talk of the Depression—that it had never affected him.

Once, after I was married, I was alone in New York one afternoon. I managed to get a single ticket for Arthur Miller's *Death of a Salesman*. I wept so uncontrollably that the man in the seat beside me did not come back after intermission. Even now I think one of the greatest lines ever written is "Attention must be paid."

I grew up surrounded by women whose task it was to see men through those difficult times and thus I had a sense of great pity for their vulnerability—men who could not find refuge in the house as we could but who had to go out every day as if there were a purpose when in fact there was none. So in time I came to feel toward Dad McCarthy something of the affection and understanding that his own children felt.

But not for Watkins.

Superficially, Gene and I came from the same kind of background. Journalists writing about us often noted that we were both small-town Irish Catholics from Minnesota who had grown up, gone away to college, and joined the larger community in the Twin Cities. In actual fact, we came from very different kinds of towns. Watkins had existed as an entity only during the lifetime of one man, Gene's uncle by marriage, old Michael Becker, who started it by building a general store at the site designated as the next stop on the Soo Line railroad. It is an unlovely place—a flat three streets running at right angles to the railroad tracks, between them and the highway, with a scattering of houses to north and south.

The little Mississippi River town where I grew up, Wabasha, Minnesota, on the eastern border of the state, had grown with the westward push of the nation. The Indian chief for whom it was named was usually pictured with his hair hanging over one eye to cover an empty socket and wearing a red cap purportedly given to him by George Washington as a reward for aid to the English colonists during the French and Indian War. The town was first settled by French traders. During my childhood the telephone book was liberally sprinkled with French names like Cratte, Levellie, LaChapelle, and Longhway. The livelihood of most of these families was connected with the river. Mr. Longhway was a fishing guide. Others worked in the steamboat yards or in the boat livery. The merchants and the owners of the few important industries—the flour mill, the grain elevator, the lumber company—tended to be people of New England backgrounds—the Lawrences, the Webbs, the Joneses, the Dills. Then there were the people like my own forebears, Irish, Scottish, Welsh, Swiss, who had come there before the Civil War for the free farmland and had made their way into the community by combining a farm with a shop in town, perhaps, or by way of the professions. These included names like my own, Quigley, and O'Leary, Shebat, and Mullen. These people had all worked out intricate community and family relationships which served them very well and continued to serve the last group of immigrants, farmers who came in the later nineteenth century primarily from Luxembourg and surrounding German-speaking territories. Wabasha had worked out in its customs and history much more complicated interrelationships than Watkins had had time to.

The women of Wabasha would not have thought of themselves as feminists, but they were important in local affairs. As in many old pioneer communities, the bridge from the farm and community service family to the professional family was often made first by the daughters who became teachers. It was characteristic of most of the pioneer Midwest that the women in the community had a better academic background than the men, since in the early days more of the women went on to get a teacher's certificate. In its early years, Wabasha was a school-centered community. The high school, originally called the academy, was the center of the intellectual life of the town. The Catholic high school, when it started, aimed at surpassing the public high school academically. Teachers were community leaders and held in high regard. The women of the community were also responsible for its cultural life. The town had its own orchestra and band as well as an opera house where local talent presented plays and operettas. There were pageants on the courthouse lawn and in the parks and a lecture series presented by the Woman's Club. My grandmother was a supporter of the town library, a favorite meeting place for young people; my mother was a founder of the Woman's Club and the monthly Newman Club. She died when I was nine, and it was early borne in on my consciousness by the older members of my family that I must be a lady as she had been. Some of the things a lady did or did not do were easy to define. A lady always wrote thank-you notes, for example. A lady did not hurt another's feelings. A lady did not stare or point. Physical defects were never alluded to. One of the most poignant memories I have and one that I cherish as real evidence of what my mother stood for concerns a grade school classmate of mine, probably of Indian descent. One day she wore to school a pink linen jumper that I recognized as having been mine the year before. It was made by my great-aunt who owned a dressmaking business and it had her careful embroidery at the neck. At recess I met the little girl under the slide as we were running for our teams. She pulled me aside and said, "I didn't want to wear this dress today but my mama said that you were your mama's daughter and you would never say anything because that would be the way your mother had brought you up." I remember being proud of my mother, proud that I had heeded her admonitions. I remember the moment, also, as one of the first insights I had into the life of another.

There were indeed differences and divisions in Wabasha, and there was pettiness, provincialism, and cruel gossip. But the differences and divisions had been muted by long years of living together. Grace Memorial Episcopal Church, a beautiful gray stone structure, was, I suppose, the "right church" if there can be a right church in a town of 2500 people. The owner of the mill was its mainstay, but it was also the church of the Longhways. The Catholic church was the church of the German immigrants; it was also the church of the doctors and lawyers, and of the one artist who lived in town. Whatever conflicts there may have been between the Germans and the remnants of the Irish like ourselves about its being a "national" church had been resolved by putting St. Boniface on one side of the altar and St. Patrick on the other. With, of course, the American flag in the sanctuary, too. There were two newspapers and there tended to be a Catholic undertaker and a Protestant undertaker, a Catholic hardware store and a Protestant one, but because of interminglings and intermarryings over the years, the line between Catholic and Protestant enterprises was never very hard nor very fast. The orphanage was Catholic and the hospital staffed by Catholic nuns, but the children in the orphanage came from all backgrounds and everyone went to the hospital when necessary.

Wabasha was a largely egalitarian community. We had maids— but no one used the word—and when maids began to disappear, there was always a cleaning lady, a wash lady, or "help." The wife of young John Dill, who came to Wabasha from Minneapolis, had as her part-time household help the locally famed Minnie Hudson. When Mrs. Dill's mother came to visit, she was astonished to see, as she sat by the open window one pleasant summer evening, a large determined woman in house dress and black tennis shoes clump by, shouting merrily, "Hi, there, Elizabeth! How are you, Elizabeth?"—and to learn that this was her daughter's cleaning woman.

We looked with fond amusement on the habit of R. E. Jones, who would lift the telephone receiver and say, "Central, give me Richard," without bothering with numbers or surnames. We accepted the fact that Jakie Mathias ranged the town carrying a pillow slip into which he put every stray feather; at the same time we were proud of his ability to make steamboat models which looked in every small detail like the originals.

That was the Wabasha of my time. I came out of it with an outlook on life that somehow combined all these disparate elements —regard for convention, a sense that art, music, literature, and civilized norms of behavior were very important but that it was also necessary to know who one was and to defend oneself physically if necessary, with a strong sense that a woman was a person and that her participation in community affairs was the norm rather than the exception.

When Gene and I went to Watkins to live after our marriage, I think that although I knew Watkins to be different, I expected life there to be somewhat like the life in Wabasha—restricted but nonetheless full of variety, discussion, and respect for eccentricity. But Watkins was indeed entirely different. I suppose it was much more like a European country village than it was like the gradually evolving American community which Wabasha typifies. It seemed almost transplanted from rural Germany to rural Meeker County, Minnesota. (Gene's sister Mildred said recently that she understood Watkins much better after having lived several years in Germany.) The church was the dominant building in the community. Beer taverns were characteristic. Almost everyone spoke English with a slight German twist or accent. At church the people prayed in German and the sermons were often in German. I remember going to church for the first time with the McCarthy family and hearing them at evening devotions break out suddenly into a gabble of prayer in a language that was not at all recognizable to me. None of the McCarthys spoke German but they were approximating what they had heard all their lives. Humor in Watkins was not based on delight in variety but on mocking differences, particularly physical oddities. Families like the McCarthys tried to see that their children went to college, but they were the first college generation of the town. There were only one or two professional people. In other words, it was a much simpler community than the one I had grown up in. Athletics was its unifying factor, especially the baseball team which made Gene and his brother so much a part of the town.

I came away from that first Easter vacation in Watkins with the feeling that the alienation of which Gene sometimes spoke had its roots in his home and his town. Yet on long walks during those few days he had shown me that there was beauty there, too. Some of his best poetry stems from the memory of that countryside and its creatures:

> The sky was a kite,
> I flew it on a string, winding
> it in to see its blue, again
> to count the whirling swallows,
> and read the patterned scroll of blackbirds turning
> to check the markings of a hawk.

As for the loneliness, I was sure that was over, as was he. After we had made our commitment to each other, I tried to give him my friends with both hands, and they had quickly become friends of his. "Your letter, filled as it was with a zest for life, helped me over a bad spot again," he wrote. "I need you so much that it would be selfish if you did not have so much understanding and capacity to live that it can run over to others. The sky is closer now and the wind seems to be blowing it across the brushy tops of the trees, catching out the dust and smoke—just as you do with people, letting me see them as better and more human and ultimately good—goodness has been theoretical to me for so long."

Riding through the countryside that spring or sitting on the bluffs looking down on the Missouri and watching the birds fly north, we made our plans. We would try to find new teaching jobs in Minnesota at better salaries—near each other and the university, we hoped, so that we could drive to Saturday classes. Perhaps we could augment our earnings by speaking and writing. Or perhaps we could stay in Mandan and save if we were given raises—but of course we were not; the Mandan school board gave raises to administrators for whom there was competition, to coaches with winning teams, to the occasional individual teacher who sued winningly and imaginatively.

By the end of the school year we were no longer willing to wait two years to get married, but the practical problems were mountainous. In Mandan I earned $105 a month for the school term; Gene, about $125. Marion Schroeder and I shared the $25 monthly rent for our little apartment. We managed to eat on a little less than a dollar a day (we received a fifteen-cent discount on the sixty-five-cent steak dinner at the railroad restaurant if we ate there regularly). Out of my check I sent my aunt money regularly—she regarded these as repayment for her help with my college education—to help with my sisters' college expenses, and also $15 each month to my younger brother, who was struggling through college on his own. This left only a very few hundred dollars a year for clothes, trips home, summer school at the University of Minnesota where I had started my graduate work. Gene had to return to summer school, too, if he was to finish his M.A. that year.

Gene's sister Marian wrote that there was a vacancy in the English department in the high school in Litchfield, Minnesota, the town where she and her friend Harriet were teaching. She thought it might pay $1200. Gene suggested that I apply and with reluctance, for I hated to think of leaving Mandan where I had been happy, I did so and received a favorable answer. Our hopes rose. Gene would surely find a Minnesota principalship once he got his master's that summer.

In a way that summer of 1939 gave us back a part of the college year together we had missed. We strolled the campus between classes, ate lunch in the crowded student union, or picnicked under the elms on the Knoll, a traditional trysting place. We studied together in the pleasant library reading rooms and sometimes spent an hour or two in the Arthur Upson Room, a memorial to a minor Minnesota poet who died young. In this romantic room students were allowed to read only for pleasure; they were never supposed to study there. It was a place made for people in love—full of whispers and the sound of turning pages. We dipped into the books here and there, sharing our favorites we had discovered alone and making new discoveries together. We liked sonnets then and were just beginning to read the Metaphysical poets.

We found old friends among the summer students and made some new ones. Among the latter I remember an inseparable couple from the university theater. They were earthy and flamboyant and found our Catholicism and idealism inexplicable and endlessly amusing. But we liked them very much and spent hot July afternoons swimming with them at Lake Nokomis and lying in the sun on its grassy shore. I cannot remember their names or see their faces, although I remember the girl's stunning performance in Irwin Shaw's *Bury the Dead*. Antiwar sentiment was still strong in Minnesota that summer.

Virginia Rankin, a college classmate to whom I felt most close, had married a young man named Bill Carlson, who, like herself, was intensely involved in the interracial movement, the Catholic Worker movement, and the co-operative movement. They found Gene and his thought very congenial, and we spent frugal but happy evenings with them hearing their plans for a co-operative housing project which was actually forming and Bill's plans to run for the legislature.

In the university atmosphere our strenuous efforts to economize seemed more like moves in a game than grim necessity. We pooled our food money and tried to eat on eighty-seven cents apiece each day. This strange total came from the prices set in the nearby student eating places. Walgreen's drug store featured a twelve-cent breakfast that usually consisted of juice, raisin toast, and coffee but was sometimes varied with sweet rolls or one pancake. An old account sheet torn from the back of one of Gene's notebooks shows that we were more often successful than not. It was possible to get an adequate lunch—sometimes a dish of stew, sometimes soup and a sandwich—at the student union. We could eat dinner for fifty cents at the Varsity, the Duchess, the Gopher, and other depressingly similar establishments. The Duchess had a particularly strange menu. One of its dinner specials was a tired fruit salad with cheese—a dish I remember because it was what we had ordered the night we saw a rat very slowly cross the floor. "Good God," exclaimed Gene, "even the rats lose energy on this food," and we walked out. After that we stretched our budget a little to eat where the food was hot and home-cooked.

Gene was awarded his M.A. at summer school graduation, walking across the stage in his rented academic gown, chin outthrust in the self-conscious gesture which had grown so familiar to me and which he never outgrew. I was very proud of him.

The summer was marred by two things. Gene found the endless job hunt very distasteful and I suffered through every interview with him in prospect and retrospect, often waiting in the car and praying dutifully, only too aware of what he was enduring. School administration as a specialized field had reached its peak and seemed to attract and prosper a breed of fussy, pedantic men much more interested in techniques of education than in ideas. If one survived their scrutiny, there remained the ordeal of interrogation by one or the other school board member, who tended to have cranky theories of his own. Gene could not and would not banter with them or try to win them over, nor did I want him to. He would not have been Gene if he had. Years later a Democratic county chairman used to recall feelingly at every state rally that he had rejected Gene as too quiet—"Too quiet! And look at him now!"—as the crowd roared—"How about that?"

Our second problem was my Aunt Abbie's strange reluctance to meet Gene. She was teaching summer school herself at the Diocesan Teachers College in St. Paul. We had long telephone conversations, as we had almost daily when I was in the Twin Cities but she pleaded the press of students and papers if I suggested that we come to see her or if I asked her to join us at dinner. It had seemed natural that I should have several long visits with her alone after the long months away, but as the weeks went on it became clear that she was really avoiding Gene. Weekend after weekend she slipped out of tentative arrangements. She had promised a friend to drive her to St. Croix or she found it necessary to visit the Malones—elderly and eccentric cousins who had merited only semi-annual duty calls in other years—or she made a trip to Wabasha. If I had found Gene's parents less than enthusiastic, he could only find Abbie's behavior chilling.

"Perhaps I should just not be able to come the next time she talks about seeing us," he suggested unhappily.

"Oh, Gene, no," I protested. "It's just that she knows she will like you if she sees you—and it will be like recognizing that something new has really happened—that I am really in love and truly going to get married."

The situation cast a little pall over my shining days. I had told the two people who meant most to me about each other. Gene had never had anyone in his life like my aunt, who could by her enthusiasms broaden anyone's world and who with her charm, interest, and appreciative discernment of quality could set him to conquering it. And I was sure that knowing Gene would convince her that he was indeed a man who was everything a man should be.

Near summer's end the shadows lifted. An acquaintance of Gene's was superintendent in the little town of Norwood, not far from

Minneapolis, and he offered Gene the principalship there, subject to the school board's approval at its annual meeting. We visited the superintendent and his wife and found the little town very dreary, but we did not think we would have to live there for long. It was a step on the way.

Abbie at long last capitulated handsomely by inviting Gene to spend a week with us in Wabasha at the old family home which she still kept, mainly for weekends of gardening and searching for antiques with one or the other of us nieces and nephews. She was at her best as she welcomed him warmly. It was her gift to celebrate life and to mark its occasions with happy ceremonies. For Gene she evoked all the past life of the old house with good talk and good cooking served with the old silver and placemats made of the worn yellow and blue damask cloths of my grandmother's time. With just a touch or two—a bowl of zinnias on the table in the living room, magazines on the porch—she made the house seem the home it had once been. Gene succumbed to the spirit of the place. I remember him looming tall against the screen door in the back entry, looking out across the yard and its border of Shasta daisies and delphinium, marveling at the life on the river beyond.

"I don't think you believed me last winter when I told you about the steamboats," I said.

"I didn't," he admitted, grinning. "I thought you were imagining it this way. I guess I thought the river only existed in Mark Twain." It was only in moments like this that it became apparent how different Gene's life of thought was from the world he actually saw and lived in. During our summer studies I had been impressed at the ease with which he identified or quoted any snatch from Shakespeare, yet he wrote me later that year that he was glad I was going to see *Hamlet*. "I should very much like to see it with you. I've never seen a professional stage play . . . Write to me all about it, *Hamlet*, I mean." Separation seemed harder as the summer drew to an end.

In the end Gene went back to Mandan for a second year. One of the school board at Norwood had vetoed his appointment at the last minute because he had not been consulted. I think we were secretly relieved that we had not broken away from everything we had known together. We wrote every day and sent each other special delivery letters for Sundays. I used to tear the letters open and skim them quickly, first for the assurances of love and then, like any exile, for the news of friends left behind. During the day I carried the letter about in my purse and read and reread the parts in which Gene wrote about what he was thinking and feeling, and I grew to know him better than I had before.

Gene had gone back, no longer an observer, but involved—usually with affectionate amusement, sometimes with genuine concern—in the lives of our friends. He related everything faithfully, with a sure eye for the flavor of occurrences and the nuances of relationships. Marion Schroeder and Lucille Walsh had both become engaged during the summer. Miss S. was telling no one until she had her ring, hence deceiving her usual Mandan escort and scandalizing Raph Thuente, who knew everything from Miss Fahey. Lucille, on the other hand, professed great surprise that people noticed her ring. Miss Frank had a new hair shade—"it reflects purple in the sunlight—most regal." Of the new teachers, Mr. Herlick, who had inherited the *Courier* staff, was a very German German and Mr. Johnson was very quiet with a rather hunted look. Gene observed that he was probably married—"such a happy sadness." He was quick to report when Nell and Lyle Weber's baby came—"It was a girl weighing six and a half pounds"—but he still had difficulty seeing good in the members of the administration. He softened his comments, however, because he knew his attitude worried me. I could not understand why he minded them so; they were at least pleasant and polite in their dealings with the teachers, very unlike the principal and superintendent in Litchfield who simply issued orders and summoned teachers by shouting down the hall after them, "Smith, Hauge, come here!"

I think even then Gene considered correct procedure of the utmost importance. When the Mandan superintendent sent around a typical personnel rating form so that the teachers would know on what they were being judged, Gene was driven to bitter sarcasm. He had posted them above his bed, he said, so that he might take check upon himself each morning and face the day with a sharp and immediate consciousness of the "qualities of major significance." He sent me a copy so that I might help him, he said, eliminate his betrayal of one of its most significant points. He had underlined "ability and willingness to conform."

But he was able to laugh when I revolted against what I considered the petty rules and the rudeness of my new principal, Mr. Bettendorf. As head of the English department in which I had worked, Gene had written one of my recommendations. Now he wrote me that my determined and extensive self-assertion was no doubt placing my new administration in a state of trepidation—and placing his fine statements about my co-operativeness in the balance. He added that he loved me for it all, and that I should be kind to the poor schoolmen.

We had planned that I would skip the traditional three-day meeting of the Minnesota Educational Association and visit him in Mandan instead. As the time neared, Gene's letters were a catalogue of train times and schedules—suggesting that it might be better to go back on the Great Northern from Fargo as it would take me directly to Litchfield or that I come on the Northern Pacific and he drive me to Fargo on the return trip, or suggesting a possible train and bus combination—all the suggestions aimed at stretching our time together as far as possible. He protested the slowness with which the days were going by. And finally grew lighthearted as the time of my coming drew nearer. "I shall see you at 6:26 on Thursday whereas you won't see me until 7:26," he wrote, playing on the time change. And teased me with what had become the traditional closing to our letters, "I love you"—saying that I might not have counted the first time he said it because he had prefaced it by saying that he was going to say it, and so said it again, "I love you."

All through that year of meeting and leave-taking—at Thanksgiving, at Christmas, at Marion Schroeder's wedding in Fargo, at the semester break, and at Easter—our letters, alternately hopeful and discouraged, went back and forth trying to share everything we saw and heard. All the images of his later poems are in them: the identification with trees and the preoccupation with their bones

—the black of box-elder twigs and the burnished dark red of rose branches in winter; the sky and its closeness; the perception of the earth turning and the relativity of time; the imprisonment in self —"Does it frighten you to think of having to be yourself for eternity—perhaps I should be frightened of joining my life to yours as an influence on your endless future." Sometimes he included fragments of poems, half-worked out, abortive with words crossed out one, two, three times until he found one good enough. He was fascinated with words and used to carry a slip of paper in his breast pocket to list those he wanted to remember or to check the meaning of.

He read voraciously but novels did not interest him except as expressions of philosophy. He abandoned Mann's *Joseph* trilogy and, when I wrote that I was reading *War and Peace*, he took it out of the library—but "I only read the first few chapters," he wrote. "You can find his whole theory of war in the last few pages."

It was as if he measured everything except the earth itself against an abstract pattern of perfection, and he found that pattern in the teachings of the Church. He wrote that he wished Irene and Milton, whom he found most congenial of all our friends, were Catholics. He feared, he said, that Milton was inclined toward an atheistic humanism which, he reminded me, Dostoyevsky had called the "mark of the Antichrist," and that he found it hard to oppose. He wished that he himself knew more history—and more of the Church and history —so that he could lead Milton to consider it as giving meaning "to life and humanity."

Although I was sure that it was proof that he was better and finer than any other man, his need to find transcendent meaning sometimes frightened me.

He wrote that heaven seemed attainable when love approached purity and unselfishness in human beings, and told me that once at Benediction that force of love had become real and sharp, more strongly our love in union with God. At such times the concept of the Mystical Body became clear and meaningful to him as the explanation of life, which otherwise might appear transient and self-centered. I felt unworthy in thinking so, but I did not want to be that pure and unselfish. I much preferred it when he wrote, "I like to watch you run, I would be so glad to see you running toward me now." Or "Tonight you were there, a presence just outside the pool of lamplight where I was reading."

My real life was lived in that daily exchange of letters and in our trips to meet each other, but my teaching life went on in Litchfield nonetheless. I would probably have liked Litchfield if I had not taught first in Mandan, but as it was, I was acutely unhappy. I first took a room with a childless couple who lived in a small bungalow. To get to my room I had to pass through their living room, which was cluttered with a welter of furniture bedecked with crocheted and ruffled doilies. My landlady wanted companionship and was annoyed at my retreating each night to my room and my typewriter. I was bent on writing for money and I did manage to sell articles to *Atlantic* and *Commonweal* that fall, but I found it hard to pray and read and write separated only by a thin door from her humming and sighing and rustling about. I knew that she thought me dull and unfriendly. Her facetious call, "Breakfast!" every morning began to seem intolerable to me. The situation was saved when one of the other teachers told me of a very small room available in the large Victorian house where she and three others stayed with a gracious widow, Mrs. McClure. Mrs. McClure herself proved to be a treasure. She was a very religious Presbyterian, but rather than being rigid, she was motherly, kind, and gentle. We all grew to love her. I had had many Protestant friends but she was the first saintly Protestant I had ever known. She never gossiped or said unkind things about others. She kept a table set on the back porch and never turned away a man who came to the door asking for food, as so many did in those Depression days. (True to her Presbyterian conscience, however, she would search about for some little job for him to do in payment.) She insisted on packing a breakfast for me to eat in the teacher's room after Mass, which I attended daily. And she listened to my confidences with endless patience and understanding.

I had always been pluralistic by experience and upbringing, but I think that in Litchfield I began to experience the first seeds of ecumenical thought—that is, to be not only tolerant of other religions but to find in them the strengths, truths, and traditions which had been minimized or perhaps atrophied in Catholic thought. I was very much helped in this appreciation by the reading in the seventeenth century I had been doing for my summer school work at the university. One could not read Richard Hooker and his explication of the *via media* without knowing that there was at least an argument for the tradition of the Anglican Church. Nor could one read the whimsical reflections of Thomas Browne, the anguished poems of George Herbert, without feeling something of the scope and civility of spirit which flourished in the English Catholic tradition. I had long and serious talks about Lutheranism with Ingrid Miller, a strong Danish girl, very knowledgeable about her heritage. Alison Moore, another of the teachers with whom I spent much time, was the daughter of a Methodist minister. Her description of the life of sacrifice and faith led by her father and mother made me appreciative of that religious strain, too.

Yet even in the motherly warmth at Mrs. McClure's and with my new friends, I was not secure from a strange affliction which was beginning to affect me. I could not seem to feel safe anywhere except in my own classroom and my bedroom unless I was near a door. Panic overtook me if I sat in the center of a theater or was caught near the wall in a restaurant booth. My heart would begin to pound rapidly, my hands grow wet, and I would feel as if there was no air. Try as I would to wait it out, I would usually have to escape. Gene wrote that I was working too hard, that our economic plight was his responsibility, not mine.

It was true that I worked hard but no harder than at Mandan, and I had the joy of teaching English all day. The Litchfield students were bright and responsive. I think that I felt what the cowardly traveler feels in a jungle, where he may at any moment be surrounded by hostiles. No longer disguised as it was in Mandan, the basic insecurity of the teacher in the public schools was beginning to haunt me, to reinforce my own unhappiness and my loneliness for Gene.

In a sense teachers were, as I wrote in my *Atlantic* piece that year, migratory laborers. However much they might like the community, however deep their involvement with their students, they had no permanent place there. Their only security lay in their contracts, negotiated anew each year. They had no tenure, no pension plan, and no reasonable expectations of advancement. If they wished to better themselves, they had to move on. They were, in reality, cogs—and easily replaceable cogs—in a machine which had institutional, recreational, and financial value to the town in which they taught.

School superintendents were really managers hired by the town to supervise one of its biggest businesses. This was vividly demonstrated in the first teachers' meeting I attended in Litchfield. We were instructed in the care of the plant and the necessity of co-operating with the janitors. We were told, for example, that we were expected to leave all the shades in our rooms at an even level at the end of the day. We were told that our absence records were of more importance than anything in judging our performance, since state aid was prorated on the number of pupil-days reported. We were also told that we were expected to spend three weekends out of every four in Litchfield, since the town paid us and expected us to spend our money there. To assure the town that we were really earning our salaries, we were instructed to be in our classrooms by eight-thirty in the morning and not to leave them before five. The school football games and basketball games were a great source of revenue and we were told that we were all expected to work at them, taking tickets, guarding gates, ushering. After this initial meeting, the junior high school principal, a woman, gathered the women teachers together to instruct them in the morality expected of them by the community. We were not to smoke, not to drink nor go to local dances, and it was strongly advised that we attend the local church. She also discussed the necessity of modest clothing.

I had further shocks. When I went to the principal and superintendent to ask about soliciting bids for the printing of the school paper which I was to supervise, I was met with blank stares of surprise.

"But there is a printer on the school board," they said.

Another member of the school board had his gunstocks and his gun cases made in the school woodworking shop.

The superintendent also suggested to me later, in a most kindly way, that it might be better if I did not go to daily Mass. It was a bit much for the community to accept. After all, I was teaching in a public school. I had learned from my aunt, who had fought a lifelong battle with repressive administrations, to turn every effort at the curtailment of individual liberties into a battle over general principle. "Was the town persecuting me for my religion?" I asked in indignation, and Mr. Harbo retreated hastily saying, "No, no, it isn't that, it was just that I had thought . . ." I also waged a little private rebellion, pretending that I did not hear when the principal yelled down the hall after me, summoning me by my last name. When he later appeared at my classroom door, I would say, "Oh, I never thought it might be *you!*"

So, sustained by Gene's support, I waged my own fight with the Establishment. The younger teachers had joined and given new life to the local chapter of the American Federation of Teachers, which had languished after the departure of the former superintendent, a confirmed liberal. The Federation was tarred with the Communist brush in those days but it was the only agency of solidarity for teachers; without it each one dealt singly with the administration and the school board.

The superintendent met with us to deplore professional people joining a labor union. I remember the courageous answer Nellie Allen, the oldest member of the English department, gave him: "A professional person takes responsibility for his work and his working hours, Mr. Harbo," she said. "I am not a professional person as long as I in effect punch a time clock. A professional person also sets his own fee. My fee, that is my salary, is set for me by others. And I must have some way of bargaining with them."

I was elected president of the local because I was willing to speak out and also because I did not have as much to lose as the married men. We tried in my brief tenure to set up relations with the only other union in town, that of the railroad men. But the railroad men were irritated and put off by our attempt to make our problems seem similar to theirs. We sought a salary scale and a regular system of raises, but our proposal was tossed aside by the administration and the board. There was only so much money for salaries, we were told, and it always had to balance off. If someone got more money, someone else had to go.

At the end of the year, buoyed by the hope that I would be married and not have to return, I answered the questionnaire given to the faculty and appended a three-page dissertation in response to the last question, "Do you have any suggestions?" for which one line had been left on the form. I set down in no uncertain terms my thoughts about everything—from the general lack of professionalism displayed in faculty meetings to the insensitivity and coldness with which new teachers were greeted. To Mr. Harbo's great credit, after his initial shock at my temerity (to which he confessed later), he took some of my suggestions to heart and at the initial faculty meeting the next year there was a discussion of the educational objectives of Litchfield High School. The new teachers were introduced and the older teachers in the system were asked to volunteer as special friends to each one. In the system, then as today, the problem is not the ill will of the individual but the lack of self-examination within the system itself.

To many struggling with the problems of urban schools today, Litchfield would have seemed a dream school and indeed it was very good. It had become a regional school to which over half of the students were bused from smaller outlying communities. In order to serve all the students, there were both college preparatory and general education courses, but the stigma of the track system was avoided in that these were a matter of elective choice on the part of the students, although the guidance counselors tried hard to steer students who were not capable of the college preparatory work away from it. In order to avoid athleticism, the curse of many private schools as well as of small-town high schools, a longer midday break was arranged and there was a full program of intramural sports which students could enjoy during this period. (Many of our students were needed to help at home on the farm at night and could not participate in the school teams.) Our extracurricular meetings were also held during this time so that the rural students could be part of the newspaper and yearbook staff and join the glee club, the drama group, and all the other activities. There was a large library and a flourishing library program; there was a full-time guidance teacher who worked with each home-room adviser; there was a remedial reading teacher.

Despite the efforts of the faculty to be evenhanded, it was clear that the school was run socially and politically by the students who lived in Litchfield. They tended to know each other well and were unified. The rural students were divided and disorganized because they came from many different communities. Ingrid Miller, the librarian, and I and the guidance counselor, Gordon Miniclier, were the most convinced Democrats on the faculty. We were convinced that the rural students should not simply accept the benefits of Litchfield High School but have a part in deciding things as well. Each year the "king" and "queen" of that most American of all folk festivals, the high school homecoming, were elected from the junior class. Since all the juniors were in my English classes, we were able to make use of a unit on parliamentary procedure to point out that the upcoming election for homecoming king and queen made an ideal laboratory test for the use of parliamentary procedure. It was clear that it would be more democratic for rural students to be among those nominated, if not elected, since they were so clearly in the majority. Once the rural students had braved the nominating procedure with the psychological support of their classmates, the election of their nominees became inevitable. They were delighted to discover the power of the political process.

Weekends were lonely that first semester and I welcomed Mrs. McCarthy's occasional invitations to the McCarthy house in Watkins. During those weekends I came to know Gene's mother well, and I think we had a real affection for each other although I do not think for a minute she yielded her inner hope that Gene would eventually be a priest. Although Carty-Ma had lived with her and her husband, he was not Carty-Ma's favorite son. All her married life Mrs. McCarthy had been placed in competition with Aunt Mary Steve, as the McCarthys called the wife of Gene's father's brother who lived seven miles away in the town of Eden Valley.

titude the immediate marriage meant that I was deserting her and my sisters and brother in time of need. She simply did not believe that I would continue to be of help once I was married. Gene's father had originally talked of giving him a half interest in the farm if Gene would manage it, but that possibility seemed to have been forgotten. In her talks with me, Gene's mother had alluded to this possibility as compromising the rights of the other children.

Everything was complicated by the shadow of approaching war; there was talk of a draft and Gene would be subject to it. But, more important than any of these practical problems was a new and hopeful possibility which changed the direction of all our plans. It seemed possible that Gene would go back to St. John's as a lay teacher. Our plans of farming as an adjunct to teaching had always been meant as more than plans for a practical solution to our personal problems—they were our answer to what we saw as the need for Christian renewal of society. The return to St. John's meant that we might join the Christian community centering around its abbey and which was gaining new life from the plans then taking shape. There were plans to make St. John's a center of adult education and economic revival based on co-operatives and on the revival of Christian rural community, all vivified with the social spirituality of the liturgical movement, the restoration of all things in Christ. There was tremendous excitement in the prospect.

St. John's is situated on a large property of over 2500 acres of forest, lake, and farmland in central Minnesota. Moreover, it was the spiritual center for the more than two hundred parishes and missions in Minnesota which were served by Benedictine priests. Over forty of these were nearby. The abbey itself was a self-contained world on its own land. It had its own post office called Collegeville and its own railroad stop. A great deal of the food was raised on the abbey farm (the abbey black bread was famous). There was a print shop for its various publications which included the papers of the new social institute, the popular liturgical library, and the internationally distributed *Orate Fratres*, organ of the liturgical movement. Down below the hill there was a little street of workmen's houses, called Flynnville by the monks and college students.

When, late in the spring of 1940, Gene was offered a position teaching education and economics at St. John's, it seemed to us that God was answering our prayers in a way better than we could have dared to hope. The salary was not very large, but it was supplemented by room and board. For the first time Gene could really save money. Litchfield was not far away, we could see each other often. Perhaps, perhaps even by the second semester, we could marry. We drove through the little street of Flynnville in the dusk, picking out the nicer houses, hoping that the abbey might substitute one of them for Gene's room when we married. At last we could be decisive. We would not wait beyond the next June of 1941 to be married.

Going back to St. John's was not only going home but also a source of liberation for Gene. He had increasingly come to feel, as I had so painfully in Litchfield, that serving the great and impersonal machine of public education—no matter how good our relations with our students or how enlightened our classroom teaching—was only half living. It was not a way in which we could make a fundamental change in our world. Gene still thought of this in terms of secularism—the all-inclusive term used by Catholic social thinkers to describe the deliberate exclusion of religion or any coherent philosophy of life from education and the world of work. It was generally held that bourgeois spirit and unchristian individualism had both resulted from the lack of any Christian social theory and had brought about the injustices of laissez-faire capitalism, materialism, the breakdown of the family, and the depersonalization of society.

Gene's application to Father Damian was couched in those terms. Teaching in a public school, he wrote, meant that one was only half teaching since the most important questions could never be raised and the most important reasons never given.

Gene had gone out from St. John's in 1935 into the world of the Great Depression, of social upheaval, without any very adequate preparation. His world had been the uncomplicated and wholly

Catholic and ethnic world of Watkins and St. John's. At the time he graduated, St. John's was a small denominational institution of no particular distinction, although the monastery to which it was attached was beginning to have a worldwide reputation for liturgical scholarship. The college was really a subsidiary—a "work," in the parlance of religious communities, and, until the deanship of Dom Virgil Michel and his predecessor, Father Mark, something of a stepchild. Abbot Alcuin, the superior of the community, and president of the college as well, was more concerned with the academic preparation of seminary teachers and missionaries than he was with staffing the college.

It was a small college of only three hundred students, half of whom were clerics, as the Benedictines called their seminarians, and it had never been accredited because the abbot believed that with accreditation would come secular interference. Gene returned to teach at St. John's in the fall of 1940.

At that time, St. John's was expanding and building its faculty and well on its way to becoming a center of adult education, a center for the discussion of, and attack on, the social problems of the day. All this had been brought about largely through the efforts of one man—Father Virgil. He had come back to St. John's as dean during Gene's second and last year in college but his effect on the students was then largely indirect. Gene's own interests were in English literature and economics, interests which did not engage much of Father Virgil's attention at the time. As a student, Gene was affected more than anything else by the renewed emphasis on the liturgy—all the ceremonies radiating out from the Eucharist as the sacred sign of the unity of all men—and by the social institutes—weekend adult education meetings. At these he acquired his interest in the co-operative movement and the rural life movement as a cure for social ills.

But he was only nineteen when he was graduated and he had spent only three years in college. His classmates of the time describe him as a loner and an observer. He did not date and he did not drink; he drew some criticism for sitting silent and listening through dormitory bull sessions. It was assumed that he was weighing a religious vocation. But he had thrown himself into his studies and into athletics, in both of which he excelled, and his college fame rested on his star quality in almost any sport. Although he had turned in his football suit after a disagreement with the coach, he ranked as an "all state" player in baseball and hockey. He was president of the Scribbler's Union, a club organized for those who aspired to write for the college paper and yearbook, and was one of the editors of the latter.

In the academic field he had had no rival. His senior biographical sketch records this in an excruciatingly arch style:

"We could make this particular write-up quite brief by merely calling your attention to the fact that this lad is being graduated cum laude at the tender age of 19. That fact speaks volumes and should suffice to give you some idea of his capabilities, but Gene was not satisfied with finishing college in three years. The really breath-taking accomplishment is yet to be recorded. In order not to heighten the suspense too much we will state now that this jolly and towering Gael made local collegiate history by registering 8 A's in his classwork two years ago, and has continued that splendid work. To him the marking alphabet of professors terminates with Alpha . . . The Watkins wonder leans toward the serious side of life, but then any fellow carrying the amount of work that Gene did could not afford to enter into all and sundry social debates, which consume so much of the average student's time."

When Gene returned to St. John's in the fall of 1940, he returned as someone very much more involved in life and as an active participant in the discussion which raged in the prefect's room, which served as an informal faculty discussion center. Basic to these discussions were the ideas of Father Virgil, who had died the year before but who had left a great blueprint for the renewal of society in his writings and in his research. Through correspondence and tireless traveling he had kept in touch with the leaders seeking change all over the Catholic world. Through teaching, lecturing, preaching, and through the publications he had founded, he had initiated some movements for change and assisted others. In his person and in his writings he had brought together the two dynamic streams of Christian renewal which had begun to flourish in the early years of our century.

The liturgical movement with which Father Virgil's name is synonymous was based on the idea that it matters how men pray together because prayer is intimately bound up with man's understanding of his relationship to his fellow man. If I appear before God, Father and Creator, as a member of a Body which potentially includes all humanity, I must eventually accept all manner of corollaries about my relationship to other men. In the terms of modern psychology, those interested in the revival of the liturgy insisted that man exists *in relationship* and that communion between man and man presupposes community. In liturgical worship the individual is lifted beyond his selfish concerns and welded into a deeper relationship with his family and his neighbors.

Ultimately, it was clear to Father Virgil, if one is aware of the implications of his worship, one must be led to the need to bring about a more perfect community among men. This, in his time and in his terms, meant a concern with social action. Father Virgil was the heir of those who in the monasteries and universities of Europe were trying to recover the concept of the Church as a living body rather than as a hierarchical structure for the dispensing of spiritual gifts and services. But he saw a connection between this theology and social action which others did not see. Ever since Leo XIII and his labor encyclicals, Catholic thinkers had been struggling with the problems of economic justice. These pioneers concerned themselves in theory with the criticism of capitalism and laissez-faire economics. In the United States this had had its practical effect in Catholic involvement in, and support of, the labor movement and in the organization and professionalization of charity. It also included the beginning of an attack on racism.

Virgil Michel, like other Christian thinkers, looked on a twentieth century where men lived in despair and upheaval and where pessimism prevailed. There was international anarchy. In his America, the richest country in the world, bread lines and soup kitchens were everywhere for the millions of men without work; farmers were leaving the land to add to the numbers of the miserable crowding in city slums. His answer was the re-Christianization of society, a reordering, a re-creation of the interdependence of the "age of faith." Significantly, all the social movements he thought worthy of support by apostolic Christians were ones which thought of modern society as crumbling and were intended to build new structures within the shell of the old—much as Christianity itself built within the dissolving Roman Empire. Such movements were the renewal of the corporate order, the personalist movement, the co-operative movement, and distributist-agrarian movement. At their heart was a distrust of the state. The "secular" and "secularization" were pejorative terms.

Like the Benedictines of the Middle Ages, Father Virgil thought of society as being rebuilt around Benedictine-centered communities. Not surprisingly—a prophet is not honored in his own country— Father Virgil's ideas had effect on the college at St. John's last of all, probably because he was allowed to put them into practical application only in the last years of his life. The conflict between his filial obedience to the abbot and his frustration at the latter's lack of understanding and co-operation had cost him his health and had driven him into the breakdown and subsequent retirement to the Indian missions from which he was recalled to the deanship.

The regular gatherings in the prefect's room included men who had been either contemporaries of Father Virgil or his students; it included men who had been stimulated by him to pursue ideas of their own. How much Gene delighted in the give and take of the nightly discussions was reflected in the letters to me, usually written when he had just returned to his room.

Father Walter was in good anti-clerical form tonight—he attacked the monastery faction which favors a complete turning to the contemplative life and the liturgy—as escapists—asserting that most of the leaders of the movement are escapists—covering up their inability to teach, preach, etcetera. He made a good point against private schools, too—explaining that they are being displaced by state schools because they have neglected to educate the poor— he includes this as one of the causes for the loss of faith among the poor during the Reformation. He thinks the same criticism can be levied on the Catholic schools today. He also took two or three swipes at the liturgists who over-emphasize the appointments, vestments, candles, altars, at the expense of the spirit. All in all, it was a good destructive evening.

I could see the scene, the ambiance very much like that in Father Hildebrand's study. The prefect's room was a very masculine retreat. Father Walter, whose field was history and who was dean of discipline, would be presiding genially. He was the "Mr. Chips" of St. John's—the man everyone came back to see—an expansive man, easily excited by ideas. He would sit, feet apart, using his cigar to punctuate his points, occasionally brushing absently at the ashes which fell on the scapular of his habit. Father Martin would be there, still fresh from his studies at Harvard, full of enthusiasm for the co-operative experiments and the folk university at Antigonish in Nova Scotia or for the latest news from Monsignor Ligutti, who was establishing co-operatives and credit unions among the poverty-stricken farmers and coal miners in Iowa. There would also be Father Emeric Lawrence, a teacher of French then serving as chaplain to the students and beginning to try his hand at writing on spirituality. And occasionally Father Godfrey Diekmann, a more austere scholar, then the new editor of *Orate Fratres*.

Emerson Hynes, who had returned with his M.A. from Notre Dame the year before, was the unofficial leader of the lay faculty. I could see him, already every inch the campus guru, tapping his pipe and drawing on it meditatively before he made his own points in his slow-speaking, definitive way. Father Ernest Kilzer, head of the philosophy department, would nod, underline, and redefine these points like a true scholastic philosopher.

Emerson had been a freshman in college with Gene. It would be hard to measure Emerson's influence on Gene but their lives were intertwined then and never really separated again. (He became Gene's legislative assistant in the Senate.) If the senior yearbook portrayed Gene as somewhat aloof, it depicted Emerson as the opposite: "First of all, he is a student as is evidenced by the 7 A's he succeeded in getting with seemingly little effort . . . In addition . . . he is the confidant of the school, his room being the haven of advice-seeking fellows, for he is a good listener except when he wants to talk."

Emerson's pre-eminence sprang from his firm intention to live out his beliefs in distributist-agrarianism and the need for the decentralization of society. He was committed to the lay apostolate and the "one foot on the land" theory. He planned to marry a St. Catherine's graduate coincidentally named Arleen McCarty. They had leased ten acres of abbey land where they planned to raise their own food and were building a cinder-block house with the rather desultory help of other faculty members and local craftsmen.

Also participants in these nightly meetings were other members of the lay faculty—Adrian Winkel, later Gene's first administrative assistant; Tom Cassidy, a waspish but entertaining little man from the East, who taught English; Vernon McGree, member of the coaching staff who shared baseball memories with Gene.

The lay faculty was not always serious. Joining in their company on weekends and at homecoming I found them less sophisticated and more given to playful foolishness than the friends we had shared elsewhere. They were hard-drinking except for Gene, who did not drink then, Emerson, who subscribed to the theory that Christians were meant to drink wine, a more natural drink than whiskey in any of its forms. Once they hit on a whimsical theory, they tended to elaborate on it endlessly, such as McGree's excuse for the basketball team's losing in a night game with Gustavus Adolphus. He declared solemnly that the light reflecting from the hair of so many Scandinavians had blinded his players. One weekend they drove Arleen and me almost to distraction by insisting that Newman's essay on the education of a gentleman must have been intended as a satire. I think that all of them including Gene half believed it. On another occasion they upheld their theory that animals could not feel pain by absurd proofs; a piece of steel thrown suddenly on dry ice would emit a sound like a scream but certainly did not feel. It was fun, but it was not conversation.

It comes to me now as something of a shock to realize that they were still in their early twenties—Gene was only twenty-four—younger than many of the leaders in the youth movement today.

They shared the common belief of youth that their elders were compromising their ideals and that the old institutions were not working. If Christian renewal was the answer to the problems of the day, they wanted its ideals pursued completely and immediately. Within the framework of this microcosm of university life, Gene and Emerson and some of the younger monks waged battles which, although they were battles in discussion only, were—in the very different idiom of Catholic social philosophy—the battles of the students today. With justice they pointed out that a plan to strengthen St. John's athletics by bringing a coach from Notre Dame —and thus to encourage further alumni and donor support—was certainly at odds with the plan worked out by Father Virgil in cooperation with Mortimer Adler to adapt the "great books" plan to the Benedictine course of study and to de-emphasize athletics.

Another clash occurred when the St. Thomas debate team engaged the team from St. John's. When the chairman asked for questions, the whole idea of debate was attacked from the floor. How could a controversial subject have two sides neither of which was supported by an appeal to morality? A hapless debater replied that debate was concerned with facts, not with moral principles, at which point the audience, led by the young lay professors, rose in denunciation and the St. John's debate coach fled in embarrassment. (He later became a Republican party official who strongly opposed Gene in all his campaigns.)

A more serious dispute arose when the philosophy department of the University of Minnesota came to spend a night of discussion with the philosophy department at St. John's. Gene wrote that he assumed that they were "slumming in the country." He listed Castell, Conger, two or three more, and Fiegel. Fiegel was reported to be one of the best logical positivists, "a contradiction in itself" in America.

The young professors had wanted to challenge the visitors on how a philosophy department could exist without some agreement on the verities. But the older faculty, mindful no doubt of hospitality, had prevented any such confrontation. The whole evening, according to Gene, had been spent in "evasive jesting." It was explained that the visit had been meant to lay the groundwork for good relations between the two departments. It was hoped that one of St. John's scholastic philosophers might eventually introduce a course at the university. "We insisted, however, that the whole business was in itself a violation of truth, sincerity, and of the intelligence and prudence of everyone present"—Gene told me. It was a true gap between the generations.

Emerson approached these disputes as philosophical problems. He had a patient man's tolerance for foibles and contradictions. But they seemed to disturb Gene profoundly. I was glad that he was so alive and engaged, but I sensed that his passionate anti-secularism and his obsessive concern when the monks seemed to fall short of the Benedictine ideal were creating a subtle barrier between us. Often, when we were together, he would hold my hand absently while he ruminated aloud about these things. One of his recurring themes was that, although the monks practiced poverty, chastity, and obedience, Christian asceticism and Christian love for the brotherhood as individuals, they had relinquished all economic and social responsibility to the religious community as a whole and that the community was as much a part of the capitalistic system as any other corporate body; that the community acted as employer, property owner, and landlord without any moral sanctions and with reference only to supply and demand. (This same criticism of church bodies has become commonplace today among the faithful in all denominations.) I often felt an outsider, still working and battling in "the world," a victim of the dichotomy set up by integralistic Catholic thinking.

In December of that year I made a change which I thought must surely bring us closer together again. The administration at St. Catherine's knew of our plans for marriage in the approaching summer, so Mother Eucharista, the president, and Sister Antonine, the dean, felt free to ask me to take Sister Maris Stella's classes for the remaining two quarters of the school year so that she could work on a textbook commission set up at Catholic University. The prospect was a delight to me. I was to take over the classes of my most admired college teacher and to guide the destiny of the very successful college magazine, *Ariston,* in her place. Like Gene I would be teaching college classes and sharing the same concerns.

When I returned to St. Catherine's, I found there the same pursuit of academic excellence as in my student years, but also a ferment of ideas. In my graduate work at the University of Minnesota, I had already been caught up in the rediscovery of the seventeenth century and the Metaphysical poets. The seventeenth was the century in which, as John Donne, its best-known poet said, "a new philosophy called all in doubt." It was a century like our own, in which the dizzying implications of recent scientific discoveries created a universal malaise and the world of thought was rocked by a new world view. It was a century of terrifying doubt and of religious revival. It was a century of experimentation in art and poetry. Its poets had been rediscovered by the poets of our century and their techniques were a favorite subject of critical essays.

T. S. Eliot had become the undisputed doyen of contemporary letters and Gerard Manley Hopkins, rediscovered, was one of the most imitated of poets. The return to tradition had been stimulated by the fugitive poets of the South—John Crowe Ransom and Allen Tate. Literature with religious themes was no longer a subject for a small coterie but was the topic of serious discussion and controversy in the most respected literary journals in the country. All this was reflected in the course of studies at St. Catherine's. When I had left, literary papers discussed Katherine Mansfield, Virginia Woolf, Saki, Ezra Pound, plays like John Drinkwater's $X=O$, with an occasional bow to such saintly writers as Thomas More who was considered relevant as an opponent to the totalitarianism symbolized by Henry VIII. When I returned the reviews in *Ariston* were devoted to Sigrid Undset, Graham Greene, Hopkins, William Butler Yeats, W. H. Auden, Eliot.

A course in the English Catholic Revival taught by Agnes Keenan was one of the most crowded on campus. The drama and speech department was being professionalized by Mabel Frey. The lively and highly literate teachers in the French department under the leadership of Sorbonne licentiates Sister Marie Philip and Anne Colloppy were discussing and teaching the work of Maritain, Claudel, Bernanos, Gide, and Mauriac. A rigorous political science department had emerged under Dr. Edna Fluegel, a Brookings fellow who had been an aide to Cordell Hull and served such ill-fated world leaders as Dollfuss at the London conference. A revolution had taken place in the sociology department when Sister Helen Angela had returned from Catholic University on fire with the teaching of Paul Hanley Furfey. In the Spanish department Sister Eleonore had departed from the classic curriculum in Spanish literature and had pioneered in the study of Latin-American authors, especially those with great social themes like Ciro Alegría, author of *Broad and Alien Is the World*. The psychology department had taken on new life under Sister Annette, a professional clinical psychologist.

It was assumed that teachers knew what they were doing, and as long as the broad outline of the course of study of the liberal arts curriculum was observed, each was free to develop in her field of interest new courses of study. When it was later decided that I was to stay at St. Catherine's I was allowed to introduce "Seventeenth Century Prose and Poetry" and an honors seminar called "Readings in World Literature," which dealt with the psychological novels of Dostoyevsky, Tolstoy, Flaubert, and Huxley, as well as Undset, and went into the *Confessions of St. Augustine* and the *Autobiography of St. Teresa*—this at a time when seminarians were forbidden to read these books. I also taught a course in free reading for people who were not English majors in which we read widely in the popular literature of the day—Hemingway, Fitzgerald, Richard Wright, Nelson Algren, Faulkner, and Farrell.

I found my work at St. Catherine's exciting and liberating. I also found it in happy correspondence with my classes at the university, where in both the English and English education departments much of the same ferment was going on. All this I tried to share with Gene in letters and on our weekend meetings, but he did not seem to take it in. It was as if he were off on a track of his own.

Since the visit of the University of Minnesota philosophy department to St. John's he had been highly critical of the university. He seemed for the first time to be aware of it as an institution as a whole, not just a source of credits needed for advancement or of law and medical degrees for private college graduates. The Hutchins-Adler theory that an education must have an integrating core of philosophy was congenial to most Catholic minds, particularly since Adler had rehabilitated Thomistic philosophy as the legitimate heir and extension of Aristotelian thought. Gene judged the eclecticism at the university from this point of view. He was troubled when he heard from two visiting philosophy students that there was no copy of the *Summa Theologica* in the university library and that Aristotle was thought of there merely as an historical figure: "His metaphysics is too definite, it seems, and his vocabulary restrictive. Plato is much more amenable to speculation and compromise."

He reported with seeming approval a plan discussed in the prefect's room for exposing false teaching at the university. It involved the bishop's appointing a person to collect and publish précis of the courses in which the falsification of theology and philosophy "is most blatant and vicious." He thought, he said, that with the support of the Lutherans and other Christians such activities would effect a definite improvement in the interest of "what is true and right." (It seems incredible that only ten years later he would be flinging in the teeth of the other McCarthy his judgment that Communists should be allowed to teach at this same university: "If college students cannot justify democracy—then democracy has indeed failed.")

This judgmental attitude troubled me, as it was to do whenever it emerged again later in our lives. (Norman Mailer, not at the time one of Gene's admirers, wrote of him at the Chicago convention that his eye was the eye of the hanging judge!) The university was very much a part of my life—my mother's school, my aunt's, and, in part, my own since I had done some of my undergraduate work there. I felt very much on the defensive and felt moreover that there was an obscure personal attack in Gene's criticism of Mr. Dunn, my graduate adviser; Gene said he had heard that in Mr. Dunn's course in the Bible as literature he discredited the possibility of its divine inspiration and referred to the stories et cetera as "the myths of the Bible." It was Mr. Dunn who had awakened my own interest in theology, making me see it not as a given, but as a living and growing thing hammered out in the lives of men. However, I did not know enough of the new biblical scholarship at the time to defend Dunn's use of the word "myth."

Even harder to cope with emotionally was the sly male ragging that the very mention of St. Catherine's seemed to evoke in the prefect's room. In part this may have been the old rivalry between the institutions founded by Archbishop Ireland (who had little time for German thought and German ways) and the Benedictine institutions. I am ashamed that when I first knew of it, I thought of St. John's as only a country college. But I think it was more than that. The monks of St. John's were dedicated men in serious pursuit of holiness. Like most men of the Church they would have denied that they were misogynistic and would have cited their devotion to the Blessed Mother and their own mothers to prove it. But they dealt with the problem of women, as men in groups ever have, by refusing to take them seriously. The attitude was so ingrown, so habitual, that I am sure they did not recognize it for the casual brutality it really was. Thus, when the psychology classes and faculty, earnest and admiring, made a field trip to St. John's to study monasticism, the only report from the prefect's room was that St. Catherine's girls affected a darker, more Joan Crawford-like make-up than those at St. Benedict's, the neighboring woman's college. What, they wanted to know, was the reason? When St. Catherine's introduced a course in rural sociology, the hope was expressed that the dignity of farm life would not be considered inseparable from "running water, electricity, tractors, and the neighbor's daughter as a maid." The gibes were insignificant in themselves, but it hurt me to have them come from Gene. He had always seemed to me sensitive to women as persons and to their aspirations.

My uneasiness was allayed because his letters were still full of thoughts and hopes I was sure he shared with no one else. At the beginning of Lent he wrote that he was going to limit his time in the prefect's room to an hour a day and spoke of our love for each other as a grace from God. On February 14 he wrote simply, "It is St. Valentine's Day. I love you," and I found at my door a huge box of red roses.

Easter was late that year, but it was still cold and gray and the signs of spring were few when I went to Watkins to spend the Holy Week vacation at the McCarthys with Gene. After the *tre ore* service on Good Friday, Gene and I went driving out into the country. We stopped by a little slough where the willows showed only a pale haze of green. There he told me that he felt called to be a priest after all. He wanted to enter the novitiate at St. John's. With those few words I was bereft of the hope and love which had sustained me and given my life center and purpose. But I could not protest the will of God.

After awhile we talked and Gene showed me the telegram of encouragement he had received from Father Godfrey. I did not quite see how I could live without him, but I felt a queer sense of relief because the veiled hostility and tension I had sensed in him were gone, now that I no longer stood between him and his goal. We fell back almost at once into our old trustful and open exchange of thoughts. "That was why I didn't like G.," Gene said with rare frankness, referring to a teacher friend of mine in Litchfield. "His feelings about you were more honest than mine." And he proposed very tentatively that I might consider entering a convent. There was dark consolation in that thought—that he still wanted me to share his future but in a different way.

Somehow I got through the rest of the weekend. Mrs. McCarthy looked knowing but said nothing until I was leaving. "You are always welcome here, Abbie," she said kindly, and I bore away the bleak knowledge that she, too, like the monks, had known Gene's plans before I did.

Until Gene finally entered the novitiate a year later—he had to save money and prepare himself further in philosophy and Latin—my life was lived on two levels. On one level I continued to be caught up emotionally with him and his plans. We saw each other often—how often, I think his spiritual advisers had no idea. (One night we ran into a prominent St. John's alumnus in a restaurant and Gene, nervous and surprised, tried to slip by without introducing me. I stormed off in tears.) My friends, too, disapproved because they thought the ambiguity of the relationship too hard on me. I suppose I hoped until the last that he would change his mind.

Whenever Gene came to see me he brought news from St. John's. Arleen and Emerson Hynes had married during the summer and were living in a trailer while their house was being finished. They were calling their ten acres "Kilfenora" after the town in Ireland from which the Hynes family came. They had a calf named Leopold—it was a conceit of liturgists taking to the land to name their animals for the feast days of the saints upon which they were acquired. Arleen was already expecting a baby. Joyful and unrestrained procreation was basic to the rural life and the family movement. They were to have ten children before they left the farm. There was at that time a concerted effort on the part of Catholic thinkers to find a positive theology of marriage in the liturgy and its sources—to look on marriage and the begetting of children not as concessions to man's weakness but as a positive participation in creation. This effort had the logical result of finding in the strictures on birth control an affirmation of life.

On the other level I was rebuilding my life. The sisters had rallied to my need. I was to stay on at St. Catherine's teaching part time until I finished my M.A. In those days an M.A. was much more of a distinction than it is now. The choice of a thesis was a very serious matter, because it was often published or, failing that, became the central core of a doctoral dissertation. Many college teachers never took a higher degree, preferring to grow as classroom teachers rather than to spend several years in the narrow specialization then required for a doctorate.

My first thought was to work on John Donne, but I was advised that he was such a popular subject that it would be difficult to make any original contribution. I had turned to Richard Crashaw—not because I found his baroque and sensuous verse appealing, but because through him I had come to know the great sixteenth-century Spanish mystics, especially Teresa of Avila.

The mystics were regarded with great suspicion by most Catholics after the Council of Trent. The popular idea was that they were impractical and given to foolish excesses. Historians like Christopher Dawson held the theory that mysticism flourished only when religion was excluded from the mainstream of history—as if it were some kind of dammed-up energy. The magisterium seemed to consider the mystics dangerous. Student theologians were allowed to read them only under guidance. After all, the mystics belonged to the Augustinian stream of Christianity, and, although St. Augustine had survived his deplorable youth to become one of the fathers of the Church, everyone knew his effect on Luther. Out of favor with both the world and the Church, the mystics' books were hard to find.

A summer school acquaintance of mine had a copy of the *Autobiography of St. Teresa*, smuggled out of some seminary library, and lent it to me. I had read it the first fall I was in Litchfield, totally unprepared for its shattering effect. I knew that one met and experienced God in prayer and in the sacraments, but that there could be this naked, blinding experience of the Divine was frightening. I sat in that narrow little room at Mrs. McClure's, shaken and fascinated. If there was any invitation extended in my discovery of mystical experience, I did not want to accept it. Clearly the price in detachment was more than I wanted to pay. It was a real spiritual struggle. I lost weight. "Marian says you are growing visibly thinner," Gene had written then. "Don't work so hard."

Now that God had taken Gene away from me I thought of that experience as prophetic. In turning back to St. Teresa as a subject of scholarship, I hoped to come to terms with her and the extraordinary demands of a jealous God.

That summer Sister Maris Stella arranged for me to take her place at the Bread Loaf School of English in Vermont. A student of hers and mine, Magdalen Schimanski, had won the first prize in the *Atlantic Monthly* poetry contest which included summer scholarships at Bread Loaf for both student and teacher. Gene lent me the Chevrolet, only a respectable four years old, insisting that it was our common property. Magdalen, my sister Ellen, who was going to intern in dietetics at Massachusetts General Hospital, and I set out for our first trip East.

It was a more venturesome trip then, before the days of motels and superhighways. Once on the open road I felt a certain lightheartedness returning. From the days of our childhood, when she was the blonde and blue-eyed favorite, my sister Ellen has faced life with a practical acceptance and an irrepressible spirit of fun. We were armed with the Duncan Hines books on restaurants and tourist homes, those inns of the automobile and the Great Depression. We ate and slept our way across Wisconsin, Illinois, Indiana, and Ohio. In Pennsylvania, awed by the furious speed of cars on the turnpike, then new, we dropped down to Gettysburg. Ellen and I toured the battlefield and Magdalen scandalized us by attending a tent revival meeting. Somehow we were lost in Pittsburgh until late at night when we found a room in a dingy house, where men wandered in and out all night cursing, stumbling, pounding on doors. Terrified, we pushed the bureaus across the doors and slipped out as soon as it was light.

In Philadelphia we were refused admission to a gas station rest room in the Negro area—"It wouldn't seem right, ma'am"—and, looking in vain for a Hines-recommended Colonial Restaurant in the newspaper, found a charming kosher restaurant instead, where they hesitated to serve us until they were sure we knew where we were. We were probably the only tourists from the West ever to spend the night in midtown Elizabeth, New Jersey, before venturing into New York City. We came out of the Holland Tunnel the next morning and stopped stock still in the bewildering traffic. A nice mounted policeman came to our aid and patiently clip-clopped blocks after us when he saw us take the wrong turn despite his patient directions. ("What do girls like you do on Saturday night in Minnesota?" "Oh, we have our simple pleasures, officer.") We missed connections with our intended host at Columbia University and ate at Jack Dempsey's. In Boston Edward Weeks of the *Atlantic Monthly* was our host. When we were alone again, we went in search of the Atlantic Ocean and spent a few moments looking solemnly out into a completely fogged-in Boston Harbor as if to mark its second discovery. Finally Magdalen and I said good-by to Ellen at Mass. General.

The language schools of Middlebury College are scattered in the Green Mountains nearby. The Bread Loaf School was a collection of white buildings and farmhouses. I stayed in a house leased to the school for the summer by the man who wrote the Earthworm tractor stories for *The Saturday Evening Post*. This fact alarmed me at first, but I soon found that it had nothing to do with the tone of the school.

John Crowe Ransom taught us seventeenth-century lyrics and everything else a poet could teach about poetry besides. I owe him the unshakable knowledge, so hard to come by, that a poem exists in itself, a made thing of words which have life and history, and that it cannot be understood by probing the life of its author or by translating it into other words.

During the week of the Cuban missile crisis in 1962 when a certain hysteria prevailed in Washington and some of our neighbors fled to the mountains, I decided to spend my last days, if they were that, doing what I really liked to do. Every day I went to the national poetry readings being held that week at the Library of Congress and listened to all the greats—Howard Nemerov, Marianne Moore, Gwendolyn Brooks, others—reading their poetry. At the reception I saw Mr. Ransom and was moved to tell him what he had meant to me that summer at Bread Loaf. He, bemused by age and, I think, a little by Bourbon, did not have much to say. After all, what was there to say after a quarter of a century and in the face of death?

Theodore Morrison directed the writer's seminar at Bread Loaf and the most interesting people in the school were there, of course. I managed one workmanlike short story which was later published and included in anthologies. At the very end of the summer I submitted the beginning of another on which he wrote, "I had no idea you could do this. Why are you afraid to write this way?" I had no idea and I never finished the story.

Robert Frost, whose farm was in the neighborhood, wandered off and on the campus and read for us occasionally. Magdalen and I went to have tea with him and the Morrisons. He talked on about poetry and life, but I cannot remember anything he said. It is only because of these queer lapses in memory that I knew only part of me was fully alive.

Yet I made good friends there, friends with whom I am still in touch after all the years, among them Tinsley Helton, an intense small girl from Kentucky who later took her doctorate at Minnesota, and Janet Moore, frail and rather fey, a convert who had lapsed, as the saying was, much to my distress and Magdalen's. Janet later had a strange reconversion—with which we had nothing to do—and is now a Dominican nun.

I encountered that summer for the first time the Ivy League mind, then almost incomprehensible from my midwestern point of view. The young Harvard and Yale men in the classes seemed incurious and incapable of enthusiasm, although they were indubitably well read and informed. "Why did you come here rather than go to California?" inquired one of the young men idly as we walked to lunch together. "Because it's almost a thousand miles nearer," I said shortly. "Really?" he inquired politely as if he had just picked up an unimportant fact about Moscow. They seemed to know so little about their own country, although most of them were soon to go to war for it. We talked very little about that, too.

In the fall of 1941 my teaching and studying began in earnest. I moved into an apartment with Edna Fluegel and contributed the linen and silver from my hope chest to our common furnishings. I commuted from St. Paul to my classes at the university and went to work on my thesis now entitled "The Influence of Teresa of Avila on Richard Crashaw," heaping the dinette table with books on mysticism and prosody, to Edna's distress.

At St. Catherine's as a part-time instructor I had been demoted from the roomy pine-paneled office I had previously occupied in Fontbonne Hall to a dimly lit room in a corridor in the basement, where heat pipes steamed and pounded over my head. To help my advisees, who became hopelessly lost looking for me, I made a sign for the door with my name and lettered under it the quotation from Christopher Marlowe, "Why, this is hell nor am I out of it." I came back from class one day to find that Mother Eucharista, the president and my former college dormitory prefect, had visited me. Under my sign was written "Praise the Lord from the deeps, ye dragons."

I am well aware that all nuns are not like the nuns I knew and worked with at St. Catherine's, who were in the main cheerful, intelligent, hard-working women, in love with their work and happy with their lot, but I have met a surprising number who are. We tend to forget that nuns are the career women of the Church—

its feminists. By their willing choice of a life of virginity, they are living testimony to a woman's intrinsic worth as a person. They choose to be defined in their own terms, not in relation to another, not as wives, not as mothers. They say, "Here I am, Lord, and this is my only life. Let me make the most of it for you and for mankind."

They dressed alike in black, many-pleated serge habits with long black silk veils, but they had surprising individuality and varied interests. The individuality was so marked that any one of us who knew them well could kneel behind the forty or fifty of them in chapel and recognize them by traits as singular as fingerprints. There was Sister St. Charles's aggressive, masculine set of shoulders; the poised dignity of Sister Antonine's head with the veil falling crisply, evenly on each side; the tall elegance of Sister Helen Margaret, her veil worn farther back and falling in narrower folds than the others.

They were interested in what they were doing and had interesting things to talk about. Sister Teresita was doing cancer research in her laboratory, studying the effect of coal tar on rats. Sister Marie Ursule was awarded a doctor of letters degree for her encyclopedic work in collecting and saving the folklore of French Canada, enabled by the trust her nun's habit inspired to cajole half-forgotten rhymes, prayers, and charms from the old people. She wrote home of bundling herself in shawls to ride the snowplow to visit some of those most isolated on remote farms. Sister St. Mark, zoologist and an ecologist before her time, roamed the campus woods, vigilant in her protection of wild life, seeking to help the workmen minimize the effect of the city which was growing close to us on all sides.

It was impossible to keep up with them all—artists, musicians, poets, scientists, and just good teachers, alive to their students and the world they lived in. Because they were women in a community, they could be supportive of each other, the girls they taught, and the people they worked with. They were capable of disinterested friendship in a way most women caught in the competitive roles society thrusts on them have yet to achieve. To them, to nuns like them, as well as to the succession of substitute mothers in my life, I owe my abiding faith in women today.

The lay teachers, a very professional lot, were more beset by rivalries and tensions between one another. Ostensibly we had full faculty status, but our actual influence was determined by our relations with the nuns. Religious orders were still authoritarian communities. The sisters owned St. Catherine's; we did not. Those of us who were alumnae, who were former students or classmates had an indefinable advantage in the way we could bypass channels and call in debts of friendship incurred in our school days. This difference tended to level out, as lay teachers stayed on and became well-known figures on the campus, identified with the college in name and purpose; in the meantime, it kept a large and varied faculty knit together when it might easily have fallen into two camps, lay and religious.

On Sunday, December 7, Gene was visiting Edna and me in our apartment. He went down to the little downstairs delicatessen to get something we had forgotten for lunch and came back with the news of Pearl Harbor. For the rest of the day we were close to the radio listening to the flashes and bulletins and interpretations as the story was pieced together. We sat thinking our own thoughts. Edna, who had worked close to things once, must have wished she were back in Washington. We were strange friends in a way, because she was a staunch conservative, convinced of rampant conspiracy. She disliked and distrusted Roosevelt, whom I admired unreservedly. I could not imagine what Gene was thinking. In the spring he had written, "The speeches in the Senate begin to sound like 1918—the same arrogance, presumption, and emotion begin to show." Americans had done nothing to avoid the war or to help end it, he thought, and he suggested that we read the Old Testament to learn how the Hebrews escaped the punishment of war. Like most midwestern college people, we had been intellectually pacifist, in favor of disarmament, even, perhaps, isolationist. However, in the face of nazism all this had changed for me. But Gene was set apart now. He was already thinking of what must be taught after the war. He was not to share the experience of his generation—a fact I think which set him unusually free later.

After Gene came to see me just before he left for the novitiate, I took him to the train for Collegeville for the last time and stood with the tears openly running down my face. "Good God, girl, don't cry," said the conductor, "he's only going sixty miles."

Gene wrote once more before he entered. "I can't do this if it isn't going to be right for you, Abbie," he said. "You must tell me if it isn't." There was nothing I could say, but I was grateful for the letter and happy that he had written it. The next week Arleen Hynes sent me a snapshot she had taken. On the back was written simply "Frater Conan, OSB," Gene's new name. He looked thin and serious but happy in his novice's habit. His hair was cropped short in the novice's tonsure.

I felt bereaved, but, in a way, as if I had stepped back into real life out of a story. I took my M.A. that summer, and, then, at the urging of my Aunt Abbie and my friends who thought I needed a change of scene, set out on a trip to the West Coast, accepting invitations from my sister and Marian McCarthy, both living there. Traveling in those early months of our involvement in the war was like a continual farewell party. Young men were leaving or were going home to say good-by to their families; families were traveling to see their sons; girls were going to one coast or the other to see their young men off. I traveled west on the Chief. Four of us soon became a group in the Pullman lounge car: a young lieutenant in the cavalry, a Jewish boy going to await the draft with his father who was in the moving picture business in Hollywood, a New York secretary looking for war work, and I. We played bridge and talked, got off the train to look for western night life in Albuquerque, and got on it again just as it was pulling out. In Los Angeles we whirled apart as casually as we had come together. The lieutenant and I watched the Jewish boy and his brother weeping without shame with their arms around each other, the New York girl scooped up by friends. He and I took a cab sight-seeing and ate in a Mexican restaurant. He bought me flowers and left me late that evening on Marian's doorstep and went off, I suppose, to the war.

It was a summer of casual encounters, but in it I found that people no longer seemed like cardboard and that I could enjoy being in a casual dating situation once again. It was stirring to be close to our great gearing for the war. All up and down the West Coast there were people whose changed lives would change our country for the next quarter century, our delayed and final commitment to Europe visible even there. The moving picture studios were alive with the possibilities of their great propaganda effort in war. With a writer friend of mine at Universal, I lunched in the dining room full of stars, vaguely regretful that I could not have done so when I was a screen-struck high school girl. With her I worked briefly as a volunteer in the hospitality house that the Hollywood English-Speaking Union maintained for RAF fliers who were learning to fly American planes. In San Francisco my sister Anne and I were entertained at dinner in the wardroom of the destroyer on which our cousin was an officer. We felt sympathy for the j.g.s, new from officer's school and civilian life, who were too eager to discuss ideas and policy to suit the crusty Annapolis men. My cousin's former ship had been one of those sunk at Pearl Harbor. "The Navy does not like to dwell on it," said his wife, whose memories of the day of confusion in Honolulu and the terror from the skies were all too fresh.

I met a few people who were troubled by the mass evacuation of the Japanese. One of my former classmates was looking after the house of a Japanese neighbor, watering the plants each day, sure that the United States could not really keep such nice people in virtual prison. But for the most part, people seemed glad to leave the questions of conscience aside and lose themselves in the community of war, something bigger than their ordinary everyday lives.

In Seattle I met a group of young Army officers from the South who had brought troops from a southern camp—we were scrupulous then about not naming camps or asking about them—to a debarkation point. They took the same train back, as curious about Washington, Idaho, and Montana as if the Northwest were a foreign country. We sat in the observation car as the train threaded its way through the Montana Rockies, awed by the bulk of the mountains, and, while night came to meet us, wondering about the lonely ranchers whose lights we saw here and there. Inevitably one boy lay greater claim to my company, and we talked until late at night, breakfasted and lunched together, and he saw me off the train in Mandan where I planned to spend the last week of vacation with old friends. The other officers came too, pressing addresses on me and reminding me of my promise to write to them when they had to go overseas. My arrival, thus escorted, lightened the spirits of Milton Higgins who met me. He and Irene found Gene's decision inexplicable and were so saddened by it that I found myself spending a good deal of time that week defending Gene and his sense of vocation. In Mandan I thought about him a great deal.

Every Catholic child is faced with the possibility of a vocation to the priesthood or to the religious life. It is not thought of as a matter of one's own choosing but as a call from God, who may draw you to it irresistibly in a manner of ways, by natural attraction to the life, through another person, through circumstance. But it is a call, echoing through life, to an existence of greater dedication and purpose. Ultimately, to refuse it is to reject Him who has known you before you were begotten, who has called you into being out of illimitable love and for a mysterious purpose. Thomas Merton wrote of his moment of decision, when he was called to answer a question "that had been preparing, not in my mind, but in the infinite depths of an eternal Providence." Although the Church gave lip service to the idea of lay vocation, most Catholics thought of vocation in terms of the priesthood or the convent.

It was a shock to me that these good friends could see only regression in Gene's entry into the monastery. They urged me not to follow suit. "What could you ask that is better than that?" asked Milton sadly as he watched me playing with their little boy.

I was even more shocked by the implication of priesthood as an escape; my former landlady Mrs. Rippel, Catholic though she was, was probably speaking from the view of the Middle European peasant. "Well, both our men left us," she said, sighing lugubriously. Irene was the most understanding when I protested and explained, but when she took me to the train she said, "All we want is to see you with a home and children of your own, you know, Abbie," and added half under her breath as she kissed me, "I think he *must* come back."

I was cheered by her words. They echoed a stubborn hope which

I could not help harboring, even though I knew it was a sin to want less than the highest good for Gene.

Back in Minneapolis I joined Tinsley Helton, whom I had met at Bread Loaf, in an apartment near the university and drove to my classes at St. Catherine's, where I now resumed a full schedule. We were busy and our range of acquaintances grew large and varied. There were old school friends of mine, teachers and instructors from both faculties I had met through my aunt, who exchanged regular visits with us; my aunt herself with her constant, stimulating interest in all we did; people at the Newman Center where I had spoken a few times the year before. We found ourselves continually marking academic milestones—prelims passed, a thesis accepted—and a little celebration with each.

But we were never far from the war. I often stayed with my classmate Virginia Rankin Carlson, whose husband Bill was in the Pacific, to help and to try to alleviate the loneliness inevitable for the young wife left behind with small children to care for alone. My brother was accepted for Navy officers' training and left. Greg Dahners, my Mandan cousin, drafted, stationed briefly at Fort Snelling, had Sunday dinner with us, looking pale and awkward in his ill-fitting private's uniform. He called when they were to move out and I went to the St. Paul station in the black of an early winter morning to bid him good-by and watch him file off through the cavernous empty station in the straggling line. "Call them at home," he said, "and let them know." He had told me that before he left Mandan his father had taken him to the bank and shown him a strongbox full of green bills. "That's for you, Greg, to buy your ranch when you come back." As I watched Greg go, I thought of that with a pang; it was his father's way of constraining fate—Greg was an only son.

It began to seem very important that every departure be appropriately marked and we sometimes found ourselves helping with farewalls for friends of friends we hardly knew. One night during a very bad smear campaign against Gene in 1952, some reporters came to our house in the middle of the night to let us know about a damaging attack to appear in a full page ad in the next day's paper. They had smuggled out a proof for us to see, so that Gene could prepare some defense. As Gene studied the ad with them and I was preparing hamburgers and coffee in the kitchen, one of the reporters came out to help me. "You don't remember me, do you?" he said. "I know I should—" I began, searching for the right political connection. "No, you shouldn't—it was ten years ago," he said, "but you helped give a party which gave me a send-off to the war. I remember, because I was feeling so low—nobody much cared—and that helped."

All this activity was a distraction, but Gene was still in the center of my thoughts. At St. John's he was fighting his own battle in the novitiate. Father Basil, the novice master, had made allowances for our former relationship as prospective man and wife and allowed Gene to write to me. This had been a happy surprise to me when I had received the first letter in California. It had seemed so abrupt and unnatural to have any communication between us cut at a stroke; yet I knew it was the norm for those who left the world for religious life. True, these letters supposedly had the aim of counseling me on the problem of my spiritual life and easing the transition to my own vocation, whatever that might be, and could be read by the novice master. After a while Father Basil limited them in number.

It has become something of a cliché in recent books and articles about Gene to speak of his time in the novitiate as time he took out from active life to read and to study. But the novitiate is neither a school nor a place of respite, and Gene did not then look on it as one. The novitiate is a place of testing a vocation. Each particular religious order has a way or spirit of its own. As late as 1968 Gene wrote in an introduction to a book by Abbot Boultwood: "The Benedictine way has never been the way of sudden conversion, but of continuing effort in combining work and prayer without sharp distinction between the secular and the spiritual."

That was the ideal. But the emphasis in the novitiate was very much on the spiritual alone. The new name given the novice signified his death to the world and rebirth in a new family. The life in the novitiate was a rigorous experience of manual labor and spiritual exercises, of work and prayer and learning to live in a community.

Gene's notebooks for the year, duly labeled "Conan OSB," list the subjects of study and reading, all done under the direction of the novice master. There were notes on assigned reading and on lectures on the spiritual life and on the history of monasticism, with concentration, of course, on the history of Benedictinism. There is a commentary with lecture notes on the Rule of St. Benedict according to which he was beginning to try to live. There were voluminous notes on the Psalms, a necessary preparation for proper participation in the Divine Office which for centuries Benedictines had prayed and recited together every day. There is a course on Mass and the Sacraments—a basic course in the liturgy.

It had always been Gene's habit when he read a book which he wanted to remember and to think about to type notes as he went and record quotations which interested him. He must have tried to read things which would help him to meditate the passion and death of Christ, because he had extensive notes on the revelations of St. Bridget of Sweden, who was supposed to have had visions of Christ's unrecorded life, and on *The Holy Shroud,* a book written about the actual sufferings of Christ, based on an analysis of the shroud supposedly found at Turin. These seem strange choices but they were probably suggested to him by the novice master. He has other notes on reading from Belloc and Pascal.

The period of the novitiate lasts for a year. Others who were novices at the same time say that Gene was a very good novice, very observant of the Rule, but that the novice master found him difficult. According to one of them, Gene read all of the back copies of *Orate Fratres,* the organ of the liturgical movement, using them as a starting point for meditation, and was constantly reprimanded by the master for reading for intellectual pleasure rather than for spiritual profit. Father Basil took his responsibility to test the vocations of those under his charge very seriously. He was somewhat suspicious of novices with superior ability and education. At the end of the year it was his duty to recommend to the older monks of the monastery— the Chapter—the acceptance of the novices who had persisted in their vocation and been found worthy. If the Chapter accepted them they became Benedictine clerics studying for the priesthood.

Gene never explained exactly why he left St. John's, but he did tell me once years later that the novice master had not wanted to recommend him because he thought him guilty of intellectual pride. It was true that the novice master had often accused him of it before other novices, but his confreres insist that he could not have been seriously rejected, that he would surely have been approved by the Chapter. However, he left before the time of appearance before the Chapter and went that summer to St. Francis Seminary in Milwaukee, a seminary for secular priests, that is, priests who do not belong to a religious order.

I was touched, when he showed me the notebooks later, that he had read the *Autobiography of St. Teresa*, Sigrid Undset's *Kristin Lavransdatter*, and the *Confessions of St. Augustine* in an intensive way during those months. They were books which had been spiritual landmarks for me and which I had mentioned often in our conversations about vocation. All through that year, Gene must have labored with his feeling for and responsibility to me. He sought out in his reading quotations and information about the great spiritual friendships which are so much a part of Catholic history. His meditation notes were studded with these quotations:

"Love desires all that is good for the beloved . . . Lovers look not at each other but at the same goal." (Gibran) "The love of man and woman is a crack which admits the love of God." (Mauriac) "Each is an aid to the other in advancing in the love of God, even to the point where they must separate . . . So those who love each other must remain concerned over the salvation of each other as long as they live. I will remember you after I have forgotten myself, to fix myself to the cross more firmly." (St. Francis de Sales to St. Jeanne de Chantal) From a note on Montalambert—perhaps the most telling quotation of all—"In the history of most saints who have exercised a *reformatory* [italics mine] influence on monasteries the name and influence of a holy woman is found. Basil and Macrine. Augustine and Monica. Benedict and Scholastica. Clare and Francis. Francis de Sales and Jeanne de Chantal." And from Abbot Marmion, "One gives up last what he loves best, or better than self."

When he wrote to me, he wrote asking me to consider becoming a

Benedictine. The reasons he gave were historical. Over the centuries they had adapted best; their rule was most human; and they had been centers of renewal whenever western civilization floundered.

For it was not the Benedictines as they were that Gene felt called to—but the Benedictines as he thought they should be, although he tried to muffle that thought in his letters from the novitiate where he was supposed to be learning to set aside his own judgment. He had written the year before that although he still tended to think the Church was right in Spain—one of our few points of difference —he knew now that there was too little thought about what had brought about revolution in the first place: "The monks were in the monasteries, and the secular clergy in the parish houses—no regard for the temporal need of the people." He had thought, too, that the renewed emphasis on teaching the humanities in Catholic colleges was our excuse for avoiding political, social, and economic questions which require positive action and personal sacrifice.

Within Benedictinism there were many possibilities. Before his entrance, Gene's advisers must surely have discussed with him the way in which truly exceptional intellectual gifts could best be put at the service of God and the order. In looking back, I was sure that Gene's almost obsessive interest in the teaching at the university reflected a new kind of mission which the Benedictines were just then exploring. He told me of the plan to establish small priories in university communities—something the Dominicans had done very effectively—where classes could be taught and where scholars could act as a magnet in the university community for true philosophy and theology. There was in his concern about what he considered false teaching much of the reformers' love which, as Virginia Woolf once said, has so much of hatred mixed into it. He read the poetry of Robert Lowell, at that time considered a Catholic poet, and reread Robert Frost, after my meeting with him. He made notes on some of the poems and a sketchy consideration, perhaps for a talk on teaching, of the comparison between teachers and poets. A teacher must give something of himself, he noted, in a way lay bare his soul as a writer does, especially a poet (Gene was always in his own teaching to find this necessity a stumbling block).

He felt called to *do* something rather than to *be* something. His vocation was a restless river seeking a channel.

His novitiate notes on St. Benedict's Twelve Degrees of Humility show that he struggled to the end with the problem of what intellectual pride might be. Years later he was to write in the notes for one of his books this comment: "Intellectual pride—always a contradiction—demanding rejection of the one distinctly human faculty—reason or knowledge—understanding." His notes from Pascal included these quotations: "One with excess of, like defect of, intellect, is accused of madness. Nothing is good but mediocrity. To leave the mean is to abandon humanity." And again, "Nothing is admired but mediocrity; whoever succeeds in escaping this will inevitably find the teeth of the majority fastened to him."

He was instinctively feeling a healthy reaction to the false spirituality which attempted to divide a man's spiritual growth from the total development of his gifts and talents. And the failure to realize that an intellectual's weakness often lies in his own all too keen awareness of his deficiencies, rather than the opposite. In the revival of spiritual direction which in the 1950s and 1960s began to use the insights of modern psychology, the tendency to glorify mediocrity and conformity was pinpointed for what it really was.

I was at the University of Chicago in that summer of 1943 and Gene came to see me a few times. I met him at the railroad station and we spent the days wandering about Chicago, eating our lunch in the sunshine in Grant Park. I think I shied away from the struggle he was going through.

It was not that my own search for vocation had not been serious; I had accepted Gene's suggestion that I enter a convent as a sign from God, since obviously our lives were meant to be intertwined. The spiritual friendships and the dual vocations cited in Gene's notes were familiar to anyone who had considered the spiritual life very seriously. And there were even more modern examples of married couples who had left each other to pursue lives of individual holiness. (The Church only gives permission for such a separation if both parties will accept the religious life.) There was the famous story of Cornelia Connelly, foundress of the Society of the Holy Child, whose husband had wanted to become a Jesuit and had prevailed on her to become a nun. When he changed his mind later, she persisted in her unsought vocation, despite much legal and personal harassment. Jacques and Raïssa Maritain had tried such a separation, but Raïssa had found life in a contemplative Benedictine community in France so trying to her health, and suffered so from the separation, that Maritain had given up his vocation to return to her. The famous Baroness de Hueck, founder of Friendship House, the first interracial apostolate of the Church in the United States, and her husband, journalist Eddie Doherty, had taken vows of chastity and transformed their movement into what is called a secular institute—a religious group who live like lay people in the world.

I loved the nuns I knew—strictly speaking, as teaching sisters, uncloistered, they were not nuns. All my school life they had been to me quite literally "other mothers" and good friends. The accidentals of religious life did not repel me. I liked the local color of convent life, the in jokes, the variety of habits, the familiar smell of starched linen and waxed floors in convents. I understood my good friend Sister Marie José very well, although I did not share her feeling when she said to me, "Sometimes when I am in chapel I shake all over when I look around at us, all women, all dressed alike. I do not think I can stand it. And yet I do not want to be anything else. I always wanted to be a sister." It was the impersonality of life in a big convent which was frightening to her. When I was a junior in college one of my best friends, now president of St. Catherine's, stunned us all by entering the convent during spring vacation without a word to any of us. There was innocent drama in her reappearance among us as a student postulant in the black, caped postulant dress, guarded from contact with us by older postulants—but I was wildly saddened by it and cried uncontrollably in bed at night. I cried, I think, not so much for her as for myself: I was afraid that I might have a vocation, too. And I had wanted more than anything else in life a warm personal love, a home and babies of my own. I had dreamed of the completion of finding one person among all others who would understand and love me, and whose life and hopes would become my own—of someone both friend and lover.

When I dutifully studied various modes of religious life, I found myself pulled two ways. I was attracted by the comparative freedom and the newness of spirit in new kinds of vocations which had come into being as responses to twentieth-century problems. In the first sad summer away from Gene, when I was at Bread Loaf I had read in *Time* of the coming to America of a new kind of nun, Dutch women who were the dedicated core of a woman's movement. They were called the Ladies of the Grail. They did not wear habits, did not necessarily live in community, moved freely about, and were not interested in the traditional women's roles of teaching and nursing. The little I read about them, with their promise of challenge and freedom, interested me very much. I wanted to explore that avenue. In Minneapolis I had taken up volunteer work with the Catholic Worker House, badly understaffed as the men were drafted or went off to conscientious objector camps. I liked the sense of the Worker community which then stretched from coast to coast. I wrote the newsletter for them and took an active part in the discussion meetings, although I could not quite reconcile myself to Dorothy Day's unyielding pacifism. There were times when it seemed to me that the Worker was the answer to Christ's call to serve the poor.

And I was attracted to the older religious orders where strong intragroup and familial affection was emphasized. Among my new friends in the group around the university in Minneapolis was Alice McDonell, a graduate student of specialized nursing. Alice had a gift for friendship. Her capacity for sympathy seemed boundless; her life was a marvelous mixture of spontaneity and self-discipline. She was, like me, interested in the literature of contemplative prayer, but, unlike me, she practiced it faithfully. We were instant friends. She was sure she had a vocation and was also exploring possibilities. Through her I gave second thought to the Religious of the Sacred Heart, whose elitism had repelled me when I first knew of them. I read the life and letters of Janet Erskine Stuart, an aristocratic Englishwoman who was their fifth mother-general.

I found there the concept of a worldwide family of religious alumnae, their families and friends, which was most attractive. And in Mother Stuart herself I saw a woman of such breadth of interest, such sensitive perception of individuality that she seemed the very archetype of mother and teacher. Such a woman must have come from a superior community of women, I thought, and a loving close community.

The Christmas after Alice went East to enter the Sacred Heart noviceship at Albany, New York, I took my engagement ring out of the box and sold it so that I could visit her and talk to the novice mistress, at that time Agnes Barry, sister of playwright Philip Barry. I also visited Alice's friend and sponsor at the Sacred Heart, Dr. Marian Newcomer in New York City. Dr. Marian, and her husband, Dr. Sidney, were well-to-do Philadelphians who had met in medical school. Dr. Marian was deeply devout and had compensated for her childlessness, a matter of regret to them both, by giving herself to various *protégés* like Alice, and founding and funding a charity called the Mater Christi Guild. Dr. Sidney was not a Catholic, and, introverted scientist that he was, seemed to me eccentric if attractive. He tolerated Dr. Marian's interests and seemed devoted to her. Dr. Marian believed firmly in the possibility of sanctity in the world, urged me not to make any sudden decision about a vocation—"Wait on the will of God, my dear"—and invited me to come and stay with her in New York and help her with the Guild until I should find my way.

Selling my engagement ring for such a journey had seemed to me an act of detachment and decision, comparable to Gene's sacrifice of my letters and pictures when he entered the monastery. It had been a sad and rather grubby business. My friend Phyllis McAllister had accompanied me to one after another of the second-floor walkups on Hennepin Avenue where the dealers in second-hand jewelry did business. We were depressed by the small amounts they offered; afterward Phyllis told me that she would have liked to buy it herself, but thought it less painful for me to dispose of it to someone who would reset the diamond.

Perhaps Gene thought my search for vocation unnecessary. In

one letter from St. John's he wrote in answer to what must have been an angry defense on my part, saying that he had not meant to criticize my aunt, that he knew he had no right to judge her. But he insisted that she probably opposed my vocation, as he suggested she had our marriage, by opposing the manner of it. It was true that Abbie had thought the idea of combining rural life and teaching —even at St. John's—visionary and could not understand why Gene did not seem to have higher professional ambitions. Now Gene thought she was happy with my graduate progress and my college teaching. "You are the one most like her—the one for whom she holds the greatest hopes," he said.

It was also true that my teaching and graduate work were satisfying in many ways. The so-called "Catholic Renaissance" was at its joyful height. To be Catholic no longer meant that one kept one's religion in one mental compartment, one's secular knowledge in another. We had only begun to sense in my college days that the Depression in America and the fragmentation in Europe, accompanied by economic chaos there, had shattered faith in the inevitability of progress and the infallibility of science. Recurring wars, the rise of nazism and fascism, the questioning threat of communism, the growing awareness of economic and racial injustice in our own country—and now finally world war—all these had reawakened interest in the problem of evil.

The Church was being rediscovered. To be a Catholic now meant that one was part of a worldwide community which shared a splendid heritage of arts and letters and in which tremendous intellectual effort was being put into the restructuring of human society to cope with modern evils. It meant that one could claim affinity with the ancient Greek and Roman and Hebraic cultures from which Christianity sprang; it meant that one could identify the universal in the tribal and ethnic cultures to which Christianity had adapted: it meant that one could affirm as Catholic everything true and good.

The Church in America, at least in an important segment of its intellectual leadership, had rediscovered its pre-Puritan past and was no longer to be thought of as at odds with science and the arts. It was the era of conversions: Evelyn Waugh, Robert Lowell,

Thomas Merton—so many others. One could think of Chris[t]
thought as a dominant and creative influence once again in Western
culture. Neo-Scholastic philosophers like Bergson, Gilson, and
Maritain were seriously discussed in the most thoughtful journals.

Evelyn Waugh, Graham Greene, Bernanos, Mauriac, Claudel,
were in vogue wherever the novel was seriously discussed—and they
were ours. Gerard Manley Hopkins was one of the most imitated
of poets. Sean O'Faolain, Sean O'Casey, Paul Vincent Carroll, and
Frank O'Connor might be deplored in their native Ireland, but
they were applauded and discussed here. James Joyce was perceived
as permanently formed by the Catholicism he rejected, as were
others whose battle with guilt was a testimony of an inverse sort.
A minor school of the breed known to us as "Catholic authors," as
distinguished from authors who merely happened to be Catholic,
flourished briefly; among them we counted Paul Horgan, Richard
Sullivan, Riley Hughes, Harry Sylvester, Joseph Dever—and perhaps the most distinguished, J. F. Powers whose short stories brought
the near perfection of that most American of forms to the service
of what we thought of as truly Catholic themes. (A few of my own
short stories, written so desperately under the need to make money,
made their way into anthologies of writers like these.) The enthusiasm for such writers affected the literature curriculum. We who
taught literature were in demand as lecturers and book reviewers.
The excitement spread to the alumnae and their friends who formed
book discussion groups; the alumnae of the honor society founded
a critical review called Books Abounding, which I edited for two
years.

Catholics everywhere were emerging from behind the intellectual
barricades and St. Catherine's as usual was ahead of its time. As
representative of the college English faculty, I had been elected
president of the Minnesota English Teachers. I was at Chicago
that summer of Gene's struggle, as a participant in a workshop on
the liberal arts, representing St. Catherine's with three others, one
of twenty selected to do the study by the American Council on
Education. Among the other participants I had struck up a special
friendship with a young doctor of divinity, a Presbyterian from a
southern college. For the first time since I had fallen in love with

Gene, I glimpsed the possibility of intimacy with another man. But anything serious was out of the question. I felt irrevocably committed by my attachment to Gene. I felt my Catholicism an impassable barrier. Yet our rapport was deep, and we spent long happy hours together, talking excitedly, exploring Chicago, building bridges out of our mutual love for certain books or pictures, discovering others together. The night before the workshop was over we talked and walked all night and sat watching the sun come up over the lake. "We were closer than I knew," he wrote later from Mississippi. I quoted him sometimes to Gene when I saw Gene or wrote to him. "I wondered about him—" said Gene inconclusively once, looking off into the distance.

When I last saw Gene that summer he had told me that he could not go on at the seminary and that he had been accepted at another Benedictine monastery, St. Bede's in Illinois. When he suddenly appeared in Minneapolis that fall, having abandoned the idea of a priestly vocation, I felt suddenly drained. He talked tentatively of ways we might be together, ways based on his seminary reading. For the first and only time in our relationship I deceived him; I suggested that he should consult his cousin, Father Louis McCarthy, a professor at St. Paul Seminary, who had acted as my friend and confessor in those difficult years. When he was on his way, I called Father Louis. "You must help him, Father," I said. "I don't know what to do. I am too tired emotionally. I don't understand what he wants and needs."

When Gene returned that evening he said that Father had been very helpful. "He knows a great deal about women," he added cryptically. "He thinks we should not talk about any plans just yet." We fell quite naturally into the easy and natural close and undemanding friendship we had shared in the two years he had been preparing for the monastery.

He went through the ordeal of reporting for the draft and being rejected on physical grounds. (He suffered in those years from a severe bursitis which left him with a limp that is noticeable even now when he is tired.) Then he started an uneasy job search. He considered going to the West Coast with his brother Austin who was reporting for Navy duty. "I have been *here* too long now," he wrote significantly from Watkins. To leave the seminary was thought scandalous then, and his position must have been painful in Watkins. A teachers college job fell through. He suspected that the recommendation from St. John's had been "too specific" about his reason for leaving there. At Sunday supper gatherings in my apartment he renewed ties with our old friends and met some new ones, all of whom tried to be helpful. In the end, his government applications, updated, bore fruit. He was recruited for Army Intelligence and left for Washington, D.C. His letters sounded lonely, but he had a flair for cryptanalysis. He could not discuss the work, but it was clearly interesting.

That winter was the beginning of a very sad two years for me. The details blur and run together now. My aunt had been seeing her doctor regularly but was vague in her discussion of illness with us. We did not find that unusual. My mother's side of the family, although always gaily affectionate, set great store on personal privacy. At the suggestion of her doctor she made a visit to the Mayo Clinic. At a dinner with me afterward she spoke generally of the need to return for X-ray treatment. I realized with shock that, in her proud and reticent way, she was telling me that she had cancer. Her searching look was at once an appeal for my understanding of the seriousness of her situation and an appeal for hope from my reaction. "It is so good that you went there," I said. "They catch things in time."

It was the beginning of long months of dissimulation. The hardest period in our lives is that in which those who were our strength and protection turn to us for help and become, bit by bit, helpless and dependent. I stayed with Abbie through successive hospital stays when she was suffering from the aftermath of radiation, through ambulance trips to the clinic at Rochester, where I slipped behind her back into the the doctor's office to ask in vain for the truth, for some estimate of time, to argue with him.

"It is best in such cases that they keep on working," he said firmly.

"But you don't understand," I protested. "Teaching is dependent on nervous energy—especially Abbie's kind of teaching. She has to have life and enthusiasm to bring out the creative in her students.

It will kill her to lose them." I fell silent at what I had said, helpless before the doctor's unyielding formula for making an abstraction of the human misery and suffering with which he dealt daily.

When a disease-weakened bone gave way and Abbie fell, breaking her hip, it almost seemed providential. She went into St. Mary's Hospital in Minneapolis and for eighteen months, except for a week or so respite when her sister or one of mine came I was there every day, witness to a long silent agony. It had hurt me to see her worry over money and her efforts at economy, when I felt quite certain that there was no need. I had taught her summer school class at the Diocesan College, a college for nuns who were elementary school teachers which she had helped Father Connole found and at which she taught evenings and summer sessions. At her behest I sold some of her precious glass collection to one of her many friends among the antique dealers. "Don't worry, Miss Quigley," he had said to me soothingly. "It eases her mind now and she can buy it back. I will put it aside."

I was appalled at the bone specialists who put her through successive operations with no reference to the malady which laid her waste and made the knitting of the bone impossible. I raged inwardly at the indifference and growing callousness of the nuns and young student nurses as her vitality and compelling charm dimmed with the passing months and her world grew smaller. Yet I carried a burden of guilt at my own frequent impatience and the way in which I sometimes delayed my daily visits and the necessary errands for her until the very last minute. Sometimes it seemed to me that my whole life was falling into shadow, that I was called to give unsought testimony to the decay and diminution which precedes death. Father Wolf, my college philosophy professor, was a carefully sequestered tuberculosis patient on the floor below Abbie. He welcomed my visits but often had nothing to say. Across the hall from Abbie, Sabina, the nurse at St. John's who had bullied and cosseted monks and students for thirty years, lay a prisoner of final illness. Priests and alumni were in and out as visitors, yet she said to me one day, "I stayed there too long."

"Did you know Aunt Annie was here?" one of the nurses, a distant relative of Gene's asked me one day. I went to visit Mrs.

McCarthy on the surgical floor regularly after that. We didn't talk of Gene, but she fixed me with a strange, sad look one day. "What does it all mean, Abbie?" she asked. "What is it for?" Yet she was never without her rosary, received communion daily, and was a compliant and grateful patient.

When Abbie's sister was with her and we began to recount some simple happy memories of family jokes and gatherings long ago, she stopped us firmly. "What good does it do to think of those things now?" she said.

"I don't understand," said Gene troubled when we talked of these things later. "Why do they deny the good there was?"

That time was lightened for me by good friends and my interests in my writing and my work. In addition to my teaching, I was publishing book reviews rather steadily, editing the small book review publication, and writing for *Today*, a magazine for college students.

One day I had a telephone call.

"Is this Miss Quigley?" a male voice asked.

"Yes."

"Is this the Miss Quigley who wrote the short story in this month's *Sign* magazine?"

"Yes."

"Well, this is Jim Powers. I write, too," said my caller.

"Jim Powers?" I said, "You mean you're J. F. Powers?"

J. F. Powers, as I have said, was a name around which excitement swirled in Catholic and critical circles. His short stories had been appearing in little magazines for some time but "Lions, Harts, Leaping Does," published that year in *Accent*, had caused a sensation. He was, for the moment, our American Mauriac or Bernanos. (When I knew him better, I found he would have preferred to be an American Evelyn Waugh!)

"I thought I might come to see you," he said.

"Why yes, of course, when would you like to come?" I said.

"Now. But I'm a convict on parole, you know," he said, "maybe you'd rather not."

I hadn't known, but a convict who could write "Lions, Harts, Leaping Does" was all right with me.

Jim was a conscientious objector who had refused alternative service and had been sent to Sandstone, the federal prison in Minnesota. He had been released on parole as a hospital worker in St. Paul. He became a regular visitor after that first call, within the hours and regulations set by his parole. He was bitter and self-conscious about that at first, but I went out and bought the six-packs he could not buy and listened as he read the manuscripts he was working on. We grew to be good friends. He puzzled me. He was deeply Catholic, but he had no time for Catholic writers except Waugh and later Flannery O'Connor, then unknown to me. When I tried to argue the morality of war, quoting Maritain, he brushed Maritain aside, "Him and his wife's friends," he said in slurring reference to Raïssa's poignant memoir, *We Have Been Friends Together*. He set me to rereading Katherine Anne Porter whom he admired extravagantly and to listening to the jazz classics he loved.

He had no time for movements or philosophies—he dismissed the liturgy because he thought the Psalms barbarous in expression, his admiration was reserved for lives he perceived intuitively as authentically lived. Thus he admired some of the Catholic Workers, for example, because they lived among the desperate, the winos, the derelicts, with no idea of improving them, and a sister he knew at the hospital who spent her free time gathering up clothes for the poor and distributing them personally with no aura of professionalism about her charity. "Why do you write about priests?" people always asked him. I only heard him answer that once, at one of my short story classes at which I had prevailed on him to talk. "Why?" he said irritably. "I can't write about love. I don't know what it's about. I can't write about what men call success and failure in things like business. I don't know what that's about. Priests—they're in the only race worth running."

Jim brought new perspectives into my life. Even Abbie rallied in interest to my reports of our conversations. The year wore on.

In early spring Gene called. "Abbie," he said abruptly, "my mother's dying. They just brought her back to St. Mary's."

"I'll be right there, Gene," I said.

Gene's sisters stayed with me that week, and Gene and I went back and forth together as if there had never been a break in our being together. I don't remember how we finally decided that we would be married in the summer. It just seemed suddenly to be a matter of fixing the details.

I told Jim Powers about it one Sunday morning when he came to late breakfast. "Well, I'll be damned," he said. "Why didn't I ever hear about this seminarian?"

"He's not a seminarian," I protested.

"He is," said Jim intractably. "I know the type. Why do you want to marry him anyway?"

"Well, if you really want to know," I said, "because I think I have a better chance of being a saint that way."

It seemed a strange answer, but it satisfied Jim.

"Oh, well, if you're going to put it like that . . ." he said.

The grief of Abbie's dying and the happiness of planning our wedding ran together through the spring. In the end, our wedding day, June 25, 1945, followed soon after her death and our ceremony was necessarily simple. It was a clear June day. My father escorted me down the aisle and my sisters followed through the small gathering of friends and relatives to the altar where Father Louis McCarthy waited and Gene stood with Emerson Hynes beside him.

We had asked to recite the vows we had waited so long to take without help from Father. We wanted to make them uniquely our own, without repeating them after him and so Gene said, first,

"I, Eugene Joseph, take thee, Abigail, to have and to hold, from this day forward, for better, for worse, for richer, for poorer, in sickness and in health, until death do us part."

And I repeated,

"I, Abigail, take you, Eugene. . . ."

"The speech work was excellent," said Mabel Frey, crying and laughing afterward.

We called the farm at Watkins "St. Anne's Farm," because St. Anne was Gene's mother's patron saint, and also because it was at St. Anne's shrine in Canada, where I had weekended that first summer in the East, that I had first dared to question the will of God by praying that Gene might leave the monastery.

"You always said not Watkins," Gene wrote me from the monastery. It was true. I had always hoped that when we began our experiment in rural life together we would be near people more like ourselves, close to books and music and conversation. The family farm was in Watkins, and that was one reason we were drawn there, although not to the McCarthys' farm, but to an adjacent one of our own. Also our returning to Watkins had run like a refrain through all of Gene's plans for our future. It was as if he had an unfinished conversation with the town and the people, as if he wanted to force them into some hitherto unrealized recognition and communion. "There must be latent good here," he said one day. "Think of all the years of praying these people have done."

I was often puzzled because although I loved my own home town and was often homesick for the hills and the river, I never thought of going back there to live.

I think Gene also wanted to wring from his father an admission of values other than those Dad McCarthy professed. To Dad McCarthy a farm was business property, something you owned and managed but did not live on. He scoffed at farmers who just made ends meet and he was driven to distraction by unbusinesslike use of the land. The sight of a tree left growing in the field would set him fuming. He could not think of farming as an occupation for an educated man and quite simply thought the work too hard. Certainly the work clearing the land and breaking it to plow, fighting storm and drouth, dry years, wet years and late years, and the cruel Minnesota winters, had been brutalizing and he must have had memories of that early time.

It was never Gene's intention to farm that way. He was caught up in the vision of the Catholic rural life movement whose ideal was the land as a source of freedom and security and as a base of community. In this view there is a unique relationship between the family and the occupation of agriculture. The farm unites the family and strengthens the marriage bond. Industrial society works against these things and, in the words of the Catholic Rural Life Manifesto, "in favor of divorce, desertion, temporary unions, companionate marriage." Farm life favors the unity of the family, binding all the members together in common economic, intellectual, recreational, and religious interest. Thus the bond of mutual love is strengthened.

The movement addressed itself for the most part to the shoring up of families already living on the land and to the improvement and humanizing of rural life. But the agrarianism that we were interested in went beyond that. It was spoken of at the time as the "Green Revolution" and was thought of as a revolt against the system. One of its apostles in whom we were much interested was Willis Nutting who later wrote *Reclamation of Independence*. It was his argument that the nature of man as well as the heritage of America demanded that men be free of outside management for the fullest development of personality. His argument was one Gene fully concurred with: our economic dependence is a dependence not on a few people but on a vast economic system of production, communication, distribution, and finance which covers the whole nation and even the whole world; since our dependence on the system is so complete, its functioning becomes our greatest concern; since it is our greatest concern, the system is bound sooner or later to be subjected to collective control. "We must adopt the way of living in which each family can provide for itself many of its actual necessities and in which those necessities which the family cannot provide . . . can be provided within the local community," Nutting wrote.

Gene's hope when we moved to the farm in 1945 was that we could become the center of a community at Watkins, but he never believed that we could or would become a self-sustaining community like some latter-day Amana or Brook Farm.

It concerned Gene greatly that St. Anthony's High School, the Catholic high school and the only one Watkins had ever had, had been closed a few years before, and the high school students were attending nearby Kimball High School where Gene had been principal before coming to Mandan. He still felt strongly about the secularization of knowledge in the usual public high school and hoped to induce the members of the local parish and the pastor, Father Bozja, to reopen St. Anthony's with lay teachers. He thought that the two of us could teach. Raph Thuente would be returning soon from the Navy and we wrote back and forth about Margaret and Raph joining us. We hoped to attract some writers and artists who could enrich the life of the community as well as the school. It was a very idealistic plan but not really impractical in that the school had an unused bank reserve of something like $60,000. It seems strange today that the revolutionary part of the idea, however, was that a Catholic school might have lay teachers. The school had been closed because the order of nuns serving it had not been able to provide enough qualified teachers for accreditation, making it hard for its graduates to be admitted to college.

These were our plans. In the meantime we had the practical problem of creating a home on our pieced-together eighty acres.

It was ironic that the legacy from my aunt, who to the end had dreaded the prospect of such a life for me, enabled us to put the farm in operation, to modernize the house, and also to be independent of Dad McCarthy. Although our aims were as always very serious and lofty, we had a good deal of fun trying to achieve them. And the things which I had inherited from Abbie—her country antiques, her books, pictures, curtains—gave the house a sense of past and continuity which I think she would have liked.

I learned early that a farm was not necessarily a bastion of privacy; I had to crawl out of bed to welcome our first caller, an old Irish farmer named Tom Kielty. Those who came by, came without warning at any time of the day and usually walked in. Often they would stay for the noontime dinner; one never knew.

The crops were already in when we arrived in June—oats and corn for the most part. There was a small garden of carrots and lettuce and although it was already late in the season we added tomatoes. Our livestock consisted of two horses, the kind that Mr. McCarthy marketed, half wild and heavy horses from Montana named Samson and Delilah. The Hyneses gave us a small rust-colored kitten whom they named Siena both for her color and for St. Catherine of Siena.

The farmhouse was a rather ugly stucco bungalow-and-a-half, but it was soundly built and situated on a rise with a pleasant view of rolling land and trees, "A proper place to bring a wife to establish a family," Gene wrote in an article that year. At some point in its history, a sun room and a front bedroom had been added and we planned to turn these into a long living room with windows on three sides which would give us command of the land in all its changing seasons. There was a long lilac hedge, a straggle of apple trees with one very beautiful large one near the house, and a bank of sumac and small elder growth nearby. We started the remodeling and put the actual physical work in the hands of some part-time carpenters from the village. They came and tore out all the downstairs partitions, leaving a welter of plaster dust and paper and then departed for six weeks to build corn cribs for the heavy corn crop which was predicted that year. We were reduced to living in the unfinished attic. Very fortunately, we had stored a bed, a desk, and some lamps there. Moreover, the kitchen was being remodeled, and I spent most of the summer cooking in the attic on an electric plate with a dutch oven.

The other inhabitants of the attic were the bats who seemed to have made it their home in the years during which the farm was not lived in. At dusk every night, they came wheeling and swooping out, brushing past our faces and shoulders and driving Siena into a delirium of excitement. Gene made it a project to kill as many as he could each night before we went to bed. The satisfaction he took in doing so and the skill he developed revealed a side of him I had never known. He appreciated the theory that bats could sense any solid object, so at first he used a tennis racket and after a while made use of an old corn popper which he had found at the farm. I did not like the bats, but I did not like the killing much either.

My cooking was still very uncertain, even when the kitchen was finished. A cake or pie was an afternoon's work, and I had no skill at producing the great bowls of gravy, relishes, and preserves, and the quantities of food that characterized country meals. Having grown up in a small town, I was acutely conscious of the fact that our impromptu guests would describe in detail the "stop" at our place (as they would put it) at their next stop.

Someone—perhaps the Hyneses—had given us a pressure cooker, a great post-World War II labor-saver for housewives. Its chief virtue was that it reduced the toughest cuts of meat to succulent delicacies in a very short time. It always terrified me, with its bewildering gauges and the clouds of steam which gushed forth when you opened the cover. But I did learn to reduce a fairly elderly chicken to the semblance of the tender boiled chicken I remembered from childhood Sunday dinners, and to do it in twenty minutes or so.

It was the custom in Meeker County for both businessmen and farmers to gather in the town restaurants for coffee or beer after the first work of the morning, so the farmer workmen who had finished their chores at home often did not get to their second jobs—such as ours—until late in the morning. By that time, Gene would be gone to the fields or to town and I would be left to cope with them.

This presented its problems if what we wanted them to do deviated in any way from what they considered the norm, and it often did. We planned to have the kitchen cabinets built higher than usual because I am above average height and it would be easier for me to work at the sink and the counter. The carpenters

Abigail Quigley at St. Catherine's graduation, 1936.

Below, Mandan High School in North Dakota, where Abigail Quigley began her teaching career in 1936 and where she met Eugene McCarthy in 1938.

In the high school library.

Eugene McCarthy, teaching applicant.

Looking south on Main Street, Watkins, Minnesota, Gene McCarthy's home town.

Right, Carty-Ma, Gene's strong-willed grandmother, a legend among her kin.

Gene (at extreme right) played championship hockey as a student at St. John's.

A month after the Christmas 1938 vacation, Gene McCarthy proposed to Abigail. Below, their engagement photo, taken in front of Gene's second-hand blue 1937 Chevrolet.

St. John's lay faculty 1940.
Gene McCarthy is second
from right on the bench.
At his left is Adrian Winkel, his first congressional
administrative assistant.
At his right is Emerson
Hynes, later his best man
and, still later, his Senate
legislative aide.

Right, Gene enjoying rural
life at their first home, St.
Anne's Farm in Watkins.
Peva, their dog, is with
him.

On June 25, 1945, after a delay of seven years, Gene and Abigail were married.

In the study at St. Anne's Farm.

looked at me in disbelief. "We wait for Eugene," they said. We planned to leave the brick of the new chimney exposed so as to give warmth to the rather shapeless kitchen. The mason, Gene's cousin's husband, looked at me uneasily, "I better ask Eugene," he said. In Watkins, women weren't decision makers.

But Gene, too, had his troubles. Because of the scarcity of skilled labor in that last year of the war, the carpenters and plumbers could pick and choose as they pleased and they looked on remodeling a house as low in priority. Aside from that, there were some jobs they simply looked on as unpleasant and put off doing as long as possible. One of these was the laying of pipes under the house. Gene could only get them to do it by going under with them himself and rallying their spirits with talk of how dry it was under there and how well made the foundation was.

Two men started to dig the cesspool but they found the ground very hard and stony. They went off for days at a time leaving their wheelbarrow and tools and suggesting that Gene might work at it in his spare time. Gene did work at it, but it was irksome to do with pick and shovel what we knew could be done in a very short time with the correct bulldozing equipment. Our cesspool problems became a byword with us, and we startled Father Bozja on the eighth Sunday after Pentecost by breaking into a fit of suppressed laughter when he was intoning the Gospel about the unjust steward who complained, "To dig I am not able."

Gene's pursuit of the bats had reminded me of a philosophical position he took while at St. John's, one that always troubled me because I was never sure whether he was serious about it or not. "There may be a philosophical war raging in the clericate, provoked by my statement in Philosophy of Education today, to the end that the animals are no more aware of their existence, insofar as we can know, than is a molecule of iron."

I was reassured, however, by his attachment to Siena who turned out to be a little cat with very human ways. She was bewitching in her kittenhood, rolling at our feet and jumping at grasshoppers and butterflies in the tall grass. But I felt a real cooling of my feeling for her when she first came triumphantly home from hunting with a small frog in her jaws. She became increasingly attached to Gene and followed him about more like a dog than a cat. She was perfectly happy on either lap but intensely jealous of our attention to each other. If we sat on the sofa reading together in the evening, she would come hurtling at us, burrowing between us. Riding in the car, she would lie like a fur scarf over Gene's shoulders, never moving, eyes alert to the passing roadside, occasionally rasping his ear with an affectionate lick of her rough tongue.

In the fall, when the nights began to cool and we had to leave our bedroom door open in order to get heat from the stove, we put a screen across the door in order to keep her out. She tolerated this for a little while, but one night there was a frantic scramble and scraping and a terrific thumping as she launched herself against the screen, knocked it over and came like a shot across the floor, up on the bed, burrowing between our heads on the pillows.

Siena was not the only one to violate our bedroom privacy. Gene had arranged for a working partnership with our next door neighbors, Oscar and Waldo Eklund, a father and son. They had stored various supplies in the attic of the house before we moved in, bags of fertilizer and seed corn and other things which had to be kept dry. We awakened one morning to hear bumblings and thumpings, just in time to see Oscar making his way down the stairs past our door, laden with sacks and grinning. "Excuse it, please," he said in a sibilant Swedish accent.

Dad McCarthy was embarrassed by Gene's alliance with the Eklunds. They were part-time farmers in a sense that the eighty acres they owned were not financially productive enough to support the family. When his children were small, Oscar "hired out," as the saying went, to other farmers and did odd jobs of all kinds. His wife had found the life too hard and had left him and gone to Minneapolis, taking some of the children with her. Oscar lived now on the farm with Waldo, his grown son, a man about Gene's age, and with his daughter Florence, a housekeeper of sorts. If one could judge by Florence, who was said to look like her, Mrs. Eklund must have been a very handsome woman. Florence was blonde and statuesque and attractive, with the looks that Britt Ekland and Ingrid Bergman have made well known to the world but which were so common in Minnesota as not to be thought unusual.

We were serious about trying to involve ourselves with the community in order to carry out our rural life mission. But it was not really easy to do. The local view was that Eugene, as they called him, had always been there after all and there was no need to make any special fuss about my coming, so we had few callers from Watkins itself. I was disappointed that Gene's many cousins did not do much to welcome us and made only minimal responses to my overtures. "Watkins people didn't know what to talk to you about, Abbie—you were always writing books and talking about things like that," wrote one of Gene's cousins to me this year. I understand now that they found me strange, but I know that I made great efforts not to be. I was less apt to talk about "things like that" than Gene was. I had never found a small town difficult before, and I thought of the happy experiences in other villages, days of teaching swimming for the Red Cross in little places named Millville, Mazeppa, Theilman, Reads Landing—all as small as Watkins or smaller—but, of course, I had never gone to live in them.

Our hope to be part of the community gave Gene a perfect excuse to play baseball with the home team—if he had needed an excuse. I knew how much he loved it. Still, I preferred lonely Sunday afternoons to following the team. I felt a stranger among the other wives, but more than that—Gene on the baseball diamond turned into someone I did not know, it seemed to me.

Years later, the wife of a prominent educator who had once taught with me introduced me to a large audience of Twin City women by saying, "You may think you are meeting the wife of a senator and a scholar. When I first asked my husband about the man Abigail was going to marry, he said, 'Oh, Gene McCarthy—he's a big, tough baseball player from around here.'" Her husband and his friends, when they were young coaches, had often made extra money by acting as umpire for the games of a small league. They found Gene a difficult player. He played with ferocity and a passion to win and would advance threateningly and vocally upon the umpire at the slightest provocation, or so it seemed to me when I was there. It bothered me, too, that the baseball field was the one place where he never seemed aware of me. Everywhere else, we maintained a sort of silent communication. Watkins was having a good year that year, and it seemed happier to wait for him to come home triumphant.

For my part, I looked forward to the threshing run as the time when I would naturally become involved with the other wives in our neighborhood. When I was growing up, my sisters, my brother, and I used to spend at least a month each summer on the farm with my aunt and uncle and three older cousins, and I remembered threshing time as the high point of the summer. The men had gone from farm to farm "on the run" with the threshing machine, some pitching bundles, some feeding the machines, some shoveling the grain. The women and children had gone from farm to farm, too, to help with the huge dinners and lunches. Each farmwife came with offerings of cakes and pies, whatever was her specialty, but the main meal was provided by the host farm. I remembered it as a time of great feasting. The men ate at the first table and the women and children afterwards. Wash basins and pitchers of water were set out under the trees and roller towels hung so that the men could wash. And they did so with great splashing and huffing and came into the house via the kitchen, scraping their feet noisily and talking farm talk about the yield per acre, the number of bushels, the prospect of rain, always a terrible threat in the threshing season.

But by 1945 things had changed. The big and prosperous farmers harvested individually by combine and only a gaggle of small farmers were still served by the communal threshing machine. When I inquired of the Eklunds as to the procedure for our threshing run, they seemed somewhat puzzled and explained to me that most of the men ran into town for lunch, that I could probably get some bakery cakes and pies to have on hand for the field lunches. But if I liked, Florence and I might work together on dinner when the men came to our fields.

The run itself proceeded rather shakily because the decrepit threshing machine kept breaking down on one farm or another, and there were long waits for parts and days lost at a time. The dinner preparation, when it was finally our turn, was not at all what I remembered. There were some other women there, but the Eklund kitchen was small and crowded. We did not spend the morning, as I remembered, shelling peas and peeling potatoes while the roast cooked. We drank a lot of coffee. Then, when it seemed time for the men to come, we opened cans of peas and set about frying great slabs of pork steak. The pork steak, the very sight of it, was almost my undoing. For the past month, I had found myself particularly vulnerable to smells, and there seemed to be an increasing number of unpleasant ones about the farm, ones I hadn't noticed when I first came. (I had been particularly dismayed earlier in the summer when Gene and I took our walks down the road in the summer evenings by the overwhelming aroma of pollinating corn.) Suddenly it occurred to me that there might be another reason, and I was thunderstruck at the realization that I was going to have a baby.

The summer held many beautiful, quiet moments when we could be together, in every sense aware of each other and of the ever changing life in the growing things around us. We tried to fit each day into the rhythm of the oldest prayers of the Church, the Divine Office. We began each day with Prime, the hour which looks joyfully to the work of the day and is full of prayers like

Let the glorious beauty of the Lord, our God be upon us, and direct thou the work of our hands; direct thou the work of our hands.

And with prayers about the goodness of creation as in Psalm 23:

The earth is the Lord's and the fullness thereof, the world and all that dwell therein, for He hath foundeth it upon the seas and upon the waters having made it firm.

At noon Gene often came in from the field or from his trips to town with handfuls of wild day lilies or brown-eyed Susans, and Queen Anne's lace—sometimes with a trailing willow branch or bearing furry-looking cattails from the little swamp on our land.

In the evening, in time-honored country fashion, we sat on our steps and watched the sun go down and the pale green sky of early evening darken and the stars come out. I began to recognize the constellations once again. I used to take sewing or reading out to the long grassy places under the apple trees in the late afternoons. Then it seemed to me that I literally could feel my nerves untangling after the long tension of the previous years.

At night we closed the day with Compline, feeling a little guilty about abandoning the Rosary but pleased by the aptness of the Compline psalm:

> He that dwelleth in the shelter of the most high and abideth in the shadow of the Almighty, shall say to the Lord thou are my protector and my refuge, my God in whom I trust.
> Like a shield His truth shall guard thee; thou shall not fear the terrors of night, nor the arrow that flies by day, nor the plague that prowleth in the dark, nor the noon day attack of the demon . . .
> I will protect Him because He hath known my name.
> He will call upon me and I will hear Him.
> I will be with him in need, I will rescue Him and bring Him to honor.
> With length of days I will satisfy Him and show Him my salvation.

These biblical prayers arranged in the Psalter of the church are really very comforting and human. The Compline hymn, for instance, calls for very specific help,

> From evil dreams defend our eyes,
> From nightly fears and fantasies.

We were very serious about building a home life based on the Benedictine ideal of mixed prayer and work, of lives which combined both intellectual and manual work, and eager to have the house finished so that we could, as the Rule says, "pursue hospitality."

Our efforts at rural life were lonely compared to the effort of the Hyneses in the shadow of St. John's where seminarians and priests and lay teachers gathered to join in the labor. But at the time, we were perhaps spared a great deal of contentious theorizing over each step of our plan and about our bourgeois spirit because we wanted certain comforts.

Arleen and Emerson were glad when they could introduce us to a young doctor and his wife who were moving to a town very near us. Edwin and Joanne Emerson became our close friends and whenever Edwin wanted rest from the continuous rounds of a general practitioner, he came to help Gene saw, dig, or paint. We were especially fortunate that he was nearby one day when we started to spray-paint the dreary stucco of the house with a white concretelike paint called Bondex. In the faulty way of mechanisms made under the circumstances of the war years, the spray gun backfired into Gene's eyes when he was high up on the ladder. He was blinded with the paint and pain. In absolute terror, I did the only thing I could think of which was to rinse his eyes continually with cold water until we were quite sure all the paint was out and then call Dr. Emerson. He felt that our quick action had saved Gene's sight.

After a polite interval, friends and relatives began to come to see how we were managing in our strange new existence. Mr. Leighton, an insurance man who was my aunt's financial adviser, made a long detour from a trip and wryly observed that Miss O'Leary would be gratified to see the way in which I was struggling to bring city touches to the country. He was especially amused at my soon-abandoned attempt to lay bricks in herringbone pattern as a walk to the kitchen door.

My sisters came to visit before they returned to their homes and jobs on both coasts—Ellen to Seattle, Anne to San Francisco. Dad McCarthy, who accepted my own defection from the city as an aberration having to do with his erratic son Eugene, was worried that we would not entertain them well. "City girls" were used to more activity, he thought. He rented a cottage for us at Clear Lake three miles away so that we could take them fishing, swimming, and sunbathing. The first time we used the cottage we found a fifth of scotch planted firmly in the center of the little dining table with a note, "Now you girls enjoy yourselves." He took them crow hunting, a sport farmers indulged in all year long with clear consciences because corn, the principal crop of our region, had to be guarded at all costs. That week I discovered in him (and, I believe, he in me) a latent, fun-loving side and we enjoyed each other much more afterwards. My brother joined us that Sunday, impressive in his Navy officer's summer whites. We embarrassed Dad McCarthy by filing into the family pew late for Sunday Mass, but appeased him later with Sunday dinner expertly cooked by Ellen, and over which we lingered long, laughing and reminiscing and telling old family stories.

Mabel Frey came using some of her precious gas to go thirty miles out of her way on a trip to her family summer home. It was at the time the partitions were gone and we were living in the attic. She made everything seem a great lark. If she was dismayed to find me in this state, she hid it well.

The carpenters had lifted the telephone from the kitchen wall and hung it in the back entry—then pulled down the entry. Mabel made her long-distance calls standing in the rain while Gene sheltered her with an umbrella.

Sister Mariella and Sister Remberta came from St. Benedict's. Sister Mariella rhapsodized about the farm as a perfect setting for scholar farmers. Sister Remberta, a science teacher, remarked severely that our manure pile was surely leached out by the weather. We were, of course, intent on using natural fertilizers. We were rather proud of the manure pile left by the previous tenant farmers. I had not even been dismayed when I slipped into it on my first tour of the farm and ruined a pair of slacks which I had included in my very limited trousseau.

By the end of the summer the house was finished enough so that we could celebrate the blessing of the home. My three students, Pat Kilp, Harriet Engfer, and Dorothy Sickel came out from St. Paul, full of high spirits, bearing house gifts. Emerson and Arleen and Father Godfrey came from St. John's. We followed Father Godfrey about in a cheerful, small procession, singing and making the responses as he intoned the ancient blessings. Father Godfrey kept punctuating the ceremony with expressions of amazement and concern that only our two Protestant members, Harriet and Dorothy, could stay in tune.

In late September we felt we could take a long-delayed wedding trip. It would eat into the little reserve of money we had not invested in the farm, but we had really done nothing just for enjoyment since we had been together again. I looked on the trip we planned as a way of sharing with Gene people and places I had come to know in the interval of our separation. So I especially wanted him to know Montreal, Quebec, and New York. We thought of it, too, as a way of connecting what we hoped to do in Watkins with apostolic movements elsewhere. Then, too, it seemed to us that we owed a courtesy call to the shrine of Ste. Anne de Beaupré, since it was very likely that St. Anne was responsible for our present happiness.

Like all long-dreamed-of trips it was disappointing in some ways and unexpectedly happy in others. Toronto, site of the Medieval Institute and where Father David, Gene's long time friend, had sent letters of introduction, we found congenial and interesting. Its dimensions seemed more human than those of the universities we knew and liked, with its English plan of a grouping of small colleges as part of the larger institution. We left with a certain reluctance the talk in the small restaurants near the campus and the people we came to know so quickly. Montreal and Quebec seemed beautiful, but foreign and cold after that. We were dismayed to find that the Jocists we sought out in Montreal, the very continental headquarters of that French worker movement, expended almost all their energies on the succor of twelve- to fourteen-year-old boys, adrift and jobless in that huge, gray city. They told us that French-Canadian farms could not support the large families and that boys of that age were often sent away by their families to find work. It was a rude shock to us who had heard much romantic talk about French-Canadian subsistence farms in the rural life movement. But Gene liked old walled Quebec as I did, and I showed him the little sideways house with flowers in the deep-embrasured window on the street behind the Ursuline convent. It was this house which symbolized seventeenth-century Quebec to me in a way that the walls could not.

Gene was enthusiastic about rural New England, beautiful from the train windows in the fall, as we went on to New York. The roar and pace of New York dismayed us both; Gene, because he found it the very epitome of what was wrong with the city, and I, because I was beginning to find myself physically unequal to the trip. One night on our way from the theater we saw a sailor fall senseless into the gutter where cars passed perilously near him. We were appalled that everyone went by as if he were not there. Gene got him up, enlisting the help of a curious onlooker, and into a bar where he paid the bartender to call for help. The bartender sent us on our way tolerantly, saying, "You get used to this, buddy—it happens all the time."

Dr. Marian and Dr. Sidney Newcomer (he hospitable but uncertain and indifferent as always about her protégés) plied us with advice and hospitality. When I fell ill at dinner one night, Dr. Marian scolded Gene for taking me on a trip in my delicate condition and insisted on making an appointment with a friend of hers who was a specialist in obstetrics. We were awed at his Park Avenue office with its sofas covered in the blue chintz some decorator had thought soothing to the sensibilities of Park Avenue prospective mothers. We did not fully understand what he told us, but gathered that there was a certain "condition" which bore watching. He advised against any further traveling and seemed nonplused when we explained that we were more than a thousand miles from home.

We were thus suddenly robbed of our first carefree days. That same day there was a letter from Dad McCarthy saying that it looked as if the corn might freeze soon. He reported that Siena was "as good as a dog." She went everywhere with him, even riding on his shoulders when he drove the tractor. Suddenly it seemed as if we could not get home fast enough. We left New York without visiting the *Catholic Worker* or seeing Dorothy Day, although we had looked forward to that very much.

We interrupted the trip home, however, with a visit to Grailville in Ohio, where the Ladies of the Grail made a celebration of our visit, as they knew so well how to do, and made much of our plans for school and community to the assembled students of their folk school. They promised to send help, once our school was really under way, and we left much encouraged. There began then a relationship between Gene and the Grail movement which was to last for many years. There was Grail help all over the country in 1968.

When winter closed in, our life became almost idyllic. It was the life we had dreamed of. The house, although stove heated, was snug and warm in the evenings with the wind and snow swirling outside. We were very happy about the baby coming. We had time to read and talk and I sewed or knitted for the baby and also for the new Hynes baby who was expected that year.

In the days Gene's farm work was quickly done and he spent his time writing as did I. We were at work on a rural life anthology and each of us wrote articles for *Land and Home*, the magazine of the rural life movement.

Our photo album of the time has a picture of Gene in the kitchen, clad in old-fashioned overalls, sitting beside our little cast-iron stove. On the stove is the little copper teakettle he brought home proudly one day from a farm auction, our first shared antique. Underneath the picture is written "The farmer in the kitchen." Beside it, another picture shows Gene in the study, head bent over his desk, above which is hung my great Aunt Nell's needlepoint picture of St. Patrick and Gene's grandfather's blackthorn stick which he had brought from Ireland.

Aunt Mary McCarthy in Eden Valley worried about my isolation on the farm and insisted that we come there for Christmas Eve dinner. Coming back that evening through a driving snowstorm, we were stuck in the snow as we neared the farm and it took a great deal of effort on Gene's part to get us out. I think we were both frightened at the proximity of danger inherent in farm life in the Minnesota winter. Both of us had heard many tales in our childhood of men lost between the barn and the house in a blinding blizzard and of people found frozen beside the road.

After our small Christmas scare, I was aware of our isolation, especially on the days when Gene had to be gone. I tired easily. In the heavy snow of winter there was no place to walk and I knew I was gaining too much weight. By the time of the first false thaws of January, I began to know what it was to be "heavy with child."

One day when I was alone, the neighbor's pigs, a scrubby bunch of no particular breed, came trotting and wheeling into our yard. They had broken out and were in search of corn. The corn was precious to us and I went out to try and scare them off. As I went heavily sliding over the rough, icy ground, flapping a dish towel to scare them, I suddenly realized how helpless I would be if they turned and charged. Pigs, to the knowledgeable farmer, are very dangerous animals. I had heard tales of men who had fallen into pens and been eaten or badly chewed before they could be rescued. When I got back into the house, I was weak and shaking.

As the time drew nearer for the baby to come, we spent hours studying methods of delivery in case, for some reason, we could not get to the hospital in St. Cloud, thirty miles away. Gene arranged with Waldo Eklund to follow him in his car if we should have to go during the night, in case the car should break down.

Our periodic visits to Dr. Schatz in St. Cloud were frustrating. He had delivered several thousand babies—more than any other doctor in Minnesota—and his examinations were competent but cursory, his instructions very few. Most of his patients were the German farm women of Stearns County. They came from large families and had large families of their own. Dr. Schatz used the language of the Catholic family life movement; he called all his patients "Mother" and when he described one of the others to me he always prefaced whatever he had to say with, "She's a good Catholic mother—fine Catholic family." But his attitude was basically fatalistic, as if it had been absorbed from the generations of experience with the women he had attended—women of peasant heritage who married, worked, bore children and died with patient acceptance and dumb strength.

He liked to talk to me about his daughter Rosemary, who had been my student at St. Catherine's. I remembered her as an intense, green-eyed girl with the perverse sort of intelligence which is always focused on a bypath of knowledge. In my Freshman English course she had distinguished herself by refusing to read the Old Testament as literature on the grounds that it was indecent, and she had been upheld by her father. I could only wonder at them both. When I talked to Dr. Schatz I felt that we used a third language, which was not the language in which either of us thought. He seemed kind, but I never felt that he understood me or my questions. I was pigeonholed somewhere in his mind and all that was necessary was being done. Babies came when they were ready.

I have an old desk calendar from that year. The date April 30 has only the notation, "Christopher Joseph."

"We couldn't save him," Dr. Schatz told me sadly, when I roused out of the whirring dark. He was holding the small body for me to see. "I baptized him Joseph. It's my name and he's a good saint."

"But his name is Christopher," I said. It was the name we had chosen one winter night because it meant "Christ-bearer."

The day lay behind me, stretching back like a road dipping and falling through peaks of pain and semiconsciousness. We had driven the long thirty miles to the hospital in the early morning dark. There was no one at the Eklunds'—they had gone to visit in the city—and there was no one else to call. My labor started and stopped all through the day. Caught in the seeming competence and routine of the hospital, we did not ask questions. For a long time Gene was beside me in the labor room. Once they rushed me into the delivery room and brought me back. After a while everything ran together. It seemed to me, hearing things in moments of consciousness, that everyone was lost. "Where is that doctor? Where is he?" I heard the old sister say in the delivery room. And later I heard Dr. Schatz, "Where's her husband? Call her husband!"

"I wish I had been there," Gene said to me sadly, walking beside the stretcher as I was being pushed to my room.

"Oh, but you were," I assured him. The sister pushing the stretcher wore the white nursing habit. It saddened me that it was flecked with blood stains and I tried to express my regret for that to her. She smiled and shook her head.

"Shock," she said to Gene, as if I were not there.

It was not until the next night that I could feel any tears. A young farm wife shared my room. She had had a baby the same day, her eighth, and she was happy because it was a big, strong boy. But she asked my permission before she would let them bring him in the next morning. "I don't want him in if it's going to bother you," she said. She watched with sisterly sympathy when they brought the small still body for me to dress. I looked in stupid wonder at the closed eyes, the lift of brow, the cheekbones, and the curled small fists all like Gene's, thinking that this was our child whom we would never know.

That afternoon they moved me to a room by myself and I finally wept thinking of Gene driving alone with the little coffin to the Watkins church and graveyard.

My brother came out from St. Paul, and the sisters at St. Catherine's sent two of my friends with armloads of white and purple lilacs.

One is not allowed a grief for a life never lived. Yet one has buried the fruit of love, and a great deal of hope and many dreams. Years later I used to wake crying in the night, thinking that I was crying for him, but a doctor told me that I was just personifying other griefs, other losses. I suppose that is so. But just this year, leafing through some of my old poetry books, I found Karl Shapiro's poem, *A Robbery,* and I find it true.

> Robber, paid agent of our hate
> I kiss my hand to you across the roofs
> And jungle of back alleys where you hide.
> You with your guns are like a boy I loved.
> He was born dead and never had a name.
> He was my little son. Night took him off.
> Hard to unlearn is love.

All through the year Gene had been working intermittently on our plan for the school. The achievement of the school was basic to our hope for building a community. Gene had been able to persuade a number of the townspeople to meet and discuss the reopening of St. Anthony's High School and Father Bozja had agreed to it if the necessary teachers could be found. We had still counted on Raph and Margaret Thuente; both Margaret and I could teach, we thought. Gene and Raph could teach and coach various athletics—we were realistic enough to know that a school without an athletic program would not be a community center in any normal Minnesota town. Responding to Sister Mariella's persuasion, the Reverend Mother at St. Benedict's granted Gene an audience and agreed to provide at least one sister for the school, preferably a sister for the field of home economics. In the course of the year, a young priest, Father Howley, stationed at Forest City came to call. He, like so many young priests, was isolated and alone in his country parish. Having been prepared at St. Paul Seminary he was not at all indoctrinated in the rural life movement or its philosophy, but he was politely interested in what we had to say about it. He was intelligent and had a puppylike friendliness which we found very endearing. He also had an openness about things that had happened to him, which was rare among the younger clergy, who tended to be very careful of their dignity. The high point of his life had been a trip he had made to Europe in the course of which he visited Therese Neumann of Konnersreuth in Bavaria, an ecstatic, a laywoman, who seemed to have received the stigmata of the wounds of the crucified Jesus and who existed for many years, as far as any investigators could determine, without any food except the Sacrament. On each Friday she re-enacted in her own physical suffering the suffering of the Crucifixion. Pilgrims who visited her often reported that she had unusual spiritual insight—could read people's hearts—and was peculiarly sensitive to evil either in the form of past deed or in character. Father Howley had been very much impressed by his visit.

His spiritual tastes were eclectic, however, so on the way back to the United States, he had stopped in England and made a special visit to the Jesuit church on Farm Street in London. Farm Street in the ecclesiastical pecking order was perhaps the intellectual and social peak. The Jesuits there were famous for their scholarship, their preaching, the ease with which they moved among the men of high station in the world. Father Howley, secure in his friendly conviction that all priests were brothers, knocked on the door at Farm Street and introduced himself as a visiting American who was eager to see the church where so much had happened. The Jesuit who answered the door escorted him through the church and, as Father Howley told of his visit to Therese Neumann, he conducted Father Howley through a side door of the church, across a little garden to another door. Father Howley, in full expectation that he was being conducted to some source of brotherly hospitality, walked through the open door to find himself back on the London street.

"I am far more interested in the passion of Christ as depicted in the sufferings of the Polish people than I am in it as depicted in the sufferings of Therese Neumann," said the Jesuit with finality as he closed the door.

For some perverse reason we thought this story hilariously funny and would entreat Father to recount it for the benefit of other guests when they came. Father Howley offered to teach religion in our school and we were grateful for the offer since we felt that it would give an added tone of clerical respectability when the time came to submit the plan to the Archbishop. This was the only thing on which Father Bozja was adamant. We had to have the full approval of the Archbishop.

Late in the spring through Father's intervention, and I think through the intervention of Gene's cousin, Father McCarthy, Gene secured an appointment with the Archbishop to talk over the program. Archbishop Murray, as Gene recounted it, listened politely, thanked Gene for his interest in the Watkins school, and said he would communicate his decision to Father Bozja. In a week Father Bozja had the answer. It was a flat no. "But why, Father?" Gene asked. "Did he give a reason?" The Archbishop had indeed given a reason. There would be no school in his archdiocese under the control of laymen while he held office there. Today it seems an incredible decision. He would rather have no school than a school conducted by the laity.

We revised our hopes, although somewhat forlornly. Perhaps after all what we were meant to have was an adult education center. Gene and Raph could look for positions in the neighboring small towns. We might eventually be able to persuade the parish to put some of the money into an adult education center. We might get help from the Grail for that kind of thing.

We were at ease on the land that second summer. I remember many things fondly. Our garden, planted so carefully and fertilized only with organic mulch. (We emphasized, as the book stressed, the vitamin C vegetables like kohlrabi, brussels sprouts, and cauliflower, and I canned jars and jars of them, only to carry them around with us for a year or two, loath to part with my handiwork and equally loath to admit that we simply didn't like them.) Our battle to save the fruit of our most beautiful apple tree in blossom as we built smudges all night long; shocking oats in our highest field with Father Garrelts up from Minneapolis as we sang "Regina Coeli"—and everywhere Peva, bounding about, following us, making short dashes of his own after rabbit or gopher and back again.

Peva had been given to us that spring by Dr. Emerson. He was a large half springer, half water spaniel. He had been the gift of grateful patients who named him in an approximation of the Bohemian word for beer because he had looked to them, when a puppy, like a beer bottle. He was an amber brown then, but by the time he came to live with us a curly, dark chocolate brown with surprising yellow eyes. He transferred his affections to us very easily, giving Stretch Emerson only the most cursory of greetings after a week or so. We thought it was because his kind of dogdom required a master with acres, but he remained faithful to us through the exigencies of city living in the next few years.

By now our project and our hopes—partly because of our writing and the grapevine of the Catholic lay movement—were becoming better known and we had visitors and guests coming to talk with us about it, coming just to stay for a while, dropping in just for a visit. A New York writer with whom I had struck up a correspondence during my brief career as a critic came with his wife and children. He wanted to be near St. John's and St. Benedict's. He was convinced that the only pure Catholicism in the country existed there, but he was repelled by the ugliness and bareness of the little town of St. Joseph in which St. Benedict's was situated. Watkins, of course, was no more appealing to him but we hopefully showed him the houses near the lake, somewhat out of town in a softer and more pleasing landscape. He fascinated us and exhausted us with his intensity and his irreconcilable despair about the Church in the East. We were made uneasy, too, by the tension which seemed to exist between him and his wife. It was the first time that I had seen the bewilderment of a woman who had left a secure and ordered existence to follow a man on a quest of his own seeking, to live as he decreed, to bear his children, and then to find herself his enemy just because she had done these things. Her every remark was met with his strained impatience. His every attack on the Irish establishment of the East out of which she had come seemed in a way to be aimed at her. We were torn in their presence. We felt they would not be back.

Franz Mueller and his wife Therese, both German sociologists and refugee professors in St. Paul, sent us their oldest daughter, Mechtilde, for the summer, hoping, they said, that seeing their ideals embodied in younger people would make Mechtilde find them acceptable.

The overflow came to us from St. John's: a convert minister and his patient Griselda-like wife from New Jersey; a young French woman who had flown unannounced and unexplained from New York for one of the rural life conferences and wanted to experience living on an American farm. We were puzzled by her name—it did not seem that of a French peasant—and she was puzzled by our books and seeming freedom from farm tasks. After a few days we discovered that she was the daughter of the Comte de Viel-Castel, councillor-general of the department of Eure, whose family home was near Chartres. She had joined the Jocist movement before the war because she was offended by the paternalistic charities of upper-class French women. "I wanted so much to do something real," she told us. She in her turn was amused to discover our academic background and refused to take our community building aspirations very seriously.

She could not see that American small communities needed rebuilding.

"You are so wholesome, you Americans—you do not understand—" and she dwelt on the degradation of the French village where even the children drank spirits. I insisted that American farmers, too, frequented taverns in the morning, and tried to prove it by taking her into one after Mass the next morning. We sat in a booth eating breakfast. The first man to come in after our arrival—a distant cousin of Gene's—went up to the bar and ordered a glass of milk. I can still hear Marie-Bonne's laughter and the perfect courtesy with which she greeted him when he came over to our booth.

After her departure we were forced to face the reality of our situation. Our money was running very low. Our half of the crop would not bring in very much. All during that year we had been eking out a little here and a little there. Concerned friends in St. Paul had recommended Gene as a field man for the co-operative grain association and he made a little from that. Some of our writing had sold. (I had been very happy when a check for two stories of mine came on Gene's birthday—they seemed a present for him sent by providence.) When the school plan faltered—we hoped temporarily—under the Archbishop's disapproval, Emerson Hynes had suggested that there might be part-time teaching at St. John's, since all the colleges were feeling the increased enrollment brought about by returning veterans. Gene had talked to the dean, who thought it might indeed be possible. Now classes were about to begin and he had not called or written. Finally Gene called him. I did not need to ask the answer when he turned from the phone. They did not need him at St. John's.

Gene stood looking out the window at our fields. After what seemed an endless time, I ventured, "What about St. Thomas?" Raph Thuente, back from the war, had written to say that he must give up the farm plan; Raph had children to think of now and St. Thomas had offered him a place in the education department. Overwhelmed with prospective students, they were adding to the faculty. He had thought Gene should consider it. But going to St. Thomas would mean giving up the farm.

Gene turned from the window. "You draft a letter," he said, "and I'll sign it." And he went out, walking toward the little marsh behind the barn.

The answer from St. Thomas came by return mail. They needed Gene and wanted him on the faculty very much.

What our year on the farm had meant to both of us and to each of us was reflected in the companion pieces we wrote that year for *Land and Home*. We both stressed the spiritual riches of farm living; Gene emphasized the correspondence between the turning of the seasons and the seasons of the liturgical year and I the peace which made prayer possible. He emphasized the joys and the emotional security to be found in ownership; I the psychological advantages of country living. Our sociologist friends would have pointed to these differences of emphasis as evidence of the differences in masculine and feminine thinking. But I think it was just Gene's way and my way.

We left the farm that fall for St. Thomas and St. Paul, and, although we did not know it then, for politics.

2 / Political Wife

We left the farm in the fall of 1946. By the end of the fall of 1948—a scant two years later—Gene was on his way to Washington, the elected representative of a district in which he had voted that year for the first time.

After the war, St. Thomas College was feeling the effect of the great influx of veteran students who were taking advantage of the GI Bill. In order to accommodate the increased faculty, the college was hastily throwing up what many colleges in the area had—a faculty village made up of surplus army housing.

The St. Thomas accommodations and those at neighboring Macalester College were planned to be better than most, since they were officers' barracks each made into two family units. However, the barracks were not completed by the time school opened and we had to fend for ourselves as best we could.

At first Gene and I rented a bedroom from our friend Phyllis McAllister. We soon found that one room provided very difficult and confining living even though we still spent weekends at the farm. After a month or so, we decided to try to find a temporary apartment. Gene heard about a basement apartment in the suburban farmlet home of Colette Bisanz, the alumni secretary at St. Thomas; Colette lived there with Margaret Hannigan, her librarian friend. It was a sketchy home but it gave us more space. The apartment consisted of a living room, a bedroom which had not been finished—it had concrete block walls—an "economy" bathroom, and an electric plate on which to cook.

Colette and Peg were experimenting with organic farming on their few acres. What appealed especially to us was that they had space for our chickens which had been a great worry to Gene when we had to leave them unattended on the farm. (Peg and Colette still talk about a mysterious disease developed that fall by some of our chickens. Through a defect in breathing they drew in air under the skins and became inflated and bounced about like feathered balloons. Gene and Peg made anxious trips to the university agricultural campus with a dead chicken or two for analysis.) We were also welcome to bring Peva our dog.

Oxboro Heath, the suburb of Minneapolis where the farmlet was located, was a good distance from St. Thomas, and Peg, Colette, and Gene were gone all day. I was without a car and the bus transportation was poor. As the fall drew on and the days became short and dark, the basement apartment seemed dreary and the days very long. Peva did not take happily to subterranean existence. He sat at the top of the basement stairs and moaned and growled unhappily. Finally, sharing his claustrophobia, I would set out with him on a walk. But I could not seem to feel at home in this formless place—neither town nor country—and found that I was suffering from vague fears and a terror of open places—probably a delayed reaction to the shock of the baby's death the spring before. I did not want to tell Gene because basically I was happy with the move to St. Thomas and I wanted him to be.

Fortunately, Peg and Colette, naturally very sociable people, became more and more friendly and desirous of our company as the time went on. They leaned heavily on Gene for advice about their little farm. We killed our afflicted chickens, and when reassured that they were safe to eat, began to share them for dinners. Gene's father also brought sides of beef for us and for them, which we had frozen and put into lockers. Little by little we became a family unit of sorts. We began to live upstairs more and more, prolonging our rural life discussions into the night or exchanging tidbits about St. Thomas with Colette—its lore and its characters. It was with genuine regret that we finally moved to the college huts shortly before Christmas.

From the moment it was known that we were moving to St. Paul, we had been under pressure to sell St. Anne's Farm to a woman who had lived there during her childhood. She knew the Eklunds and was anxious to return to the farm with her husband and live in semiretirement. The man who rented Dad McCarthy's farm was equally anxious to have Dad annex our other forty acres. The offers became increasingly good but we were reluctant to give up what had been our first home together. Gene had not abandoned his idea of a rural community. As time went on we were drawn into a rural life group; Peg and Colette had met the other members through their search for a Christian rural community. The group's most persistent member was a fireman named Joe Byrne who was addicted to causes and schemes and whose thin, pretty wife, Berry, was the willing victim of the consequences of project after project. Until our advent they had been talking in theory since none of them was able to buy a farm large enough to be the beginning of a community. Now if we were willing to sell St. Anne's Farm and buy another one, their hopes might become reality. We went to their meetings biweekly and began to spend our weekends and late afternoons looking at farmland in the country near the Twin Cities. In the process we learned a great deal about the surroundings of the cities themselves. Within short driving distance there were surprising pockets of rural living. I remember our coming upon a pig farm, late one Sunday afternoon—something I had never seen before. The farmhouse stood stark in a bare farmyard cluttered with rusted machinery and old car bodies. White, sluglike hogs were crawling over a huge mountain of garbage. It was years before I could eat pork with equanimity again!

In another direction from St. Paul, in a suburban area called Golden Valley, we found a remodeled farmhouse, a picture-book kind of farmhouse under huge maple trees. It was filled with antiques which the owner was willing to sell with the house, but alas, there were only seven acres and we were committed to a farm large enough to be the base of a community.

To the south of St. Paul on the hills along the river there were prosperous-looking farms with comfortable old farmhouses, but whenever we stopped the car and got out to look, the sounds of planes overhead or the stench of the South St. Paul stockyards made it all too clear that the city had won and that rural living in this area was already doomed. Finally, in Dakota County to the south and west of the city, we found one hundred and sixty acres, the traditional Minnesota quarter section farm. We bought it. The house was square, ugly, set too high on its foundation. But the farm had a marshy lake and a strip of hilly land along the road which seemed ideally suited for division into one-acre holdings which our fellow group members could buy for their houses. There were good fields and the farmer, who took a great liking to Gene, showed us his account sheets. Under his management it had been a good working farm. It had given his family a good living and had brought in a profit. We thought the fact that the farm lay within the boundaries of the first Irish parish in that part of the state was a favorable omen. The other members of the prospective community liked the location and it would probably double as an investment since it was within the growth area of St. Paul.

We sold the Watkins farm and bought the new one. We were destined never to live on it.

In the meantime we were finding life in Tomtown, as the faculty village of St. Thomas was called, the most carefree and enjoyable we had known. We were surrounded by people we found interesting. Gene had the camaraderie of the faculty restaurant at noon, plus the stimulation of the students who were back from the war and of the new faculty members who came from all over the world. Our old friends from Mandan, Raph and Margaret Thuente, lived next door with their two little boys, John and David. On the other side of us lived Dr. Heinrich Rommen and his wife. Dr. Rommen was a famous professor, a refugee from Germany who was an authority on natural law and a pillar of the early Christian Democratic party; he had been one of the bright young men in the party during the days of the Weimar Republic. Rudolph Schwenger, the head of the sociology department to which Gene was nominally attached, was an Austrian scholar who had been driven out of his homeland by the Nazis.

Our home consisted of a combination kitchen-living room with a

138

small bathroom, one large bedroom and another small one. That first year we were able to use the small bedroom as a combination guest room and study, and the space seemed all we needed. We shut off the kitchen area by turning a kitchen cupboard backward and painting its back pale yellow to match the living room walls. With my Aunt Abbie's theatrical gauze curtains at the high windows, her chintz-covered living room furniture, a mahogany table, and a red rug from her dining room, our house looked very pretty.

There was no scarcity of company and good talk. We often had people in for dinner and for sherry parties. When it was a big group we served dinner from platters set on the floor and carved our food on broiler pans.

But even as we continued our plans for a Christian rural community, other forces and influences were beginning to enter our lives. One of the new professors at St. Thomas, a professor of political science named Marshall Smelser, had taken his doctorate at St. Louis University and had come under the influence of the first social-action Jesuit priests there. Marshall was a historian. He shared with Gene an admiration for Benedictinism in history. However, Marshall believed in combining Benedictine ideals with the political process. He had interested Gene in joining Americans for Democratic Action, which at the time seemed a new and exciting organization coping with postwar problems. Americans for Democratic Action was orginally conceived as a means of liberal opposition to communism. This opposition was to express itself not only in combating the imperialism of Russian communism, but also in remedying those evils in society which made people turn to communism. To Marshall and to Gene, this line of thought could not have been more congenial. The concern with adequate housing, just wages, care for the aged, job security, and enlightened welfare was in complete harmony with the thinking of the new generation of Catholic social scientists. In their view all discussions of social theory centered on whether or not the proposed remedies for social problems were good for the family or not. In Catholic social thought, the family was the basis of all society and the source of all society. This resulted in the acceptance of certain ideas as natural and Christian, ideas which were still considered novel if not dangerous almost twenty years later when they emerged as a base of Gene's philosophy: the idea of a guaranteed annual wage, for example, and the idea (already put into practice at St. John's) that a man's basic salary should take into account the number of people in his family. There was also in this Catholic thought the calm assumption that an international society, in fact a world government of some sort, was not only desirable but was intended by God. Another idea was that if capitalism was not actually evil, it was certainly very faulty as a system. There was, at least in theory, a condemnation of nationalism and racism in America. And, finally, there was a great preoccupation with war as an evil; if pacifism was not openly advocated, it came very close to it.

The Minnesota chapter of ADA was an important one because its head, Hubert Humphrey, then the mayor of Minneapolis, was one of the founders of the national organization and, next to Mrs. Roosevelt, its most enthusiastic organizing speaker. The young Catholic liberals from St. Paul were welcome additions to the newly formed chapter. When the state officers were elected, Marshall nominated Gene for the post of treasurer and Gene was elected.

When he went forward to be introduced, wearing his one good blue suit, he heard one of the members ask another, "Who is he anyway?" "Oh, don't you know?" was the reply. "He's the one with the money."

Gene found in ADA a new perspective. In it he glimpsed a way of reaching the levers of a society whose wrongs disturbed him deeply.

Gene's thinking about government was being clarified during this period. At St. John's, identification of modern evils had been clear enough, but the solutions seemed to lie in a return to what had been lost. Underlying this was the thinly veiled attitude that the government was at best a necessary evil. Gene had taken a gloomy view of what the young people called "the system"—the union of capitalism and big government which manipulates popular democracy. He read books such as Francis Campbell's *The Menace of the Herd* and

Private Faces/Public Places

Lawrence Dennis' *The Dynamics of War and Revolution*, and commented on them with some approval.

Now, with his new colleagues Rudolph Schwenger, Heinrich Rommen, Marshall Smelser, and Herman Schauinger, he found a different perspective. (Herman Schauinger was a specialist in early American Catholic history and brought to Gene's attention the positive belief in democracy held by such early giants as Charles Carroll of Carrollton and William Gaston of North Carolina.) These were men who thought that history was irreversible, that in history one could discern the movement of Providence—in other words, that the Lord was the Lord of history. In their political science and sociology, they did not deal with abstractions but with men in social, industrial, and political development. No two men could have been more conscious that men in history were capable of barbarous regression than Heinrich Rommen and Rudolph Schwenger: both of them had had important careers cut short by the Nazis. Dr. Rommen, a perceptive pioneer in the application of the theory of natural law to the development of democracy, had been a founder of an institute for socioeconomic order which was suppressed by the Gestapo in 1933. He subsisted by writing and working as a clerk until he escaped as a refugee in 1938. Rudolph Schwenger, a sociologist who specialized in the social aspects of industrial problems, had been the editor of *The Magazine for Culture and Politics* in Vienna. It was a periodical which, under his editorship, vigorously opposed the theory of National Socialism. After the *Anschluss* he was imprisoned and tortured by the Nazis. He never fully recovered from that experience. These two men had fully participated in the life of their times. Despite the shattering effect of nazism on their personal lives, they remained optimistic about man's ability to improve things through self-government and social development. Dr. Rommen was enthusiastic about the possibilities inherent in the American Constitution and referred to the Supreme Court as the tenth wonder of the world. He often chided us for not appreciating certain democratic aspects of American life which he felt Americans took blithely for granted. As a scholar he was fascinated with the fact that any one could have access to the books in the Library of Congress. "That would not be possible, no, that would not be possible in Europe," he would say, puffing vigorously on his cigar. He loved the equality demonstrated in our neighborhood in St. Paul where, as he put it, professors and laborers lived side by side.

Gene's debt to Heinrich Rommen was profound. In his new awareness of the application of the theory of natural law, Gene could go back to Maritain and discover a new basis for his own political thinking. Jacques Maritain, who had lived in Toronto and in Princeton as a refugee from Pétain's France and the German occupation, had a great effect on Catholic liberals in this country.

Although Gene's first book, *Frontiers in American Democracy*, was published after he had been in Congress twelve years and represents a distillation of the thinking, writing, and speaking he had done during the congressional years, his debt to the men at St. Thomas is clear. In the opening section of the book, he suggests that a negative protective function is not the only justification for government:

It is not even the fundamental or primary one. Man needs political institutions. This need is not the consequence of his depravity; neither does it depend on the relative goodness or badness of any particular period of history, although these two conditions, general depravity and the level of goodness and badness, will have immediate and practical effects on government and government actions. Man's need for government remains a positive one . . . a society of saints would still need positive human law. Grace or the absence of it does not wholly destroy nature or make the essential social or political institutions such as the family and government unnecessary. Aristotle's observation that man is by nature a political animal is sustained by history. One community rises on the ruin of another. As he observed, the state comes into existence originating in the bare needs of life; it continues in existence for the sake of a good life.

Government has a positive and natural function to assist man in the pursuit of perfection and of happiness. Government accomplishes this purpose by promoting the common good.

At the same time that Gene was hammering out in terms he could personally accept, a theory of the state as necessary and good, a theory basic to his own career in politics, a conflict was developing in

Catholic thought generally with respect to the relationship between church and state. The Church had accepted the separation of church and state in America in practice, but not always in theory. There was ample evidence in the writings of Catholics to uphold the popular belief that if Catholics were in the majority, they would seek a favored position for the Church. It seemed very hard for Catholic thinkers to free themselves from the proposition that if the Church was the true Church it should then be given a special position in the state. This thinking was reflected in the concordats with the Italian and Spanish governments and even in the Constitution of the new democracy in Eire. It seems an obviously untenable position, yet the men who fought through to a better one, Father John Courtney Murray and Jacques Maritain, were violently opposed by Catholic conservatives and their teachings were suppressed and sometimes banned.

"The state does not, then, have the right or the responsibility to impose what any majority considers true faith upon all of its subjects," Gene wrote. "It should encourage and aid, to the extent possible, all its subjects either in their own activities or through the instrumentality of other institutions, to advance in spiritual perfection. This it can do: first, by avoiding unwarranted interference, and second, by positive aid without dictation or discrimination."

Gene was active politically even while he was engaged in philosophical debate. Indeed, it often seemed to me later that in politics he arrived at a decision for action or came to a conclusion in theory intuitively and later worked out the philosophical foundation.

A struggle to unite the shattered remnants of the Farmer-Labor party and the old Democratic party in Minnesota, a union which must be credited to Hubert Humphrey's efforts, was in progress. Although the new party called the Democratic-Farmer-Labor party already existed, the struggle to control nomination for offices, appointments, and finances was still in progress. When a party is out of power in the state but in control nationally, it is not always true that the representatives of the national committee in the state are anxious for revitalization of the party. There were powerful elements opposed to the renewal in Minnesota. First of all, there were leftist elements of the old Farmer-Labor party who were reluctant to take the new hard line toward the Communists and who had co-operated with the Communist party within the state in the bitter labor struggles of the early 1930s. These were later to become the Progressives who almost led the Minnesota party into the column of Henry Wallace in 1948. Then there was the national committeeman himself, not a native Minnesotan but an appointee from Washington, and understandably reluctant to share his appointive powers. In the absence of a strong party the Labor Temples, as the headquarters of the American Federation of Labor in both Minneapolis and St. Paul were called, had been able to pick the nominees for office because they controlled the vote. There was only one Democratic congressman out of Minnesota's nine at the time, John A. Blatnik, who was from the traditionally liberal district where Minnesota's Iron Range is located. St. Paul, where St. Thomas was, and its surrounding county comprised Minnesota's Fourth District. It had been represented briefly for the first time since World War I by a Democratic congressman, but he had been quickly retired in the Republican year of 1946 by a handsome Navy veteran, Edward J. Devitt. Devitt was a lawyer and, like Gene, a St. John's alumnus. But unlike Gene, Devitt was a native of St. Paul. He had had strong support from the Postal Workers, another political force in the Twin Cities, and from the Railroad Brotherhood of which his father had been a member and which was traditionally a conservative union. To the Humphrey forces in Minneapolis, St. Paul was the traditional bastion of the old Democratic party and was largely foreign territory. The few officeholders in City Hall who were interested in strengthening the party turned to the colleges for help. Both St. Thomas College and Macalester College, at which Humphrey had taught briefly, had great influence in the city. They were looked on as city colleges and objects of city pride. There was none of the division between town and gown which sometimes exists elsewhere. Part of this resulted from the ethnic identification with the Minnesota colleges, part from the deep-seated Minnesota respect for education and educated people.

Gene and Marshall and a good many of the other teachers, as well as the veteran students, leaped into the organizing fray. They found ready allies at Macalester, notably G. Theodore Mitau, a young professor of political science who had fled the Nazis in Berlin, and his wife, Charlotte, who eventually became a county executive of the party. Our friend Bill Carlson was already a veteran of the St. Paul political wars, having served several terms in the legislature, and he was an ever present source of information on personalities and areas of the city. We began to understand the subtleties of the situation and the importance of the struggle that was taking place in 1947.

Mayor Hubert Humphrey, who had always wanted to be a senator, needed a strong party base as well as labor support and strong congressional candidates in other districts. It was also apparent—and this was more important for Gene and the young academics in St. Paul—that the left was attempting to seize the party structure for its own purposes. We were not unfamiliar with such strategy. It was a period of struggle between left and center in many organizations, and we had experienced just such a struggle in the teachers' union, and we knew about the Reuthers and their battles in the CIO.

There were other ideological battles as well. Gene, Marshall, and Ted Mitau were taken with the idea, as Orville Freeman was, that our parties hold their representatives to party decisions as did parties in Great Britain and that ultimately the party decision on issues should be binding on the representatives of the party in the legislatures and in Congress. Meeting followed meeting and one involvement led to another and to as colorful a cast of characters as I have ever known. Party officers, ward chairmen, courthouse officeholders, powers behind all sorts of small and large thrones seemed to come flocking into our hut.

There was Frank Thill, a crusty and tough old labor organizer who dated from the days when scabs were beaten and threatened. He had once backed the brave but perspiring Ted Mitau into a corner at a meeting, shouting, "I'll break your neck, Mitau." There was Tom Walsh, a wily and well-established lawyer who had profited from his Democratic contacts and seemed always to have a drafted resolution in his vest pocket ready to pull out at the strategic moment. There was Blanche McGovern, respectable and stalwart keeper of the party files. Blanche was reputed to keep the files under her bed and in fact refused to give them up when the new coalition elected a county chairman. There was Kosciusko Marsh, a druggist, who had been a functionary in the days of Farmer-Labor glory. He was a power in his ward and was given to making emotional speeches, declaring that Floyd B. Olson was looking down on us from Valhalla. Bob and Bart Hess, brothers and leaders of the CIO, sat in a trailer across from the Minnesota Mining & Manufacturing plant, battling the company's lawyers with only a laymen's legal handbook for support.

There was Frank Marzitelli, a power in the Italian community, and Mary Monsour Leavitt, of the Lebanese. Gene began to gather a group of special friends and supporters from the people he met at the meetings. One was Ray Devine from the machinist's union. He was another former Floyd B. Olson man, more, one gathered, because of Olson's organizational abilities than from basic admiration for the man and his stands. "He would call you in the day after an election," Ray said, "and go over it with you precinct by precinct. Why didn't this one deliver? Why did that? What a mind he had," Ray would say admiringly.

Another was Johnny O'Hara, a huge burly ex-prize fighter who had a minor local reputation. Johnny was now a bartender, belonged to the bartender's union and had influence there. He had various other part-time occupations. At one time he sold balloons. At another he drove a truck delivering bags of potato chips and peanuts to various bars and restaurants. He sometimes came to organization meetings in this truck, a fact which proved fortunate one evening when one of the ward chairwomen, a very choleric lady, had what seemed to be a stroke in her excitement over some parlimentary problem and had to be hastily taken to the hospital. Johnny's truck was pressed into service. Most trying to me, who so frequently received their calls, were two women who had had, if one could believe their own stories, enormous power and influence in organizations and clubs in previous years. One was a woman of real brilliance but she was at a period in her life when her prolonged talking could take almost sadistic form and there seemed to be no polite way of extricating oneself from the conversation. The other at one time held me on the phone so long that I could hear her husband expostulating in the background. "Wait a minute, dearie," she said to me cheerily, "I have to put the dog out." There was a decisive sound of a door slamming and no further sound from her husband.

Although I was caught up in the excitement of the political struggle, Gene's increasing involvement troubled me. I had found myself very happy in our new life at St. Thomas. St. Paul was home to me and full of old friends. The cozy security and spartan simplicity of our academic community suited me very well. One had all the advantages of a full social life with none of the complication of what we used to call "bourgeois standards." The housekeeping in the huts was minimal; our entertaining was simple. I had time to teach a course at St. Catherine's, to journey to St. Benedict's once a week to give an honors course, to do a little translating and editing for Dr. Rommen.

Gene's first uncertainties about St. Thomas and his work there had disappeared almost at once. In the first weeks the dean, an old family friend, had dropped by for a cup of coffee to tell me confidentially that Gene was perhaps too quiet. "Perhaps you could suggest that he be a little more assertive," he suggested. A year and a half later, when Gene had the whole campus energized in his campaign, the dean accused me of taking him too seriously. Gene had begun some graduate courses at the university which he found less than stimulating, but he grew more buoyant as the interchange on the faculty grew and as his student veterans began to respond to his more provocative ideas about society. I foresaw a life of academic distinction and leadership for him and I was happy. Best of all we were expecting another baby.

Ellen was born on October 30, 1947, after a long anxious wait. For some reason my babies always arrived from two to three weeks after the date predicted by the doctors. Ellen was a round, plump nine pounds and seven ounces with brown eyes, large and startling in so young a baby. When we returned to the hut from the hospital on a cold November day, Gene, sure that the late fall weather would be injurious to his precious new possession, leaped from the car, seized Ellen, and made off to the doorway. Inside, he made straight for the bedroom where he laid her on the big bed to unwrap her. Peva's reaction was pitiful. He had leaped joyously to meet me, but as he followed us into the bedroom it was clear that he sensed that the new being in the bundle had supplanted him. He sank into a corner with his head drooping lower and lower. Contritely we showed him Ellen and he sniffed half-heartedly at her, accepting what he could not change.

The arrival of the baby changed our lives in many ways. We were no longer free to come and go at will. The hut grew very small. Ellen's bathinette crowded the tiny bathroom; her playpen jutted into the living room, her crib occupied our study. There were diaper bags and drying racks and small pink woolens drying on the stove and, it seemed, formula constantly being sterilized in the kitchen. Although I had faithfully read Dr. Spock and knew what to expect theoretically, I found my slow return to full strength and the inevitable post-baby weepiness hard to cope with. Finally, one day, distraught more than usual at my ineptness and inefficiency, I sat down and made out a schedule. I found that the care of Ellen alone took eight hours. Anything I did over and above that, I told myself, I should be self-congratulatory about. It was easy to tell myself this but very difficult to accept psychologically. I could not believe that I could accomplish so little every twenty-four hours.

Gene never had any qualms about helping with the baby. He seemed to look on no task as peculiarly woman's work. But he was gone a great deal, to his classes and to the ever increasing organizational work of building up the new party. Thus, at last a prisoner of domesticity, I followed the effort from the sidelines. Our hut became a veritable message center with the telephone constantly ringing and students stopping by to pick up meeting information or strategy assignments.

What was in the process of being built was the Minnesota party which Theodore White described in 1960:

> When Freeman became governor in 1954 and Eugene McCarthy, United States Senator in 1958, they (the members of the new DFL

party) had not only given their state one of the finest, most responsive, most practical yet visionary parties the nation's government knows, it also made their Minnesota Democratic party a model of clean and practical politics. It was stimulating citizens' groups across the north central belt of the United States. Loved by intellectuals, untainted by scandal, solidly backed by the money and troops of the great labor unions, loved by the farmers in Minnesota, their state party seemed to possess a formula for unbroken victory.

But in St. Paul and Ramsey County, the fourth district of Minnesota, as 1947 drew on into 1948, it was not all that clear. The elements were many, various, greatly at odds with each other. The American Federation of Labor warred with the CIO. The Postal Workers were waiting to see. Even our close friend Bill Carlson, whose strongest election support came from labor, looked on the party building effort as quixotic. Still, Gene and his strange band of allies kept at it. Going from precinct to precinct, introduced grandiloquently by Koscie Marsh as "the man who broke the Japanese code," he picked up a supporter here, two or more there, identified a potential precinct leader there, and everywhere, of course, were the students. The precinct caucuses held in the spring of 1948 in Ramsey County were a triumph. Orville Freeman, the state chairman, who telephoned us constantly demanding to know what was going on and was probably sure that nothing was because of Gene's typically laconic answers, was pleased and astounded by the results. Ramsey County was clearly the stronghold of the new party.

We gloried in the stories about the caucuses. The mayor Edward Delaney had been refused a delegate seat in his own precinct where the caucus had been attended by such unexpected Democrats as my old friend Agnes Keenan. The new Democrats had been warned that it was a trick of the old leftist leaders struggling to stay in power to meet early, declare a quorum, adjourn to another place, and tear down the precinct sign. Nurses from the hospital had followed such a group to a garage and outvoted them. In our own precinct, twenty or more students had thundered in and, seeing Gene, had inquired, "What do we do now, Prof?" They were not unusual incidents— such tales are told in every reorganization effort—but to us they were fresh and they added fillip to hard-won victory. When the county convention was called, the mass of new delegates hardly knew each other and the old party names meant nothing. They elected the one man they all knew for county chairman. It was Eugene McCarthy. The St. Paul *Pioneer Press*, which usually ignored Democratic party politics as much as possible, was startled into a black headline.

My father who had become county chairman as a culmination of lifelong devotion to the politics of the old Democratic party, was pleased and aggrieved at the same time. "I don't think you people realize what that means," he called to say. "That's a very big job." "Oh, we know it is, Daddy," I replied blithely, with all insensitivity of the younger generation who takes it for granted that it can do in a year what took its parents a lifetime to accomplish.

The real power struggle now began. Precinct caucuses, ward and county chairmanships were all very well, but the nomination of candidates for public office was serious business indeed. The Labor Temple indicated that it was all very nice of the college boys, as they called the young professors, to have done the leg work. They could now go home. The men of the Labor Temple would take over. A second struggle was instantly in progress; it was more deadly and far less lighthearted than the first. But the academic people, the issue-oriented women, the people from the old politics who had tasted victory once again were not willing to let it go at that. It was for the party to pick and endorse the candidate, not for one power group or another. "I'll run myself if I have to," said Gene, and I was serene in the belief that he was speaking theoretically. One of the old ladies of the party had shouted prophetically when he stepped to the podium to accept the chairmanship, "There's our candidate against Devitt!" And Ray Devine and Johnny O'Hara, by now devoted friends and followers, had suggested the same thing. But I thought that Gene was interested in politics only as a laboratory exercise and as a matter of principle. At first—as I did again in 1968— I listened to his explanation of the necessity for party endorsement if the people were to be truly represented and if the democratic process were really to work as I listened to any of his expoundings on philosophy. It did not occur to me that he was seriously contemplating a change in his life. When I realized that it was more than just talk, I tried to reason him out of it. Reluctantly I came to accept what they pressed upon me, the fact that all the gains would be lost if someone like Gene were not nominated.

I talked to Adrian Winkel, Gene's old St. John's colleague who had joined us at St. Thomas. "Even at St. John's, Abigail," he said, "Gene always seemed to want something more direct and more immediate than teaching."

Gene reported on a conversation with Humphrey one night after a meeting in Minneapolis. Humphrey was noncommittal. "It's rough if you're not a veteran," he had said. (He himself had been a target of political advertisements questioning his deferred status while he was mayor.) We went one evening that summer to sit on the porch of the Freeman's duplex in northeast Minneapolis, taking Ellen with us. While I tried to rock Ellen to sleep on my lap, Orville said that he, like Gene, thought that the principle of party endorsement, so hardly won, should be sustained at all costs. "But," he warned, "we can't afford to lose labor support. This is Humphrey's year. It's his chance for statewide office." Gene was quiet, but in the car going home he told me that he was quite sure that labor would come along, once one could show them the possibility of winning. I was terrified. I thought him too idealistic for politics.

At the nominating convention, in the midst of great confusion and struggle, Gene became the endorsed candidate for Congress of the Ramsey County Democratic-Farmer-Labor party. My pride in him was great. But my happiness was marred by the hurt and confusion felt by my best friend, Virginia Carlson, who thought Bill had been treated unfairly. He had wanted the nomination and had assumed that Gene supported him. "Gene never talked to Bill," Virginia insisted, when I tried to explain Gene's feeling about party endorsement.

The Labor Temple endorsed a candidate of its own and a primary struggle began. It was a rocky time for the new party. Hubert Humphrey appeared at a rally in St. Paul and said that we had two fine candidates. It was a realistic move for a man who needed labor support for his own campaign but it was disillusioning to many of the young people. Fortunately, labor was divided. The CIO and the Machinists were as outraged as the new party members were by the monolithic stand of the AFL. The CIO was new and the Machinists were a small group but they had young and scrappy leadership. Gene rented a front room with a separate entrance in a rooming house near St. Thomas and set up a campaign office there. It was before the days of television and campaigns in St. Paul ran on mailing circulars, distribution, and public appearances at as many meetings as possible. It was difficult to be invited to meetings. The idea of joint appearances or debates between candidates was almost unheard of. You invited your candidate and shut out the other if possible. Politics was still considered a slightly shady occupation and most organizations would allow only the incumbents to appear and then only because of the grace of office. The League of Women Voters and the Unitarians, it is true, did run pre-election candidate meetings, but if the incumbent failed to appear, his opponent was not allowed to speak; the incumbent frequently saw to it that his challenger thus had no audience. It was said of Humphrey at the time that he solved this problem by appearing in the back of the hall and shaking hands when his opponent was speaking in the front. Gene followed this example in a quieter way by shaking as many hands as he could. We wrote Gene's literature ourselves and ran it off on the mimeograph machines in the St. Thomas' offices at night, paying only for the materials. Our chief advantage, and one which Gene's opponent underestimated, was the prestige and influence of the colleges with which our names were associated. Not only did Gene seem to have solid support from the faculty at St. Catherine's and St. Thomas but from Macalester College and Hamline, the Methodist university, as well. I think we invented the coffee party that year, except that we called them house parties and held them at night in order to reach the men as well as the women.

On primary night we convened in Ray Devine's small row house and Johnny O'Hara, the bartender, and Tony Blaha were posted in City Hall to watch the votes come in. At first it was an even match. Gene and his union opponent were neck to neck. Gene and Ray ticked off the wards and precincts, commenting approvingly on the ones that went the way they had expected. Then with a sudden and drastic drop, Gene was behind by more than a thousand votes. "They say you've lost, Gene," reported Tony glumly. Gene sat pale, thinking. I, like most of those in the room, thought that it was indeed over and I felt a certain sense of relief. "It's all right, Gene," I said stretching out my hand, "we can go back to working on our rural community." He took my hand but as he did so, turned to Ray and said "That can't be right. Call Tony and ask to have him check it. I know those precincts." Then he added to me, "Let's pray."

The feeling in that room was so intense that some of the women, hearing him say that, got down on their knees and we all followed suit. As we prayed, the phone rang. There had been a mistake. Gene was five hundred votes ahead and he had won the primary election. "I can't believe it," said Ray Devine afterwards. "It was his first election and he knew where every vote was." The primary was the real victory. After that labor closed ranks as Gene had predicted it would, and the ensuing campaign against the Republican incumbent was almost predictable. But the twenty-thousand-vote plurality was the result of leadership and planning.

It seemed clear that Gene had a natural flair for the political possibilities of any situation.

On a visit to St. John's after the election, we went through the ceremony which made us Benedictine oblates, lay members of the Benedictine community. Gene took as his oblate patron and Benedictine name Thomas More. And I, Gertrude, for St. Gertrude, great contemplative of the Benedictines, the closest I could find among them to my admired Teresa of Avila.

"It must be the first time in history that a congressman of the United States has been a Benedictine," said our friend Emerson Hynes with satisfaction.

We all had a happy sense of embarking on a new day in which "all things would work together for them that loved Christ."

We left St. Paul in December and drove across country on our way to Washington with Ellen, then fourteen months old, to spend Christmas with Mildred, Gene's sister, and her husband, Henry, in Larchmont, New York. Of that trip I can recall only the frequent stops we made in order to walk up and down with Ellen to tire her out. The change in her life seemed to have stimulated her to an almost frenetic and constant activity. I remember our threading through the Christmas crowds in dingy towns in Ohio, Pennsylvania, and northern New York, following the frantic small figure who darted here and there, pointing and crying, "Look, Daddy, look."

On New Year's Day, in our innocence, we set out from Larchmont for Washington to find our new house, which Mildred, on a flying trip to Washington, had rented for us. Gene was to take the oath of office the next day. There was no New Jersey Turnpike then, no Chesapeake Bay Bridge. The only way to Washington was via the narrow black-top roads through New Jersey and Delaware and across Chesapeake Bay on the ferry. For hours before we reached the ferry, we were caught in bumper-to-bumper traffic. We ran out of snacks for Ellen, and all the roadside restaurants were closed. Occasionally, as the afternoon darkened, we caught sight of a small grocery or neighborhood store, lit up and open, but we dared not stop long enough to buy something for fear of losing our place in the ferry line. When we finally crossed Chesapeake Bay, we discovered that it had grown late and dark and we were still miles from Washington.

We stopped to eat on the outskirts of Baltimore and pressed on across the old Baltimore-Washington road with its huddles of cinderblock buildings, store-fronted frame houses, one sordid and dingy motel after the other. In desperation we called the owners of our rented house to see if we could stay there that night, but they had not yet moved out. We finally found a motel in which we could bear to stay with Ellen and made our way on into Silver Spring in the morning.

At 11 o'clock we were still searching for the house. Gene had to be at the Capitol by 12 noon. He consulted a policeman, hailed a cab, thrust the map into my hands, and left. With the pressure of haste lifted, I soon found Woodland Drive in suburban Silver Spring and our house. A neighbor brought the key and lent me milk and bread so that I could feed Ellen. I piled pillows on the floor of a closet and set a chair across the door so that Ellen could take a nap in safety. Then I went to take stock of my new home. I did not know that the big problem of my life for the next ten years would be "where *is* home?"

The title of Ellen Proxmire's book *One Foot in Washington* is an apt description of congressional life in post-World War II Washington. But there had been a time earlier in the century when official life in Washington coincided with the congressional session. Congress met for a few months of the year; the congressmen and the wives who accompanied them to Washington stayed for the entire period. It was a time of solemnly paced lawmaking during the day and intensive, if rigidly patterned, social life in the evening. The social life was like an intricate choreography, with prescribed rounds of formal calls, of receptions, of entertaining and being entertained according to the prescriptions of protocol and seniority, and with a carefully balanced reciprocity among the three branches of government.

So important was Congress considered to be to the life of Washington in those years that the Congressional Club was chartered by Congress in 1908 for the express purpose of making Washington more attractive to congressional wives many of whom, at that time, considered it a stuffy and dull provincial capital. The club was housed in a mansion just off then fashionable Sixteenth Street, and for years its functions were as obligatory as those of the White House. Many of us who live in Washington today recall with amazement the nationally headlined feud over precedence between Dolly Gann, official hostess for Vice President Curtis, and Alice Roosevelt Longworth, wife of the Speaker of the House.

Washington had changed in many ways since Speaker Longworth's day. And Congress had changed with it, not only in its position with regard to the other branches of government, but also in its own composition. During the Roosevelt years and World War II, Washington became truly a national and world capital. The executive branch had swollen beyond recognition as had the military.

Theoretically each newly convened Congress is a new legislative body. The Eighty-first Congress, the one elected in 1948 with Gene, was overwhelmingly Democratic, elected in response to Truman's assault on the preceding Congress as a "do-nothing Congress." It was a far younger Congress than any elected before. It was a Congress full of veterans, many of whom were issue-conscious members of the American Veterans Committee. It was a Congress responsible to new kinds of constituencies—to labor constituencies which had reached their full power in the postwar years and to younger, more alert and demanding constituencies in general.

By the time we arrived in Washington in 1949, it was customary to organize the wives of each new Congress into a club called by the name of the Congress. Ours, therefore, was The 81st Club. It included the wives of the new representatives and also the wives of senators who might have served in the House but were new in the sense that they were new to the Senate.

There were over one hundred twenty-five members of The 81st Club in that first meeting twenty-three years ago. Many of those in the Eighty-first Congress were men who came to dominate and shape the history of our country in significant ways during these past twenty-three years. Lyndon Johnson, newly elected senator, and his close friend from Texas Representative Homer Thornberry were members of the Eighty-first Congress. Hubert Humphrey was there. So were Paul Douglas of Illinois, Gerald Ford of Michigan, Lloyd Bentsen of Texas who soon left the House but returned to Congress as a senator in 1970. Karl Mundt of South Dakota and Harold Velde of Illinois were to play continuing and important roles in the conservative wing of the Congress. Representative Richard Simpson of Pennsylvania and Senator Andrew Schoeppel of Kansas were to lead the Republican campaign forces for a decade or more. Daniel Flood of Pennsylvania became an important voice in the House Foreign Relations Committee. Richard Bolling of Missouri cut a swathe as a supposed intimate of Speaker Sam Rayburn and an aspirant for future leadership. Representative Sidney Yates of Illinois was synonymous with the liberal wing of the Democratic party. H. R. Gross of Iowa became the gadfly of the House on spending and the budget.

Over the years, members of the Eighty-first left Congress and built reputations in other offices. One of the most interesting was Abe Ribicoff, who became an outstanding governor of Connecticut, later a member of the Kennedy cabinet—the first governor to come out for Jack Kennedy for President—and then returned to the Senate. Foster Furcolo of Massachusetts also became governor of his state, although his career was not as happy. John Shelley of California became mayor of San Francisco. And no one would have thought, in that January of 1949 when they were all so pleased with each other and with their victories, that the interrelationship of Hubert Humphrey, Eugene McCarthy, and Lyndon Johnson would develop into the crescendo of conflict which was the campaign of 1968.

Among the wives of the Eighty-first Congress I was to find some of my closest friends. It is hard to know on what such friendships are founded. Like other friendships they are based on common experience, association, often on the fact that husbands find each other congenial. But friendships between congressional wives rest most solidly, I feel, on the fact that they share a unique experience which they cannot communicate to people who have not also shared it. For that reason the friendships often reach across party lines, although because loyalty to one's husband and his career comes first, these bipartisan friendships are always a bit wary and conditional.

Even under the circumstances of such a different time and a different kind of Congress, some of the old controversies continued to rage on the society pages in 1949. One such issue was whether or not to pay formal calls. The prewar pattern had been quite set. The ladies of the Supreme Court received and served tea from four to six on Mondays, congressional wives on Tuesdays, cabinet wives on Wednesdays, Ladies of the Senate on Thursdays, the diplomatic corps on Fridays. The wives of the new congressmen were polled as to whether they intended to revive the old formal custom which had disappeared with the war. Muriel Humphrey stated flatly that she did not intend to make calls—that where she was brought up, newcomers were called upon and did not make the calls themselves. I felt constrained to say that I would do whatever my Senate colleague thought proper.

There ensued clucking reports of new Senate wives who did not call or who were not aware of their proper calling days and were caught scrubbing the porch or washing the windows by older wives who arrived carrying card cases. Exaggerations surely, but they underlined the passing of a Washington in which all official ladies lived within a small geographical circle northwest of the capital.

We of the Eighty-first Congress were scattered far and wide throughout the Washington area, in whatever housing we could find and afford; there were very few residents of fashionable Georgetown and Kalorama among us. Even Cleveland Park, just beginning to change from old residential Washington to what Russell Baker later called "the chintz and brains section," attracted very few. Washington, like the rest of the nation, was still in the grip of the postwar housing shortage. Because our means were limited and many of us were parents of young families, we gravitated to the new suburbs of Washington or found apartments in the garden complexes which had sprung up during the war.

The Congress is quite literally a cross section of the nation, and each new congressman comes to Washington carrying with him the experience, the habits, and the expectations of his own part of the country. It depends a great deal on how strong his roots are and in what they are placed, whether Washington changes him or whether he adapts to Washington in significant ways. Our new Minnesota contingent of Democrats was typical. Roy Wier, the aging labor man who had been elected in a Minneapolis district settled into a hotel efficiency apartment on Capitol Hill. The Humphreys, with a six-year Senate term to look forward to, dared to sell their house in Minneapolis and use the money for a down payment on a comparatively large house in a new development just off East-West Highway on the fringe of Chevy Chase. Fred Marshall, the sturdy farmer and farm organization representative who had been elected in central Minnesota, cannily bought a pleasant house in nearby Virginia; it was completely furnished, and he sold the furniture he did not want for as much as all of it had cost—a fact which impressed the rest of us with the advantage of coming to Congress with money. Buying in Washington was still something of a political taboo—it was thought to be certain political death if constituents thought you were settling in. (Lady Bird Johnson once told us that she had moved in and out of ten apartments in five years, before they had dared to risk the luxury of owning a home.)

In 1949 it never occurred to Gene and me that we could do anything but rent, anchored as we still were by our commitment to our projected farm community. We wrote to John Foley, later a Maryland congressman, who was then practicing law in Washington, asking him to see what he could find for us to live in. He replied with details about a sad collection of houses in town which he had been able to see. Some, usually rented to diplomats, were dirty and in bad states of disrepair except for the rooms used as reception rooms; others were open to children only under certain conditions; all the houses rented with long leases full of restrictive clauses about subletting, no "non-Caucasians," no Jews, no Orientals, etc. We were appalled. And even for this selection, the rents quoted seemed far beyond our means. Finally, Gene's sister Mildred made a flying trip to Washington and called us to describe some of the winter rentals available. We took the one she recommended—a three-bedroom, two-story brick Colonial house in Silver Spring, Maryland. A retired government worker financed his winter vacation in Florida by renting it for three months each year.

We rented that house from the Dixon Realty Company, now world famous because it is owned and managed by Mrs. Jeane Dixon, the famous clairvoyant. Superficially, it seemed to be a comfortable and well-furnished house, but actually it was a house which needed an owner's ever-present and loving care. The dining-room table was strategically placed over a large hole in the purple and blue "oriental" rug and, thus, was situated off center in the dining room, making it impossible to seat more than four people. Occasional tables in the living room had wobbly legs and were propped up against the wall. We solved the dining room problem by removing and folding the rug away and polishing the floor. We removed the wobbly tables and rearranged the living-room furniture into a congenial grouping around the fireplace. The agent who dealt with us was a retired army colonel and when our lease was up three months later, he reported our scandalous changes to Mrs. Dixon who showed, I thought, a singular lack of second sight when she called me herself to protest.

Because of the new long sessions, congressmen and congressional families had one foot in Washington and one foot back home, not only in the sense that they had to maintain physical homes in two places but also because they were torn between the two places, spiritually and psychologically. The young congressional people of our generation found this need to maintain a presence in both places a great hardship. We were parents of young families for the most part who had not yet established and purchased permanent homes. Traveling back and forth with the children was hard on them and hard on us. Because of the children we could not do without help, but the help we could afford was inadequate and hard to find. "I don't need all this allowance for office staff," Gene used to say only half humorously. "I could use it better for help at home."

In 1971 a skeptical Washington *Post* writer set about interviewing the wives of House members. Admitting that she hoped very much that they weren't going to plead poverty on $42,500 a year, she found that they were not, but that "they did make a strong case that $42,500 doesn't mean a life of servants, catered parties, leisurely games of tennis, and White House dinners." I read the story with a sense of pained and amused recognition. "It isn't just the routine madness of 'Housewife USA'—car pools, PTA meetings, chauffeuring kids to music lessons, waxing kitchen floors, cooking heaven only knows how many meals a year—that congressional wives experience. Because of their husband's jobs they have considerably more personal expenses, more duties and demands on their own time, and handle an increased load of family rearing and household tasks than most wives. They bewailed the expense of traveling home with the family and the major expense of maintaining two homes. One said, 'No matter what you do, you have to pay for the other. Even if you rent your home back there, you have to stay in a hotel when you go back. There are still two property taxes, two sets of furniture.'"

The problems now are just as they were then twenty-three years ago when the $12,500 dollar a year salary made life for a congressional wife even more difficult.

On our anniversary in 1956, I gave Gene a scroll with the following inscription:

11 Years—1945–1956

It was a diagrammatic representation of our peregrinations and of the personal adjustments that had been necessary for us to make in our many homes:

Addresses	Children	Campaigns	Places
1946	Christopher		Quebec &
St. Anne's Farm			Montreal
5345 France		St. Thomas	
Oxboro Heath			
1947	Ellen		
75 North Cleveland			
986 Portland		**1948**	
75 North Cleveland		Campaign	
1949	Mary Abigail		
Woodland Drive,			
Silver Spring			
14 Woodmoor Drive			
White Bear Beach			
1948 Selby			
Porter Street, D.C.			
Battery Lane,			
Bethesda			
1946 Selby		**1950**	
1951	Michael	Campaign	
3517 17th St. N.E.			
Rehoboth and			
107 Hesketh,			
Chevy Chase			
1946 Selby			
107 Hesketh			
1946 Selby		**1952**	
Custer Road		Campaign	Florida
3507 Raymond St.			
2014 Summit			
2103 Iglehart	Margaret Alice	**1954**	
		Campaign	
1955			Europe
3507 Raymond St.			
2103 Iglehart			
3310 Ohio Drive			
TOTAL—27 Moves			

The following have lived with us:

Margaret	Berti
Martha	Mabel
Anne Bronander	Hattie
Therese McCanna	Cousin Esther
Ida	Betty
Eileen	Aunt Ellen
Peg Hannigan	

In the past twenty-three years most constituents have acquired a relative sophistication about the need for their representatives to take up residence in Washington, but when we began our congressional life, most constituencies wanted their congressman to be very much a part of his home district, a man clearly of themselves. But they also wanted him to be in Washington during every minute Congress was in session, earning his salary by representing them.

It did not occur to us that forming friendships in Washington would be altered in any way by Gene's congressional status. In general, our friendships based on previous associations grew out of two groups: the network of Catholic liberals with whom we shared mutual friends and acquaintances and the less diversified group of "new" Democrats typified by the ADA of that time and the AVC. These associations often overlapped.

We looked on the people who had come to Washington with us as part of our extended family. Gene's administrative assistant, Adrian Winkel, had taught with Gene at St. Thomas and St. John's, and he and his wife, Isabel, had shared our experience of living in the huts. His secretary and legislative aide was Loraine O'Donnell, his cousin. There were inevitable charges of nepotism, but Loraine's law degree and loyalty made her invaluable during that time of learning, and her independent family income allowed her to work for far less than she could have commanded elsewhere. We shared family celebrations with them.

Most of our friendships, though, came from a coming together of like-minded people—most of us out of the Midwest—who had developed out of the new Catholicism an attitude toward service and government.

Mary McGrory, then new in Washington as a book reviewer for the *Star*, found us when she was looking for material on congressmen who could be called writers. I secretly think Mary had initiated the assignment for herself as an excuse to wander the Hill, to which she was irresistibly attracted by her Boston-bred fascination with the political scene. She met Gene, who told her that he didn't write but that I did. She came to see us and a long, close friendship ensued. For twenty years she was in our home and we in hers. She was always present at baptisms, first communions, confirmations, and birthday parties and we were fixtures at her gaily improvised buffet suppers where the talk and the singing were of a quality of entertainment found nowhere else in Washington.

Those were the halcyon days of our friendships, when the children were little and we were all younger, days of spontaneous get-togethers and simpler associations, before any of us had tasted power or close association with it. Mary went to the beach with us, shared picnics in the park with us, and occasionally, out of compassion, baby-sat for us or took the children to the zoo.

When we invited the Hubert Humphreys to one of our first Washington parties, Hubert noted our guests' government and newspaper connections and said to Gene approvingly, "You've worked up a nice little connection—there's a line here into almost anything you'll need for help or information." It was a new thought to Gene; for us, friendships just happened in those days.

At that time we wanted all our friends to like each other and saw no reason why they should not. In the first session of the Eighty-first Congress Senator Humphrey was the new and brash member from the Midwest who, with his brilliant civil rights speech at the 1948 convention, had been spokesman for those forces which split the party (to its ultimate good) into Democrats and Dixiecrats. Hubert was finding the going in the gentleman's club of the Senate very rough. His first speech had been marked by a serious rebuff. By prearranged signal, all the other senators had left the floor. The same press which had hailed his coming was beginning to harass and ridicule him. We were certain that if the reporters knew him, they would like him. So we asked Mary and Edwin Lahey, then chief of the Knight bureau, and several other newspaper people we knew to come to our house to meet him and we urged them to bring friends.

Hubert was at his best that evening—warm, friendly, personal, affirmative about others, full of attention-gripping inside stories of past and current political battles.

"But how do you keep your organization going?" asked Ed Lahey seriously at one point. "I mean, who gives out the Christmas baskets in Minnesota?" Edwin Lahey was a Nieman fellow and wrote with great intellectual authority, but he persisted in speaking in a Runyonesque shorthand.

"The Salvation Army," said Hubert laughing. But we Minnesotans were mildly shocked by the implications of the question. For the first time it was clear to us that we had come from a political context in Minnesota almost impossible for reporters from the big machine cities to comprehend. In our academic view, such things were certainly not the business of a political party.

That particular mixing of friends worked out happily, but others were not so successful. It took me years to learn what Muriel Humphrey once told me succinctly, "Our friendship is like two hexagons fitting together. We are very close on one side." She probably spoke from hard experience as the wife of a mayor.

Among our new liberal friends we counted liberal lawyers Joe Rauh and Jim Lanigan, and writers Jim Loeb and Gilbert Harrison, new then to the *New Republic,* and a wide group of young congressional and committee aides, labor union intellectuals, and people from independent committees formed for one liberal purpose or another. There was a certain reserve to these friendships. No one from the East seemed to quite believe that one could be both a Catholic and liberal, and there were those who tended to look on us as infiltrators of a sort. It was a truism at the time often quoted humorously but quite accurate, "Anti-Catholicism is the anti-Semitism of the liberals."

An ex-Catholic was one thing; a practicing one, another. I still remember the hush at one dinner party when all the guests had been vociferously discussing a censorship threat of some kind. My voice fell into the sudden dinner table silence, "Why, even our bishops have taken a stand against that kind of thing." "Your bishops?" queried the host. "What do you mean?" "Why the Catholic bishops, of course," I answered. He looked at me in simple astonishment. "You mean you and Gene actually consider yourselves Catholics?" he asked as if he found that incredible. "We do," I said shortly. It was an uncomfortable moment. Years later the same man worked his way through a crowded garden party to grasp my hand and ask with true solicitude, "Abigail, how is *our* pope?" Pope John, who lay dying then, had wrought the change . . . and perhaps we had helped.

It was a new experience for us to find ourselves stereotyped because of our religion. Prejudice in our part of the Midwest took the form of a squabbling among equals—in its simplest form a "my father is stronger or better or smarter than your father" kind of rivalry. Underlying it—I am sure, because we all started out in the pioneer territories as economic equals—was a sort of blind acceptance of pluralism. We knew from our intermingling that no group had a monopoly on rascals or saints. And we did not take our festivals very seriously. St. Patrick's Day was a day for wearing a bit of green in good fun. One of the favorite stories of my childhood was told by my aunt about how the Orangemen borrowed the McLachlan's white horses—the best in town, even if they did have a Catholic owner—for the Orangemen's parade. Other ethnic groups had to be encouraged to perpetuate or recall customs and celebrations out of their past by such community-sponsored activities as the annual St. Paul Festival of Nations. For in our Minnesota sense of things, it was all rather interesting but it belonged to other lands, other places.

It was with some consternation that Gene realized that ethnic ties could lead to such congressional behavior as tacking riders onto bills for aid to the United Kingdom—demanding that England give "the six" back to Ireland as a condition—and that the congressman who did these things meant them as serious legislative maneuvers. It was the sort of thing Gene himself might toss around as an interesting idea, based on some concept of abstract justice, but not one he would have felt called upon to support, either because of his name or the substantial minority of Irish voters in his constituency. We were both amused that the British ambassador, Sir Oliver Franks, thought it an act of political courage when Gene introduced him at a Foreign Policy Association meeting in St. Paul while members of the Ancient Order of Hibernians picketed outside. We were regular guests at the embassy after that. But the passionate seriousness of the ethnic groups in Congress was instructive to us, revealing the crippling effect that economic and social slavery had on immigrant groups in big cities and industrial towns.

All this is not to say that we were innocents unaware that we were the objects of possible exploitation in those early years. In the very first months we were trapped into a wasted evening by an official of the Minnesota State Society—the state societies of Washington are stories in themselves—who insisted that he and his wife escort us to the society's annual ball. We spent an interminable cocktail hour in their apartment, on exhibit for unexplained people—perhaps good social contacts, perhaps business acquaintances—our hosts sought to impress. We arrived at the party too late for the receiving line and were met with ill-disguised dislike on the part of the committee, whose members interpreted our delay as congressional arrogance.

Sometimes, like other new congressional people fresh from victories which seemed so important, we overestimated our importance. Jim Lanigan, who had served as an observer in the 1948 Minnesota campaign, called to invite us to dinner and Gene was reluctant to go, but I told him that I thought it was only kind to do so because Jim had been helpful and now probably wanted to produce the congressmen he had helped. His small apartment was crowded with people serving themselves from the casserole and salad buffet then considered *de rigueur*. (Entertaining then—at least in Democratic circles —still bore the informal imprint of Mrs. Roosevelt, who had served hot dogs and potato salad to the King of England. Stewart Alsop wrote an article for *The Saturday Evening Post* cataloguing and lamenting the ubiquitous and repetitious casseroles of Georgetown.) Among the other guests we recognized only Representative and Mrs. Richard Bolling of Missouri who immediately assumed stature when

Barbara Bolling said that she kept Mrs. Truman's private number in the bottom of her powder box. I sat at a table with a red-haired older woman who kept talking about "the Boss" and a fair-haired and politely inquiring young couple whose name I did not catch. They asked about our campaign and I expatiated on it, pausing at one point to grieve over Henry Wallace's fall from grace. "I felt so bad about it," I said. "We used to admire him so, didn't you?" "Well, yes," said the young man. "He was my editor, you know." The young man was Michael Straight, publisher of the *New Republic*. And the red-haired woman turned out to be Grace Tully, FDR's secretary and confidential aide.

Gradually things fell into place. We began to manage the complexities of the congressional social life. House members were more visible then on the Washington scene, and we began to find it an interesting life.

Our first experience of a royal visit was when Queen Juliana of the Netherlands came to present a Dutch carillon to the American people as a gift of thanks for our help during World War II. She addressed the combined House and Senate and I remember being very proud of her as a woman for the strength of her speech. The dignity of the occasion was mixed with the folksy errors which seemed to be the hallmark of Congress and which make it perhaps the most representative and American of the branches of government. The Queen had been announced by the inimitable "Fishbait" Miller, doorkeeper of the House, with a stentorian, "Ladies and gentlemen, the Queen of the Netherlands." He then trotted before her to guide her to the podium and when she had trouble lifting her veil to read her speech, he bent forward gallantly, saying, "Let me get it for you, Queenie."

At the huge reception at the Army-Navy Club in Virginia for the Queen later that afternoon, a large printed sign was displayed saying, "Americans do not curtsey to royalty." There was no sign saying that royalty was not accustomed to being spoken to without having spoken first. So many of us going through the line congratulated her on the speech of the morning. I think I must have been one of the first because of her startled look. She thanked me gracefully and

I think because she had been a resident of Washington as a refugee during the war years, she was not surprised by this American effusiveness.

We found some of our closest congressional friends among the Southerners and the Texans. I spent a good deal of time with Virginia Sims of South Carolina and Mary Alice Herlong of Florida. They lived near us, and in those days of comparative penury we were all one-car families and the men used to ride back and forth to the Capitol together. Hugo Sims, a hero of the 101st Airborne in World War II, was the youngest man ever elected to Congress. Virginia, his wife, was pretty and young and uncomplaining in her acceptance of her role as mistress of the household and mother of their small children in a rather shabby little house on a court in Silver Spring. They had brought with them their maid from South Carolina. Hugo was uncompromisingly liberal in his attitudes and Virginia accepted them without question. Still, she combined the unquestioning maternalism of the Southerner toward the black with efforts to conform to the interracialism which was still to her largely theoretical. At that period in our social development, interracialism consisted largely in an effort to treat people fairly in economic matters. What it meant in Virginia's life was an uncomplaining tending of Carrie's frequent illnesses and hours of "carrying" Carrie to the hospital, to the doctor and the dentist, a constant search for companionship for her, combined with pride in the fact that they paid Carrie the prevailing wage and "Hugo says that if we have steak in the dining room, Carrie has steak in the kitchen." If this seems primitive in today's context of race relations, it is important to realize how far advanced it was in comparison with the mindless and violent adherence to the status quo manifested years later by other Southern women in the tragic confrontations in Louisiana, Alabama, and Mississippi, and in Orangeburg, the Sims' home city. It was initially from Virginia that I learned my first reluctant admiration for southern women. She had spent most of her life in a secure and privileged position in a small and stratified southern town. Yet she struggled valiantly with the often inimical environment of the Washington suburbs and the challenges of the congressional life, as well as with the new concepts imposed upon her by her husband's political stance. Hugo, on his side, was deferential to the southern leadership of the Congress. It always intrigued Gene and me to see the almost instant acceptance given southern newcomers by reason of their accent and bearing. They addressed Representative Rankin of Mississippi, then almost a czar in the House because of his chairmanship of the committee which dealt with veterans affairs, and Speaker Rayburn as "Mr. John" and "Mr. Sam." But Hugo did not hesitate to vote against them and to side with his fellow members of the AVC, the liberal veterans who had come back from the war with a passion for a different kind of justice.

One time when I told Virginia that I had to hurry home to prepare dinner because we were having friends in to meet my fellow alumna Ikalina Moore and her writer-husband—Negroes—Virginia was at once horrified and sympathetic. "Oh, Abbie," she said in the accent which delighted me because it somehow gave two a's to my name, "do you have to?" She raised the question of what our part-time helper, Martha, might think. Motivated by her question I explained to Martha that our honored guests for the evening were Negroes and did that make any difference to her. "No, ma'am," she said emphatically. "I'm not one of them." I never knew who "them" were or what "they" were like but I was glad that Martha took that stand. That evening our other guests waited for an hour and a half while the dinner grew cold and I feared that some strange misunderstanding had occurred between me and Ikalina. When she and her husband finally appeared, they explained that they had driven around until it got dark so that they would not embarrass us by coming to the front door when our neighbors could see them. That was still the situation in Washington in 1948; Virginia's assessment of our situation was closer than mine.

Eloise and Homer Thornberry were also among our close friends and it was largely through Homer that Gene was drawn into a loose friendship with most of the Texas group. The Texans enjoyed special status in the House because of their naturally close relationship with the Speaker. They constituted a large delegation and a table in the House restaurant was informally reserved for them. Gene used to be asked to sit at this table frequently and became, in a way, a sort of honorary Texan. He used to attribute his right to sit there to his Great-uncle Charles McCarthy who had scandalized his Minnesota family during the Civil War by deciding to go South and fight with the Confederacy—not because he approved of slavery but because he believed in the sovereignty of the states. After the war—perhaps because he chose not to or perhaps because he was afraid to return to Minnesota—he went west to California by way of Texas. Carty-Ma, Gene's grandmother, was always proud of Charles (the family insisted that she called him "Charliss" in her Irish brogue) because of his enterprise and independence of mind and it was one of the high marks of her life when she went to visit him in California. The children must have heard a great deal about him in their early years.

Our first meeting with President Harry Truman was at the Congressional Club presidential reception, an occasion which was then still a matter of obligation for the President. Secretary of the Navy Forrestal was among the cabinet members there. I remember his earnest and anxious concentration when Gene talked to him about the intelligence community and the importance of a central agency. Forrestal's tragic plunge to death from the tower of the naval hospital in Bethesda, Maryland, some time later demonstrated an important fact to us: men of power are seldom protected from their own infirmities by the men subordinate to them—not even in the sad circumstances of mental exhaustion.

We wives were feted at teas, not only at Blair House where the Trumans were living while the White House was being renovated—it was President Truman with his great sense of history who first started bringing that lovely old house back to life—but at various embassies as well. The embassies provided our experience of living in the grand manner, and I was often glad for my mother and aunts' instruction, which I had tended to scorn when young, and for St. Catherine's finishing school emphasis in my time there on formal dinners of many courses and formal teas. How easily I might have been at sea between the fish forks and coffee spoons! In the climate of the times, people in Washington had not regained the pragmatic view of diplomacy which exists today, and ideologues of either liberalism or the right wing tended to avoid certain embassies. We were among those who avoided the Spanish at the time, but when Ellen was in her first year at Stone Ridge, the daughter of the ambassador, the Count of Motrico, was her classmate and she went as a matter of course to Cristina's birthday party. I tried to prepare her for the new experience of a children's party in the elegance of an embassy which was among the most formal and alive with footmen. "Cristina's mother is something like a princess," I said clutching at her fairy tale books for a frame of reference, "so don't forget your curtsey." "I was the politest one there," Ellen reported that night, "I curtsied to all the butlers." It seemed that the American children had been highly diverted when they discovered that if they asked for a drink of water, a white-gloved attendant would bring it on a silver tray, and they had kept up a constant demand all through the party. As she took part in this delightful new fun, Ellen's bobbing had, I think, been a sop to her conscience.

Our first real friendships with diplomats tended to be with those from the Scandinavian countries, from Britain, and, strangely enough, from Yugoslavia. Our acquaintanceship with the latter in a time when the Iron Curtain countries were virtually in social quarantine was because of their relationship with John Blatnik, our senior Democratic congressman from Minnesota. John's parents were Serbian immigrants who came to Chisholm, Minnesota, from Yugoslavia. He was fond of telling that he was born on the first floor of a house where his mother cooked and kept house for twenty-four Serbian roomers who worked in the mines with his father. John and his sisters had grown up and gone to college, but were bilingual and had never lost touch with their web of connections in Yugoslavia. During the war, John as a member of the OSS had been parachuted into Yugoslavia to get in touch with the Partisans and maintain liaison with them. The new regime in Yugoslavia was now made up of people who with whom he had shared that dangerous life in the mountains. We spent evenings listening with fascination as they reminisced, joining as best we could in the songs they sang—songs they had sung around the campfires. The wife of the ambassador had been a girl Partisan in the mountains at sixteen. Anti-Communist feeling was running so high that when the ambassador was invited to the annual Yugoslav festival in northern Minnesota, no state or local official could be found to tender him an official welcome at the Twin Cities airport. So Gene had one of his assistants, who was in St. Paul, meet the ambassador and his wife and drive them up to the Iron Range country. It was a courtesy they never forgot.

The congressional social interplay with the White House was very cut and dried and not particularly gay or glamorous. But, of course, we valued it highly. At the annual congressional wives reception we went through the receiving line and then stood eying each other in the state dining room, the more bold among us stashing away matchfolders labeled "The White House." This was before Mrs. John F. Kennedy had reinstituted the more correct "The President's House." At one of these teas during our husbands' second terms, Eloise Thornberry and I, looking at the newer wives and remembering our own first-time uncertainties, decided to do something about it.

"You go one way," Eloise said, "and introduce every two you pass and I'll go the other." "I'm Abigail McCarthy," I said tentatively to a woman standing near me and found that she was Mrs. Jones, wife of a new administration appointee. I introduced her to the congressional wife next to her and went on my way, exhilarated by the little eddy of activity and the murmur of conversation in my wake. Eloise and I passed each other midway, smiling happily at each other, and came full circle smug in our sense of doing good. "I'm Abigail McCarthy," I said cheerily to one last tea-drinker, standing alone. "I'm still Mrs. Jones," she answered.

It did not take much Washington experience to learn the utility of the social life. The executive, legislative, judicial, military, diplomatic, and press organizations were such busy worlds in themselves that social engagements provided bridges, and a tenuous but not always permanent glue of community. In the little talks I used to give at home in our district entitled "Life in Washington" I would try very hard and very seriously to explain this fact. And I found several quotations very useful, not only for my hearers but for myself . . .

guidelines of a sort. One from Mary Van Rensselaer Thayer was an especially apt description of Washington in the 1950s: it was the only world capital "in which brains and achievement counted for as much as birth and money" and where you might find a Dior original and a copy from "Kann's basement" equally acceptable. Another I thought telling was from a Swiss embassy minister who had told me that he looked over his social calendar each day and tried to anticipate who would be at which reception. "Then I find him as soon as I can. Often five minutes with that person over a highball will save hours of office time and do much more good for my country." Still another was the harried complaint of a South American diplomat: "Our social secretary is left over from the 1920s. I cannot convince her or my government that the society writers are important to our diplomatic success here. Of course, this is not true in other capitals, but it is true in Washington."

The little speeches I began making then to club and school groups about life in Washington were, in a way, educational devices. I used them as I had an illustrative short story or essay with which I caught the attention of my college classes to lure them into deeper discussion. When I talked of Washington life, of its rituals and its levels, and the social relationships of the various branches of government, I was really saying, "What your congressman is doing is important and merits your serious attention. The legislative process is part of our hallowed constitutional democracy; it is tested and shored up by tradition. All these important people in these incidents I regale you with are seriously concerned with your Congress. Shouldn't you be, too?"

For in the 1950s politics was held in very low esteem. In part this was because of the historical American attitude decried by Gene in his first book, *Frontiers in American Democracy*:

> The suspicious, reluctant attitude which Americans have toward politics is not merely superficial. It goes much deeper, for instance, than the sense of dismay the public manifests at the revelation of unbecoming conduct on the part of certain public officials. The American attitude toward politics shows more clearly than anything else the American belief in the innocence of Americans—a belief which has

been a moving force in the American mind since the time of the colonial settlements . . .

American suspicion of government is intensified and deepened at the sight of political activity. Politics is somehow considered the enemy of innocence and of simplicity . . .

Politics was also suspect, it seemed to me, because of the disdain in which public service and the men who chose it were held by the men of business who controlled power and public opinion in the North and West. What harm had been done to the presidency by the party who contemptuously gave the office to men like Warren G. Harding and Calvin Coolidge, what harm by the same men who let the city machines develop through callousness and neglect! The rehabilitation of politics as a career for gentlemen had begun with Franklin Delano Roosevelt, but conventional wisdom still held that politics was hardly a fit occupation for a good and intelligent man. "I don't like to see him with those crooks, Abbie," said Gene's father to me, looking at a picture of Gene walking with Senator Humphrey and the President of the United States. And many a schoolboy held the idea expressed by sixteen-year-old Robert Dahl at the 1956 convention of the Minnesota Association of Student Councils, "There is a lot of corruptness in government now and I wouldn't care to go into politics."

The Minneapolis *Tribune* had taken Bob to task, but half-heartedly and with infuriating condescension: "Yes, there's a lot of corruptness (sic) in government these days, but don't get discouraged. . . . We need to cleanse politics of its corruption, Bob. We need to guarantee adequate pay to those who assume high government responsibilities. We need to lift political campaigning out of the gutter. . . ."

I think we would all have welcomed a serious effort to give adequate compensation to holders of public office, but most of us wives would have agreed with more feeling to the statement of the Democratic mayor of St. Paul: "They don't know how easily most of us would sell out for just a little courtesy and respectful treatment." Our friends from the South where government was an honored occupation could never understand our need to defend the choice of a political life. They did not have to accept, as did some of us northern wives, a qualified social ostracism as the price of our husband's choice of life. It was in the 1950s that David Riesman wrote:

> . . . Politics seems to me to be one of those callings where celibacy can be defended on practical grounds. For while the wives of some kinds of doctors and executives must put up with irregular hours and tense lives, and while the wives of college presidents must sit through many boring rituals, all these women have at least the modest compensations bought by their spouses' high income and success. Politicians, however, along with ministers and school offi- cials, can but seldom give their wives an anxiety-free middle-class existence . . .

The normal anxiety which underlay each campaign was augmented by the secret and nagging fear about which Stimson Bullitt wrote in *To Be a Politician*, the book to which Riesman's words were an introduction. It was not so much the loss of livelihood which I used to fear in those successive campaigns, but rather the possible psychological devastation for Gene of a loss of vocation. Gene had come to politics through such labyrinthine wanderings. The defeated politician had no sure berth to return to, Bullitt pointed out. If he had been a teacher, he would find the return to the academy difficult because there is a tendency to feel that an ex-politician might corrupt the young.

During Gene's first two terms, St. Thomas College had continued to carry his name in the bulletin as "on leave," but the campaign of 1952 brought that to an end.

The difficulties of family living in the congressional context sometimes seemed enormous and without solution. Only recently I was discussing with Bethine Church, wife of the senator from Idaho, and Barbara Eagleton, wife of the senator from Missouri, the double life of the congressional wife which continues to this day. "It's a constant juggling," said Bethine, "between the official and the public and the private. One never seems to do either well." Although our thinking about social action had been broadened and integrated into the secular experience by the association with Dr. Rommen, Dr. Schwenger, and others, Gene and I, too, held fast to the prevailing theology of the Catholic family. Children were a gift from God: put your trust in Him as to when they should come. The general, even enthusiastic, acceptance of this view among the young Catholic academics of his American acquaintance troubled Dr. Rommen, although he adverted to it only once. We were sitting in a circle on the grassy strip between our huts one blastingly hot August night. From all sides we could hear the fretful crying of children unable to sleep in the ovenlike heat within.

"In Europe people do not take this talk of the clerics seriously," he had said. "It is not historically sensible." We were dismayed that he, the great proponent of natural law, could dispute it in the Vatican's biological interpretation. One's stand on birth control was almost the touchstone of one's Catholicity, and family life was the great subject of Catholic discussion groups with which we were in touch even after we went to Washington.

When Gene was elected to the Senate in 1958, there were the inevitable solicitations from TV producers for us to take part in shows built around new senatorial families. Most of these shows were up-dated versions of what we used to call the "empty cereal bowl picture" in newspapers, several of which had been done with us in the past under such titles as *A Day with Congressman McCarthy*. The whole family, unnaturally brushed and shining, was supposedly gathered around the breakfast table conversing earnestly about the day ahead. In the projected TV show, the families were to be grouped around restaurant tables and visited in turn by inquiring reporters. We refused the opportunity, knowing too well the danger of the suddenly tongue-tied child or of the child with the unexpected frank answer. Midwestern children did not seem to take easily to the public parade. (When Senator and Mrs. Walter Mondale of Minnesota accepted a similar offer when he was new to the Senate, their Eleanor climbed under the table and refused to come out.) Florence Lowe, the interviewer, finally suggested that our Michael, then seven, appear with Forrest Church, son of the senator from Idaho, in a more in-depth interview following the family part of the show.

"How does it feel to be the son of a senator? What do you think about it?" began the interview.

Forrest Church, fourteen or fifteen at the time, answered solemnly that it was a great opportunity to learn by being so close to history in the making. It was also great to be a help to his father who was working so hard for what was good and right.

When it was Michael's turn, he said, "Well, I don't know. When I was born and became conscious, he was already in it, you know."

"In what?" asked the interviewer, somewhat startled.

"In being a congressman," said Michael, "so you see, I can't say what it's like because I don't know anything else."

The girls, Ellen and Mary, thought this an incredibly stupid answer. They were always very hard on Michael, and, of course, jealous of any attention he got by virtue of being a boy. But he was entirely accurate. Ours were congressional children. They were born into a life of moves and campaigns, in which organized family life suffered and tension necessarily mounted, and into a life in which I fear all too often they were made conscious that whatever they did might reflect on their father. All except Ellen were born into that life and her first year had been marked by Gene's first campaign.

Even the circumstances of Michael's birth marked him as a congressional child. It was precipitate—so precipitate that the doctor met us at the hospital door and had me rushed into x-ray. Gene, who had come home to take me to the hospital, couldn't wait for the results; he was needed on the floor of the House for the vote on the universal military training bill.

"It is difficult for anyone in Congress to schedule a certain time for being with his family," Gene said in an interview at that time. "Most of our time together is scheduled by ear. We all enjoy picnicking and hiking and I probably have as much time with my childern as do most professional people."

Our life with the children was a life apart, compounded almost equally of delight and worry. Based on our own convictions, rooted in Gene's social theory, and as a result of our own childhood memories, we felt certain things were vital for the children: to have a sense of home as a place of life experiences and traditions, a security built on loved places, and the feeling of identity and acceptance which comes from an extended family. From the beginning we made much of family celebrations like birthdays, Thanksgiving, Christmas, and Easter and incorporated the sense of continued celebration and learning through celebration which was at the heart of the liturgical movement. We celebrated not only birthdays, but feast days—the days of the saints for which the children were named—the season of Advent, the Twelve Days of Christmas, the Lenten season. Gene read from or improvised on the Collect for the day or the Gospel at evening dinners and at Sunday dinner which we made the family event of the week.

Along the way we developed some secular family traditions of our own which became important to the children—a yearly trip to Rehoboth Beach and to the Skyline Drive in the Washington area and to Lake Sylvia in Minnesota where the Carlsons had a cottage. By all this we hoped not only to root the children in the strength of their own faith and tradition, but also to counter the strains on them of the congressional life—our necessary absenzes from them, the frequent moves in Washington, the moves back and forth to Minnesota. But because we tried to make pattern and routine their security, and although we had enough close friends and relatives so that they had a sense of extended family, they found their security in us perhaps more than they would have if the strains had not been present. Gene often said that we really needed a house with one bedroom, so often would we wake in the morning to find that sometime during the night everyone, even the toddler in the crib, had crawled into bed with us.

Eventually, although we struggled against it, we had to give way to television, which we monitored anxiously and tried to control. The television programs had one very good result; they gave the children a common basis of experience with their cousins and neighborhood friends when they moved to Minnesota and back again each year.

There were inevitably two great problems. How to give the children a good education, a problem for parents everywhere in those postwar years and particularly pressing in our circumstances, and how to give them a sense of geographical home.

As to geographical home, we came to realize that despite the closeness of some of our adult friends to the children—mostly friends dating from our precongressional life—and, despite efforts to have them see the family of other friends frequently as well as their cousins, both in Washington and Minnesota, their real security would come from closeness to friends of their own choosing near enough to be continually available. I happened on a Harvard study of the time on happy families, which concluded that happy contemporary families in the mobile society to which we certainly belonged were happy because they were part of an interlocking group of as many as ten or twenty-five other families in whose homes the children felt almost as free as they did in their own and in which they were welcomed at meals and to stay overnight. For a time we had this situation in Minnesota when we lived on Iglehart Avenue in St. Paul. That part of Iglehart Avenue was a two-block stretch of large, solid, middle-class homes arched by the spreading elms which make the ugliest St. Paul streets beautiful in the summer. The other parents there were for the most part professional people—a large number of them doctors. They were interested in their own children and welcomed ours. It was a neighborhood of intensive and organized play. There were informal projects; trick-or-treating on Halloween, Christmas caroling and an annual improvised Christmas play in which all the children had parts and which all the parents attended. It was given in one basement recreation room or the other. The parents all had separate worlds of their own, but we saw enough of each other and there were enough big neighborhood get-togethers—sometimes a barbecue in the fall and a series of holiday parties—to make us feel the same unity the children felt. The associations on Iglehart were warm and the children's friendships endured through the inevitable absences.

We had a similar happy Washington experience when we were living on Cortland Place in the District of Columbia near our present Cleveland Park neighborhood. Soon after we moved in, we were called upon by two small boys, Mary's and Ellen's ages exactly—Carlos and Santos Goni. They were the children of an Argentine diplomat who lived across the alley. Carlos and Santos and Ellen and Mary became almost immediately a foursome. They were in the same classes at schools and walked back and forth together each day. There were also two smaller brothers, one a little younger than Michael, but a willing playmate, and another, Margaret's age. My particular love was the former, Joseph, fondly called "Uki." He arrived on the doorstep the first day, rang the bell ceremoniously and announced to me, "I am Joseph Mr. Goni and I like cookies. Do you have any?" In no time at all we were spending a part of every weekend with the Gonis.

Later, when the Gonis had returned to Buenos Aires and we visited them there, I found on returning home a note in my purse which read: "Dear Mrs. McCarthy, come back Saterday (sic) and take me back to the United States. Love, respectfully, Joseph Uki." It was a sad little missive, and it symbolized the partings and uprootings which our lives visited on our children who only asked for pleasant, sunny days together, undisturbed by the demands of office and country. Some children come through the pressures of the congressional life untouched, but the odds are against it and the tragedies are many. They are part of the folklore of Washington.

*E*ach house we occupied in Washington had become the center of a constellation of memories, of the friends and neighbors and the events which took place while we were in that house. Nineteen fifty-two—the year during which we lived at 107 Hesketh Street in Chevy Chase—was to me one of the most momentous in Gene's career. It was the year of his initial confrontation with Senator Joseph McCarthy of Wisconsin, who by bullying tactics of investigation, innuendo, and claims of guilt by association, had the State Department, the Administration, and the Congress frozen into a trance of ineffectiveness. Studies of this period now emphasize the fact that Senator McCarthy was only the most flamboyant exponent of an attitude and a policy of action which ran all through our government at that time, on both the Democratic and the Republican sides.

This is perfectly true. Our government has never seemed to trust the American people to be dispassionate yet still unwavering in the face of an enemy, whether that enemy is an abstraction like communism or an attacker like Japan. It was President Truman who established the temporary commission on employee loyalty in 1946 and in support of the work of that commission and his moves against international communism, Truman is quoted as making some very inflammatory statements in his speeches of the time: "We must not be confused about the issue which confronts the world today . . . It is tyranny or freedom . . . and even *worse*, communism denies the very existence of God. Religion is persecuted because it stands for freedom under God. This threat to our liberty and to our faith must be faced by each one of us. . . ." "We must beware of those who are sowing the seeds of disunity among our people . . . we must not fall victim to the insidious propaganda that peace can be obtained solely by wanting peace . . ." "Our homes, our nation, all the things we believe in are in great danger."

But even though Mr. Truman said these things, I, for one, and I think I was rather typical, did not hear them. A call to arms in that flat Missouri accent and that matter-of-fact voice simply was not convincing and I think Mr. Truman meant to alert, not to alarm. It remained for Joe McCarthy to see the great possibilities of the issue, to exploit them cleverly and cynically, and to divide and paralyze the nation. It was nightmarish to those of us whose youth ended in disillusionment about the progress of Western civilization when we saw an admired nation from whom we had taken our music, science, and graduate educational system turn into a mad mire of repression and barbarism during the Nazi era. The atmosphere of suspicion and distrust spread everywhere. People living in my own block were asked to watch their next-door neighbors, and erstwhile friends noted the comings and going of visitors and the license plates of all who came and went. Worst of all, the Communist-hunt took on the aspect of a religious crusade, as President Truman's speech shows. To make it more confusing to liberals who abhorred the McCarthy methods, the fact remained that there *was* a Communist enemy, both without and within.

Riding the wave of the time, Senator McCarthy seemed feral by instinct and almost gleeful over the fear and consternation he inspired. It is still anyone's guess how much of the glee he manifested was a result of the fact that he was, in a sense, the representative of the ethnic element in our society so often disparaged and despised, or that as the representative of the farm states, he had at last commanded the attention of the Establishment and made it sit up and take notice.

Considering the atmosphere of the time, Gene's detachment, the coolness of his appraisal were unique. Our liberal friends were often driven to try to prove that they were more anti-Communist and more truly loyal than Joe McCarthy: witness Hubert Humphrey's authoring the bill to outlaw the Communist party in this country. Or they refused to accept that there might be any subversion at all or that if there were subversion, it could lie within any circles with which they were in touch. This was the period of Dean Acheson's famous statement, "I will not turn my back on Alger Hiss." (Gene wickedly parodied this statement in 1958 when Dean Acheson espoused Eugenie Anderson's candidacy for the Senate nomination against Gene: "I did not expect Dean Acheson to turn his back on Eugenie Anderson.") One night at dinner at the Gilbert Harrisons' we heard Joe Rauh, now the grand old man of civil liberties, describe the way in which he, as defender of Alger Hiss, had had a typewriter completely constructed in Baltimore to show that Hiss's typewriter could have been duplicated and the papers for which he was responsible forged.

Gene's attitude was that Joe McCarthy was only a popular figure acting on premises held by more powerful figures. He often pointed to the kind of campaign waged by Richard Nixon for the House against Helen Gahagan Douglas. He also often said that any time the members of the United States Senate wanted to silence Joseph McCarthy they could; and that he would be effectively destroyed the day the newspapers put him on page seventeen instead of page one. Gene was particularly irked by one incident when he was to speak at an outdoor picnic in Silver Spring. When he arrived he found microphones set up, television cameras in evidence, and a gathering of reporters. When the reporters discovered that it was Representative Eugene McCarthy and not Senator Joseph McCarthy who was speaking, they took down their cameras and equipment and departed.

"You might stay," he said to the departing reporters. "What I am about to say has application to the very thing you're interested in." And his speech that day was indeed applicable. The rally was a meeting of the Holy Name Society, a society of men within the Catholic Church pledged to avoid blasphemy. Gene's thesis was that the ultimate blasphemy was to submit our fellowman to indignities, to blacken his reputation, to take away his livelihood in the name of God—a thing that he held that McCarthyism was doing. But the speech went unreported. A few months later Theodore Granik, who was around a good deal in liberal circles and had heard Gene quoted, decided that it would be an attention-getting idea to have a McCarthy-versus-McCarthy debate on his television program "American Forum of the Air." Gene agreed at once. (Living with this detachment of Gene's was, I always said, like living with an accident about to happen.) I was terrified. Our friends called to urge me to dissuade Gene, if I could. It would mean the end of his career, they insisted. Hubert Humphrey called. Paul Douglas, then the courageous and battling senator from Illinois, called. Homer Thornberry called. I don't know how many others talked to Gene directly.

I had never been able to attend any debate or candidate-to-candidate confrontation in which Gene was involved. In the first campaign I was simply too much identified with him, and in addition I was pregnant. I felt I could not stand the emotional strain. The pattern persisted. So I saw him off to the studio that Sunday afternoon, having heard him go over his notes and describe the telephone call he had received from Senator McCarthy the day before.

"Hello, Gene, this is Joe," the latter had said. "We don't want to cut each other up too badly, do we? After all, we're on the same side in a lot of ways." Was the ingratiating, half avuncular approach an effort to disarm Gene? Or was it possible that Joe McCarthy was not sure of the strength of the liberal Catholic element which Gene represented?

"I'll take my chances, Senator," Gene had replied.

Now, at home with the children, I sat by the radio quite literally praying. Admiral and Mrs. Brent Young next door had a television set, still a luxury in those days, and had come over several times to urge me to join them. The admiral was hopping with excitement. He had taken a great liking to Gene, and he and Patsy, his wife, had more or less taken it upon themselves to advise us about the intricacies of Washington society. Now, their protégés were very much in the limelight. I could hear their phone ringing constantly; the houses were separated only by a narrow driveway. I turned on the radio just once and heard Gene saying firmly, "Now just a minute, Senator, I'm entitled to half this time." This only compounded my terror and I turned the radio off. Once I was sure that the program was over I joined the admiral and Patsy. They were jubilant as we watched the credits and the small audience fade from view as the program ended. Gene and a small entourage of friends and staff soon arrived in good spirits and we rehashed the program and the day over Sunday night supper. The next day the Washington *Star* television review column, written by Harry MacArthur, summed up the encounter as follows:

Two notable events took place on television during the weekend. Each, in its way, may have far-reaching effects. One was the TV debut of Bing Crosby and the other was a demonstration that Senator Joseph McCarthy is not invincible in television debate.

Senator McCarthy has always been a fearsome opponent. His manner aggravates many people, usually his foe in a debate more than anyone else. The result is that he usually reaches the end of one of these broadcast sessions seeming a calm, reasonable and even persecuted man while his opponent is reduced to incoherent rage.

Senator McCarthy starts out with the friendly disarming approach, full of affability and first-name calling. Preliminary debate gets under way and he just happens to have with him something bearing on that first point. From a voluminous briefcase he produces a thick document. It seems to be flowing with seals and ribbons as if notarized several times and is fearfully inpressive.

The Senator reads. His opponent may be certain that something is being quoted out of context, but there isn't a thing he can do about it at the time. He can say it, but he can't prove it. Senator McCarthy has that big document. . . . This has led more than one McCarthy opponent into frustration and fumbling and looking bad by comparison.

Representative Gene McCarthy seems to have found the formula, however. There probably was no true victor Sunday night. It is not likely that many McCarthy supporters buy any other McCarthy. Representative McCarthy emerged unruffled and unscarred though. That is tantamount to victory in this league.

A few weeks later, we headed home to begin the 1952 campaign. Just before we left I heard Gene in a radio speech from Pennsylvania making the point that he felt Communists should be allowed to teach in our universities if education meant anything at all! He was serving on the Post Office Committee at the time and had authored an amendment to a bill concerned with subversion among government employees, which stipulated that security risks could be employed in non-sensitive positions. Security risks, at the time, were defined as people who might be subject to blackmail either because of personal weaknesses like alcoholism, simple loquacity and the like, or vulnerable for other reasons—because they had relatives behind the Iron Curtain, for example. Gene held that it was wrong to deprive these people of government employment because of simple vulnerability; although they should certainly not be employed in a code room, they could drive trucks or dispense coffee in government cafeterias. His basic position went deeper, however.

As he said later: "Government, even unpopular and corrupt government, can command and secure external obedience to the laws, but no government can successfully command interior loyalty or love of country."

He was referring to the loyalty oath which people were also required to take in the wake of the fear of communism but what he had to say was basic to his whole approach to the loyalty problem: "Genuine loyalty is more than an external affirmation, more, too, than a habit uncritically accepted. It is a free and generous act of an informed citizen. It is love of country—of its institutions, its laws, its traditions, the land. More importantly, loyalty requires a special regard and concern for fellow citizens, and certainly part of this respect is trust of neighbor, the assumption that he, too, is devoted to his country and its people.

"In a democracy mistakes and failures should be the consequence of too great leniency, rather than of too much restraint; the result of excessive trust, rather than of excessive suspicion and mistrust; of too much freedom, rather than of too much interference and control. Democracy, when the hard choice must be made, must run the risk of being betrayed or destroyed by its own people rather than itself become their betrayer and destroyer."

These were good words based on a dispassionate and thoughtful consideration of the problem of loyalty. But they seemed to have no relevance to the passions of that most disturbed time. We went home that fall to face the "worst smear campaign waged anywhere in the country," according to columnist Drew Pearson.

When we first came home it would have seemed impossible that such a campaign could have been engendered and nourished among a people so sensible and independent-minded as our fellow Minnesotans. There was much less fevered anxiety, much less frantic talk in Minnesota than there was in Washington. It was the year of Adlai Stevenson's first try for the presidency. The party leadership, specifically Senator Humphrey, asked Gene to assume the chairmanship of the Stevenson campaign in Minnesota because Gene's own election was deemed certain and his seat in the House "safe." It was true that his opponent, a young man named Roger Kennedy, was already making the rounds of various meetings and that he had distributed a sheet attacking Gene on several points. But it was so poorly researched that it contained five or more factual errors and it was easy for Gene to refute the whole attack as based on misrepresentation and distortion.

There were, however, uncalculated factors at work. Underlying everything was the strange and inconclusive Korean War, a kind of warfare Americans had never experienced before. The whole Republican attack on the Democrats that year was made in terms of the latter's supposed failure to deal properly with worldwide communism. Each local campaign was a segment of the national campaign in a way which is not usually true in a non-presidential year. Gene's opponent, a young Yale graduate and lawyer, seemed remarkably elastic in his approach to the problem of his candidacy. He was supposed to have counseled with Senator Joseph McCarthy and certainly his tactics were remarkably similar to those of our neighboring senator. His campaign was masterminded by Warren Burger, at that time aspiring to be a United States district attorney and now Chief Justice of the United States Supreme Court. Furthermore, Roger Kennedy was tied to the Establishment in St. Paul in more ways than one. He was the nephew of the wife of the publisher of our monopolistic newspaper and, on both his father and mother's sides, he was the son of prominent, old merchandising families in St. Paul. His own initial ineptitude in campaigning—that is, his listing of charges without proper research—began to be rectified by his more skillful, and Machiavellian, advisers.

(It is only fair to note that he later regretted the campaign and said to Gene and his assistant that he had been badly advised. In 1968 he paid a tribute to Gene in a campaign film.)

In those first years of our involvement in politics, it often seemed to me that the attitudes of Republicans and Democrats to political life were fundamentally different. Republicans who had control of the strings of real power in the country seemed to feel that they should own the government, too, or at least control it, but that politics was not a vocation to be pursued seriously. It was all right as a fling for a younger son or for a junior executive but it was not by any means the pursuit for a man of property. (Nelson Rockefeller and his brothers were to challenge this view by their candidacies but they have not wrought widespread change.) The fundamental Republican attitude was summed up in the approach of the committee who advertised for a candidate with certain qualifications—a merchandisable candidate in the terms of the time—and had their advertisement answered by Richard Nixon. This was the habit of mind which lay at the base of the rage at Roosevelt as a "traitor to his class." The Establishment in St. Paul had not liked Gene's initial election (executives at Minnesota Mining circulated his opponent's literature throughout all their offices and laboratories but refused to let Gene's be similarly circulated). But its full ire was not brought to bear until 1952. Gene's following had increased from the original corps of students, academics, and labor to include many independent-minded Republicans to whom Gene's issue-oriented approach was attractive. He was beginning to be institutionalized and to build seniority in the Congress. It was completely consistent of this Establishment that its members did not seem concerned about the fact that their contender in 1952 appeared to have few qualifications for office at the time and seemed temperamentally unsuited to the campaign.

We were used to the newspaper's opposition. Indeed, we would have felt strange about its approbation, considering its policies. But we were unprepared for its cynical attack. Young Mr. Kennedy's backers evidently decided, after his first inept showing in debate with Gene, that Gene had to be destroyed by zeroing in on his amendment providing for employment of security risks. It was an easy attack to make in many ways. It took a great deal of explanation to unravel for constituents the intricacies of the bill in question. The very term "security risk" made its own condemnation. Our first signal of what was in store for us came when Gene appeared to debate his opponent before a candidates' meeting held at Hamline University in St. Paul. Gene and his aide, Adrian Winkel, came home from that debate shaken and disturbed. The candidate had not appeared to meet Gene, but Warren Burger had substituted for him. Burger, whose legal approach used every trick of courtroom debate, so confused the audience that Gene was never able to make his position clear. Gene was outraged by the substitution of Burger for his opponent and even more outraged by the attack on his patriotism and loyalty. He had never had patience with the technique of debate, and over the years it always bothered me that he would persist in reacting to his opponent's questions, rather than in seizing the opportunity to make his own points.

From then on in the campaign, it was one thing after another. Full page ads appeared in the paper, signed by some of the most prestigious lawyers in St. Paul, saying in effect that Gene's amendment was treasonous in effect and intent. These ads also appeared in different forms as flyers with more flamboyant headlines: IS YOUR CONGRESSMAN A TRAITOR?

Ellen, who started kindergarten that fall, came home the first week and said to me piteously, "Mama, what is a Communist?" And I knew that some child on the playground had told her that her father was one.

Television was used for the first time in a congressional campaign in St. Paul that fall. I turned it on one day after lunch to see Gene's opponent interviewing two soldiers home on leave from Korea. "And how did you feel," he inquired solicitously of one, "when you came home and found that your congressman was giving aid and comfort to the enemy?" The soldier, who needless to say had been well briefed, expressed his distress and his concern about how disheartening this sort of thing was for his buddies still on the battlefield. I felt sick. Most frightening to me was to see Gene growing thin and more distraught each day over the attack.

Slowly the tide began to turn. St. Paul had a community of intellectual refugees to whom the opposition's techniques smacked of Hitler and the regime he represented. Many in this group moved forward strongly to offer help. And for the first time to my knowledge, the Church people came forward in defense of political truth in a political campaign. When we first came home we had met the new head of the department of theology at Macalester, Dr. Robert McAfee Brown, and his wife. On a day when our spirits were at their lowest in the campaign, Adrian Winkel called up from the downtown campaign office and said to me, "Say, there was some man in here by the name of Brown who said he knows you and he'd like to do something." And I cried out in great relief, "Brown—you don't mean Robert McAfee Brown? That would be a gift from heaven!" So it proved to be, because Bob Brown, on fire with a sense of justice assaulted, gathered a committee of clergymen and professors who issued a statement condemning the abuse of truth in the campaign and calling on the people of St. Paul to examine the issues on their merits, to refuse to be swayed by false attacks. They went on the radio with this statement and distributed it at church doors. Help also came from another source, from the women in various organizations, especially in the League of Women Voters, who had come to know Gene and his stands through their studies of candidates and who through their study circles or league units had a grasp of the fine points of legislation. Many of these women found themselves ashamed and outraged when their husbands, members of law firms, found that their names had been affixed as a matter of course by their senior partners to the advertisements attacking Gene. One Sunday morning when such an advertisement appeared, one of these women called us very early.

"I'm so upset," she said. "I've been literally sick ever since I saw that ad and the names affixed to it. And Jenny Smith [fictitious name] is so upset that she can't get out of bed. Her husband's name is on that ad. He is coming over to see you about writing a letter to the paper disclaiming it."

By that time, our combination living-dining room was filling up with outraged neighbors and ward workers, several of them profane in expression, clad in plaid lumberjack shirts, the uniform in Minnesota of the working man on his day off. Our volunteer press people were there, in the process of drawing up an answering ad. The room was littered with ash trays and coffee cups, lists and mock-ups of new advertisements. I alternated between feeding the babies at the kitchen table and pouring coffee for the workers in the living room.

We took turns going to Mass that day as was our custom when the children were too small to go, and Gene was at Mass when the precisely dressed young Ivy-League lawyer, Mr. Smith, appeared at the door. I felt sorry for him as he stood under the unfriendly eyes of the Democrats in the living room, and I asked him to wait for Gene in our small study. He sat at the desk, wrestling with the composition of his letter and from time to time, I brought him a cup of coffee and stopped to chat with him. I knew that what he was doing required a tremendous effort of will. He was crossing a line as a matter of conscience, an indefinable line but one much harder to cross than many visible boundaries. He was leaving an inner circle for a world uncharted, unknown and, for him, not at all rewarding. He was aligning himself with those men in the living room from whom he had always counted himself apart and fortunate to be so. In his talks Gene sometimes quoted C. S. Lewis on the inner-circle, from a speech Lewis had given to Cambridge undergraduates about to leave the university. It was a speech I had come across first in my teaching at St. Catherine's and it had made a powerful impression on us because of its very clear articulation of a fact on which our society rests but which we very seldom advert to in our discussion of groups. The most subtle and most compelling of all temptations, Lewis had said, is the temptation to the inner circle. Men will lie, betray their wives and friends for admission to that circle. For one man the inner circle may constitute one thing, for another man another thing; some may prefer the inner circle of science, others the inner circle of business. But the charm of the inner circle lies in the fact that others may not enter, that only a select few are admitted. Mr. Smith was leaving his. He was leaving it because of his wife's conscience and because of her effect on his.

I learned many things from the campaign that fall. I learned first of all what the overt power of the Establishment can do in a community of supposedly free men. We had experienced the passive opposition of the Establishment in the two previous campaigns but we were unprepared for the full force of its attack. When Gene's supporters scraped together enough money for full page ads answering the attacks, the ads were held up for three or four days while the newspapers lawyers "studied" them, and their impact was thus blunted. Father Vincent Flynn, the president of St. Thomas and a family friend of mine, who had been marvelously courageous in encouraging Gene's entry into politics, was almost literally coerced into giving the invocation at the luncheon kicking off Gene's opponent's campaign. Ostensibly that was all he was doing, but he was miserably aware as were we that the presence of the president of St. Thomas at that luncheon gave the public the impression that the college was disavowing its former professor and in effect, blessing the attack upon him. But the college loans were held by the local banks; people who sat on its board of trustees were also important Republicans.

College friends of ours who held white-collar positions in the town's lesser hierarchy and who had helped happily in Gene's previous campaigns now asked to have their names withdrawn from our lists. "After all, Abigail," one of my friends telephoned angrily to say, "we have children, we have to eat. What right have you to ask Jack to risk that for Gene?" "I didn't ask, Betty," I said unhappily, secretly frightened at her hostility and knowing that things would never be the same between us again. No sooner would we answer the charges against Gene's loyalty in one place then they would crop up again in another. Battalions of young businessmen were sent out to speak at the service clubs, veterans' meetings, employees' groups, secretaries' associations, church groups. The phone rang incessantly, and again, and again, and again I repeated the definition of a security risk and the terms of Gene's amendment, setting the distortion straight as best I could.

I learned also that people support a candidate for many reasons and that the little people of the world often find in a campaign not only what is good—a larger meaning for their lives—but also sometimes an outlet for pettiness, old grudges, and that most human, if ignoble, of urges, the urge to tear the mighty down. All through that fall we were kept aware of what the opposition was planning by the invisible people, the people the Establishment takes for granted, the people who wait on them in restaurants, the people who check their hats, open their car doors, caddy for them at golf courses, work for them in offices. (I was reminded of this when I read in the memoirs of Joseph Kennedy's nurse that the Kennedy family held business conferences aboard the family airplane with no one else there. The Joseph Kennedys, whose roots are outside the Establishment, know people!) It was in this campaign that the newspaper workers came in the middle of the night with a fresh proof of a smearing advertisement so that we could be prepared. It was also during this campaign that Gene was called late one night to a meeting of newspaper men and TV and radio reporters who had gathered together the $2000 required for an ad which was to be an exposé of the publishing family and its tactics. The money was on the table, the copy was ready; it was well written and documented. But Gene refused to use it. Robert McAfee Brown wrote of this later in his article called "Confessions of a Political Neophyte," published in *Christianity and Crisis* the next year. He interpreted the incident as evidence of Gene's high principles and idealism. "I also knew it was bad politics," said Gene dryly when he read the piece. "Those people were just working out their own grudges and you just lose people if you seem to be using the same kind of smear attack."

When President Truman made his campaign visit to St. Paul, I learned two new things: that nothing exceeds the power of the presidency in drawing attention and that the apathy and inattention of the average citizen is beyond comprehension. The President, of course, had been briefed, very graphically, by Senator Humphrey on the local situation, so he inserted into his St. Paul speech a very spirited defense of Gene. "I know," he said, "the citizens of the Fourth District will reject this attack on Gene McCarthy, a fine citizen, an outstanding Christian layman, a fine family man whom you all know." To say that such a man could be guilty of any form of subversion, Truman implied, was dastardly. It was the only time that fall that a defense of Gene appeared on the front page of the evening paper.

All during the campaign I had been saddened by the conviction that a classmate of mine who lived across the street and whose little girl was in kindergarten with Ellen was undoubtedly involved in the campaign against us. Her husband was a Republican stalwart. I had seen nothing of her, and her little girl never came across the street to play. On the night of President Truman's visit, the phone rang. It was Debbie.

"For heaven's sake, Abigail, what in the world is President Truman saying such awful things about Gene for?" she said. "But he didn't, Deb," I answered. "He was just answering the attacks on Gene." "Well, I didn't read it very carefully, I admit," she rejoined, "but it was all about something about subversion and so on. Imagine, saying such a thing about Gene!" She had actually been oblivious to the whole campaign, to charge and countercharge, and was evidently heading merrily toward Election Day to vote for Gene for friendship's sake, no matter what her husband might think.

What I learned most of all in that campaign was the full cost of being a political wife. Up to that time the campaigns, the moving back and forth, the problems had been perhaps unusual, but in many ways not more unusual than those of people involved in working for the Army or Foreign Service or for companies whose professional employees are moved about a good deal. But this was different, frighteningly so. Gene was a target for hatred and vituperation and so was I, as identified with him. It is much harder, I found, to accept the attacks on another than on oneself. It is hard to endure the attack; it is hard for a wife to answer it in a seemly way. By the very fact of public life, one seems to lose humanity in people's eyes. And so do your children. How was I to explain to small Mary in nursery school that when Sister tried to introduce her mother to another parent, the lady turned and walked away? How was I to make up to Ellen, who had trotted off to kindergarten so happily, for the tensions in the adult world which she did not understand but which turned some of her classmates against her, which caused her to be left out of some birthday parties, and which caused mothers, picking up their children, to turn and stare at her as she passed.

The strain told. One sunny fall afternoon when Gene was exhausted from campaigning, we played hooky and drove north along the St. Croix River and its lovely valley. We came upon a small, old country church with a little weed-grown cemetery. We drove into the churchyard and parked there in the quiet and the sun. In a few minutes, Gene was asleep, sprawled back in the driver's seat in an attitude of simple exhaustion. I got out of the car and wandered through the little graveyard, reading the old tombstones, grateful for the relief of the country quiet in which the only sound was the calling of crows. I came across a small gravestone with the legend ELLEN O'LEARY, AGED 5, 1866. The names were family names although that small, long-ago Ellen O'Leary had nothing to do with me. Somehow the coincidence of names and the thought of the small child dying on the frontier so long ago snapped the control I had maintained. I burst into tears and wept for small Ellen O'Leary and for my own children and for myself.

Gene won that election by an overwhelming majority. "You Republicans let me down," stormed his opponent at the Republican election party. And later, in an interview with *U.S. News & World Report*, he said that he would have won except that it was impossible to destroy the high regard in which the incumbent was held! It would not have been impossible, Gene insisted soberly, if he had had a bigger district or if it had been a state-wide campaign. The day after election I lost my voice and it did not come back for five weeks, a long enough time to begin to concern the doctors. It was not that I had talked so much, it was the strain, they said, and fatigue. All I know is that I was never able to face a campaign with equanimity again.

By this time in our lives, Gene, always haunted by the idea of vocation, had worked out a philosophy of the vocation of politics which satisfied him. I remember how moved he was when he read Bernanos' *Diary of a Country Priest* and came upon the passage in which Bernanos, through the words of the soldier, accuses the institutional Church of robbing the men of chivalry—"The protectors of the city, not slaves to it . . . Righters of wrong, hands of iron!"—of vocation.

The emotion-fraught scene between the soldier and the priest fit in with what Gene had been thinking for a long time: the idea that vocation applied only to priestly vocation was at the root of Christianity's failure to serve the world.

"It is important," Gene said, "that a clear sense of vocation be developed by Christians and Christian leaders. The general significance of calling or vocation does, of course, still exist today. Two things, however, have occurred which weakened its effect. On the one hand, its meaning has been so generalized that it has come to have little significance for individual Christians: on the other hand, where its meaning remains specific, it has been restricted in application to the calling to the priestly, the religious life. Actually this loss of the awareness of vocation is another subtle manifestation of the secularization of our society. It is not something which has happened overnight. It is not wholly the product of the materialism of the modern age.

"Along with this progressive loss of the sense of vocation there has been a corresponding loss of the meaning of profession and neglect of the practice. This in a sense is another sign of the denial and rejection of sacramentalism. Profession was essentially a public and formal acceptance of a vocation, a public and formal acceptance that this was the way by which the individual Christian was to work out his own salvation and promote the common good."

Gene made it clear that he was not advocating jumping back into a nicely ordered, highly stratified society. But he insisted that what was necessary was a revived sense of vocation and a formal or informal acceptance of that calling as well as of a general calling of all Christians. Overspecialization, he thought, had brought about fragmentation, lack of synthesis as well as lack of a sense of order and relationship.

True to his own words Gene had, in a way, in these speeches professed to his calling—to the vocation of politics. A person who did this must remember that politics is part of the real world and he must be realistic: "The ideal is seldom realized and often cannot be advocated." Compromise is, in the political sense, not a bad word. Compromise is a mark of human relations not only in politics but almost in every institution or social relationship involving two or more persons. "Genuine compromise is not a violation of principle, not a compromise with principle, but with reality." Another error he pointed out which a Christian turning to politics might make was confusing politics and its secular content and purposes with religion. There was no such thing as a purely Christian politics or Christian state.

What were the marks of a Christian politician then? He should be judged by the standards of whether he had advanced the cause of justice and helped at least to achieve the highest degree of perfection possible in the temporal order. He must in a way be a theologian, a philosopher, and a moralist himself and he should listen to the voices of these disciplines.

As he proceeds in action, his general guide must be to make his decisions in the hope that they may help to make an imperfect world somewhat more perfect, or that, at least, if he cannot make an imperfect world more perfect, he can save it from becoming less perfect or finally from becoming entirely evil and perverted. He can try to prevent degradations; to prevent decline; and, if possible, he can hope to move things forward and upward toward right and justice. That is the purpose and the end of political action and of the compromises that go with such action . . . these seem difficult standards and demands and their fulfillment requires sanctity. There is, however, no other measure which is valid for Christians in politics or Christians in any other way of life.

Gene's ideas about the vocation of politics were part of an important area of discussion in the 1940s and 1950s, a rediscovery of the fact that laymen are part of the Church. At the same time there was a resurgence of interest in the theology of marriage, an effort to prove that marriage and sexuality in the true Christian view were not just alternatives to "burning," as St. Paul so unchivalrously put it, or poor alternatives to the priesthood and the religious life, but good in themselves. Movements centered on the family flourished; these included the Cana Clubs and Conferences and the Christian Family Movement. Inevitably, perhaps, the conclusion often was that if the priesthood was a vocation, then marriage was also a vocation. If a man's vocation was to marriage and family life, then his work in the world took on secondary importance, although he could of course take into account his interests, talents, opportunities. But all this was subordinated to the care and education of his family. Gene had rejected this idea for himself early. When I had last minute doubts just before our marriage, he had written to me that he did not look on marriage as a vocation and that he had told this to Father Walter and to the novice master when he was leaving the monastery. Nor did he look on our marriage as his responsibility to me because of our earlier engagement. "If I have any responsibility," he had said, "it is not to take on a certain state but the responsibility to love." Marriage was a sacrament and a state of life; it was not a vocation.

There was a difficulty in this, although I did not see it then. If his vocation was to politics and marriage was not a vocation, what was my vocation? The whole question of woman was then latent in our lives. Laying aside any theological considerations, it was taken for granted that to be the wife of a man in politics and the mother of his children was not only a full-time occupation but a worthy calling in itself. Lady Bird Johnson had given voice to this for all of us when she said in a speech to congressional wives, "I am sure that we would say the life of any congressional wife revolves around three things: husband, children, and home . . . as wives of busy men whose daily business is the nation's business, our best chance to find the significant is to help our husbands achieve their own legislative aims." She had asked Lyndon what he felt were the three most significant things in his career and he had said that helping push and extend the draft act in August of 1941 when it passed only by one vote was one of them; the Civil Rights Act of 1957 was another; the Space Act of 1967 was the third. "I recommend," she said, "that you ask that same question at home. It is well to be reminded that all of the fragmentation of self—as Anne Lindbergh describes the daily living of today's homemakers—adds up to something."

I think we all agreed to that even as late as 1963 when Lady Bird said it. It was part of the American political tradition that in one sense a man and his wife were both "elected." We need only recall the days when Ohio voters welcomed the Tafts on his first Senate election with a huge sign saying "Congratulations, Bob and Martha." Those few wives who led independent lives with independent careers were for the most part wives of the very rich congressmen or senators to whom politics might be a vocation but not a living. Running a business which added to the family's fortune, as many wives did including Lady Bird with her television station, Betty Talmadge with her meat business and Emily Malino Scheuer with her decorating, was not thought contrary to the pattern. In 1968 I voiced the same point of view when I said in an interview, "Honors, writing—they're by-products of the mainstream of my life which has been to be the wife of an involved man with four involved children." It was in 1970 that a congressional wife thought to question this attitude publicly, when Arvonne Fraser of Minnesota told a New York reporter, "A lot are unhappy here. They have no life of their own and wonder, who am I? Am I just somebody's wife? Or is there something more?"

We worked very hard at what we thought was our vocation, we political wives. We held campaign schools at the Democratic Wives

Forum and at the Congressional Club, trading campaign experiences, learning how to dress for platform appearances, learning how to use television, radio, and how to deal with the press. Katie Louchheim discovered us as a useful tool in her days as head of the women's division of the Democratic National Committee, and we were grateful because professional political women, like the national committee women, for the most part tended to look on wives as a necessary evil but an evil which sometimes got in their way. Katie's initial discovery occurred, I'd like to think, before she returned to politics in 1952, when she was working on a projected article with Christine Sadler Coe for *McCall's* about congressional wives, and came to the Democratic club to hear one of our campaign panels. We Minnesota women, partly out of necessity, had pioneered the new and more independent kind of campaigning in which we often had a separate itinerary from our husbands and made speeches discussing the issues, always, of course, with a disclaimer—"I think Gene would say . . ." or "Orville says . . ." or "Hubert thinks . . ."

We were very, very careful never to take a stand on our own. But still, we had gone a long way from the days of "Miss Lucy" George who went along with Senator Walter George and sat on the platform "to show them I don't have a cleft foot."

The new approach insofar as it was new seemed to fascinate Katie and she asked me to lunch to talk about it. When she became vice chairman she remembered the Democratic-Farmer-Labor Forum which I had helped form in our Minnesota district to give a home and a focus to the new women active in the party. It appealed to her as a way around the old war horses of the party—evidently formidable and venerable ladies like those in our Ramsey County DFL Women's Club flourished everywhere. So she encouraged us to form the Democratic Wives Forum. At a farewell party she said:

> Long ago I realized how very important you were. Some of you have heard me tell about how I discovered congressional wives. I was a hopeful writer and only a part-time politician in those days. As a writer, I did some interviewing. I soon found out that you wives knew more about politics than most politicians. It was like discovering gold—so naturally I went back to stake my claim as soon as I got appointed.

Now I'd like to say a word to you lucky husbands. I hope you all realize how indispensable these ladies are to you, too . . . My husband might well say . . . that he regrets having only one wife to give to his party.

But every one of you have solved that problem. For none of these ladies ever abandoned her wifely duties. So that especially between now and November, every husband in this room will admit his wife is indispensable. But what I hope all of you realize is that indispensable means politically indispensable as well.

But that was exactly the trouble. Were we politically indispensable? And did our husbands realize it? Or want it?

Very few of us thought in the terms Marvella Bayh expressed so frankly in an interview in 1971: "I've always longed for a career of my own because I never really did have one. Some women don't have a need for it, but I was an only child and I was always made to feel that I could have a career and could contribute. I live completely through him . . . But I suppose it would be a rude awakening if something happened to him. Not only would I lose a husband, a best friend and a breadwinner, but my own career."

I was struck, reading this, at how completely accurate it is as a description of the situation of the political wife. The political side of her life is a career in itself. She works in the field of public relations; her job is to interpret, reflect, and round out the image of the public man. Besides that, she is often confidential adviser, behind-the-scenes organizer, and sometimes speech writer. She often represents him, if not always at public functions, then at benefits and semisocial occasions like official receptions.

I remember how proud and happy I was in 1952 when Robert McAfee Brown said to Gene and me, "Sydney and I were so impressed when we first met you by what a perfect married team you were, how well you complemented each other." It was what I really wanted to do more than anything else, to be totally part of Gene's life, to make my talents serve his which I thought of as wholly unique. One tenet of the Catholic rural life movement which had appealed to me strongly was the insistence that in farm life true marriage was safeguarded because in the rural situation man and wife were real partners and needed each other. This seemed to be true of the political life as well.

I did not want a career of my own. I had come to marriage with a modest reputation as a college teacher, lecturer, and reviewer and with ten years of work experience behind me. It was taken for granted that I could always teach again if I had to; Gene often scandalized eager insurance agents in those early days by saying that my M.A. was my insurance and that he didn't need to take out any more than he already had. None of the things I could do harmonized very well with the circumstances of the political life except writing and there was very little of the requisite energy left for that. I was perfectly happy to help Gene as I could. I used to help with speeches and articles, not so much with the text itself—Gene's own style was so distinctive—impersonal, compressed skeletal, and Latinate—that only he could write it—but in outlining ideas, finding references, calling his attention to background books and articles. And the traditional American wife's role of keeping in touch with relatives and friends expanded to take in our expanding political family and friends. We felt strongly that the Christmas card should not be a political tool, for example, but the personal list grew and grew.

Inevitably, inexorably, unless the wife becomes her husband's actual office aide or confidential secretary (and many do), the congressional husband and wife begin to live separate lives. To some wives this change comes with shocking suddenness before the life has developed any compensating factors for her. "I cried for three months," admitted a congressional wife, interviewed recently in The New York Times. In the beginning her husband was out most of the time meeting people, being seen, learning the ropes, and most of his invitations did not include her. "I was alone, I didn't know anyone, and had no one to talk to," she said. "When he did come home, and I was dying for conversation, he would ask, 'Would you mind if I take a nap?'"

"You develop interests in things you can do without him," said Jane Muskie to me when we were talking about this one day, "—or you go mad!"

Even at first Gene never felt that these multitudinous engagements were so important, and he early began dropping into the predinner reception to greet everyone necessary and then coming home to have dinner with me and the children. When he thought the dinner important enough, we went together. Our concept of Christian family life was still precious to us; we said evening prayers with the children and he helped put them to bed. From the beginning we had mutual friends who shared our ideas and ideals, and I never felt isolated. Gene's natural love of home gave me a feeling of great security and I was entirely untroubled when Mrs. Edward Thye, wife of our senior Minnesota senator, said, "I never see you with your husband. It doesn't look right, you know." I knew it was more important to be with the children and, in any case, I didn't care to be at the Chamber of Commerce dinner, the Fire Insurance Underwriters' dinner, the Savings and Loan Association dinner, the hundred and one lobby receptions where congressmen were more demeaned than honored. It bothered me to see Gene subjected to the "You'd-better-listen-we're-the-tax-payers" approach. I was content to attend the official congressional and White House affairs and we went to small dinners together. It was at these that we really came to know people well.

But the legislative life is demanding in itself, and keeping in touch with the constituency often means that a husband must be in his home district more often than his wife—or that he must be back in Washington when she is at home. The husband and wife cease to be a team working together; they begin to play complementary roles. In my own mind I came to terms with this as a normal expansion of the marriage roles we had talked of so solemnly when we planned our married life. In public life the roles expanded beyond the boundaries of home and work, but the goal was the same. There are some things one wife can do to help her husband, others that another can do. The wife's role remains supportive yet responsible as in the adaptation of the Benedictine rule for oblates: "The husband is the abbot; the wife, the cellarer —both with great responsibilities for the community." Sometimes the complementary role is so subtle and all-pervasive in a political life that it is not recognized until it surfaces dramatically in a time of great need or stress: one remembers Lady Bird Johnson's anticipating Lyndon Johnson's first public statement after his aide and long-time friend Walter Jenkins was trapped in a morals offense. The tone of understanding and compassion was irrevocably set; the public attention focused on the suffering family. There was also her statement when they emerged from the plane which carried the body of John F. Kennedy from Dallas. It is the statement and her demeanor of sad dignity which one remembers from that moment so impossible for both her and her husband. Who has become President under more difficult circumstance? Jacqueline Kennedy's theatrical grace and courage at the same time made one realize how much of the unique mystique of Camelot was hers— the mystique which convinced the whole world that we were in a time of new beginnings. And I think of Muriel Humphrey's post-1968 statement, "He is not what he was; he is not what he will be"—a masterly concentrated message of reality and hope about her husband's situation and future which, for me, at least, and surely for other readers, lifted him out of a morass and carried him forward.

The complementary role of a wife was most visible in the case of Mrs. Roosevelt, but it is necessary to recall the opprobrium she suffered for it, exactly because it was overt and visible. The cruel jokes, the naked hatred she evoked certainly served to intimidate lesser women. No one of us Minnesota DFL wives would have affirmed for ourselves in the 1950s what Senator Birch Bayh so cheerfully ascribed to wives in the interview I have quoted: he freely said that his wife was his best political confidante and adviser. "In public life you are surrounded by admirers. They are worshipful and it's easy to get carried away. But there is a sense of security to have someone who loves you and helps you keep your feet on the ground."

It was more or less true in each of our cases, but our husbands belonged to a party whose chief strength lay in farmers and union men, who would have felt such a confession a sign of weakness, and our husbands, college men or not, would have felt their position weakened by such a statement. Yet we were fortunate in that

we were expected to take active roles, to campaign, and to participate in party politics. Jane Freeman, who had had a career in
student politics at the University of Minnesota, sat in as active
participant at party councils, and Arvonne Fraser, wife of Congressman Don Fraser (then a state senator), graduated from the Young
Democrats to a place on the state executive committee. She acted
as her husband's campaign manager and eventually managed campaigns for other candidates.

Arvonne's ability and acceptance was rare, however. Gene's assistant, Adrian Winkel, put it succinctly, "I don't know what it
is about Arvonne—she's one woman you don't mind working with
or for."

Generally, however, we recognized that columnist David Broder's
dictum held true: a woman's role in politics is rough, especially
if her forte is organization. My own flair for organization, discovered in Gene's first campaign, seemed best used behind the
scenes, and then best used in the volunteer efforts which were
always part of his campaigns and kept him somewhat free and
independent of the state and county party organizations. I liked it
that way. From the first I was terrified by the clashing drives and
open confrontations which seemed part of the work in the party.
Although we recognized the moral obligation to work in and with
the party, it always seemed to me that working with the women
and volunteer organizations was a way to promote civility, objectiv-
ity, and issue-orientation. It was also clear to me that people from
these groups usually ended up with a personal loyalty to Gene. It
did not occur to me then that there was something ultimately cor-
rupting about a wife's hidden role like this because of its essential
falseness.

In those years I was never comfortable with the official wife
role, either. After every interview I lay awake in a black nightmare
of anxiety, fearful that I had said something which would do Gene
irreparable harm. A phrase or a statement which I deemed unfortunate would literally rise out of my consciousness to strike me
with a paralyzing fear and sense of inadequacy.

Occasionally I gave talks on the duties and responsibilities of the

was to give me some understanding of what addiction can mean in the lives of our young people today. I was forty when Margaret was born and in the preceding months a doctor, noting my fatigue, had prescribed a combination of Dexedrine and Amytal—at once a tranquilizer and a stimulant. I thought the effect miraculous. I was always cheerful and tireless, at least until the effect wore off in late afternoon. Muriel Humphrey, whose energy had always been my envy, confided that her doctor also prescribed them for her and that under campaign conditions she sometimes took another toward evening. So, after Margaret was born I continued to take them. Doctors were unaware of the dangers of "uppers and downers" then, although I do remember that my Washington doctor once said that he thought it was best not to get dependent on them, that they were a rather strong medication. Naturally, the miraculous effect grew less and less. But Margaret was almost three before I realized that I had seriously exhausted myself physically and that my nerves were overstrained. I was overcome by irrational streaks of irritability and I would become anxious without cause. "You aren't a race horse, you know," said my sister Ellen sensibly, "and if you were, you would be disqualified." I stopped taking the pills, but it was several years before the irritability and anxiety disappeared.

I found respite from the pressures in the widening circle of friends which each move and each campaign brought to us. I don't think life offers any greater experience than the joyful sense of recognition when one finds in a new acquaintance a real friend, or when an old relationship deepens into friendship, or when one finds an old friendship intact despite the passage of years and many absences. "Try people," I had said to Gene in our first real conversation. Now, although the political life robbed me of the pleasant ease of long and continuous shared life with my friends, it gave me the mobility and the opportunity to live on many levels which made rich new friendships possible.

When I was young I thought of friendship as a matter of total loyalty and unchanging preference and I was often disappointed. But as an adult I had come to see that it was more the refraction of some total faithfulness and joy of which we all had some primordial notion. The exchange of trust and the experience of understanding between two people was like a sign or witness to the possibility of eternal caring and understanding and communication. Whenever I met someone with whom it was possible to get beyond the exchange of tribal signs—"Ah, Akron . . . do you know so and so? . . . Bermuda . . . where did you stay?"—and the sniffing out of common experience—what school, what club, what profession, what specialty—and plunge into real talk, I felt I had found a friend. Sometimes I saw them often again; sometimes there was just the memory of one happy time, from which I had come away excited by new perspectives and new feelings about myself and Gene and our work in the world. I think I could move so freely into these friendships, accepting the possibility of their short duration, because I looked on our Washington life as always subject to a sudden end, as if we were audience participants in a drama on which the curtain could descend at any minute. It was endlessly interesting and the actors were fellow characters. My attitude did not go unnoticed. "I like your wife," a chic and sought-after embassy wife told Gene once, "she really looks at me as if I am a person. So few do that here." Scottie Smith, then Scottie Lanahan, F. Scott Fitzgerald's daughter and perennial commentator on the Washington scene, put it differently when I asked her advice about a benefit chore I was asked to do. "Oh, for heaven's sake, Abigail," she said, "you won't have any trouble with the publicity. Just ask some of the press girls to lunch and they'll melt before that Alice-in-Wonderland air of yours."

Robert McAfee Brown and his wife Sydney had become close friends. I was especially glad of this because our talks with the Browns, who were Protestants, began to change our perspective on ecumenism. Since I had first met Gene and experienced what could be called a conversion to his more integrated and total Catholicism, I had lived mentally and spiritually in a more enclosed world. We thought wholeness discernible. We thought of ecumenical development as the eventual and inevitable return to the true Church. And the best thing we could hope for a friend was conversion. Now all that began to change.

In the aftermath of the strenuous 1952 campaign we spent many evenings with Bob and Sydney discussing the abuse of religious feeling and the mistaken morality which had made such a campaign possible on the local scene and distorted the Eisenhower victory. (Eisenhower's personal popularity was so great that he certainly could have been elected without the kind of campaign which was waged on his behalf.) Quite naturally we began to compare the basic concepts which underlay our beliefs. Who was Christ? What do we mean when we say "the Church?" We invited Father Godfrey down from St. John's to meet them. And they went up with us to visit, a little wary, a little doubtful of our insistence that they see this monastery of monks hidden in the woods.

When Bob wrote *American Dialogue,* the first book on ecumenism to become popular reading in this country, he said that if dedications were in order he would dedicate it "to Gene and Abigail, that the dialogue which they helped initiate might continue." And he confessed quite frankly in the introduction that if he had not come to St. Paul and to the Midwest he might never have met Catholic laymen and priests with whom he would have found common ground in the pursuit of justice.

For my part I found his sense of witness and his reliance on Providence a revelation. "We don't know how Christians will come together," he said. "We only know that He wants it. He said, 'Let them be one, Father, as Thou and I are one.' All we can do is take the first step." It was the personal rediscovery of the new covenant and of the God who is the Way. On the purely natural level it was my first glimpse of what a movement truly is—an organized coming together of people for a common purpose, but one which cannot and must not be rigidly planned and structured since each step forward changes the relationship of every part and person to all other parts and persons. Over each hill there is a new vista.

The 1952 campaign was for us the inauguration of the Eisenhower years. Gene had found that our experience reflected an aspect of the national campaign which he thought a disquieting extension of the American presumption of innocence. "After the convention, the 'political' Republicans having indicated their willingness to join the crusade, were enlisted for the ultimate battle against those who were to be labeled the real forces of evil—the Democrats. Along the way strange compromises were accepted as is often the case in crusades once they have been launched."

He referred, of course, to General Eisenhower's appeasement of Joseph McCarthy, despite his slanderous attack on his old friend and superior officer, General George C. Marshall. And certainly he had in mind the participation by high-ranking Republicans in the smearing tactics of his own opponent.

It is hard for many people today to make the distinction between religion and religiosity, the latter a dangerous parody of the former. The religiosity of the Eisenhower administration often drove Gene to slashing irony at political dinners in the ensuing years. Gene had found in irony that "compensatory worldliness" which made it impossible for political realists to discount him as an impractical idealist. He had also found his way to the hearts of the rank and file party faithful who, once they caught on to his style of humor—the satirical twist, the delayed barb in throw-away lines tossed off quietly and casually—came to delight in it and look forward to it as staple entertainment. And he had found in it an inverted way of revealing what was at the heart of his concern without opening up his inner thoughts. More and more often the statement of the ideal, the call of leader to follower or of struggler to comrade in action, was left to a final sentence or two in a speech, a summary paragraph in an article.

I appreciated his need to find such a mode of expression; and I could see its effectiveness. But I preferred the sober discussion, the clear logical presentation, and the appeal to reason and right which characterized his academic speeches. I preferred the prophetic idealist behind the witty speaker. And it often distressed me that as the applause got louder, the laughter more constant, ad lib gibes seemed to go a little too close to the bone. Friends as well as foes became targets. My anxiety amused him—"There you were again, twisting your hands under the table." It had always diverted him that my hands betrayed my feeling when my face did not; he would point out my tightly clasped hands in a smiling press photograph, something no one else would notice.

But I had to admit that the Republicans of the 1950s were often ideal subjects for irony. They had announced, according to Gene, that they were going to remake the party in the image of President Eisenhower, "an interesting undertaking—a kind of reincarnation." Then came Arthur Larson's book *A Republican Looks at His Party*, and "in it they found that they already were what they thought they had to make themselves. This simplified their problem a great deal." Gene called attention to what he called the "wonderful phrases of Republicanism": progressive moderation—"a gradual slowdown"; their statement that they were "standing firmly astride the authentic American center, grasping the American consensus," to which he added dryly that it was a frightening image if looked at too closely—an aside I did not fully appreciate for years.

The 1950s were also the Stevenson years. This meant that we, who belonged by definition to the liberal, academically influenced, and issue-oriented wing of the party, were no longer part of a small minority. In retrospect one tends to forget that Adlai Stevenson was a realistic politician, a one-time governor of Illinois, and that his candidacy for President was the result of backroom compromise worked out as a solution to the impasse presented at the 1952 convention by two strong candidates, Senators Estes Kefauver and Richard Russell. Stevenson's eloquence, his literate mind, the appeal he made to conscience brought erstwhile independents flocking to the party, proud to be Democrats with him. He became the symbol of the "different" politician, since the more dogmatic among his followers suffered as much as did the Republicans from the syndrome of the 1950s: the failure to admit that politics is a necessary and honorable part of the quest for the common good. Adlai Stevenson brought his followers closer to this admission as had Gene in a more limited arena.

Stevenson's gift for friendship with a wide variety of people brought many disparate groups together and, since we were of that company, our circle widened. Gene was clearly a Stevensonian in 1952 and again in 1956 when he joined Hubert Humphrey and

Orville Freeman in endorsing a second candidacy for Stevenson, although Senator Kefauver had won the presidential primary that year in Minnesota.

The Stevenson years of the Democratic party were also the Johnson years as far as Washington was concerned. Although Lyndon Johnson was virtually unknown nationally when he helped choose Stevenson as a candidate in 1952, he became a real power in the Senate as Majority Leader.

Washington seemed divided into two camps then. One was at the headquarters of the Democratic National Committee, where under the aegis of Chairman Paul Butler the Stevensonian Democratic Policy Committee would meet to formulate goals and objectives of the party. The other was on Capitol Hill where Senator Johnson and Speaker Rayburn held the belief, and acted on it, that the center of the party lay with its elected officials and that its legislative goals, and its foreign policy goals, were formulated there within the realm of the possible. Most senators and congressmen agreed. The two wings of the party did not trust each other.

Gene stood between them with something in common with each. As a matter of history he felt that the center of the party lay in the Congress where its record had to be made. Although he still thought highly of the ideal of the party responsibility, he had come to see that the nature of the division between the American parties was not ideological. "Both parties, of course, are committed to the principles embodied in the Constitution. Their differences are chiefly about practical policies for implementing it." However, because ours is a government of men as well as of law, he thought it needed "the continuous attention of thoughtful men" and therefore that the Democratic members of Congress should do more than follow the leadership.

Gene used to say in those years that most congressmen were at least a cut above the people who had elected them and that the Congress as a whole represented a much higher intellectual average and level of integrity than the country as a whole. Our liberal friends used to listen to this assertion with open astonishment and disbelief. How much of our present dilemma and tragic division rests in this subtle denial of representative government is open to surmise. What strange national quirk led us to idealize the amateur and the outside expert as shapers of our destiny rather than the men who had been elected by the people and were responsible to them? I was always moved by Speaker Rayburn's address to each newly elected group of House members in which he reminded them proudly that the House of Representatives was the "people's branch" which returned every two years to the people for review of its record and for renewal.

Gene fit well into the House. His concern for tradition and institutions made him properly respectful of its traditions and at the same time concerned that its machinery be used properly in service of the people who were its source of power.

When the senators honored Gene in the traditional round of laudatory speeches when he left the Senate in 1970, Senators Mike Mansfield and Lee Metcalf of Montana, both of whom had served with him in the House, made special mention of this period.

Senator Metcalf said, "Not enough mention . . . has been made of the early McCarthy, Gene McCarthy as a leader before 1968 . . . As a freshman congressman in 1953, I went to see the then Representative McCarthy to talk about committee assignments." He was already a leader, said Metcalf, and one of the only two Democrats from the "whole great western area" on the important Ways and Means Committee. "That first meeting was an important one," continued Senator Metcalf. "He could see that I was in need of help and guidance and he was generous and kind enough to give it to me. He called me back to his office and under the guise of discussing some of the legislative problems before the Eighty-second Congress he gave me wise and experienced advice. Whenever a question arose there someone would always say, 'Let us see what Gene has to say about it.'

"An example is a liberal statement that was issued in 1957 just before President Eisenhower's State of the Union and Budget messages. Several congressmen including former Secretary of the Interior Stewart L. Udall, Frank Thompson of New Jersey, James Roosevelt, and others wanted to have a Democratic program. So we all went to see Gene and he wrote a draft of a program that was adopted substantially in its entirety . . . during the Eighty-fifth Congress it became known as the 'McCarthy manifesto.'

"A study of the McCarthy manifesto will show what an innovative and imaginative legislator Gene McCarthy was. Looking back with the advantage of 20/20 hindsight we can see that he had the wisdom and sagacity to foresee the impact of programs denied to many of us."

Now in the 1970s it is especially interesting to read what this statement of the 1950s called for in certain areas of great concern today: for example, the encouragement and facilitation of world trade with appropriate help to American industries affected adversely by the liberalization of policy; Federal help for medical education and expanded health services; housing for low- and middle-income groups and senior citizens; expanded urban redevelopment; consumer protection; the protection and conservation of resources; the settlement of Indian claims and the honoring of Indian treaties; and much more. It also anticipated the legislative achievement of the 1960s in the field of civil rights, calling, as it did, uncompromisingly for the elimination of legal and unconstitutional discrimination affecting the right to vote and the right to engage in gainful occupation, the insurance of the full protection of the law for the enjoyment of security of person and of the rights of citizenship.

. Legislation rests on precedent. The Democratic Study Group of the House grew out of, as Senator Metcalf put it "those who wanted to talk it over with Gene" and who met and discussed legislation in his office. They became a formal group and Gene was its first chairman. Called variously "McCarthy's Mavericks" and "McCarthy's Marauders," they persistently sought this sort of legislation and succeeded little by little in attaching amendments, improving phraseology, and introducing concepts which became part of the law of the land in the 1960s.

Despite his position of leadership in the House, Gene decided to run for the Senate in 1958. He felt, he said, that as a member of the Senate he would be better able to speak about programs and the nation's need for them. And the foreign policy of this country had also become more and more important, and therefore the role of the Senate had become increasingly important.

Gene's last years in the House had been marked by increasing involvement in our country's foreign relations. In the postwar years, various ad hoc organizations had been set up to allow congressmen more direct involvement, such as the NATO Interparliamentary Conference, the British-American Interparliamentary Conference, and others. Legislation required an increasing knowledge of foreign affairs—especially, interestingly enough, agricultural legislation which dealt with sugar quotas, cheese imports, food for foreign aid, and a spate of other things. In the Ways and Means Committee, where tax bills originated, our balance of payments and the international monetary system were a matter of constant concern.

We personally had been international in our interests from the beginning and had welcomed the opportunity which Washington afforded to know people from other countries. Early in the 1950s I had been one of the first members of one of the international groups which were the happy idea of Marian Adair, wife of the then congressman from Indiana. My group consisted of twenty women (it was later enlarged to twenty-two) who were either wives of senators and Congressmen or wives of diplomats. The diplomatic wives were enthusiastic about the opportunity these groups afforded to know Americans well in an informal way. Over the years the men became even more enthusiastic. "We meet more influential Americans through our wives than we ever would otherwise—and diplomatic people outside our own sphere of interest, too," the husband of one of our Mediterranean members said to me in 1971; we met at a wedding at the Iranian embassy which neither of us would have attended were it not for the close familylike relationships developed by our international groups. It seems strange to remember now that we had to coax and cajole American members in the beginning in order to get a representation of both Republicans and Democrats and of the various regions of our country. Isolationism had lingered on in social life after it disappeared from national policy.

Our first trips abroad were under the auspices of the Interparliamentary Conferences: The first was to England in 1955 and was like the homecoming which a trip to England always is for those who have taught and loved that language and literature and to whom all the place names are echoes of the familiar.

In the years that followed, these trips were joyful interludes for us—respites from worries about a growing family and from the pressures of public life. It was *de rigueur* then—and it still is—for columnists to decry the "congressional junket," and I suspect many a horror story was leaked from State Department sources over the years. But I think congressmen abroad are very much like their compatriots—not much worse and often better—and much of what they learned was useful. We had our own horror stories about the entrenched bureaucracy. There was the congressional committee chairman on an investigative trip who was only able to evade watchful departmental escorts by going out the men's room window. And Gene and I on our first trip to Italy hired a little car and a driver for a trip to Subiaco, where St. Benedict's own monastery was situated—clearly a personal trip—only to arise at dawn to find the car and driver dismissed and replaced by our determined escort and his bored, sleepy wife, who changed the character of the day to which we had looked forward, and which was meant to be no burden on the taxpayers. One gathered the impression that congressmen were not to wander loose if it was possible to prevent it.

If there was criticism of congressmen's travels, there was even more of travels by congressional wives, although most of us tried hard to distinguish between the personal and the official and use our own funds accordingly. At least one ambassador in our experience was to note in his department report that the wives' presence had value. The first Mexican-American Interparliamentary Conference occurred in a time of so much anti-American feeling in Mexico that it was thought wise to hold it in Guadalajara rather than in the capital. At its end it was with obvious relief that the ambassador cabled:

SENATOR MANSFIELD, REPRESENTATIVE SAUND [JOINT CHAIRMEN OF THE DELEGATION] AND COLLEAGUES SOLIDLY EFFECTIVE IN BREAKING DOWN RESERVE AND SUSPICIONS AND IN ASSURING COUNTERPARTS

U.S. DOES NOT COVET ANYTHING IN MEXICO . . . BUT MADE CLEAR
PROBLEMS MANY YEARS IN THE MAKING CANNOT BE SOLVED TO FULL
SATISFACTION OR QUICKLY. . . . PARTICIPANTS' WIVES CONTRIBUTED
MOST SIGNIFICANTLY FRIENDLY AND COMFORTABLE FEELING. ENTIRE
USDEL REPRESENTED COUNTRY WITH GREAT CREDIT.

The congressional virtues of living amicably with opposition and
being both friendly and frank in debate were sometimes of great
value as in this instance:

> . . . ON PARTING FEELING OF DOUBT THAT MEETING WOULD NOT AC-
> COMPLISH MUCH REPLACED BY SINCERE BELIEF SOLID FOUNDATION SET
> FOR BETTER UNDERSTANDING EACH COUNTRY'S PROBLEMS AND ATTRI-
> BUTES AND THAT ADDITIONAL MEETINGS OFFER HOPE CONTINUED
> PROGRESS . . . NO INCIDENT . . .

It was at this meeting that Gene's growing reputation in Latin-
American countries became noticeable. The Mexican delegates asked
that he make the valedictory speech for the American delegation,
but he yielded the honor to a senior member of the delegation.

The desire of House members to participate more directly in
foreign affairs was a natural one, but on the surface in 1958 the road
to the Senate for Gene seemed rocky indeed. To come to the
decision to run in Minnesota seemed to fly in the face of conventional
political wisdom. No Catholic had ever been elected to such high
office in Minnesota's history. The incumbent senator, Edward Thye,
had been a popular governor and was a well-liked if not outstanding
senator. He was of Norwegian descent and a farmer with impressive
ties to farm, ethnic, and church organizations and was looked on by
rural and small-town Minnesotans as one of their own. There was no
great competition to run against him. The DFL state committee, including Governor Orville Freeman, Lieutenant Governor Karl Rolvaag, and Senator Humphrey, was perfectly willing to meet and approve Gene's candidacy early in the year after our senior congressman,
John Blatnik, had declined the chance to run.

Once Gene had announced that he hoped to be nominated by the
state convention, the Honorable Eugenie Anderson, former national committeewoman and former ambassador to Denmark, announced that she would also seek the nomination. This caused

Governor Freeman and Senator Humphrey to withdraw their original approval of Gene's candidacy and to announce their neutrality. The ensuing struggle was given a great deal of publicity, and, after Gene won the nomination on the second ballot at the convention, probably helped him in the campaign which followed because of the interest which had been aroused. Former Farmer-Labor Governor Hjalmar Petersen ran against Gene in the Democratic primary, but this again was more helpful than harmful, because it gave Gene more statewide attention and distracted people's attention from the Republican candidate.

Gene's victory that fall of 1958 was hailed as a precedent-shattering landmark election. Actually the religious issue had played a very small part in it, an analysis of the vote later showed. A very small, hardly discernible percentage of Catholics might have shifted their vote for Gene. And Protestants had stayed with their party and economic groups. The members of the press, I think, were looking at the wrong indicators, as they were to do in 1968. And they were conditioned by occupational failings—the tendency to rewrite each other and the failure to do very deep research.

In the primary Gene's vote in some of the rural counties had outrun the vote of the Republican incumbent. This surprising fact was the subject of speculation in political columns for three days. How had this city congressman, who had never had a rural constituency, become so popular among the farmers? Finally one of the reporters called Gene for his comment.

"Can you account for your vote in Meeker County?" he asked.

"I think I can," Gene answered. "I like to think that the fact that I was born and grew up there had something to do with it."

Despite the fact that there was little statistical evidence that Gene's election proved much about a Catholic's chance for high office in a predominantly non-Catholic state, interest in it on that score persisted. (It is hard to realize how many old fears and misunderstandings were later exorcised by the very *fact* of a Catholic as President; some of the charges and presuppositions seem absurd now, but they were then the stuff of substantial public debate—

the material for headlines and television talk shows.) Interviews with Gene on this subject abounded and, perhaps because of his election, the subject had more of a national airing than it would otherwise have had. In one interview with Donald McDonald, Gene made some interesting points which revealed, perhaps, that the issue was being kept alive artificially, and that it did not cut as deep as it once had in the heartland of America. He noted that those who professed to fear a Catholic majority always drew their examples from the extremes and overlooked contrary examples—among other things, he noted that liberal France was Catholic and that Catholic Connecticut enthusiastically supported Abe Ribicoff, a Jew, as governor.

McDonald: Did you encounter any religious bigotry in your recent campaign for the Senate? Samuel Lubell, in his pre-election articles, said that he had run into it in talking to voters and so he was not sure which way the election was going. . . .

McCarthy: That's the kind of thing you can get a lot of talk about if you raise the question. Of course Lubell's thesis, I think, is that people vote religion and national origins, so when he goes out to make a survey, he's trying to prove his thesis. . . . It's my general opinion that if the issues are clear and if the differences are clear then religion is of relatively minor importance in a campaign.

But he held that religion did make a difference in the political life:

McDonald: . . . I should think that one's theology and philosophy would determine a man's general outlook at least.

McCarthy: I think that's quite right. I would say that in the first place you would expect to find some reflection of the whole great body of teaching in the Catholic tradition relating to government and politics and the question of social justice and, well, even the simple distinctions between commutative and distributive justice. If you don't have a conception of distributive justice, it's extremely difficult to reason with regard to certain problems.

This point was really involved in the debate over wheat to India several years ago. One member of Congress took the floor and made the rather interesting point—the government had no right to carry on charitable works for the citizens. . . . I responded by saying that really we should not establish that this was an act of charity, that all we were proposing to do could very well be justified in terms of distributive justice. I said that the question of the state of famine existing in India and the surplus production that we had, was really a question in terms of justice.

After 1968 various chroniclers of Gene's presidential campaign —notably Richard Stout and Jeremy Larner—tried to establish that his Catholicism made a difference in his character as a politician. The exchange above the comments which followed come much closer to explaining that the difference, if any really existed, lay in Gene's more clearly defined premises. Gene touched again in this interview on the ever-recurring themes in his speeches and writing: that a Christian in politics should be particularly careful about being truthful, not to misrepresent. "And beyond that—well, you can be truthful and still pervert the people; you might appeal to the emotions at a time when people should be extremely rational, extremely calm." He made the application then in terms of the Communist issue—but the point might well be recalled in regard to his refusal to personalize the race issue in 1968.

Quite inadvertently, it seemed, Gene became a spokesman in the debate which raged in 1959 and 1960: should a Catholic be nominated in 1960? As early as June of 1958 he appeared with Francis B. Sayre, Jr., Episcopal dean of the Washington Cathedral, on the network show "The Big Issue." They were opposed by Dr. John A. Mackay, president of Princeton Theological Seminary, and Glenn Archer, executive director of Protestants and Other Americans United. The latter two argued quite seriously that a Catholic President could not be loyal to his Church and to his country at the same time. In the same period Gene debated more than once with Paul Blanshard, then the scourge of the American hierarchy. He often quoted Dean Sayre who had said that the questions were raised as if only Catholics might have problems with loyalty to the state—as if everyone else could do anything ordered by the state, "and as though they were completely subordinate and subject to the determinations of the government, which is not true. What should a true Quaker do about a declaration of war?"

By June of the next year, 1959, the concern was no longer over the possibility of *a* Catholic candidate for the presidency but over the approaching candidacy of John F. Kennedy. In a long and wide-ranging interview in the *New Republic* under the title "A Catholic in Politics: Conversation with Senator Eugene McCarthy." Gilbert Harrison put pressing questions to Gene: Is there a Roman Catholic "political line" in this country? Would a Catholic majority deprive non-Catholics of their freedoms? Gene's clarification, point by point, could not help but have been useful in dispelling some of the opposition to John F. Kennedy on the ground of his religion.

The 1960 presidential debate was still ahead of us in that November of 1958. To have reached the Senate was both fulfillment and respite for the moment at least. A reporter from *Time* tracked us down at the ranch in New Mexico which had been recommended to us by Stewart Udall as a good place to vacation with the children. His mission was to fill out *Time*'s files on Gene and, after interviewing him exhaustively he came to the edge of the swimming pool where I was floating idly and put a few perfunctory questions. Did I look forward to the social life of a senator's wife? I didn't expect it to be much different from that of a congressman's wife, I said, although I knew that we would be more visible. For we had told each other that we were determined not to let the Senate change us. Gene even insisted that we would not accept invitations from people who had not invited us as a congressional couple. We laughed about the Washington hostess who had said in an interview that she looked forward to entertaining the new senators—and characterized Gene as such "a spiritual dinner partner." But in the end, of course, the Senate by its very nature brought about changes.

I became officially a Senate wife when Muriel Humphrey introduced me at the first meeting of the Ladies of the Senate, much as her husband as senior senator from Minnesota had escorted Gene down the Senate aisle to take his oath. The Ladies of the Senate meet every Tuesday during the session as a unit of the American Red Cross and have done this ever since World War I.

They are presided over by the wife of the Vice President—at that time, Pat Nixon, who sent each of us newcomers a hand-written note of invitation. Pat, who had been a Senate wife herself, was well-liked by the Senate ladies. She was always there, always crisp and correct in her Red Cross uniform, and sometimes showed surprising political astuteness and sometimes a good sense of humor. We used to complain because we had to walk down the hall in the Old Senate Office Building to a public lavatory to wash our coffee cups after lunch; it seemed neither dignified or sanitary. Mrs. Nixon cannily appointed a committee led by Mrs. Dennis Chavez, whose husband, the senior senator from New Mexico, was chairman of the Senate Public Works Committee, to explore with the Capitol architect the possibility of installing a kitchen sink and perhaps a restroom in the quarters where we met. Shortly thereafter I arrived one morning to find the officers in a state of agitation laced with fits of merriment. The architect, carried away by the request from such an important source, had sent us plans for a luxurious suite of rooms complete with a so-called "splash pool" and rows of hair driers.

"They forgot the movie magazines to read under the driers," snorted Pat Nixon, and we all laughed. But it was a serious matter. Suppose the press got the idea that we had requested any such thing. Ruin for our husbands! The plans were returned with a stern refusal, and we were all pledged to secrecy. When, a month or so later, the story turned up, headlined on the front page of the Washington *Post*, we were aghast. The text of the story revealed that it had been lifted from the newsletter of Mrs. Prescott Bush, wife of the senator from Connecticut, whose letter was picked up by a number of Connecticut papers. It spoofed the architect mildly and absolved us, so we were somewhat mollified about Dottie Bush's scoop.

The newsletter was a favorite and effective device used by congressional wives to keep in touch with constituents who were not apt to read the political news with any degree of interest or who wanted to know more about their representatives in Washington than their local newspapers were willing to tell them. One of the most effective was that of Mrs. John Sherman Cooper, wife of the senator from Kentucky. It seemed a good idea and I wanted to try it. Gene had introduced my first one by writing, "Abigail has written this one. If you like it, if you have friends who should be on the mailing list, please let us know." A good part was reprinted in the St. Paul paper and some other papers throughout the state:

These past months have been the busiest we have lived through as a family in Washington. There was the stepped-up activity which came from Gene's representing a whole state rather than one district. But added to that, this 86th Congress was off to a faster start than any in recent history. There never seemed to be a warming up period.

Every senator plunged immediately into hours of committee work and floor debate—plus the extras which are a part of Senate life—correspondence, office appointments, and so on. Then, too, as you've probably read, Washington has played host to more heads of state, prime ministers, and foreign missions in the past few months than at any time since World War II. That meant more official receptions and dinners—more joint sessions of the House and Senate.

Last of all, the mere fact that there were so many new senators—seventeen—intensified Washington social activity. Everyone who must deal with the Senate—the members of the Executive Branch, news commentators, diplomats—wanted to see the new ones. All of us were made very conscious, I think, that, interesting as it is, the Washington round is part of the working life. In the great complexity of federal government itself, and in the multiplicity of international agencies which make Washington the center of the free world, the only way working relationships can be set up is by meeting people personally.

Therefore, there isn't much idle chatter at small Washington dinners, but there is usually a great exchange of mutually useful information. Sometimes the period after dinner seems to go on forever, because the men are so intent on what ever topic draws them together that they quite forget to "join the ladies." The ranking guest is up and off at 10:30, and everyone leaves almost immediately because there is work in the morning and the distances are great.

One day in the supermarket I met both Mme. de Torrenté, wife of the Swiss ambassador, and Señora de Lacarte, wife of the ambassador from Uruguay—each with a chauffeur pushing her cart and each with a list in hand going in and out the aisles with practiced efficiency. Mary, our ten-year-old, was with me, and Margaret, our three-and-a-half year old, was pushing our cart, which made for anything but efficient progress on my part.

We had been at both embassies within the week, and I confess that I had thought how easy it must be to entertain in a huge embassy dining room with butler and footmen at hand, and presumably a wonderful cook in the kitchen. But as I greeted these ladies and watched their hurried progress, I realized that there was really nothing festive about dinner parties for them—it was all in the day's work, and a very steady day-in day-out thing. And no such thing as family shopping expeditions either!

The letter went on to tell about Gene's first speech in the Senate and about Minnesotans coming to Washington—Antal Dorati, then conductor of the Minneapolis Symphony in a guest appearance, and a concert by the Concordia College Choir.

Now it seems to me a solemn sounding letter. I think I always had an idea that one must not let constituents think that we were wasting time or just enjoying ourselves. But the truth was that we were having an interesting and comparatively relaxed time. I have scrapbooks of our invitations which I will sort out someday, but for now there is a crowding of unrelated memories: Mary McGrory and I crowned with laurel—Mary had won a critic's award that year—at a victory party; the social drama at a dinner when fellow guests restrained columnist Joseph Alsop, our host, who had ordered a State Department official out of his house because he found the latter's implication that he was using his guest as news sources insulting; Gene singing the old Irish war ballad "The West's Awake" in duet with our long-time friend, Liz Acosta; the hearty back-slapping humor at the parties of the Class of 1958—the Democratic senators elected that year and dubbed later "the fearless fifteen" by doughty little Senator Stephen Young of Ohio in an elegiac moment; Christmas carol singing at the Walter Ridders' home on the beautiful Potomac Palisades and New Year's parties at which the doors and windows were traditionally thrown open so that we could hear the bells of Washington Cathedral ringing in the New Year; endless excited discussions in one living room or another; splendid embassy desserts of spun sugar or towering frozen molds; the excitement of watching debates and the tally of close votes from the Family Gallery; Washington beautiful in the heavy snows of those years and beautiful with flowering trees in the spring as I made my way to luncheons accompanying Muriel Humphrey, Jane Muskie, Lu Engle, and sometimes, Lady Bird.

And sometimes the wildly improbably happened. When Nikita Khrushchev came to visit the United States, the Congress almost literally fled the capital to avoid holding a joint session, despite President Eisenhower's plea that the Soviet leader be met with every courtesy. Anti-communism was still the badge of orthodox Americanism. Only the Foreign Relations Committee stayed long enough to hold a reception for him. Those of us wives who were left behind in Washington debated what we should do about the reception at the Soviet Embassy. It was an especially difficult question for Muriel Humphrey. After all, Hubert Humphrey had been most royally received in the Kremlin and had held an eight-hour dialogue with Khrushchev which had catapulted Hubert on to the cover of *Life* and given new importance to his possible 1960 try for the presidency.

Muriel and I decided that we would go, but very late, hopefully after the press had melted away. But, as we neared the embassy we found that Muriel had forgotten her entrance card and we retraced our way to Chevy Chase to retrieve it. So we were very late indeed. We arrived to find that the members of the receiving line had retreated to an inner room, a sort of glassed-in conservatory. Members of the Washington press corps were standing on each others shoulders to peer through the clerestory windows, so we went by almost unnoticed. I seized on a passing official and said, "Mrs. Humphrey and I would like to leave our names for the Chairman. Mrs. Humphrey would especially like him to know that she came to pay her respects." And we turned to go with great relief. But the official would not hear of our going. Before we knew it Ambassador Menshikov was summoned and we were whisked into the inner room to join Chairman and Mrs. Khrushchev, their daughter Rada and her husband, the Cyrus Eatons, and the Nixons. We looked at each other in desperation, envisioning Minnesota headlines: MRS. HUMPHREY AND MRS. McCARTHY AT INTIMATE PARTY WITH COMMUNIST LEADERS.

The Chairman seemed in a testy mood. The morning papers had speculated that he was unhappy about Menshikov's inaccurate briefings about conditions in America. And everyone knew that he had been angered by Vice President Nixon's use of the so-called "kitchen debate." He snapped at the ambassador who presented me with what appeared to be some jovial play on our name, and I understood from the interpreter that he had said that he knew very well that there was "a second Senator McCarthy." While Muriel conversed briefly with him, I found myself alone with the Vice President who was standing apart looking lost. He said that he had felt that it was unfair of him to monopolize the Chairman's time and that he wanted to give others a chance to speak with him. Under the circumstances, it seemed as good an explanation as any. In a moment Mrs. Nixon rose and yielded her place on the sofa with Mrs. Khrushchev to Muriel and me.

Mrs. Khrushchev looked pleasant and motherly but her first words to us were that she found American women very disappointing—that there seemed to be no professional women among us. I protested politely that her trip had not been well planned in that regard, that we did have women doctors, lawyers, professors, and owners of businesses. "Why," I said rather stupidly to Rada, who seemed to understand English, "we even have organizations of university women and business and professional women." They stared unbelievingly. Now, in the day of our renewed awareness about the unequal status of women, I realize that they had expected much more from a country of our vaunted progress. And I felt sorry that we were so uneasy about the effect of our visit that we did not take time to enjoy it and take advantage of our opportunity to have a real conversation with them.

Eleanor Roosevelt wrote ruefully of her life in Washington when her husband was in the Navy Department: "It is hard for me now to realize that dinners or contacts with people in society could ever have seemed so important as they did in those first years. I can only explain it by the fact that, so far as I could see, they were the only connection I had with the work my husband was doing, and which I felt was important, though I knew nothing about it at that time. . . .

I think for the good of our own relationship, and of my husband's work we did far more of the social round in Washington than was either necessary or wise." (The last is a sad statement, and even more sad in the light of recent revelations about Eleanor Roosevelt's married life in just the period of which she writes.) Society with a capital S had disappeared from Washington in the years between 1918 and 1958, but the reasons for the social round were approximately the same. . . . Vance Packard's claim that men and women are most separate at the opposite poles of society had even more meaning for me in the context of Senate life. To those Senate wives who came from the issue-conscious and educated middle class where the highest degree of partnership in marriage had developed, the increasing distance from the actual work for shared goals was painful. Often one or the other confided to me that they treasured the minutes spent in the car on the way to or from evening engagements as the only time they really had to talk things over with their husbands. More and more we valued the social life, campaign work, and our contacts with constituents through hospitality, personal correspondence and more organized efforts like the newsletters. They were our ways of sharing in our husband's life.

The Senate life meant changes for Gene's office staff, too. "I don't like it over here," complained Jean Stack, his personal secretary, in one of the first weeks. "Everybody acts like the clerks at Garfinkel's," referring to a Washington woman's specialty store where, the girls in the office felt, they were treated with unseemly hauteur by the aging saleswomen. But Miss Stack was soon to adjust, adapted as she was to the interplay of that curious complex which one Washington paper named the "Third Branch of Congress"—the congressional and committee staffs. The New York *Times* Magazine went farther: "the staff men run Congress." The House had been important, but in the Senate the staffs felt much closer to real power.

Haynes Johnson wrote: "They are the men who run the congressional offices and committee staffs, answer and sign the senator's mail, write the speeches, arrange for interviews, become involved in patronage, help select witnesses and shape hearings, advise and brief members of Congress on technical and complicated issues that affect every American, deal with important constituents, lobbyists, ordinary citizens, and contact other comparable staff men in government agencies on a multitude of problems that are the grist of government work."

On the face of it, Gene's staff did not seem quite specialized enough, or diversified enough, to be a part of such a complex. Mary Richardson Boo, herself briefly his press secretary, wrote of it in an article published in July of 1961: "McCarthy, who is 45, has a young, well-educated staff. All of the top members are 'retired school-teachers,' according to McCarthy. His legislative assistant, Emerson Hynes, a former college sociology teacher, is 45. Administrative Assistant Dick Boo, a former college English teacher, is 33. Other ex-teachers on the staff are George Cashman, a former college English teacher; and Jean Stack, a high school social studies teacher before becoming McCarthy's personal secretary in the House."

Those in that list were all Minnesotans with school connections with Gene except Jean Stack. But because she had come with him from the House side she had a position of seniority. Like many another secretary in the world, she had become invaluable to Gene by her gradual assumption of all the details of our personal affairs which he found too time-consuming or onerous—insurance, leases, income tax, bills, honoraria. This meant, naturally, that I had less and less to do with the decisions in this area of our life. But it relieved me of work, too, at a time when I was very busy with the house and children. I finally did not even see the statements from our joint checking account and became accustomed to signing mortgages and tax statements on the line pointed out by Gene when he brought them home. Inevitably as the years went by and Miss Stack grew older, she became jealous of her prerogatives. A lawyer who did some work for us once tried to improve our insurance arrangements and improve my understanding of our financial affairs. He was astounded when she pursued him into the outer office after he finished talking to Gene and upbraided him for his interference. He was quite shaken when he told me about it. "Good God, Abigail," he said, "she controls my access to the Senator."

"Don't you understand, Mother," Mary had said to me once,

when I was puzzling over some petty misunderstanding with the office staff, "the name of the game—even on that level—is power." I had indeed come to this understanding very slowly.

As I have said, in the early congressional years, the office staff had seemed like our extended family. We were young together; we had mutual friends and interests. I thought our goals the same and that we were all working together for the things Gene stood for in politics. Gradually, however, they had become part of the special world described by Haynes Johnson: "In time as they stay on the Hill they tend to travel in the same circles, attend the same private Hill club, even form formal social associations and meet for theater and cocktail parties. 'You begin to look forward to those three or four lunches a week with the lobbyists at the good restaurants,' said one committee aide, 'to the $25 bottles of scotch, the football tickets, the occasional junkets, and if you don't watch out you get pulled into the lobby frame of reference. And there's another problem. You can begin to lose sight of the important goals because you love the game so much.'"

An unfortunate concomitant of all of this is that the relationship to the officeholder alters. He is no longer friend and associate but the source of power. Everything—even the opportunity to do good on the part of the most disinterested and incorruptible staff member—depends on the relationship with him. As one man said, "It's something like being a member of the king's court in the old days. The staff men are the keepers of the jewels, the confidants and counselors to the mighty." And another, "I'll tell you this, there's more intrigue in a congressional office than anywhere outside the Kremlin."

I was reluctant to believe what one wife wisely told me—that staff inevitably came to look on the officeholder's wife and family as rivals, because they, too, had claim on his time and, even more threatening, were an avenue to him. "It's not that they see it that clearly," she said. "They sincerely believe that they're better for him than you are —they think he shouldn't be bothered with family and wife and their problems. They have to make him larger than life in order to justify spending their lives that way." But I was sure that our staff, mostly devout and idealistic like ourselves, members of the family life and liturgical movements, would never be like that.

But the Senate and the new staff members created a threatening situation even for our old friends. Each new person had to be absorbed into the old framework or frozen out; each new activity was an implied criticism of the old order.

To my hurt surprise, my newsletter, which was received well at home—as we thought of Minnesota—if we could judge by letters, was one such irritant. Old friends told me that they had received calls from one of Gene's assistants excoriating them for encouraging me by praising it. This was the beginning of a series of equally hurtful revelations. Relationships which had sustained me for years turned out to be no relationships at all. Most upsetting of all was the fact that Gene thought the whole thing amusing.

If, when we first fell in love, I had meant new life to Gene, he had meant love and perfect friendship in one person. Loyalty and dedication had been prized ideals to me when I was growing up—reinforced by the books and poems which were to me a kind of second life. I had believed Gene the epitome of these ideals. It had always seemed to me that he was too fine to be deceived by the traditional artifices and subtle manipulation which I, like other girls, had accepted as part of the man-and-woman relationship in my dating years in high school and college. I had assumed perfect openness and trust. His attitude now, typically masculine though it was, was shattering to me. Nothing later was such a blow.

A short time later, Jerome Eller, who was very much a part of the Hill special world, told Gene that some of his staff were deceiving him about Hill regulations about employment. Gene naturally took this evidence of behind-the-scenes manipulation very seriously and made some changes which incidentally made my relationships easier. At about this time Lawrence Merthan, whom I had known since his college days and whom we had visited in Europe where he had spent the postwar period as a foreign service officer and later as an official of a private foundation in Germany, joined the staff. He had been counsel for Gene's special committee on unemployment problems. And in 1963, Jerome Eller came on the staff as Gene's administrative aide.

I abandoned the newsletter and turned my attention to other things which, although they had grown out of our mutual interests, were not so directly a part of Gene's public life. We had been drawn more and more into the ecumenical movement. I accepted posts on various committees and did some speaking. (Eventually I was one of two laymen appointed by Lawrence Cardinal Shehan of Baltimore to a national committee on education and ecumenism. I did some work for the National Council of Churches and edited and contributed to a symposium published as a guide to ecumenism under the title *First Steps in Christian Renewal* in 1967.)

In these years Gene was hospitalized once for pneumonia and had other illnesses which caused him to cut down his schedule in Minnesota. Inevitably there were rumors that he had all sorts of mysterious maladies and that he was going to retire. There was much speculation in the press, usually set off by a slurring statement from a Republican aspirant to the Senate seat. This upset Gene's closest supporters, who continued to urge me to make frequent public appearances as a sort of countermeasure. I had a slide talk on Washington which women's groups and schools seemed to enjoy, and the children often accompanied me when I gave it in order to see different parts of their home state. It was a modification of one originally prepared by Carrie Davis of Tennessee, who let other congressional wives buy the slides and notes. Those of us who used it gradually adapted the talk to our own states and added slides of our own. By the time of Gene's second run for the Senate, my participation in the actual political life at home was almost entirely of this peripheral nature.

In 1960, at the Democratic convention in Los Angeles, Gene nominated Adlai Stevenson for President. He made a ringing speech to the convention, calling on the delegates not to reject the man who carried the party banner in 1952 and 1956:

> Do not reject this man who, his enemies said, spoke above the heads of the people, but they said it only because they did not want the people to listen. He spoke to the people. He moved their minds and stirred their hearts, and this is what was objected to. Do not leave this man without honor in his own party. Do not reject this man.

Gene gave the speech because he was asked to do so by Senator Mike Monroney of Oklahoma, leader of the Stevenson draft and later by Adlai Stevenson himself. Gene was aware, he said, that the chances for a Stevenson nomination were remote, but it seemed to him that the Democratic convention should, if Stevenson wished, consider him for nomination even though it might turn out "to be no more than a tribute." And a tribute it was. Read closely today, the speech can be seen as much a plea for an open convention at it was for the nomination of Stevenson.

The Stevenson speech confirmed the supporters of John F. Kennedy and many political observers in their belief that a feud existed between Gene and John F. Kennedy. By 1968 the existence of this feud was almost taken for granted. The writers of *An American Melodrama* wrote:

> Perhaps the origin of the quarrel lay in the bitterness that Mc-Carthy must have felt as he watched Kennedy rise by successively

laying claim to the very attributes that McCarthy was most proud of in himself—his religion, his liberal political faith, his academic constituency—and to which, with some reason, McCarthy felt he had the better claim. If so it should be said that once McCarthy had dared to oppose them in 1960, the bitterness was fully reciprocated by the Kennedys.

This is the stuff of myth and for its substance, it relies on a quip Gene tossed off early in 1960. It was embroidered on by a reporter, he says, to come out "I should run for President—I'm twice as Catholic as Kennedy, twice as liberal as Humphrey, and twice as smart as Symington." What he actually said was "I'm twice as Catholic as Kennedy and twice as liberal as Humphrey." No one seemed to think then that it meant that he had a feud with either Humphrey or Symington; why should the quip have betrayed a special enmity for Kennedy?

Whether Kennedy shared completely the punitive attitude of his brother Robert and aides toward Gene because of the Stevenson speech I do not know. Certainly, John Kennedy was the product and practitioner of the Massachusetts brand of politics so successfully exported to the rest of the country by the Kennedy organization—a feudal sort of politics at best, built on personal loyalties rather than on issues—and he shared with his brothers the Kennedy family attitude so aptly characterized by Sargent Shriver in 1970: "I'm open to everybody. My wife Eunice says it's because I wasn't brought up the way she was—it was always us against *them*, whoever *they* were." Yet I would doubt it. President Kennedy had a speculative, objective mind and a well-developed sense of history. He surely saw what any objective reporter should have seen —that prior to 1960 it was not he who stood between Gene McCarthy and the presidency if he aspired to it, but Hubert Humphrey, Gene's fellow-Minnesotan. He would have seen the sensible justice of Gene's own words (sometimes men are the best sources of explanation for their own actions):

My participation in presidential politics has reflected not only my beliefs, but also the fact that in three Democratic conventions before 1964 I was called upon as a Minnesotan and one active in our political party to support various efforts and undertakings of Hubert Humphrey.

In 1952 at the Democratic convention in Chicago, I placed in nomination, as a favorite son, Senator Hubert Humphrey of my state of Minnesota.

In 1956, I was a supporter of Senator Humphrey in his bid for the vice-presidential nomination, which was thrown before the convention by the presidential nominee, Adlai Stevenson. My participation was very limited; the contest was principally between John Kennedy and Estes Kefauver. It was the first occasion, however, on which I found myself *quite by accident and geography* supporting the candidate opposed by John Kennedy.

In 1960, I was again, by virtue of essentially the same circumstances, made co-chairman of the Humphrey for President campaign in the primaries. I participated in the campaign in Wisconsin and in West Virginia.

It is hard for popular historians writing today to conceive of a time when John Kennedy was just another man aspiring to the Democratic nomination. Yet that was what he was in 1960. He had to slog through bruising primaries and delegate meetings to prove himself a winner. In Wisconsin in 1968 they were still talking about how hard it was to get a crowd out for an event planned for Kennedy in the early days of the 1960 primary—a handful of six or eight in Chippewa Falls, a top of sixty in Green Bay even when he was accompanied by Jackie. When he finally won the election, it was by the slimmest margin in history, a fraction of 1 per cent. It was only because of the personal decision of Richard Nixon that the vote was not contested. This seems unimaginable today as we look back on his glamorous and fabled years as President. But Gene's support for Stevenson has to be put in this context.

It is perhaps also hard for a new generation of journalists to realize that Hubert Humphrey was a popular, even a beloved man, and that the ties of personal and regional loyalty made fellow Midwesterners, especially Minnesotans, the willing servant of his ambitions. It was only after the primaries of 1960 that the façade of this loyalty began to crack, with the canny cultivation of Governor Orville Freeman as a potential vice-presidential candidate and his selection as nominator of Kennedy.

The story that Gene aspired to the vice presidency that year is also nonsense when looked at in historical context. "It was obvious," Gene wrote, "that John Kennedy, had he not been nominated for the presidency, would have been the vice-presidential choice of either Stevenson or Johnson or of any other candidate who might have been nominated."

John Kennedy was a political realist as is evidenced by his choice of Lyndon B. Johnson as vice-presidential candidate in 1960. Despite the extraordinary explanation to the protesting Michigan delegation —that he had not expected Lyndon to accept—and the even more extraordinary explanation given by Kenneth O'Donnell, one of President Kennedy's special assistants, that Johnson would be more trouble as Senate Majority Leader than as Vice President, I am convinced that he knew he needed Lyndon Johnson's support to win. No other Southerner had the same support in the South and the legislative credentials to be acceptable in the North. I also think that he knew his own time was limited and that Lyndon Johnson had unique qualifications for the presidency. In like manner, whatever John Kennedy may have said to his family and friends about Gene—and I am blessed in not knowing with certainty what this was—he was certainly aware of his usefulness and his gifts.

Jack Kennedy was serving in the House of Representatives when Gene was elected in 1948. They were casual friends during that time. He was then a rich and highly eligible bachelor sought after for Georgetown dinner parties, and Gene, though almost immediately well known as an outstanding and well-thought-of newcomer in the House, was relatively poverty-stricken and mired in the domesticity of young parents.

We lunched with Jack Kennedy one day when I happened to be visiting the House with Ellen who was only two or three years old. Ellen fell off her chair and he reached under the table and picked her up without pausing in his conversation. He had the indifferent but capable attitude of a young uncle used to children but not particularly involved with them.

At another lunch he introduced Jackie who was working as an "inquiring reporter" at the Capitol. She was wearing a thick gray sweater and wore her very curly hair pulled back into a knot at the time. We had no indication that she was special; he was dating many girls, among them Mary McGrory occasionally. When we received our invitation to the wedding in Newport, it seemed to us out of the question to go, since we were in Minnesota with many commitments for the summer.

We saw them from time to time at dinner parties in the ensuing years. I remember especially one dinner party in early 1960. It was clear that they had invited us with the object of softening Doris Fleeson, our friend and at that time a very powerful political columnist who was adamantly opposed to the Kennedy candidacy. The evening was not successful in that Gene inadvertently evoked Doris' rage about a vote on which the then Senator Kennedy had not been right in her opinion, and Jack muttered under his breath, "Cut it out, will you? You're supposed to help me with her."

He was candid in discussing his aspirations and his chances, apparently understanding the fact that prior loyalty committed us to the support of Hubert Humphrey. But, as we were leaving, he drew me aside to ask whether I would head his woman's effort in Minnesota. I was genuinely astonished. I thought he was the candidate most likely to win, but the Minnesotans of the 1948 campaign were still a close-knit team and our party was looked on as one of the most unified and grass-roots state parties in the nation. I said, "Why, Senator, I couldn't do that. We have a candidate in Minnesota."

"I know," he said. "Not now, but later."

Later, however, the tactics of the West Virginia primary had alienated the people like us, and the Stevenson effort was growing.

In at least one instance, in the appointment of Orville Freeman as Secretary of Agriculture, Kennedy followed Gene's advice rather than that of Hubert Humphrey who was supporting a farm organization man. The appointment also ran contrary to the Kennedy axiom, "Never go with the loser." I can still see him standing in the hospital room talking to Gene, who was ill with pneumonia after the exhausting campaign of 1960, in which he had traveled over 60,000 miles soliciting disaffected Stevensonian liberals for votes for the Kennedy-Johnson ticket. "And almost all of it in the places where only the DC-3s and the Convairs fly," he had said later.

"But how about Freeman for head of the Veterans Bureau?" John Kennedy asked. "After all, he lost in Minnesota." "I don't think it's good enough," Gene answered. I was sitting in the corner with my knitting, but I interposed timidly, searching my mind frantically for a title to call a President-elect ("Jack" was certainly not proper in context of the conversation). I decided to go the whole way, "Mr. President, people would never understand. After all, he nominated you. It's an emotional thing." This seemed to me a very important argument to make. As the great mythical quality of the Kennedy years has developed in the nation's memory, few perhaps remember that one of the arguments advanced against John Kennedy as a Democratic candidate was the he was cold. "He isn't, you know," Sargent Shriver told us one night during a pre-election visit to Minnesota. "He's like my wife. They really feel deeply." And Henry Brandon, a Kennedy friend, wrote of him that year, confessing frankly that he had been amazed to discover "his driving ambition." He had thought of him, he said, as a curious mixture of playboy and earnest student of history and politics. "Essentially, he is a pragmatist, a tough-minded idealist, a utilitarian humanist. He may lack warmth, he may be cold and calculating, but those eager to work for him suspect or at least hope that he would follow up ideas with action." But in his candidate days, Kennedy's speeches in his pre-nominee days were not particularly stirring and they were delivered in a flat Boston accent with little or no passion. The doubt about his warmth still lingered after the close—far too close to be comfortable—victory, tainted as it was by the allegation of the manipulation of the vote in Cook County. A rejection of Orville Freeman, who had nominated him, seemed a needless underscoring of this doubt.

Shortly after his election, President Kennedy proposed to the president of the Gridiron Club that Gene be the respondent for the Administration at the annual Gridiron dinner. The Gridiron, a select group of fifty from the Washington press corps, each year prepares a satirical revue dealing with current political events and presents it at a dinner honoring publishers and important political figures. It can be an uncomfortable ordeal for the President who is, of course, always invited. Some Presidents have refused to come. Others have responded with their own speeches. It was a flattering and formidable assignment for Gene. His speech was brilliantly biting and witty, but it was so packed with mordant and trenchant satire that I doubt that his audience appreciated it.

Although Gene's wit was a staple at Minnesota political dinners and was already celebrated in the Midwest and in New York and California, this audience, impatient for its traditional broad and farcical entertainment, was unprepared for it and therefore largely unappreciative. The President later said of Gene's speech, according to Gridiron president Robert Riggs of the Louisville *Courier-Journal*, that it was the most sophisticated political commentary he had ever heard.

During the fall of 1961, President Kennedy made a visit to Minnesota, in order to be honored at a $100-a-plate dinner—a traditional way of raising money to pay off campaign debts. The Humphrey Senate campaign and primary campaigns had taken a heavy toll in Minnesota and donors badly needed the psychological lift of a presidential visit. Such a visit is always an occasion for a struggle among the various factions within the party.

The President was scheduled to attend Mass at the St. Paul Cathedral and a number of Democratic party Catholics wanted to accompany him. Among those so intent on praying with the President were lawyer Pat O'Connor, later Humphrey-appointed head of the Democratic National Committee; Cortland Silver, a St. Paul jeweler who always described himself as half-Irish, half-Jewish; Fred Gates, the vending machine millionaire who was Senator Humphrey's best friend and man Friday; and the state AFL-CIO leader, Robert Hess.

The trip was advanced by Ray Rasenberger, a young Washington lawyer we knew rather well because of our children's friendship. He reported to us that the President had said, "No, I only want Gene and Abigail with me because I know damn well they always go to church." The others were to sit near by. The Mass was to serve two purposes. It was an expedient way of showing courtesy to the junior senator and a way of drawing the line as to companions. On the long trip between Minneapolis and St. Paul, the President's casual conversation reflected that interesting mind of his —politically practical, curious about men and events, and cheerfully cynical. He commented on the sparseness of crowds along the way and the implication was clear that the Minnesota party might have done a better job of crowd-raising. He was interested in Minnesota history and squabbled mildly with me when I said that the Town and Country golf course which we were passing was the second oldest in the country. He was interested in where F. Scott Fitzgerald had lived and he was frank about his own casual Catholicism. He teased me about the Missal I was carrying and said, "That seems to be the thing now—Teddy carries one around that he can hardly lift with both hands." (When in 1964 a photographer made me a present of a picture of our entry into church that day, I surprised myself by bursting into tears.)

The reassessment of the Kennedy administration is just beginning; we can see it now as an Administration still committed to the ideology of the Cold War, the Administration which committed us initially to Vietnam. But it was an Administration which lifted all our spirits and gave the world new hope for exactly the reasons John Kennedy foresaw when he talked with Henry Brandon in 1960:

"Youth—I've come on the political scene at a time when the leadership is old. The President is old, his health has been affected, his leadership is not wholly successful, and therefore I think there is a desire to turn a new page and start with a newer leadership, fresher, and we hope more vigorous."

It was the loss of new beginnings embodied in a worthy human being which started my tears that day.

Once in the pew, the President started when the congregation broke out into a strong-voiced *Missa recitata* and said, "God, nobody briefed me on this." Out of deference to the President who did not know the responses, Gene also stood mute through the service. The crowds had been thick as we approached the cathedral and the President had been welcomed at the side door by Bishop Keefe, the Auxiliary Bishop, the Archbishop having already left for Rome and Vatican Council II called by Pope John XXIII. Bishop Keefe, torn between Pope and President, stayed during the first part of the Mass so that he could deliver a welcoming and appropriate homily, at the end of which he said that he must be off himself to the Vatican Council and took his leave, disappearing across the marble sanctuary floor into the dark recesses of the cathedral. His predictions in the homily for the prospects of the Vatican II were most cautious, and the President commented *sotto voce* that he didn't think the Bishop quite got the pitch of the new thing.

The circumstances of this Mass seemed somewhat prophetic to me the next year when Gene was asked by the White House to go to Rome to feel out the prospect of a presidential visit. But, more important, to find out whether the Vatican really disapproved of American co-operation with the Italian government's "opening to the left"—the *apertura a sinistra*—which was the hopeful and much discussed stance of the Christian Democrats in control at the time. The State Department held that this posture was disapproved of by the Vatican.

John Kennedy, as a Catholic President, felt that he could not send an envoy to the Vatican, but he was convinced that good relations there would be helpful to the implementation of his foreign policy. He was skeptical also of the intelligence on Italian affairs coming from the American Embassy.

Gene had other reasons for going to Europe at the time—reasons which would provide adequate "cover" for the trip. There were always things for the Finance Committee to investigate; and it was only natural that in his capacity as a well-known Catholic layman, he would want to visit Rome and Vatican II, which was attracting so much attention at the time. In Rome there were also FAO meetings to attend.

We took Mary, who was then fourteen, with us. Lawrence Merthan, Gene's legislative aide, who had a great deal to do with the arranging of the visit, accompanied us. It was a joyful time to be in Rome. The city and the people seemed to bask in the geniality and goodness of the surprising man who was Pope and everywhere there was a conviction that a new day had dawned.

Rome was full of our friends, not only among the bishops, but also theologians and writers. People we knew or with whom we had connections thronged the hotels and rooming houses. Bob Kaiser of *Time* and his wife had an apartment which they shared with the spectacular Archbishop Roberts of Bombay, known rather irreverently as "Ban-the-Bomb" Roberts. We had dinner there with various *periti* (experts), writers, and Protestant observers. At the time it was generally assumed that Bob Kaiser, Archbishop Roberts, and our old friend Monsignor George Higgins collaborated with Father Xavier Murphy, C.Ss.R., on the "Xavier Rynne" articles in the *New Yorker* which bypassed the Council secrecy in fascinating detail and probably had some effect on the course of the Council itself.

Dé Groothuizen of the Grail had entertained us at lunch with Hans Küng, the young German theologian, then as much the center of controversy as he is now. We sat in the observers' tribune at the Council itself with old friends like Robert McAfee Brown and Dr. John Bennett, dean of the Union Theological Seminary. By the time the carefully planned-for meeting with Pope John was set and the even more important meeting with Secretary of State Cicognani, we had a very good idea of the temper of the Council and of the Vatican itself.

Mary McGrory was in Rome on assignment to cover the Council. She and Larry took Mary about when we were otherwise involved. With her customary flair, Mary McGrory had made a home for herself in a little hotel called the Eden and had discovered sights, restaurants, and people which she was bent on our sharing. She had fallen in love with Pope John, savoring every anecdote of his humanity. Her favorite restaurant was the Abruzzi, a place of sawdust floors, bare white tables, and good food, which specialized in the pasta of Pope John's native region. When she heard that we were to have a private audience which would include our daughter Mary, she insisted on accompanying us. I was a little upset at the prospect; it seemed almost sacrilegious to bring an uninvited person to a private papal audience, but I could understand her desire very well. We finally decided that all Irish could claim relationship in the general sense, and word was conveyed to the appropriate office that the senator and his wife would be accompanied by his daughter and a relative.

The papal translator who met us was Irish and from Ireland. He welcomed us with some reserve, I thought, perhaps disapproving of the overly warm welcome being extended to an American senator. Cardinal Cicognani welcomed Gene very warmly indeed. He had met Gene at St. John's and he had, in his own days as papal delegate in Washington, known of Gene's theological and philosophical stands. He and Gene retired to his office for their discussion, leaving Mary, Mary McGrory, and me to the rather chilly hospitality of the monsignor who spent most of the time trying to find out who Mary McGrory was. I found him less than congenial and did not feel quite so sacrilegious as I parried his carefully veiled questions with vague answers equally as careful. Mary McGrory countered his curiosity by launching an attack of very specific questions as to his own background, linguistic abilities, education, home, and so on. She pushed him into reminiscences of Ireland and recounted her own adventures there. When we finally went into the Holy Father, he rather lamely introduced Mary as the senator's *sobrina* (cousin).

Pope John, who must already have been ill from the malady which finally killed him, welcomed us with cordiality and verve—which what could only be called a sprightliness in manner and gesture which one would expect to be surprising in one so heavy; but in truth he was light on his feet and appeared more round than fat. (Pictures were always unkind to him.) He welcomed Gene as one of whom he had heard much that was good and one who had very good friends including, as he said, twinkling, "the Secretary of State, Cardinal Cicognani." He turned to me to say that he had heard much about me, about my writing and speaking. This was in Italian and the monsignor did not think it significant enough to translate, but Mary McGrory did.

The Pope led us to the audience part of the chamber and seated us first, fussing a little hospitably as he did so, and only then climbed on the platform to sit in the thronelike chair of audience.

He talked charmingly to our Mary of his sisters, who were, he said, all named Mary—with names like Maria Emilia, Maria Assunta. One of his sisters who had died early, he said, was very good and his mother had always taken him to her grave to pray that he might be as good. He added humorously that he had another sister who was not so good, who was in fact "a little witch." Again, the monsignor seemed to feel that this should go untranslated and it was only as we were finally leaving the chamber, with hands full of the gifts the Holy Father had given us—velvet-cased medals and rosaries—that Mary McGrory said to him, "Santissimo," and continued in Italian, "did you say your sister was a little witch?" Whereupon he laughed and said, "Oh, yes, but it was, you know, a joke."

When the Pope switched to French, it was clear that he felt it was time to come to the diplomatic point of the audience, the discussion of the President's message. Gene, who had always fancied that he actually spoke French since he studied with Father Clarus Graves at St. John's long ago, had assured the translator that he did. (He once gave a speech in French to the Chamber of Commerce in Casablanca. It was enthusiastically, if uncomprehendingly, received.) So the translator ceased functioning at that point. The Pope inquired delicately as to the President's health. Gene assured him in English that the President was well and was doing well. After that, silence. Mary McGrory and I looked at each other in consternation. Wasn't Gene going to say anything? Apparently, he wasn't. Mary McGrory signaled to me frantically to say something. I dearly wanted to but I was sure that it was the most inappropriate of things to do. What would the Pope think?

The Holy Father saved the situation. He launched into a disquisition on what he had heard about the President, about the fact that he was much interested in him, of the fact that there was much new in the world and that he thought the President would do new things, that he had had the pleasure of meeting the President's mother, his sister, his sister-in-law, but not the President himself. The implication was clear. Gene said he was sure the President would like to meet the Holy Father and the Pope switched back to Italian for the concluding part of the audience.

I will always remember that, when we were leaving and as I kissed his ring, he said to me in English, "Good-by, Abigalia." I thought he said it in sympathetic tones and I was convinced that he had seen my distress in the audience chamber. Mary McGrory hardly waited for the elevator doors to close behind us when she began expostulating with Gene about his silence. Why hadn't he conveyed the President's message to the Holy Father? "I thought he knew what he was doing," said Gene. "I didn't think he needed me to tell him anything." That didn't seem to be the point. The Pope's knowledge had not been the issue, I thought. But Gene had ever been impatient of conventional formalities. The language of gesture and the symbolic was always foreign and distasteful to him. (I realized later that he had come to the conclusion that it was demeaning to seek to make the Pope more useful to an American administration.) He told us that Cardinal Cicognani had rejected the President's offer to identify someone in the Embassy as his unofficial representative if the Vatican would designate someone on their side so that there could be more direct communication. "This is not a political Pope," Gene quoted Cicognani as saying. "He thinks political matters should take care of themselves. He is concerned with the heart of the Church."

It was Larry Merthan who carried the results of this meeting to the White House. It was duly conveyed to us later by Mary McGrory that the White House felt that Gene had snubbed the President by not making the presentation himself.

Of our trips abroad the one we made to Chile, during which Gene was conducting an informal investigation for President Kennedy, is the most vivid in my memory. Its pattern is such a simple travel chronicle, the tale of a mildly unusual congressional trip, yet its purpose had such far-reaching implications.

I was home in Minnesota when Gene called to say that he had been asked by the Administration to go to the Third International Christian Democratic Conference which was to be held in Santiago. Over the years, Gene had been in touch with the various leaders of the Christian Democratic parties from Europe and South America. They usually came to see him when delegations from the various countries with strong parties came to the United States—because his writings on the Christian in politcs were known to them. (They were put in touch with him informally, sometimes through George Donahue, of the board of the Committee for an Effective Congress.)

In those initial years of the Alliance for Progress, members of the Kennedy administration were eager to assess the strength of this third force in Latin America and to get some information on the strength of its leaders. As usual, they were doubtful of the evaluation of the State Department, which, as the Kennedy papers make clear, they looked upon as the defender of the status quo. Relations with an opposition party are difficult to establish and maintain outside the diplomatic framework, however. Having heard of Gene's contacts, probably through White House assistant Ralph

Dungan, a close friend of Larry Merthan, the President wished Gene to attend the Congress as an informal observer.

The trip to South America seems a strange one still. One zigzags across the bulge of the equator to end the journey in our own hemisphere in a climate very like ours, in cities like and yet very unlike ours, and with everything strangely upside down. The seasons are at odds and there are different stars in the sky.

At that time jets did not go beyond Lima and when we boarded the plane for the next leg of the trip to Santiago we found it a smaller plane crowded with a chanting and shouting group of young people who watched us take our three reserved seats in the back with deep interest—they were university students on their way to the Congress in Santiago from Venezuela. The hostile reception Richard Nixon had experienced in Caracas in 1958 was still vivid in every American mind, and I was made uneasy by the realization that we were three obviously affluent North Americans, alone on a plane in a crowd of excited, gesticulating Latinos, some of them clad like Cuban guerrillas. Neither Gene nor Larry spoke Spanish and mine was rudimentary at best. We became the object of long speeches which seemed to concern North American and South American relations. We conveyed sympathetic responses as well as we could by nods and smiles. The steward came back to act as translator and to ease these young people toward their seats.

Gene's appearance was apparently reassuring. When it became clear that we, too, were on our way to the Congress in Santiago— a meeting which seemed to them to assure worldwide support for quiet revolutionary change in Latin America—they adopted us with a great show of camaraderie. They invited us to join in their songs. One or the other would come back at intervals making wide gestures of friendship and conveying with signals what the correct relations between North and South America—hands held side by side, "Sí!"; one hand on top of the other, "No!"

As we approached Santiago the pilot announced that we would not be able to land because of fog. The universal groan from the passengers indicated that this was a frequent occurrence. The small plane flew through what Chilenos called the *cordillera*, the one true pass between Chile and Argentina. It was dwarfed by Andean peaks on each side and buffeted about by the capricious winds of the pass. Mount Aconcagua towered bleak and black and inimical to human kind, not like any other mountain landmark, it seemed to us.

We came down into the little sports capital of Mendoza in Argentina into a small airport where confusion reigned, flight after flight having been rerouted there. The airline promised us that we would return to Chile as soon as the fog lifted. We ran into the Chilean ambassador to Washington and his wife who had been vacationing but who had decided to go on to Rio and back to the United States rather than wait for return clearance to Santiago. "Twice through the *cordillera* in midwinter is too much," said Senora Müller cryptically, leaving me to cope with the hidden terror which rides with the mother who is thousands of miles away from her children and in fear of never seeing them again. (This powerful surge of maternal feeling—more biological, I suppose, than anything else—never ceased to surprise me when it came upon me. Once, when we were at the opera in Paris, I was seized by such an overpowering feeling—it came on in an instant—what am I doing here when my children are there?—that I shook as if with a chill.)

As time went by and any return seemed more and more unlikely, Larry had discovered that there was an American military advisory group at the Argentinian air base nearby and he got in touch with them to announce in his most authoritarian terms that an American senator was in Mendoza. After what seemed an interminable time, a car and an agitated major arrived from the air base and things began to fall into place. Feeling weary and very grubby, we went home with the major for drinks. This was our first experience with the far-flung military advisory role that was, in the years to come, to precipitate such tragic complications for the United States. The officers and their wives were pleasant people from small towns in the United States and their attitude was that of colonial functionaries anywhere. They enjoyed the privileges of a ruling class.

Mendoza is a Spanish colonial town situated in vineyard country below the gentler eastern slopes of the Andes. It had been a favorite skiing center for Perón and his followers and was still very much a resortlike town, conscious of its charm and its visitors. We walked its polished, tiled sidewalks that night, and again the next morning, marveling at the freshness of the air, the vitality and geniality of the people we met.

Back at the hotel we found a carnival atmosphere. The youth delegation was in possession of the small lobby and milled in and out from short excursions into the streets of Mendoza, pleased over their unexpected visit to Argentina. Once sure of a bed and having had our first showers in two days, we took a table in a restaurant where, after an excellent meal of Argentine beef with the wine of the region, we sat up late enjoying the singing contest between our student fellow passengers and some of the local Argentinian youths.

The next day we braved the *cordillera* again and finally arrived in Santiago to be met by a Christian Democratic delegation and the United States chargé d'affaires, Minister John Jova and his wife, who were mildly worried about what such a breakdown in travel arrangements had done to the nerves and temper of that most dreaded of creatures in diplomatic circles—a United States senator. They were relieved by Gene and Larry's obvious affability. Gene was rushed off to a press conference and they took me with them.

There had been an anxious briefing for Gene as he left the plane. The Bay of Pigs was still very fresh in Latin-American minds and Chile was a country with a strong Communist party whose press had free play. When Gene and his escorting press officer came, it was apparent that Gene had confounded the hostile reporters to some extent by drawing a close parallel between Minnesota and Chile, referring to our past conflicts with absentee mine owners and shrugging off the conflict between the two most important Christian Democratic leaders, Eduardo Frei and Radomiro Tomic, with a quip about Tomic's forebears: "We have troubles with the Yugoslavs in the DFL party in Minnesota, too," he said, "but the troubles are always before election—we're all good friends afterwards."

About the Bay of Pigs? It was perhaps not the right time to invade Cuba. When was the right time? "Eighteen ninety-eight," answered Gene.

The Jovas, later good friends of ours, were carefully noncommittal about the purpose of our visit but very knowledgeable and helpful about the people we might want to see. That evening we met members of the various Christian Democrat delegations from all over the world at a reception given by Horacio Walker Larraín, the grand old man of the party. (Indeed the Larraíns, one of the oldest Spanish families in Chile, seemed to be everywhere in the arena of Christian reform. Eduardo Frei's wife, a charming, vivacious, and motherly woman, was a Larraín, and her brother, Monsignor Larraín, had founded hospices for the street children of Chile which he directed with the devoted assistance of women volunteers and university students.)

We dined with the Freis the next night. Theirs was the modest home of the university professor. We were enormously struck by Frei himself—a handsome, hawk-nosed, energetic intellectual with the qualities of leadership which, as it was said of him later, would have made him a world force had his country been one of the major countries of the world.

It was easy to fall into discussion with the Christian Democrats. They had the same questions we had long asked about world capitalism and the technological revolution which had enriched many but left the poor poorer than ever. They had the same interests in the distribution of land and wealth and the necessity for the restructuring society. In addition, they were—at least, the Chileans were—practical politicians.

There was, however, to us the puzzling gap between theory and practice which seemed to prevail sometimes in the Latin-American countries. There was a very attractive couple there that evening at the Freis. The woman was a dazzling, slender brunette in a Parisian-made black frock. She was the mother of thirteen children, she told me, and laughed—"You see it is easy for me. In America you could not do it. Here I can have a maid for each child!" He taught, as so many of them did, part-time at the university, but owned, I was told, one of the largest *fincas* in the country. He was the author of a book on land reform. When I inquired innocently if he had instituted land reform on his *finca*, he said, "Oh no, it is not yet time."

It had been arranged before we left the United States that I make use of my time in Chile by learning as much as I could that would be helpful for Gene's report on the country. Our friend Kate Alfriend, the Washington executive secretary of CARE, had arranged for me to visit some of their projects in Chile. In fact, it was one of her hopes that traveling congressional wives might act as informal observers of American help abroad and report it, since CARE had no funds for traveling observers. The Embassy arranged other contacts and I had some of my own. The next morning I started on my little expedition while Gene and Larry were busy at the conference. I breakfasted early with Carmen Miró, a young woman from Panama who had been a student at St. Catherine's and whose family were now political refugees. Carmen was working for the United Nations in Chile. She startled me in the midst of her passionate discussion of the social problems in Latin America by saying in a casual aside, "Of course, the Vatican must accept birth control." Like many pre-Vatican II Catholics, I thought the Church immovable on this question.

The report I wrote after our return startles me today more than anything else because so many of the conditions I described are so little changed according to current reports. I wrote: "The few days I spent in Santiago, Chile, left me with a confused impression of a busy, modern city beset with centuries-old, almost insoluble problems," and then I went on to describe the poverty of the co-operatives, the problem of the passivity of the poor, the legacy of centuries on the great rural *fundos* and the mines where the *patrones* and the employers thought and willed for the workers. I visited clinics, nursery schools, self-help housing projects, and rural institutes.

"Land reform is inevitable in Chile," I concluded my report. "In the meantime a nation which could well feed itself must still import food. The system of food distribution, now under study, may some day make available through efficient storage and refrigeration, the wealth of protein in sea food off Chile's miles of coastline. Until that is done, however, thousands go hungry. A CARE food program could make a great difference in a country in which there is such need and much hope."

The food problem in Chile was frustrating to many casual North American observers. When I returned to the hotel one afternoon there was a call for Gene which I took in his absence. It was a young man from Minnesota who was studying the co-operative potentialities in Chile: "You won't believe it, Mrs. McCarthy, these people aren't much more than fifty miles away from the sea at any given point for a thousand miles, yet they have no means of getting this cheap protein to the hungry and no way of refrigerating it and preserving it. It's a crime."

The same forces in Chilean life which were supporting the rural institutes were supporting the co-operative efforts; the international arms of American labor unions were also. But the leaders of American business established or with investments in Chile, in concert with the conservatives led by President Jorge Alessandri, seemed to look on any of these reforms as an open door to revolution.

When Gene returned to Washington, he was convinced that the Christian Democrats presented a good choice for Chile, that they had practical plans, that they were adept politically, and that they were in touch with the people. The Administration, already tempted to give covert help to the Christian Democrats in the forthcoming Chilean elections because of the strength of the postwar Christian Democratic parties in Europe as alternatives to the Communist party, felt the next step was to evaluate the leaders personally and to build support for such aid in the Congress.

Therefore, it was arranged in complicated ways that a symposium on Latin America be held at Georgetown University and that Senators Frei and Tomic be invited to speak. Dr. Heinrich Rommen, our old friend, by now a professor at Georgetown, joined them in a symposium on Christian democracy. I remember the long wait one Sunday afternoon as Gene tried to get through a call to Santiago about some last minute hitch in the plans for the Chileans arrival.

Once they were in Washington, everything went very smoothly, Gene gave a luncheon for them on Capitol Hill to introduce them to members of the Senate, especially members of the Foreign Relations Committee. He recounted with amusement afterwards Senator Frei's tendency to bolster his remarks with quotations from the papal encyclicals—"Not exactly the evidence with which to impress Senator Fulbright." We gave a dinner party for Senators Frei and Tomic to meet Senator Wayne Morse of Oregon, at that time chairman of the subcommittee on Latin America, and selected members of the press including, of course, Mary McGrory. Ralph Dungan of the White House staff and his wife were also there.

The highlight of the trip as far as the visitors were concerned was a private tour of the White House which included a back-door visit with President Kennedy in his office. As far as we were to know officially the scenario ended there. Subsequent events made it clear that President Kennedy's impression of Frei was a positive one, and that Frei was to receive help in his campaign for election as President of Chile—heaven only knows how. We did not really want to know. Gene wanted to be of service to the Administration. He was enthusiastic about Frei. But there was in all this, in retrospect, another kind of innocence and what came to be in the subsequent years Gene's battle cry: "The abuse of institutions." There was in these missions—on the part of the Administration—a rather cynical use of Gene and his personal associations. It was perhaps the reason he stubbornly refused the Administration full psychological capitulation.

The first person to call me was Mrs. McCarthy," confided Lyndon Johnson to Walter Cronkite in an interview about his announcement to the nation that he would not seek his party's nomination. Richard Dudman, Washington chief of bureau for the St. Louis *Post-Dispatch*, brought me the pre-broadcast transcript so that I would not be astonished when I heard these words in their context and with the implication with which Lyndon Johnson invested them. They were indeed astonishing. But by the time of that broadcast, I had long since ceased to feel astonishment at anything. It was a statement with an undertone of petty malice. It did not surprise me but it saddened me. I had been, in my time, an admirer of Lyndon Johnson. I had admired his take-charge quality as Majority Leader, believed that the motives were good which led him to champion and win the cause of civil rights in Congress and to battle so mightily for the poor and for those deprived of education. I felt that both he and his wife acted within a Texas frame of reference; I felt that they were often unfairly criticized for regional characteristics and habits of thinking.

I called the White House from Wisconsin the night of Lyndon Johnson's announcement purely on impulse. I was genuinely moved, and I believed that he had come to the decision sorrowfully, nobly, because he thought it best for the country. I think I meant to ask for Lady Bird, glad that I could say something heartfelt and good about the President. But the President was on the line almost at once and I said what was in my heart at the moment, that I admired him profoundly for his decision and that I knew what it must have cost him. I was almost immediately sorry because there was in the President's voice such a note of suppressed triumph that I could not miss it. It was the familiar voice of one who felt that he had once again stolen the march on everyone—the voice of a man who operated in the supreme confidence that he could outmaneuver anyone.

"Honey," he said, "I'm just one little person. It's not important what happens to me."

Even as I protested uncomfortably, even as he asked about Gene and I said, "He isn't here yet, Mr. President, but I'm sure he'll want to talk to you," even as the conversation went on almost as I had imagined it would, my mind was racing and tumbling with the thoughts and suppositions awakened by that voice and a larger-than-life protestations of humility. Did he not see the divisions in the nation after all? Did he think it all political maneuvering: Was he doing this only to stimulate a draft for himself in Chicago? It was all supposedly explained in the former President's book *Vantage Point*, but the questions stick in my mind.

Then he was saying, "Let me put Bird on." There was a long pause and I knew, as surely as if I were there, that Lady Bird did not really want to talk to me, that she was wounded and angry at the course the President had been forced to take, and that in her mind I was classed among the disloyal friends who had brought him to this pass. Then she was on and I was repeating what I had said to the President, meaning it at least for her, feeling that it was as important for her as it was for me to feel that her husband acted from the best of motives. I was taken aback when she said, referring to the sons-in-law, "When you have two boys out there, you know what Vietnam is about."

Could she really not understand the many, many young men who recoiled from the war as a matter of conscience? Still, I understood what she was trying to tell me and I understood her coolness and restraint far better than the President's tone.

It became conventional wisdom later—especially after the President's telecast—to attribute his announcement that night before the Wisconsin primary to a combined effort to avoid almost certain defeat in that primary and to maneuver around future primaries by laying the groundwork for a draft at the convention. Remembering the President's voice that night I think that this is perfectly possible, but I also believe with Bill D. Moyers, who wrote, "I think the only answer that really makes sense is the most simple answer of all. He believes that it is necessary for him to step aside if the country is to succeed in achieving the two things he most fervently sought in 1963: unity and reconciliation."

We always forget that a man can be many things at the same time, that he can combine in one person very noble thoughts and very ignoble behavior. Eliot Janeway the economist and Senator Vance Hartke of Indiana had always insisted that the President would wilt under a direct challenge. This was probably true. Lyndon Johnson had no taste for a direct contest. Long years in the vote counting of Congress had habituated him to arranged victory. Nor could he change the nature which made him take glee in the thought of Hubert Humphrey struggling to hear through the faulty transmission in Mexico City this announcement which would mean so much to him, of Gene with the edge being taken off his victory in Wisconsin, of Bobby Kennedy robbed forever of the role of giant killer. In order to achieve this effect, he had had to keep his announcement secret from his closest friends and advisers, revealing it even to Lady Bird only just before the telecast.

I think that it was in this last aspect—the willingness to let the trust of friends and associates go by the board for the sake of an effect—that Lyndon Johnson's true weakness lay.

The events at the 1964 Atlantic City convention, at which he pretended to be hesitating about his choice of Vice President, seemed rooted in just that attribute. Atlantic City and its aftermath was the culmination of our long and ambivalent relationship with the Johnsons. During the House years, Gene saw quite a bit of Senator Johnson because of his friendship with Texas congressmen, especially Homer Thornberry who was very close to him. But I probably saw much more of Lady Bird because she was a member of my 81st Club to which we were both most loyal and of my international group which we both enjoyed very much.

"Women can afford friendships," Gene said once philosophically. "Men can't seem to have them."

In a way this is true, but it is true because women, unlike men, are willing to accept a friendship with qualifications. They accept the fact that their lives are determined by relationships, that before they are persons they are somebody's wife, somebody's mother. And that no matter how much they may love a friend, that friend has to be sacrificed if there is a choice to be made between her interests and the interest of a husband. This can sometimes be heartbreaking, as I learned in the time of the first campaign when Gene's candidacy jettisoned Bill Carlson's hopes. But for the most part, we don't even think about it. That is the way it is. My friendship with Lady Bird Johnson was qualified then by many things—by disparity of regional interests, disparity of position—she was a Senate wife while I was a House wife, Vice President's wife for most of the time I was a Senate wife, and ultimately the President's wife—but most of all because we could not be friends as couples.

I was always and am still unreserved in my own admiration for Lady Bird. I considered her next to Lindy Boggs of Louisiana in my private list of the great women of Washington. I admired her self-discipline and the energy with which she directed her life. Through the years I saw her progress from the motherly and slightly plump mother of small children to the chic, slim, and well-dressed woman she was when her husband became Vice President. In my experience she was unfailingly kind and thoughtful. She used to pick me up for luncheons in the days when I was pregnant, knowing that it was difficult for me to drive and park. At her luncheons right through the White House days, she remembered people who had been forgotten by others: somebody who had dropped out of the capital scene because she was divorced or because she was widowed, for instance, or the mother of a congressman, forgotten wives of former Cabinet members. She was an easy conversationalist, a good listener although she never traded the smallest gossip or the confidences which are the human stuff of conversation. After she had formed our small Spanish class which included me, Mercedes Douglas (at that time), Bethine Church, June White, wife of the columnist

William S. White, a very small group which met weekly for three hours, she used to emphasize her delight in those mornings, calling them the time she stole for herself alone.

Yet in twenty-two years I can only remember two or three times when she dropped her guard enough so that our exchange was truly woman to woman. One of these times was when Gene was still in the House. Lady Bird and I were going someplace together and she asked if we had been at the Louisiana Mardi Gras Ball which is held each year in Washington as a preview of the real Mardi Gras in New Orleans. I said no, that we had been invited to the opening of the Cone Wing of the Baltimore Museum the night before and went on to say that it was such a beautiful wing and so well suited to the display of the Cone sisters' marvelous collection of early Picassos, Matisses, and so on. She stopped me with the abrupt question, "But does Gene like that kind of thing?" When I said that he did and that I thought he really knew a little bit more about that period than I did, she reflected a minute, then said flatly, "Lyndon just wouldn't understand that."

I think she often listened to the rest of us for clues as to how other people met their personal problems and for insights about other people's feelings, but she maintained a well-learned reserve which I am sure stands her in good stead to this day.

Lyndon Johnson had always manifested a certain uneasiness about Gene. Although he certainly knew from Sam Rayburn that Gene had been welcomed by the House leadership to the powerful Ways and Means Committee as "a most reasonable man," Senator Johnson did not seem at all eager that Gene should become a fellow senator. Gene after all was the founder and leader of the House liberal caucus which sometimes challenged the leadership. In the Senate campaign of 1958, Gene received the barest of support from the Senate Campaign Committee which was headed by ex-Senator Earle Clements of Kentucky but really under the control of the Majority Leader. So apparent was this fact that Senator Mike Mansfield of Montana, when he seemed sure of his own victory, had the last contributions to him from that committee transferred to Gene's campaign. On election night in 1958, Gene's election was not one of those announced by the Senate Campaign Committee. At five in the morning, I remember his mounting irritation when he answered a call from Senator Clements. "Well, you can call it or not if you like. Humphrey says I've won, Freeman says I've won, the New York *Times* says I've won, and *I* think I've won."

It was true that the Republican incumbent Senator Thye was reluctant to believe that he had lost and refused to concede until late that afternoon, believing that his election would be saved by the farm vote from the northwestern part of the state; however Gene drew a normal Democratic vote from those sections. When the Majority Leader finally called with his congratulations, Gene reported with wry emphasis, "He says that now there will be two tall men in the Senate."

Because we had promised the children a dude ranch vacation and, I suspect, because he didn't want to go, Gene refused the invitation to meet with other newly elected senators at the Johnson ranch in Texas. "It's too much like being summoned to court," he said at the time.

That year the Majority Leader broke with tradition by giving each of the new incoming senators a position on a major committee, and despite Gene's show of independence, he was given a place on the powerful Finance Committee. Also, he inherited one on agriculture which was good for a Minnesota senator. It is not generally known— at least, I did not know it until that year—that seniority and protocol have something to do with incoming senators as well as with incumbent senators. A senator who has served in the House has precedence over those who have not and a senator who has been a governor also has precedence. The three top Democratic members of the "Class of '58," as they like to call themselves, were then Clair Engle of California, Gene, and Stephen Young of Ohio, all of the House of Representatives. Ed Muskie, former governor of Maine, was right behind them. Not only did Gene come into the freshman class of 1958 with these advantages but he was soon made chairman of a special subcommittee on unemployment problems, for which substantial appropriation had been wangled through the Senate by the Majority Leader. Gene's solid but quietly handled achievement as chairman of this committee may not have been what Senator Johnson had in mind.

In 1968 Frank Gannon, former research director for the teamsters who had also served in the Department of Health, Education, and Welfare, came strongly to Gene's defense when his record was attacked: "The truth is, as Mr. McCarthy cogently notes, that his Special Committee on Unemployment Problems outlined both the architectural design and the concrete program which lie at the social welfare base of both the New Frontier and the Great Society."

As I think back over this long relationship, one scene is especially vivid in my mind. It must have been prior to 1960 because Adlai Stevenson was still the titular head of the Democratic party, and Agnes Meyer, the redoubtable widow of the owner of the Washington *Post*, was giving a large reception in his honor at her house on Crescent Place. The house is one of the large, grand old mansions of Washington and the reception was on the grand scale. Everybody in Democratic, liberal, and press circles was there. There had been a vote that day in the Democratic caucus of the Senate in which seventeen of the senators had held out against the Majority Leader, most of them among the new senators. We were there at the reception when the Johnsons arrived and the leader was obviously in a black mood. He ranged about glumly for a while exuding, as was sometimes his wont, the exaggerated patience of a man who has much to bear from ingrates and those lacking in understanding. I don't know when I became aware that Mrs. Johnson had left the party. I think they had probably started to leave together and he had turned back intent on confronting those who had treated him so badly that day. Suddenly he and Gene were toe to toe in the middle room of the great house, where Stevenson sat on a corner sofa in conversation with Mrs. Meyer and several of us gathered nearby. We could not hear the initial interchange but as voices rose and the room hushed, I could hear Gene trying to dismiss the matter with jocularity. But the leader was not to be appeased. He inveighed against Johnny-come-latelies and people who didn't know how the wheels had been greased for them by their betters. Gene, who dislikes any kind of direct confrontation, held his ground. He started in a low tone to establish the facts of that day's maneuver and the principle which underlay it. But Senator Johnson was having none of that insubordination. His mien was threatening and his voice rose menacingly. Then Philip Graham, the son-in-law of the hostess and publisher of the Washington *Post,* a friend of Johnson's, tried to intervene and to lighten the incident. The Majority Leader shrugged him off. Mrs. Meyer drew near. There was now a small circle formed about the two towering senators. Trembling, I moved in just as Senator Johnson said, "I'll take care of you, never fear," and Gene said, "You do just that." I intervened in the only way I know how, mindful of my hostess' distress and the watchful eyes of the press. I took Gene by the hand and laid my hand on Senator Johnson's arm and kissed him on the cheek and said, "Senator, there are all these ladies waiting to talk to you, you must not let Gene monopolize your time." Slightly mollified, he put an arm around my shoulders and said, "Well, anyway we love you and Muriel." Why he chose to involve Mrs. Humphrey at the moment, I will never know. Perhaps both Minnesota senators were a problem to him.

The tension eased and people fell back into small chattering groups as they do at Washington receptions. We worried about what might appear in the press the next day, but evidently the Meyer premises were sacrosanct because there was nothing. The town itself was agog as only Washington can be. The next day Marie Ridder, wife of the head of the Ridder papers Washington bureau, called me to say, "I was simply petrified, Abigail, and I lost all respect for Adlai Stevenson. He just sat there on that sofa and did nothing." "But what could he do, Marie?" I asked.

"Well, I don't know," she said, "but something. After all, he's the head of the party." Her thought underlines a problem in the philosophy of party politics, particularly during those years. The Democratic Policy Council, which was instituted by the national party chairman, Paul Butler, and was headed by Adlai Stevenson as the party head, was in almost inevitable conflict with the Democratic majority of the House and Senate where the history of the party was really being made. The philosophy of the party was in one place, the practice in another. And because of a force which no one had yet measured—the influence of the media—the leadership of the party was being assumed by yet another force personified by John Kennedy.

In the years that followed, Gene's relationship to both Johnson and Kennedy was conditioned by his absolute refusal to give any kind of symbolic obeisance to them as persons. He had refused this fealty to Hubert Humphrey as well. He was, I am quite sure, incapable of giving it to any man. His refusal often took tiny symbolic forms. His refusal to report personally to the White House after his missions abroad for John Kennedy was one instance. When Lyndon Johnson became President, he refused to join him in his famous "skinny-dipping" sessions in the White House pool with what I think must have seemed the thinnest of excuses: "Abigail expects me home," he said. It was an exasperating quality, the quality of a totally free man, of course, but also the quality of a man who sets limits to loyalty. It must have been very much on Lyndon Johnson's mind in 1964.

In the introduction to Katie Louchheim's book, *By the Political Sea*, she has this to say of that period:

"One afternoon in the summer of 1964, congressional helpers and friends had been invited to the family floor of the White House to mingle with the wives of the Organization of American States. The President made one of his unexpected entrances. The chatting faded away and all eyes turned toward him. He first walked to the sofa where Bird sat between Latin American leaders' wives, placed a kiss on her brow. He then went around the room, shaking hands. At one point he reached over heads and hands to bestow a kiss on Phyllis Dillon (Douglas Dillon was still Secretary of the Treasury) and Betty Fulbright, wife of the Chairman of the Foreign Relations Committee of the Senate. Senator Eugene McCarthy's wife and I stood in his path. He shook hands with us.

"In a later recounting of the scene, I said that Phyllis Dillon got a good-bye kiss (Dillon had tendered his resignation), Betty Fulbright, a longtime friendship kiss, Abigail McCarthy, a 'don't count on your husband as a Vice Presidential candidate' shake. 'And you?' I was asked. 'I was in the wrong pew,' I replied."

But behind that incident and Katie's interpretation of it, there was much more than she saw. President Johnson often invaded his wife's gatherings with the left-over energy and restlessness of the host whose guests have gone home when he still has things to talk about. When I reached home that afternoon, I saw in the early edition of the Washington *Star* the headline which told us that the President had ruled out all Cabinet-level appointees as possible vice-presidential prospects, thereby eliminating with one swoop Robert Kennedy who, hard as it is to remember now, felt it his right to be chosen, and Adlai Stevenson, ambassador to the United Nations. That left in contention, at least as far as the press was concerned, only two men—Hubert Humphrey and Eugene McCarthy, both of Minnesota. I'd like to think that the President came on me that day unaware, that he had not expected to see me there and that he was, for the moment, taken aback and unable to bestow the usual social kiss, so much a part of the Washington routine, because he knew what he intended to do and had a twinge of guilt.

To me the headlines were the explanation of the President's air of subdued elation. He had successfully dealt with his most difficult problem, the unspoken claim of Robert F. Kennedy to the vice presidency, a claim supported by so many of the men of the former Administration in Washington and a claim which so many who mourned for the promise and élan of a fallen President hoped would be honored. How much it had cost Lyndon Johnson to deal with this problem is detailed in Theodore White's *The Making of the President: 1964*. He could not feel himself truly President until it was clear that he held the presidency without help from any Kennedy and the people around Kennedy. Yet he did not wish to seem to repudiate the Administration in which he himself had served. The Attorney General had been informed of his decision privately, but because he was adamant in his refusal to let the public think the decision had been his, and not the President's, as the President suggested obliquely, the President had finally decided on the device of eliminating everyone in the Cabinet from consideration, thus making no special point of the rejection of any one person.

But by this device he narrowed his options. Although he continued to name a wide variety of other possible candidates, he had focused the white light of national attention on two men and created a situation of extreme tension among Minnesotans who supported them both—and he drove them farther apart. He continued to urge Gene to line up support, to consider himself still a possibility. The White House was in almost daily communication with Gene's office or with one or another of his supporters.

But to me that day at the White House, his intentions were very clear. My intuition told me that whether he chose Hubert Humphrey or not, he was clearly not going to choose Gene McCarthy. And Katie Louchheim's intuition supported mine.

"When did you first know that he had finally decided?" Larry Merthan asked me several months later.

"June thirtieth," I said, remembering that day.

"June thirtieth!" he exclaimed. "That was five weeks before any of the rest of us!"

Katie read the incident as a mark of personal disfavor; Larry read it as a mark of my political acumen, which he often lauded. To me it was simply one more indication of what political wives are for—to be where assistants cannot go and to bring home what word is found there.

For weeks before that gathering in the White House, I had been aware of nuances in greetings at teas and receptions; some of our close friends frankly begged me to urge Gene to withdraw from consideration for the vice presidency. They did not want him to dance "while that Texan shoots at his feet," as one of them put it. It was clear that others were worried.

One day I had put the question frankly to my friend Lindy Boggs, whose husband, Hale, was privy to the highest Democratic party councils. Lindy herself was an intimate at the White House. For over thirty years the Boggses and the Johnsons had shared the political life as representatives of adjoining states. I knew her assessment would be as close to the truth of the situation as anyone's could be, given the President's love of surprise and the way in which history might change things at any moment.

"Tell me honestly, Lindy," I said, "there really is no chance now that the President will pick Gene, is there?"

She hesitated, then said smoothly, "Well, if he doesn't, there are going to be some very disappointed Louisianians among the people I know." It was true. Some of the people actively working for Gene were from the South, among them young Democrats from New Orleans. Gene purportedly had other supporters from the South and West, notably Governor John Connally of Texas. They were supposed to believe that if the President must balance his ticket with a northern liberal, it should be someone less abrasive in personality to the South than Hubert Humphrey. And some of the Southerners had noted Gene's expertise in taxes and finance and respected him for that. His links to them went back to his days on the House Ways and Means Committee, and they had been aware of his work on unemployment problems on the Senate Finance Committee, which had been largely overlooked in the North where few commentators had patience with the intricacies of that kind of legislation. The South and Southwest had been not long ago economically a colonial area.

All this lay back of Lindy's answer. But I knew what she was really saying. If she had believed that the choice of Gene was still possible, she would have said so. But she could not afford to say anything, even to me, which could later be quoted and, in any way, spoil the President's scenario for the convention. For it was a scenario. To be fair to the President, it is important to remember that it was necessary that he have one. It was still important to him that there be a sense of drama and suspense at the convention, so that bored and nostaligic delegates would not be swept off their feet by the sudden appearance of Robert Kennedy—or, in the incredible press rumor of the time, Jacqueline Kennedy making a plea for his nomination. The appearance of a continuing contest for the vice presidency was part of the strategy. Undoubtedly he felt, too, that uncertainty was necessary motivation for Senator Humphrey and the Minnesota delegates, Walter Mondale and Geri Joseph, who were charged with the painful task of negotiating the challenge of the Mississippi Freedom delegation. (In a strange parody of the drama, Senator Humphrey, before appointing his successor in the Senate later that year, allowed speculation about his choice to run for some time, largely as a concession to the support for Congressman John Blatnik. The able and affable hard-working congressman from the Iron Range was the senior of all Minnesota Democrats. Time after time his district, because of his tireless campaigning, had saved us in close elections. In point of service and in recognition of ability, the appointment should have been his. But the debt incurred at Atlantic City made the appointment of Minnesota's young attorney general, Walter Mondale, a foregone conclusion. ("John never really had a chance, did he, Abigail?" Gisela Blatnik asked me sadly later. "I tried to keep him from hoping too much, but what can you do?")

There is a Cassandra-like quality to the wife's waiting in cases like these. There is nothing you can do. You cannot insist on what you know, because you do not surely know it. In politics a man rides on appearances as surely as an actor does, and, as someone has said, with none of the actor's excuses for temperament. His wife's behavior is part of the appearance to be maintained. His mood of confidence must be sustained. And though he may disclaim hope as Gene did, so many other hopes ride on his that he is constantly fed by their reading of the signs, their reporting of what they regard as significant comments. I did not even know who these people were. My only link to them was Larry Merthan, still Gene's closest adviser, and Bill and Kay Nee, Minnesota friends who handled public relations for Gene's political campaigns and whose efforts to prepare for the Minnesota campaign had been synchronized into the preparation of material for the delegates—a response to the exhortations from the White House: "Let people know about you." I had done whatever I was asked to do.

When the President and Lady Bird had come to Minnesota for the celebration of Svenskarnasdag (Swedes' day), I appeared at a press conference arranged by Bill and Kay to brief the women of the Minnesota suburban and small-town press, who had been somewhat ignored in the advance preparations. I had gone through the interviews in Washington which were a necessity for the wire services and the big dailies to have in their files "just in case." Although the efforts to put together the volunteer group for Gene's approaching Senate campaign took almost all my spare time, I had undertaken a few trips at the request of the women's division of the national committee into areas which had sent special requests to Gene's office. On one of these, a trip to make awards in the "4-for-'64" registration drive in Cleveland, I met Mrs. Susan Perry, a young divorcée somewhat at loose ends who was doing advance work on a volunteer basis for the committee. Her cheerfulness and upbeat approach to the inevitable difficulties of dealing with the press and the schedulers struck me immediately. She flew back to Washington with me and I asked her if she would work in the Minnesota campaign in the fall if the campaign could come up with enough money. For I kept thinking that after the convention there would be the Minnesota campaign. In all my public statements I tried to stress old Minnesota ties and friendships. Whatever happened, there would have to be a coming together, a healing process. Over and over I said that it was, of course, a great honor to be considered for the vice presidency and that I could not help being very proud that Minnesota had produced not one, not two, but three of the men being considered (Before the elimination of the Cabinet, Orville Freeman's name was among those mentioned, too).

Now as the convention approached, I felt relieved that it would soon be over. At the last minute Gene decided that the children should be there. They were in Minnesota. I called our friend, Mabel Frey, head of the speech department at St. Catherine's, and she gathered them together. Michael and Mary were at camp. Ellen, sixteen then, surveyed their clothes, planned the packing, took them on whirlwind shopping trips. With Mabel they flew to Washington and then to Atlantic City to join us. I had been driven to Atlantic City and smuggled into the hotel through a side entrance. I had instructions to evade the press; the time of Gene's arrival was to be kept a secret. I didn't know why. All I remember is that Jean Stack, Gene's secretary, was there when I arrived, with the door an inch ajar, and that she reached out and pulled me into the suite, quickly shutting the door. The suite was big, and I felt it very empty despite the welcoming flowers and baskets of fruit.

Conventions and campaigns become a series of unrelated scenes and acts to the people participating. Those at center stage are most isolated of all because they cannot wander about from camp to camp piecing things together. They are dependent on the news brought to them. For the next few days I was a prisoner in that hotel suite, meeting people, being interviewed, acting as a decoy for the press stationed outside the door, while Gene slipped in and out to the headquarters set up by his people in a motel outside the city. It seemed to me that I was acting a part in a cruel charade. In his book about 1968 Gene told the story briefly:

> Before leaving for the convention at Atlantic City, I had my staff check with the White House to make it clear to those with whom we had been speaking that I did not want to embarrass the President at the convention and would be glad to drop out. I was asked not to do so. We set up a limited headquarters, not at a convention hotel but at a motel on the edge of town, principally to keep in touch with the White House and to keep the candidacy alive.

He and Senator Humphrey appeared together on a network TV show on Sunday and the President and Lady Bird called and talked to them both. Characteristically, Gene had outlined his idea of the constitutional prerogatives of the Vice President; Senator Humphrey had been passionate about the need of the Vice President to be personally loyal—an *alter ego* to the President. Lady Bird was supposed to have told Gene that he was her candidate; I think it much more likely that she had said that she liked his particular TV appearance that day.

No one seemed sure how the President intended to make his choice known. Muriel and I appeared at a women's reception together, moving through the crowd which pressed around at our entrance, autographing programs, smiling, even when one woman said to Muriel ungraciously, "We want McCarthy where I come from," and another—I still remember that she was from Florida—pulled her program back from me, saying, "I don't want *your* name, dearie." Convention delegates are chosen for their willingness to stay committed, and their wives follow suit. "That was beautiful, that was just beautiful," said Kay Nee approvingly when we came out. Again, I was not sure why it was beautiful.

Michael was caught at the elevator by TV interviewers who asked why he thought his father should be Vice President. Michael, fourteen, surprised us, watching him, by saying that he thought his father knew more about the economy than anyone else and launched into an account of what Gene had to say about the balance of payments, dredging out of his memory some casual remarks of Gene's at the breakfast table or over the Sunday papers. A call came to Gene's staff from the Humphrey staff room: "We'll trade you two Frances Howards for one Michael," an ungallant reference to the senator's sister, who was working hard for him.

It was decided that we must make a public family appearance—perhaps the press asked for it—and we went with the children for a stroll on the boardwalk, ringed by newspaper photographers and TV men. This inevitably drew a crowd which made the walk impossible and we retreated to the suite again. I marveled at the picture in the Minneapolis paper later. How could I look so serene when I was so filled with dread? The strain was beginning to tell on Gene. And it seemed that the President was going to extract every bit of drama from the suspense, drawing it to some frightful denouement which would be excruciatingly painful for both winner and loser. I felt the age-old helplessness of the wife unable to forestall pain for the husband she cherishes.

"The melodrama . . . was staged and produced entirely by Lyndon Johnson," wrote Theodore White. "In its mixture of comedy, tension and teasing, it was a work of art; it was as if, said someone, Caligula were directing 'I've Got a Secret.' It is difficult to see it as any appropriate way for handing on succession to the mightiest office on earth; but as excitement and a study of personality in power, it was unmatched."

I desperately wanted Gene to withdraw. So did others who cared about him. But I was driven almost to despair by the realization that no one will counsel anyone that close to power frankly. George Dixon, Gene's closest friend among the columnists, came to see us and kept saying, "It should be you, if he had a grain of sense, it should be you." It had the flavor of a visit of condolence, but George could not bring himself to say that clearly. Ed Lahey kept shaving close to the truth as he saw it, saying, "You must remember, Gene, the guy lives on polls. Polls are his stuff of life. He keeps his pocket full of them." Gene's brother-in-law called from New York, saying vaguely in a troubled voice, "Keep him steady now, Abbie, Johnson is no man to fool with." We went to a lunch with Adlai Stevenson who looked miserably unhappy when he saw his nominator of four years before. Gene's old friend John Courtney was so concerned that despite a serious heart condition he took time out from a necessary trip to New York to come to Atlantic City and seek Gene out at the motel to say, "Remember who you are. Play this one out like a gentleman." Finally, on Tuesday night as he was having a pre-dinner drink with me and Mary McGrory in our suite as the children ran in and out, Gene asked us abruptly, "Should I withdraw?" I looked at Mary. She knew of my anxiety about the manner of the ending of what she felt as strongly as I was a cruel farce.

"That's what Adlai thinks you should do, Gene," she said quietly.

"I think I will in the morning," he said. I was relieved but I argued that he should do it as soon as possible, before the President moved.

Later that night some of the staff and old campaign friends from the motel came by to tell Gene that the mood there was angry and that some of the Michigan delegates wanted to put Gene's name in nomination from the floor. I had a moment of panic, but Gene vetoed the idea after questioning them idly about the delegates involved. They stayed talking and Gene held them late with satirical parodies of convention speeches and sketches of speeches never made but which should be made. They made a game of it, each improving on the other's ideas. When they left, Gene stayed up listening to a late night program of Al Hirt's trumpet playing, which he admired. He urged me to go to bed, asking me to call him at six o'clock to work on his statement. It was the first night in a week in which I had slept. When I called him the next morning, he went out to the living room and brought back a scrawled and scratched over piece of paper.

He gave it to me. It was his statement written during the night. It was a graceful withdrawal. He asked me to get Mary McGrory on the phone and he read it to her. She also thought it very good. The President could not reasonably fault it; Gene rested his withdrawal on the President's own words.

Gene's telegram read:

DEAR MR. PRESIDENT. THE TIME FOR YOUR ANNOUNCEMENT OF YOUR CHOICE OF YOUR VICE PRESIDENTIAL RUNNING MATE IS VERY CLOSE. I HAVE, AS YOU KNOW, DURING THIS CONVENTION AND FOR SEVERAL WEEKS NOT BEEN INDIFFERENT TO THE CHOICE YOU MUST MAKE. THE ACTION THAT I HAVE TAKEN HAS BEEN TO THIS END AND TO THIS PURPOSE: THAT YOUR CHOICE WOULD BE A FREE ONE AND THAT THOSE WHOM YOU MIGHT CONSULT, OR WHO MIGHT MAKE RECOMMENDATIONS TO YOU, MIGHT BE WELL INFORMED. THE GREAT MAJORITY OF THE DELEGATES HERE ARE, AS YOU KNOW, READY TO SUPPORT YOUR CHOICE. IT IS MY OPINION THAT THE QUALIFICATIONS THAT YOU HAVE LISTED AS MOST DESIRABLE IN THE MAN WHO WOULD BE VICE PRESIDENT WITH YOU, WOULD BE MET MOST ADMIRABLY BY SENATOR HUMPHREY. I WISH, THEREFORE, TO RECOMMEND FOR YOUR PRIMARY CONSIDERATION SENATOR HUBERT H. HUMPHREY.

Gene gave it to the staff with instruction to let our White House contacts know about it first and then release it to the press. In all the years of dealing with Gene's staff and campaign workers, I had never changed anything he wanted—once I knew what it was. (Often I had to guess, or take my cues from hints and half-expressed wishes.) But, when Gene left the room that day to get ready for the "Class of '58" breakfast, I turned to Larry Merthan and said, "Larry, please listen to me—release it to the press at the same time. The President will tell them not to let Gene withdraw—he'll drag it out to the very end and it will be dreadful for Gene."

And, indeed, the White House spokesman had said at once, "Don't send it and don't give it to the press." And had seemed distraught to hear that it had already been released. Why this respectfully couched message, carefully constructed to leave the President continued freedom, should have sent him into a towering rage is a question. Yet a former White House aide who was there told us later, "Sending that message was the smartest thing you ever did. Boy, what an explosion you caused! But it was a good thing that you sent it. Otherwise you would have been ruined."

What the President had in mind only he knows. Gene speculated laconically in his book,

> Senator Thomas Dodd of Connecticut was asked to fly from Atlantic City to Washington on the same plane as Senator Humphrey. There were some who thought that had I not sent the telegram I might have been on the plane, serving much the same function as Senator Dodd served—to keep alive the illusion that there were other candidates for the vice presidency.

Gene did not wish to elaborate for the press before the President's call came making his choice official; it was sure to come, we thought, soon. So we arranged a rather complicated plot so that he could evade the press after the breakfast. We went into the dining room reserved for the "dauntless fifteen"—the senators elected in 1958—their wives and aides, passing the stationed reporters quickly, with Gene brushing aside their queries with a "Later, see you later—they're waiting for me here." It was relaxing to be with our Senate friends; we had seen little or nothing of them since the convention began. Halfway through breakfast Gene left the table and conspicuously borrowed a dime from someone at another table. He disappeared toward the telephones. When we were sure that he had got away, Larry and I moved quickly to our car and the driver pulled away, stopping just long enough to be sure the press car was following us. We stopped and went inside a church. I was glad of the opportunity. I wanted to pray for many things, but especially for courage and strength for the widow of Senator Clair Engle whom we had memorialized at the breakfast. Senator Engle, the ranking member of the class of 1958, had died of a brain tumor that year. He had served in the House with Lyndon Johnson and been proud to serve with him in the Senate, but in his last illness he had waited in vain for a call from the White House. His wife had been vilified as scheming and ambitious by the press and some California politicians because she refused to persuade him to resign. "How can I take away his hope, tell him he is finished?" she had said to me and some of her other friends. "Do they really think I would refuse for a

274   Private Faces/Public Places

few more months of being a Senate wife? You and I know that it isn't that great." But her stand had complicated matters for the Democratic party and for the President, and there had been little sympathy.

Later that morning Muriel came to see me. "It's time for you and me to appear together," she said. "Let's go to one of these receptions together." I explained that I had to wait in the suite until Gene heard from the President. "You mean the President didn't know Gene was going to send that wire?" she said. I shook my head. She was puzzled. The President had sent Jim Rowe, acting as messenger, to them the night before. She thought that we, too, were acting under instructions.

The day dragged on. When the President finally called, he asked Gene to nominate Humphrey. Gene assented with some reluctance. The speech he gave that night was a good speech for the start of a national campaign, far too well-crafted to have been thrown together that afternoon.

> We, the Democratic party are the party of history. We accept the traditions of America. We accept the history of the South—of the old and new and of the changing South. We accept the North and we accept the West. We accept all of this America as our America, and beyond that are willing to accept responsibility in every part of the world in which we have some power to influence people for good or to help them achieve the good and full life . . .

This was how he saw our party in 1964. He contrasted its strengths with the philosophy and performance of Barry Goldwater, the Republican nominee, citing his votes of "no commitment" on the Test Ban Treaty, on civil rights, and finally in the "great effort to eliminate poverty."

But the President had made sure that Gene's speech would not repeat the effect on the convention that Gene's speech for Stevenson had in 1960. He had already himself taken the gavel from Speaker John McCormack, presiding that evening, and given Humphrey's name to the convention, thus breaking the suspense in which the delegates were still held. (Beside me in the gallery, Florence Rolvaag, wife of Minnesota's governor, had been uncertain of the nomination until that moment.) Now, as Gene spoke, I watched in helpless sympathy as the President distracted the crowd and the television cameras by moving from one part of the platform to another, greeting people, clasping hands, as Gene spoke doggedly to an unhearing audience. Only David Brinkley recorded what Gene had said that night and again in the book he wrote about the conventions of that year. Few remembered that Gene had said to his party in 1964 what became his message in 1968 . . .

> I call upon you here tonight, Democrats all, to affirm America. This is a time for all of us to enter into the fabric of our own time and to accept the challenge of the history of the twentieth century, to declare and manifest our belief that the power of reason can give some direction to the movement of history itself.

3 / *Changes*

*H*ad it not been for the shadow of the war in Vietnam and its increasing escalation, 1966 would have been one of our happiest years. For me it was one of the happiest of my mature life. Gene was beginning to recover the buoyancy and energy he had lost in a long illness. Ellen was getting along well in college. Mary was graduating from Stone Ridge with honors and had been accepted at Wellesley, Radcliffe, and Stanford, all in one week. Michael liked Georgetown Prep and his friends; Margaret was again building friendships at Stone Ridge. Best of all, there was no election in prospect for four years (the Senate elections would be in 1970). It seemed that at long last we could relax and enjoy our friends and family.

In the summer of that year in what is known as the "little season," we gave Ellen a small coming-out party. Many of her friends, both in college and in Washington, had come out and Ellen, after some hesitation, decided that she would like to do so, too. Because neither Gene nor I was from a family with a tradition of debuts, we chose to do it in the simplest way possible, the old-fashioned tea and reception given by the parents without benefit of a social director. Thus, we could adhere quite literally to the nice part of the presentation tradition—the introduction of our now-adult daughter to the friends of our generation.

Ellen, perhaps because as the oldest she has been so close to us, is, in a sense, our old-fashioned child. She really took an interest in our friends and cultivated her own friendships with them. For her, then, the debut seemed appropriate. We held it at the Congressional Club where other congressional daughters had been feted by their parents in times past. In this way we thought we could make it perfectly clear that we were not compromising our egalitarian background, but that we *were* observing the customs of the country—Ellen's country.

It was a happy party and a healing one. Gene was touched and pleased by the outpouring of friends, a happy mixture of senators, congressmen, diplomats, and people from the press, parents of friends of the children. Ellen has always been very close to Gene and the pictures show him looking proud and pleased as she greeted people. He is there, genial and joking with Vice President Humphrey, in earnest consultation with Charles Lucet, the ambassador from France, bending solicitously over an Asian diplomat with a language problem, jovial and back-slapping with some of our old Minnesota friends.

Ellen had invited her favorite college professor, Dr. Milton S. Rakove, and his wife. Dr. Rakove was frankly delighted to be in a room with the Washington great and near great whom he recognized—Senators Mike Mansfield and Harry Byrd, Mr. and Mrs. Walter Lippmann, Perle Mesta, the ambassadors of Great Britain and France and Spain, and Ellen felt, for once, that there were more advantages than disadvantages to being a senator's daughter. Gene had every reason that day to feel that whatever the petty harassment of the Administration, as a well-known senator with a ranking position on the Finance Committee and a member of the Foreign Relations Committee, he commanded a position of respect in the nation's capital, and affection as well, for there were many there that day who came because they liked us as well as they respected his position.

The first nosegay Ellen carried that day was the one from her father and then, the one which came from the White House. It was evidence of the cooled relations between the Johnsons and the McCarthys that the nosegay was there but the President and Mrs. Johnson were not.

By the end of the summer I felt that all was well enough with the family so that I could set a date for a long-postponed operation to end a debilitating condition which had snapped my vitality and caused occasional hospitalization since shortly after Margaret's birth in 1954. I flew out to Minnesota for a final examination and almost put the operation off too long by going to one last weekend meeting. In the end I was rushed into the hospital and Gene had to fly out suddenly from Washington. It was a successful operation and we issued a press release to end any speculation such as had accompanied Gene's hospitalization of the year before. There was a heartening outpouring of messages, flowers, and gifts from our friends in Washington and Minnesota and my hospital stay was almost like a vacation—the first vacation in years. When it was time for me to leave the hospital, Vice President Humphrey flew us back to Washington in his private plane.

The fall of 1966 was already beautiful in Bethesda and as I picked up strength day by day, life seemed very pleasant indeed. And Gene was relaxed, cheerful, and attentive.

Mary, who worried us through the summer by her apprehensions about facing college, was very happy at Radcliffe. "I was born for this, Mother," she said in one conversation. When Gene was invited to give the William Belden Noble Lectures at Harvard Divinity School in November, we went to Cambridge for a very interesting few days. It was impossible not to feel the pessimism, unrest, and mounting division within the academic community. It was interesting that Gene's three lectures drew standing-room-only crowds, especially the last one on the moral aspects of foreign policy. The lectures were, I thought, Gene at his very best, and I secretly rejoiced that the bitterness and cynicism of the post-Atlantic City period seemed to have receded and that a renewed sense of leadership was replacing them. In the first lecture on religious belief and political action, Gene reiterated and in a sense quoted himself on the way it is impossible to separate religion and politics in the conscience of one man. His examples were in a sense those cited in his writing but they were given new form and there was a new eloquence:

> Knowledge of the Bible, the Koran, the Ten Commandments, or
> of the spiritual and corporal works of mercy does not, of course,

give the religious man in politics a ready answer to all his problems.

. . . This conflict between conscience and the unjust and all-embracing state is age-old and, indeed, runs through the history of Western civilization. The list of the great, the brave, and the prudent who, exhausting all alternatives, fell back at last on the dictates of conscience goes back at least to Socrates, who is admired for his stand against the state and honored for his declaration, "Men of Athens, I respect you, but I must obey God rather than you." Not only do we honor those who stand on conscience, we consider a stand against injustice the obligation of the responsible citizen.

He dealt again with the old problem of the separation of the religious man from the world, the problem of detachment which had caused him so much worry long ago:

. . . The excuse of rejection no longer stands. The world today is not arrogant. It has been brought low. The world today is not suffering from illusion. It has been disillusioned.

There is, of course, still a need for the long view, for the search for absolutes, but there is a great need for the application of that knowledge which we do possess to contemporary life and problems. The dead hand of the past is less of a problem today, although we still use it as an excuse, than is the violent hand of the future which reaches back for us today, imposing most serious demands.

There is little time to escape and few escape routes still open. . . .

. . . By necessity of history, rather than of choice, those who have long been pilgrims of the absolute have now been forced to become pilgrims of the relative as well.

Religious and intellectual leaders today cannot retreat in ignorance and half-truth or go back into their own protected caves. Leonardo da Vinci could speculate on the principles of aerodynamics without giving any thought to the possibility that his knowledge would be used to construct intercontinental ballistic missiles. Descartes could develop new theories of mathematics without anticipating that his conclusions might be incorporated in nuclear bombs. Men of the past did not have to anticipate what might happen to their ideas and their conceptions when subjected to the power of computers. Nor did they have to worry about chain reactions as men do today, not just in physics but in biology, philosophy, theology, and in the structure and function of society.

Gene thoroughly enjoyed those days at Harvard and found there an audience which understood him and was concerned about the things he was concerned about. Dean Price of the Divinity School recognized this in his introduction on the third night. It was a lecture on the moral aspects of foreign policy:

> By this time, Senator McCarthy needs very little introduction from me to this audience. He has given himself over the last three days in this community in an altogether remarkable way: not only by means of these lectures and by answering the many questions which they have brought out, but also in a breathtaking number of daytime engagements. Senator McCarthy has been his own best introduction to Harvard, and I have very few words to add, for he has allowed us to see something of himself: a well-balanced mind, a cool head, and a free heart. . . .

It has been said that Gene was among the last of the so-called "doves" to take an outright stand against the war in Vietnam, but nobody can reread this lecture given in 1966 and not realize that he had decided to oppose it at that time. However, it is true that his statements were so abstract and philosophical that they left me as well as the students with a feeling of inconclusiveness. But Gene was right when he said later that people who thought that he was late in speaking out had not been listening.

It is hard now to recapture the atmosphere of Lyndon Johnson's Washington in 1967, just prior to Gene's announcement for the presidency. During any Administration, the power of the presidency is deeply felt in Washington. Many Washingtonians with influence are dependent on the presidency: the press for sources of stories, the legislators of both parties for favors for their districts, and the members of the bureaucracy for their jobs. Even people who have made a great show of independence become aware of this dependency when the presidency is threatened in any way. Being opposed to the incumbent or being out of favor at the White House can easily make one something of a leper. In the Johnson administration, this was even more true than in any other I remember, and we had lived in Washington through the Truman, Eisenhower, and Kennedy administrations as well.

This was largely a matter of the President's personal style. As far as one could judge as an observer, he seemed to hold firmly to the belief that one had to control people by having some power over them. His constant attention to domination in one form or another, and it was domination—of the press by one news conference after the other, of Congress by the constant calling of conferences, consultations, meetings of the leadership, a multiplication of social invitations which were in effect a summons and were often accompanied by briefings—began in the end to numb the people it was intended to affect. But at the time about which I write—1967—the demand for unquestioning loyalty to the President became in a way ominous and threatening. There seemed to be an unspoken edict: support my war, avoid my critics.

In Johnson's years as Majority Leader, he frequently boasted in off-the-record sessions that no telephone call went in or out of the Senate wing or the office buildings that he did not know about. News people who visted his ranch and telephoned out their stories told half humorously of incidents when they could hear heavy breathing on the line as they did so. One woman reporter was quoted as having said, "Was that all right, Mr. President?" when she finished. The story was probably apocryphal but was widely believed.

By the summer of 1967, it was taken for granted that most office phones and the phones in officials' houses were tapped. This was probably absurd, considering the number of man-hours that would have been involved in such wide-scale surveillance. Yet the fact that it was believed and acted upon is evidence of the unhealthy miasma of fear and doubt which hung over the city.

The wife of a high official in the Administration who had been my friend told me quite seriously that we should communicate with each other by note or personal visit in some neutral place. After Gene's announcement, she arranged for me to meet her in New York in Grand Central Station where it would seem that we had bumped into each other by accident.

Social life became uncertain to the puzzlement of foreign visitors. "But I don't see why you care, Kay," said Lady Pamela Barry, British publisher, one night at a dinner party at the Achesons' when Mrs. Graham, publisher of the *Post* half-humorously told her that she had been dropped by the White House because of recent editorials on the war. "I would never *dream* of going to Number 10 Downing Street!" But Washington was not London and people *did* care.

Even at official functions an atmosphere of uncertainty prevailed. One was never quite sure what would happen. There was a widely publicized incident in which the President challenged and up-braided Senator Frank Church at one of the briefing buffet suppers for the Congress. And Betty Fulbright, wife of the chairman of the Foreign Relations Committee, gave a nervous interview to the society pages denying that her husband had left yet another reception in anger at his treatment there by the President.

The so-called Senate "doves" as critics of the war had long since been *persona non grata* at the White House and they began to feel during the final months of 1967 that they were unwelcome almost any place in Washington as well. These facts would be petty and unimportant in themselves except that they were other manifestations of a widespread malaise in Washington caused by the war.

I was troubled by the uglier forms of protest. It seemed to me that the President of the United States had a right to be heard and to travel in his own country and that attacks on his wife and family were certainly indefensible. I thought the behavior of people who accepted invitations to the White House and used the occasion to attack the President's policies was reprehensible, and it seemed to me that in many cases, the most vocal of the protesters had done little to prevent the situation in which the nation found itself.

When the clergy and laymen concerned about Vietnam convened in Washington in February of 1967, Gene had reminded them that the influence of the Church and of religious leaders had only been felt in American politics, "over the period of the last four or five years."

In the case of civil rights, for example, when the issue was before the Congress in 1949 and 1950, there was no significant Church support, there were no marches; but when the support did come ten years later, it came with great force and contributed strongly. Support for the Test Ban Treaty had not been so slow in coming, Gene noted, and it had a great effect on Congress. The moral issues involved in both these cases were relatively simple in contrast to those involved in Vietnam, and the solutions were direct and simple—the passing of specific legislation.

In comparison, protest against the war was diffuse and generalized. In the absence of realizable goals and solutions, its increasing personalization and violence was frightening. And yet, as I thought about it, wasn't the problem that people wanted to be heard and there was no one to hear? Testimony, speeches, the chants of protesters—all fell on deaf ears.

If the form of protest adults chose might be questioned, I had come to understand that the situation was quite different among the young. During '66 and '67, I realized through Mary, Mary's friends, and Ellen's that young people could not possibly see things as we did. Everything we thought or did had a parallel or a precedent in World War II. They could not remember that war. And it was the people of their generation who were asked to sacrifice their lives for something we believed—and which might not be true. There were times when I saw, in a flash of insight, that this was a form of human sacrifice—that we were willing to offer up our young on the altar of some idolatrous illusion. At other times, the old values would return and I would be troubled by the arguments of those who believed that our duty lay in Southeast Asia. Yet I had come to realize that in the lifetime of our young, the world had changed forever. They were born in an age in which the total destruction of mankind was scientifically possible, in which human life was a danger rather than a gift because of the population growth, and in which nature was no longer thought of as inexhaustible in its riches. They carried a burden which we never carried in our youth.

Mary came home with friends from Radcliffe and Harvard for the October 1967 Peace Mobilization (or, as it is better known, the Pentagon March). In Washington the opposition to protest took a particularly ugly form as police and troops massed to defend the Pentagon. The story of the march itself has been very well told in Norman Mailer's *Armies of the Night*. But I think the real story lay in the homes where hospitality was offered by parents through their sons and daughters to the young people who came from far away.

There was a great incongruity between these vital, dedicated young people who sat around our tables discussing the plight of their country and the preparations we saw made for them and the descriptions given of them in the Washington press.

They were difficult to talk to, those young people. It was chilling to realize, for example, that they believed quite seriously that World War II camps were being reactivated as concentration centers for dissenters. It was even more chilling that the imprisonment of the more troublesome marchers, the use of gas for the first time, a strongly stepped-up outburst of criticism directed at the protesters gave some substance to their fears.

When I put Mary on the plane the day after the march, we saw young David Bruce, the son of the ambassador to Great Britain at that time, also leaving the city after having participated in the march. He was only one of many children of Administration-related parents who were in Washington for that weekend. A day later I heard from a Washington columnist that she had been called and urged not to mention the fact that he was present because it would react against his parents. This was the climate of the times: a petty response to a pressing disorder. In only a short time the President was to threaten reprisal against protesters with these words, "If they are going to use storm trooper tactics, it will be dealt with and will be dealt with properly." Vice President Humphrey was to assail the "walkers and talkers." Senator Bourke Hickenlooper of Iowa was to attack Benjamin B. Cohen, venerable adviser to Franklin Delano Roosevelt, by saying that his proposal for a United Nations solution to the war was a proposal for "abject surrender, utter defeat, and an abdication of our responsibility to the people of South Vietnam." Republican congressional leaders called for stern measures against the demonstrators who "committed acts of violence or otherwise affront decency." On October 27, even Senator Robert Kennedy criticized the anti-Vietnam war demonstrators as going too far and using useless tactics.

It was clear that conventional Washington wisdom held that support for protest was fading and that, in any case, it represented only a vocal minority of the population. At the same time, however, letters were pouring into Gene's office and I am sure into other offices in Washington which indicated that discontent and disillusionment with the war was far more widespread than anyone could believe.

I have often wondered about the mail in other congressional offices. Certainly Gene could not have been alone in what he received and Senator Kennedy must have received much more. Perhaps this mail was not analyzed carefully in other offices. Perhaps it didn't seem to indicate a real, earnest, and purposeful opposition to the President and his policies. But looking back now at the mail received by Gene in November 1967 from only one Minnesota city, our home city of St. Paul, reveals the depth and variety of the concern not only about Vietnam but also about what the war was doing to America and American life.

Some of the letters were very predictable and were not the kind of mail which alone would have convinced or encouraged any man to take a lonely stand: the mimeographed group letter from a Committee of Concerned Democrats; a telegram from a group, United Against the War in Vietnam; and a printed, signed statement issued by the office of the Individuals Against the Crime of Silence. But even the printed forms had notes scrawled on the back, the sort of personal note which is a signal to the recipients of mass mail, especially to the representatives of the people in Congress, of the extent to which the concern expressed in the letter is real.

The form letters and the petition letters were the letters of people seeking a candidate with their views. These were to form one nucleus of the emerging campaign and were probably the people who, in later months, were dissatisfied with a candidate who did not conform completely to their views. It was the other letters, however, which were really meaningful. There were letters professionally typed for businessmen. There were letters scrawled on drugstore stationery and on notebook paper. There were letters laboriously hand-typed in the evening hours by students and workers. The letters from students and intellectuals were probably the kind of letters being dismissed in Washington by the party regulars. It is clear from many of the letters that the students had not yet found each other and that they did not know of their own strength. Many of them felt somewhat help-less and were only glad that a responsible adult was espousing the cause against the war in a practical way.

Intellectuals clearly thought of themselves as a minority and of Gene's proposed candidacy as a desperate effort indeed. One coun-seled him, "I recommend that you enter several primaries so that at least history will record that there were American legislators and voters opposed to the present foreign policy."

These lonely students and intellectuals in early November would certainly have been heartened by some of the other letters, like the one from the woman who described herself thus: "I am a square, thirty-nine-year-old, churchgoing housewife—politically independent, too." This was the voice of the "liberated housewife" who was to play such a large part in the campaign all over the country.

There were voices of other women, also: the mothers of sons in the service and the mothers of the future generation. And there was a kind of woman's letter which became very well known to us throughout the year, a letter from the wife of a high public official who could not take a stand, "A quiet personal note of admiration for the action you are taking. I share your moral convictions. And here's to Mary-don't-sit-there-do-something-about-it-McCarthy"—a reference to our vocal daughter Mary.

In much of the reporting in 1968 and in the fall of 1967, dis-satisfaction with the war in Vietnam and with our country's foreign policy were linked to dislike or even hatred of the President him-self. It seems significant to me that there were so few letters like that among those expressing gratitude for Gene's intentions. I hope really that it was indicative not only of the New Constituency, but also of Gene's personal constituency.

But the letters which would have given the Administration pause if its members could have seen them were the reasoned and thought-ful assessments from active Minnesota Democrats. Minnesota Demo-crats, as a rule, are people devoted to the party not for reasons of patronage or for reasons of power base, but because they have a long tradition of participation in politics. Minnesota and Wisconsin have come closer in the past to the ideal of participatory politics than any other states I can think of (with the possible exception of Michigan).

Many of the letters contained pledges of support. Some of them had dollar bills hastily stuffed into the envelopes. Others pledged to send "$50 immediately and $200 in the future." The steady stream of such contributions (probably never realistically accounted for) was to be one of the hallmarks of the campaign and a reassuring, constant testimony to its volunteer nature.

As I reread these letters, I saw that all the strains, all the forebodings, all the strengths, all the weaknesses of the campaign year of 1968 were foreshadowed in these encouraging letters sent to Gene before he announced his candidacy. And also, all the strains of the New Constituency—young people, intellectuals and professional people, women, members of the clergy, people who had never participated actively in politics before. It is very unlikely that in the press of events and because of the many speeches he was making at the time, Gene had any time to read these letters analytically. The letters I cite here were from only one city in Minnesota. They were pouring into the Senate office from all over the United States at the same time.

The letters coming in from other parts of the country followed certain patterns of origin. It was no surprise that there were hundreds of letters from California and from New York. It *was* surprising that there were so many from places like Russellville, Arkansas; Bavedu, Colorado; Laurel, Delaware (the last from a man who described himself as a "Caucasian whose ancestors came over in 1640").

It has always puzzled me that there were so very many from all over Pennsylvania, although this certainly was reflected later in the Pennsylvania primary.

And there were, I thought, a surprising number from Massachusetts, from unexpected people there like Catholic priests who certainly didn't think of themselves as activists, because, as one of their members noted, "As a priest, there is nothing I can do for you except pray." Hardly the note of the new clergy.

Perhaps some day someone will do a thesis on why there were so many letters from doctors and so many offers from doctors all through the campaign to help in any way they could. One of our most staunch supporters in the Indiana primary was to be the head of the state medical association, a courageous Irishman named Dr. Patrick B. Corcoran. It has always been a political axiom that doctors interest themselves politically only in the causes espoused by the American Medical Association, and these have usually been causes protecting the economic welfare of doctors. Only psychiatrists have tended to speak out for liberal and humanitarian causes. It was a great surprise, then, to have the letters pouring in from doctors of every background and specialty, from Fellows of the American College of Surgeons, from internists, from pediatricians, from eye, ear, nose, and throat specialists, from dermatologists, from orthopedists. I can only hazard the surmise that doctors were, in the best sense, concerned for life and that they looked on Vietnam and what it was doing to American life as a threat to life that made their healing art ultimately irrelevant. I would at least like to think that that was one of the reasons.

*A*lthough Washington is famous for its springs, I think fall is its most beautiful season. It is the one time of year when Washington weather can be said to be invigorating and the city seems to respond after the summer with new bursts of purposeful activity. The days are consistently bright and clear, on every street the eyes beguiled by the more exotic colors of fall below the Mason and Dixon line—the red of the dogwood trees, the flashing orange of pyracantha berries, the rusty red and green of the Virginia creeper on old walls, the occasional scarlet and yellow glory of the maple which will bear its leaves like beacons for weeks unlike the sudden brief blaze and disappearance of the maple leaves of the North. My associations with fall had always been happy. Throughout my early life it was the time of new beginning because, I suppose, it coincided with the beginning of the school year.

Throughout our Washington years, fall, when it was not a campaign year, was always a happy time, a time when we had some leisure for friends and for the children. For years we had made it a family custom to spend at least one day with the children and their friends on the Skyline Drive in the Blue Ridge Mountains of Virginia. We followed the trail to the top of the different mountains each time and the children had developed their favorites: Mary Rock, Old Rag, and Big Stony Man. But there was no time for any of this in the fall of 1967.

As I look back at that period, I realize that I was deeply troubled. Gene sometimes said during that fall and winter that his lonely course need not involve the family, but that was to deny reality. No public man can choose to take such a course without drawing his family in his wake.

I was troubled because of the personal cost of dissent in Lyndon Johnson's Washington and in the Democratic party he led. I was troubled because of the inevitable sunderings of old friendships and associations that Gene's contemplated step could lead to. I was troubled by many of the people who approached Gene and urged him to run. They seemed to be concerned not so much for finding a real solution within the system as for making another kind of demonstration of their protest by filing an anti-Johnson candidate. It seemed to me that they asked Gene to cast aside his public career of twenty years in order to make a case for them. I was troubled, too, because there were so many Kennedy-haters among them. I could not see at that time that anything but protest was possible within the system as we knew it, nor, I think, did they. In this, Gene's vision was better than anyone else's at the time because he alone seemed to know that a try at the presidency was possible. But he did not say so.

I was troubled most of all by the increasing personalization of Gene's attack on members of the Administration.

The New York *Times* quoted him as saying that Secretary of State Dean Rusk's clarification of the Administration's Vietnam policy was hardly a clarification "since the style and language are those of the Secretary." He was interviewed by his old friend Ed Lahey, chief of the Washington bureau of the Knight Newspapers. The story was headlined all over the country: A BITTER SENATOR PERILS DEMS; MCCARTHY AT NO RETURN POINT? SCALPEL OF SATIRE CUTS LBJ. "In past years," wrote Ed, "McCarthy's comments about Mr. Johnson and other associates of public life had been framed in quiet and intellectual wit. McCarthy is now using a ball bat."

Ed Lahey loved Gene McCarthy as an older man loves his son. He was too good a newspaperman not to see the importance of the story he was writing, but between the lines one could read his concern for his old friend, his vision of the inevitable effect of Gene's seeking the nomination even as a symbolic gesture, and his concern at the change in Gene himself: "The most interesting phase is the deep personal feeling that McCarthy conveyed. He seemed dead serious in his criticism and quite bitter . . ."

Mary, very much involved in the anti-war movement in Cambridge, called almost nightly. As I ruefully admitted in speeches later that year, I said to her one night,

"Mary, I know that somebody should challenge the President. Something must be done. But does your father have to be the one to do it?"

Her furious answer came back, "Mother, that is the most immoral thing you ever said."

The reverberations of Gene's stand in our personal life had begun when the possibility of his running was only hinted at. At the time of the Arab-Israeli Six-Day War in the spring of 1967, we attended a reception at Katie and Walter Louchheims'. Katie at that time was the deputy assistant secretary of state. At one point, I was caught in a cluster in a corner with Liz Carpenter, press secretary to Mrs. Johnson, and unofficial press secretary and oftentimes speech writer for the President himself. She remarked pointedly, looking at me, that she expected it would be interesting to watch the doves—her use of the plural was a concession to tact—justify the support of Israel when they refused to justify our involvement in Vietnam.

I attended a luncheon given by Mrs. Robert LeBaron, a pleasant Washington hostess who has made the large luncheon a specialty. These are congenial gatherings of Republicans and Democrats, diplomats and resident Washingtonians. Her luncheons, given at the Sulgrave Club, were usually held in a large room adjacent to a lobby at the top of a long, curving staircase. As I mounted the stairs into the cheerful hubbub of chatter, I came face to face with the chatelaine of the Spanish embassy, Marquesa Mercedes Merry Del Val. She was celebrated in the press then as a reigning hostess of Embassy Row, and although she probably considered us a little less than chic, she had always gone out of her way to be especially friendly. Perhaps it was her assumption that anyone named McCarthy was probably a particular friend of Spain's. Now, however, she registered recognition with a very brief handshake and quickly turned to some-one else. Her frigidity was quickly compensated for by the warm welcome of Mme. Michalowska, the wife of the Polish ambassador. Mira Michalowska is a charming, intelligent woman, a recognized writer, whose son attended Carleton College in Minnesota. These facts were enough to make us mutual friends, but I was, of course, acutely aware that Poland was probably much more enthusiastic about my husband's stand than was Spain and much more indifferent to the standing of its embassy at the White House. (During the Johnson administration it was interesting to see Spain and Venezuela, both of which had embassy social secretaries with Administration connections, become the front rank embassies.)

At almost the same time, I ran into the wife of a Washington lawyer in the beauty shop of Saks Fifth Avenue. She served with me on a charity board. I greeted her cheerily as always in the dressingroom and met with blank non-recognition and then a brief hello. It was clear that I had made the metamorphosis from asset to liability.

Gene and I had long been scheduled to attend a black-tie dinner at the home of Leonard and Dorothy Marks. Leonard was director of the United States Information Agency and Dorothy had served for the past two years as president of the Woman's National Demo-cratic Club. I had served on her board and grown to know her well. Invitations to black-tie dinners in Washington usually go out a month before the event itself, and I wondered in the accelerating pace of events whether it would be considerate on our part to find an excuse not to go. By circuitous inquiry via mutual friends, I ascertained that the Marks still hoped we would come. The party was crowded with Administration figures and with White House favorites like Nancy Dickerson, who was then still with NBC. It was a fairly happy evening, although there was some wrangling during cocktail hour about Gene's attack on Dean Rusk. Edward Bennett Williams, a prominent Washington lawyer, was there and he diverted Gene into a baseball analogy which more or less amused everyone and took the emotional content out of the situation. During the course of the evening I remember remarking half humorously to Bess Abell, daughter of the former Kentucky Senator Clements and Mrs. Johnson's social secretary, that the whole thing was certainly not my idea.

Two days after the dinner party, a Washington columnist called, asking me to give her an interview on my disagreement with my husband over his policy and quoting my statement to Mrs. Abell. This rather shattering interpretation of my diffidence as public opposition made me realize once and for all that there was no longer any such thing as friendly or frank discussion in the social atmosphere of the time. I had to take my stand and make it clear as Gene was making his own.

I had long planned a short vacation with Dorothy Marks and two other friends in Florida prior to an Atlanta meeting of the Church Women United, where I had promised to speak. Now, for reasons which had nothing to do with politics, the other two had to drop out of our plan and I have always felt that it was brave of Dorothy at the time to go ahead herself and of Leonard to agree that she do so.

On the eve of our departure for Atlanta I was put under rather strong pressure by Helen Dudman, then woman's editor of the Washington *Post*, to give an interview to the *Post* about my feelings on Gene's proposed campaign. Helen had rather cannily arranged that the interviewer be the sophisticated and social Jenny Moore, wife of the Episcopal suffragan bishop of Washington, a member of my ecumenical prayer group. We had seen a great deal of Jenny in 1966 and 1967 since we moved to Cleveland Park. I had seen her book, *The People on Second Street*, in manuscript and knew of her ambition to keep writing. This left me with no viable means of exit.

It had become increasingly clear that I should make my stand public and that if I were to do so, certainly it would be best to do so in a friendly interview for a paper which seemed to be increasingly hostile to Gene. As I look back now on what I said in that interview it is clear that I was sending messages to friends in Minnesota and in Washington—messages pleading the cause of the dissenter in our society and protesting the cost to the dissenter. Jenny, who was friendly in her approach but wanted to write a lively interview, described me at the time as having "an element of the intellectual's vague detachment" in my manner "but involvement, too." She quotes me as saying: "Like any wife and mother I yearn for unity in a political sense as well as in my family, but that is not always the law of life, because growth requires purposeful division. Responsible dissent is the essence of democracy . . ."

There is in that interview my message to myself, I think, in the quotation that faith and experience have taught me one must not be overcautious.

There is my message to Minnesota: "We never have much idea what is in store in life. The tradition of Midwest politics is freedom: ours is not a machine background. In Minnesota, people tend to be more devoted to issues than personalities. I grew up in a pluralistic society: I resent homogenization."

There is my message to old friends: "I can't help but be painfully aware that this step of Gene's creates hardships for friends and political associates and it may be hard for some to understand."

And finally there is my message about Gene to his critics: "Gene was not afraid to be alone before. People forget. The relaxed understatement of his manner is so marked, it sometimes becomes confused with unflattering qualities. People don't know how deeply he feels and are surprised when he takes such decisive action."

It was on that note and with a feeling of trepidation that I left Washington that day. Gene drove me to the airport. We met Leonard and Dorothy there and made somewhat stiff conversation, but Dorothy and I got on the plane with the feeling of schoolgirls escaping for a holiday. It was my last carefree trip for a year and a half.

The reason I had been able to plan the trip at all was that I was scheduled to speak at the fall board meeting of Church Women United. On Tuesday of that week I flew back from Palm Beach to Atlanta. Here there was further evidence of widespread disaffection with the war among ordinary Americans, if Washington and the press had only had the eyes to see, and if those waverers like myself had only had the faith to believe.

It is strange that people have been so surprised at the emergence of the Church as an instrument of change: Richard Neuhaus, Lutheran theologian and pastor, who sought a New York congressional nomination in 1970, says that there are "two highly pragmatic reasons for a revolutionary reformer to be interested in the Church." The first is that the Church is a large part of the world—"the largest complex of voluntary associations in the United States of America." The second reason is that "in terms of its resources and personnel, of its facilities to communicate with and educate large numbers, and of its international constitution, the Church is crucial in revolutionary reform."

There is in the very reason for being of the Church an underlying sense of mission which, although it may lie dormant for long intervals, demands change and renewal. Ruth McKay, president of the Church Women United in New Hampshire in 1968, put it well when she said, "Most of all, I am a woman of the Church. As a serious woman of the Church, I see the mission or the work of the Church to be the Body of Christ. And if this is true, as I believe it is, then we need to be about the work that other Body was about—in other words, to be healing the hurts of mankind. It seemed to me that war was the largest hurt facing the world."

Church organizations of women tend to be much more grass roots in membership and program than do Church organizations of men. Perhaps the largest of these organizations is Church Women United, a coalition of women of many denominations and from the fifty states which can claim to be a channel to twenty-six million or more. In the 1960s the organization had changed its name from United Church Women with its implication of bureaucratic structure, and had begun to transform itself into a movement, thus opening its membership to hitherto ineligible women: young women, minority women, women of achievement in the arts, sciences, and business, and women like myself kept by the demands of a particular kind of life from being very active in Church organizations. They extended its ecumenical embrace to Orthodox and Catholic women. As a result of this change I had been one of the first four Catholic women to be elected to the board of Church Women United.

By the fall of 1967 I had already served as a member of its peace consultation under the chairmanship of Barbara Ward. So had Coretta King, wife of Martin Luther King, Jr. We had prepared support for a program of development. Development, we agreed, was basic to world peace. In the summer of 1967 a further step was taken at the triennial assembly—a mass meeting of delegates—held at Purdue University. We voted the condemnation of the use of indiscriminate weapons such as napalm, and we condemned any escalation which might lead to wider war. How insignificant this seems now! And yet when we went on to frame a peace resolution at the Atlanta board meeting, it was obvious that some of the board members were having second thoughts about any peace stand because of the sharpening of issues and the element of serious confrontation in their home states between pro-Administration forces and the dissenting critics. Among the strong supporters who argued for the peace statement which I helped frame were Ruth McKay, Ruth Kodani of California, and California state president Loris Coletta, Clarie Harvey of Mississippi, Olive Collins of Alabama, Julia Piper of Kansas, Clara Nicholson of Massachusetts—all new faces to me then, but people I met again in 1968.

Another point of disturbed debate was the call of the Jeannette Rankin Brigade to the Women's March on the Capitol. The call was framed in language which seemed inflammatory to many of the board and it had indeed been framed without any prior consultation with the Church Women.

Although I did not realize it at the time, the meeting was a graphic demonstration of the way in which the constituency of 1968 was being formed. It was a preview of the way in which renewed structures—or perhaps it is better to say the removal of rigid, old structures—could free individuals to grapple with the really overriding issues. The Church Women in Atlanta were crossing a bridge between the old and the new. In some areas they were taking new steps; in others they were lagging.

On Wednesday before my speech, I had a lengthy lunch with Coretta King whose husband had just gone into a retreat with his fellow workers in the Southern Christian Leadership Conference to pray over and discuss their plans for the Poor People's March.

We talked of Gene's projected candidacy and of his call to discuss it with Dr. King.

That night Walter Cronkite prematurely broke the news of Gene's impending announcement. Since my arrival at the meeting to speak at the luncheon the following day had been announced to the press, the hotel was instantly besieged by reporters from the various media demanding interviews with me.

I avoided the calls for two reasons. First, I hadn't a clue as to what my husband was going to say the next morning (the press conference was called for ten o'clock). Secondly, I was afraid that any attention focused on me would draw attention away from the meeting itself.

I discussed this with Margaret Shannon, the executive secretary. Her attitude was that it couldn't really hurt, that attention would be drawn to the fact that the Church Women were there by the very simple fact that I was being interviewed. But she agreed it would be easier if I had some orderly way to meet the press, so Maza Tilghman, the press relations staff person of Church Women United, began to take all the calls and arrange for a press conference which would take place immediately after the final luncheon and thus after all the events scheduled by the meeting.

Fortunately, none of the reporters in Atlanta had any idea what I looked like or where to look for me. So I had the dubious pleasure of walking by the cameras and the people in the lobby, watching them scan the faces as they went by, fairly secure in my knowledge that they couldn't possibly pick me out of the crowd.

In the morning meeting on the final day, Mrs. Dolbey, the president of the Church Women who was a former acting mayor of Cincinnati, announced that my husband was announcing for the presidency and asked for the good will and support of the women there for me in the days ahead, as friends if not supporters; she said she knew too well the abrasiveness of public life, especially for the women involved, and she felt that everyone there in good conscience could give him the support of prayer and good will.

I was very much touched by this, and it was my first inkling of the way in which many Church Women were to see the campaign in 1968—as a matter which involved principle and issue rather than party or personality. I think that of any group of women in 1968 the Church Women who took part in the campaign probably went farthest in what they did and took greater personal leaps than women who had always been involved in secular movements or in politics. For the Church Women were primarily apolitical and, if they participated in politics, it would usually be in the party into which they had been born. The effort to discern what was actually involved in our foreign policy, what relationship it had to Christian principle, to take a stand, then finally to move into active participation really involved a long, spiritual, personal journey for many.

I spoke at the luncheon on the development program espoused by the Church Women and left immediately afterward to meet the members of the press. Maza had talked to them about what questions they were going to ask and what ones I would not answer. She had ruled out questions of personal nature.

Perhaps, because Atlanta is the South and the South has traditionally been more committed to whatever is America's defense policy than any other part of the nation, I found the reporters polite but far from sympathetic. None of them seemed to me to be understanding of Gene's position or of the position of the anti-war people in general.

The press conference was like a confrontation. The newsmen seemed actually incredulous and almost hostile about what Gene had done. They seemed to hold me, in a way, responsible. Tony Howard of the London *Observer* was to write many months later, after the candidacy was a matter of history, that the Washington correspondents seemed to spend the year trying to prove that their initial reaction to Gene's candidacy was valid, that his action was foolish, unsupported by any real strength of opinion in the country, and disloyal to his party leaders. As he said, this attitude tended to distort the reporting of the campaign from the very beginning. And its historical significance was that in its relationship to the feelings about the war, about the necessity for peace, a great undercurrent in the country went unreported.

My experience in Atlanta, as I remember it, was evidence that this was true of all newsmen—not just the Washington correspondents. To this day, I feel that only the foreign correspondents, who watched us with detachment and with perhaps greater attention to research of what was actually happening, detected in those first moments what the candidacy really meant.

The newsmen in Atlanta were Southerners; they were polite to ladies as a matter of course. I detected their incredulity and their hostility only in the way their questions were phrased. They asked, for example, "How can your husband do this without fragmenting his party?" "Won't what your husband is doing give aid and comfort to the enemy?" And I met for the first time that ever-present question, "Isn't your husband really just a stalking horse for Robert Kennedy?"

As a political wife for twenty years, I have learned to deal as pleasantly as possible with questions like these, to make my own points if I can. The clippings from the press conferences and interviews in Atlanta show, I think, that I held my own.

And, happily, I found that although I had been deeply troubled about the course Gene was proposing to take in the months prior to his announcement, I had absorbed through my skin (one might say) his reasons for doing so. In this moment of truth, I found that I could give those reasons convincingly, for I had made them my own.

Gene had made his announcement less in terms of personal candidacy for the presidency than in terms of issues, planning to go through the channels provided for such a discussion—the presidential primaries. It was intended to be a different kind of campaign from those he had waged previously as a candidate for office. It was with this in mind that I had told both Jenny Moore and the interviewers in Atlanta that I did not expect to be as involved in or as active in this campaign as I had been in others.

Marion Sanders said in an article on women in politics in *Harper's* that a man running for office has a priceless asset: "That built-in housekeeper, secretary, chauffeur, and campaign manager—a wife."

This is a rather good approximation of my role in the years when Gene was running for the House, but I remember my activities in his Senate campaign rather differently. It seems to me that I became a den mother to the inevitable strays who attach themselves to campaigns as well as frantic behind-the-scenes planner of volunteer activities and telephone confidante of unseen advisers, contributors, and disturbed volunteers who needed the reassurance of some personal contact with the candidate. If not with the candidate, someone close to him. But, in late 1967 I was less the wife of a candidate than I was the wife of a prophet, and a prophet who was without much honor in his own country—the Senate of the United States and the Democratic party. One can search the books of the Old Testament from Isaiah to Malachi and find very little in the way of precept or practice to guide the wife of a prophet.

When I returned home, I discovered that the campaign had moved into our house. It was not only that our house seemed to be filled at all times with advisers, well-wishers, and people seeking a place in the campaign, that the telephone rang incessantly, that Gene's schedule changed from day to day, necessitating constant changes in family plans, but also that long-scheduled events that would have passed unnoticed in another year took on political significance and I found myself constantly on stage. And I had no time to prepare to be the wife of a presidential candidate!

I thought ruefully of the plaint of another political wife who had once said in a rare burst of confidence: "If I had known that this was going to happen to me, I would have changed my nose and my nickname."

I thought of many things I would like to have done, too. But here I was, limping on one foot because of a bone injured in our move the summer before, with a wardrobe adequate for the needs of run-of-the-mill Senate life but certainly not adequate for such a glare of publicity, and with a schedule already full and getting fuller. I drove the family Pontiac to my engagements. I had no press secretary, no appointments secretary, none of the entourage which seems to come automatically to a national candidate, and this fact seemed an affront to some of the news people and political figures trying to get in touch with me.

I found myself in almost the same position as I was in Gene's first campaign for Congress. The campaign was as yet without a center and people sought it at the house. The campaign came into the house most compellingly in those first days via Mary McGrory's telephone calls and visits.

We had always talked at length two or three times a week. Mary's writing gift was very great; by 1958 *Time* had dubbed her the "queen of the corps" because most of her male colleagues were willing to admit that she was the best writer among them. (Carroll Kilpatrick, then of the Washington *Post,* had sent her a humorous, despairing telegram imploring her to stop writing as a favor to his "fellow stumblebums," and James Reston of the *Times* said that her "poet's gift of analogy" made her a superior writer and he tried to hire her.) Mary herself said, "I have very few opinions, but powerful impressions. I am poor at summary, significance, relating— all I can do is respond." These responses were distilled into provocative sentences almost impossible for a reader to forget. "He walked like a prince and he talked like a scholar," she wrote of John Kennedy after his death; and of Senator Everett Dirksen, "His great enemy was boredom and he won every engagement."

I have always thought that the source of Mary's gift was the bardic, Celtic quality of her writing, a very sophisticated version of the oral tradition. Every column was first talked before it was written. Every friend of Mary's has been the recipient of telephone calls late in the evening or around six when she was working on copy at the *Star.* I used at first to think that she was asking for my opinion in these calls, but I came to realize that they were a means of creative effort. The interpersonal give and take was an essential ingredient of the process by which she fixed the essentials of the experience or the impression. It was a way of reaching for the right word, the telling phrase, the picture. In private life, Mary, as raconteur, was even more compelling than the Mary of the written page. One could be held spellbound by her account of a conflict with an upholsterer over a hassock. Drama is the stuff of her life: the most ordinary incident could be invested with color, suspense, meaning, as she turned her mind to it.

There was a certain arbitrariness in this quality when she abandoned impressions and espoused opinions. She tended to think of her friends and acquaintances in terms of the roles she cast them in. One was forever the gallant widow, for example; another, the perfect nun. Woe betide the friend who betrayed his or her role! In this characteristic, I think, we can find the source of her disillusionment with Robert Kennedy in 1968. It was with outright disbelief that she responded to what seemed to her his indefensible calculation and weighing of consequences. Bobby, who should have been the tilter at windmills, the defender of the young, was betraying his role by playing the wily politician.

For Mary was essentially issue-oriented. She had initially been a Stevensonian Democrat for this reason and supported Stevenson even in 1960. She used to argue with people looking for a winner that year, who brought up Jack Kennedy's name at dinner parties. She felt very strongly that he had not earned the right to run because of his relatively undistinguished career in House and Senate. Now she felt strongly about the Vietnam war, and when Gene had made his Berkeley speech calling for Dean Rusk's resignation, a postcard with cheers had come flying across the ocean from Mary who was in Europe on vacation.

In the pre- and post-announcement days Mary provided a link to the Kennedy camp. She acted informally as a go-between between Gene and Senator Kennedy and his associates. Most of this was on her own initiative, in that she had both a journalistic and personal interest in what both men were going to do. I remember one night when we three were visiting together that Gene said to Mary, "Well, tell him that if I run, I will only want one term. He can have a free run in 1972." In Mary's call the next day she admonished me that this was wild talk indeed, that the Kennedys would think it beyond belief as a suggestion. To me it seemed frightening talk, although I could dimly perceive that it was fully consistent with Gene's concept of the presidency. I saw in the remark—casual as it was—much more meaning: Gene was not just raising an issue. He was seriously running for President.

In this period Gene had two talks with Robert Kennedy and came away from them convinced that the latter was not going to challenge the President. I heard of Senator Kennedy's reaction to the second meeting from Mary. He had set aside an hour to discuss the primaries with Gene—the possibilities and the pitfalls. He had at hand lists of key people. Gene had talked in generalities, stayed seven minutes (by actual count, I gathered) and left!

Mary who had long cherished the hope that the two men might come to understand each other better, even to like each other, thought it was disappointing behavior on Gene's part—to put her reaction mildly.

At the time I relayed Mary's news to Gene, but not her concerns, except to verify a detail or two I might wonder about. It was a very tricky time. As Paul Wieck wrote in the *New Republic*, Gene was having to deal with the Washington syndrome, "with people in the press and in the party structure and in the government who were wilfully out of touch with the climate of opinion outside of Washington . . . The Washington syndrome has strong withdrawal symptoms." Gene was finding the support from those he had reason to count on less than enthusiastic.

None of the people who had been discussed or approached hopefully as campaign managers and organizers had agreed to help, although some of them had urged Gene to take the step he took . . . not Kenneth O'Donnell, Fred Dutton, Thomas Finney, Jr., former Governor Terry Sanford of North Carolina, former Postmaster General Edward P. Day, Senator Vance Hartke, and Representative Don Edwards. "All the classical excuses were given," Gene wrote with some bitterness. "Family obligations, professional commitments, etc. One individual said he had just joined a law firm and too much depended on his being in the firm. Another used the argument of his general financial and business interests, and some, that they had received political favors of one kind or another from the Johnson administration." Gene never liked to approach people directly for help, and such a series of rebuffs, even indirectly received (as I think most of them were), was difficult. Even worse were the members of what he called the "Nicodemus Society"—a reference to Nicodemus in the story of Jesus, who "supported the cause only between sundown and sunrise"—which included, at the time, even his former aide and long-time close friend, Larry Merthan, now an officer in the public relations firm of Hill and Knowlton. It is little wonder that the open support and help of such well-known people as John Kenneth Galbraith, Richard Goodwin, and Robert Lowell meant so much to him later.

Partly because of these beginnings, Mary McGrory eventually proved to be the most influential person in the campaign—influential because of her effect on public opinion and influential because of her relationship to people within and without the campaign structure itself. In these days she was a constant talent scout for the building campaign organization.

It was Mary who brought Blair Clark, soon to be campaign manager, to the campaign. It was with her that he came to the candidate's suite at the Chicago meeting of Concerned Democrats on December 2. We had known Blair for some years, but very casually and through Mary. They had been friends for a long time.

On the way back from Chicago, Blair came to the house with Mary after they had lunched together. We talked rather idly about what Blair might do in the campaign and of people he might enlist. Mary and I left Gene and Blair talking while we went walking. As we scuffed through the sodden leaves still thick on Cleveland Park sidewalks in late fall, Mary talked of Blair. Blair was a pleasant person of many friendships and connections. He had been a Harvard classmate and friend of John Kennedy's. His wealth had made it easy for him to go from one interesting occupation to another. He had edited a paper and had been an executive at CBS. (Those who remember the Kennedy-Nixon debates of 1960 could recall Blair as one of the friendly interlocutors.) He had acted briefly as press aide for his friend Averell Harriman in one of his campaigns. For the past two years he had been drifting about Europe having an interesting but idle time. From Mary's point of view, he needed saving from his own aimlessness. (Mary tended to be somewhat directive toward her friends, always with their good in mind. Paul Niven, another television personality and her devoted friend, and I used to commiserate with each other about this at times.) Now Mary thought that Blair's interest in the campaign was providential; he would be good for the campaign and it would be good for him. On Sunday that week Gene met again with Blair in New York and asked him to be campaign manager. Blair agreed to act on a temporary basis. He, as well as others, thought then that a bigger political name would finally emerge for this task.

"What do I get for bringing Blair Clark to the campaign?" Jerome Eller, Gene's administrative assistant, reported Mary as asking him. He was not happy with the question. At that time Jerry tended to think that the campaign could be masterminded, if not actually run, out of the Senate office, with perhaps the help of the temporary financial office which had already been set up by John Safer and June Degnan, two old friends of Gene's. Jerry was another daily presence on the telephone. Actually his thought was probably consistent with the theory of a limited campaign which Gene talked about, but it was not very realistic.

In the inevitable mythmaking and fairly hasty, perhaps lazy, reporting of a presidential campaign in which one reporter tends to rewrite another, the idea seemed to have become firmly fixed in everyone's mind that Jerome Eller had been Gene's aide and confidant since the beginning of his congressional career. Actually he had joined the staff shortly before the 1964 campaign, and it was only after Larry Merthan left the staff for lobbying in 1965 that Jerry began to go with Gene as an aide on trips.

Jerry had been a student at St. John's after Gene left in 1944; they had not known each other there. When he came to Washington on the staff of Congressman Fred Marshall, the congressman for a central Minnesota district, Father Godfrey had written asking that we look him up, and we invited him to dinner. At that time he was writing a novel. Although he stayed on as a congressional aide year after year, he continued to write a little, and wrote a regular Washington column for *America*, the national Jesuit review. We saw him occasionally through the years, and he was in close touch with Gene's staff because of their common connections.

Now in 1968 he was facing a national campaign, having gone through only one state-wide campaign and only one with Gene, the race for the Senate in 1964. It was a good campaign—Gene had the largest majority in Minnesota history—but Jerry had had the resources of a well-organized state party and a volunteer organization which had been two years in the building as well. As the difficulties mounted in late 1967, he called every day to discuss ways of mobilizing and using volunteers. I listened, but I resisted involvement, because Gene had said he did not want that kind of campaign. I did not feel I could go against his wishes. But at one point I suggested that he ask Arleen Hynes, wife of Emerson Hynes, our long-time friend, now Gene's legislative assistant, to co-ordinate volunteer activity. Arleen, the mother of ten children, is a marvelously disciplined and organized person who works with other people very effectively. She held office in the American Association of University Women and had done volunteer work for specialized agencies like Family and Child Services. She had helped organize the volunteers for Gene's '64 campaign. Jerry thought the request would come better from me, so I talked to Arleen. We had been friends since our courtship days and had tried to keep our families in close touch by alternating Thanksgiving celebrations each year at their house and ours. She, like Blair, thought she could assume the responsibility on a temporary basis—surely we would find some well-known political person to take over! Then Jerry was concerned with where the volunteers would work. The only campaign office at that time was a small suite in the Capitol Hill Hotel. Arleen searched, Jerry searched. Even John Safer, whose business was the management of investment properties and necessarily had all sorts of real estate connections, searched to no avail.

There are certain requirements for volunteer offices. They should be accessible. Their location should be fairly safe so that volunteers can work at night—night work is the stuff of life in a political campaign. There should be easy and convenient parking, because housewives who are paying baby-sitters to free them for campaign activity cannot afford further expense. But nobody in Washington with such facilities vacant wanted to rent to a candidate challenging the President. At one point John Safer thought he had secured an empty supermarket near the Georgetown section of Washington—an ideal location—but when the board of the chain met they vetoed the agreement on the grounds that it would affect the chain image adversely to rent a store to the McCarthy campaign. Finally I said that they could use for the time being the third floor of our house, where Walter Lippmann had had his offices. Tables and chairs were rented. Charlie Callanan of the Senate office began a regular run back and forth each day with accumulated mail. And volunteers from the Cleveland Park neighborhood moved in, a dedicated group of women, who later called themselves the "Attic Group." They were aided by neighborhood high school students who took over at four o'clock, often working into the evening. The campaign was in the house with a vengeance!

Mary McGrory called to say that Jerry had reported my capitulation to volunteer work with a triumphant word to her, "Abigail's on. She's on!" "I don't recognize my old friends when Jerry talks about you two," sniffed Mary. "It's as if you were some giant and giantess." And perhaps the campaign *had* mysteriously enlarged us for Jerry. Gene was the agent of a totally new life, lived, as it were, on a very wide screen.

A third daily caller was Dr. William Davidson, a psychiatrist who at that time held a post in the State Department that he had secured with Gene's help. He had entered our lives during the 1964 campaign when he and a fellow intern in psychiatry turned up evenings in the campaign office as volunteer envelope stuffers—a relief, they said, from the pressures of their work at the hospital. He thought of himself, he often told me, as an "intercessor," a necessary link between people who could advance each other's causes. All great men needed someone to perform this service, he said.

William Davidson had a curious history. He and his wife were both from broken families and were converts to Catholicism. They had met as fellow students at Duke University and became Catholics, he had once told me, after a strange spiritual safari which began in Jerusalem and worked back through some of the great historical Christian centers of Europe. Some time in the early years of their marriage they had explored the idea of entering religious communities. His wife had tried living with the Trappistines in northern New England or Quebec and he, I believe, had been associated with a new community of Benedictines. These things eventually had not worked out and they had ended up coming to the neighborhood of

St. John's because of the attraction of living a Catholic family life near a monastic center. He had been a surgeon then and practiced surgery at St. Cloud Hospital and acted as college doctor for both St. John's and St. Benedict's. They had built a spectacular $90,000 house near the grounds of the latter college. It was the marvel of the surrounding countryside.

One of their children had died as a result of an accident in that house. This experience, he said, had led him to leave the St. John's area and to take up the study of psychiatry at the University of Minnesota, while his wife taught at St. Benedict's and took care of their other children.

When he left Minnesota, he had wanted to go on to the Harvard faculty, and he did secure a year's appointment there in a government-funded program having to do with medical services in a poverty area. It was during this time in Boston that he divorced his wife and left the Catholic Church. His interests turned to the peace movement and he became acquainted with the peace group known as Mass Pax. During this time he had kept up an intense relationship with people in the Senate office and with us as far as he possibly could.

Through the summer and fall of 1968 Dr. Davidson had been a self-appointed advocate of Gene's candidacy. He said that I should see it as the will of God and the fruit of prayer. I do not remember the exact gist of his argument, but I do remember that he threw in a great deal about St. John of the Cross and other mystics. This rather irritated me because I thought he was adducing arguments he did not really believe, but which he thought would convince me. I thought the discussion of the challenge to the President should be in terms of "things seen" rather than "things unseen." What I thought I could see was a very lonely course. I did not think as Dr. Davidson did that Gene had only to make the step and other peace-minded senators would follow. It seemed to me completely lacking in any kind of political realism to suppose that they would take such a risk in support of someone else if they would not take the risk for themselves, either as primary candidates or as the favorite sons of their own states.

Now that Gene had announced, Bill Davidson's concern was the credibility of Gene's effort and he called every day with suggestions as to tactics, personnel, public relations. As the campaign went from primary to primary, Bill Davidson became a fixture of it, sleeping on a couch in our suite in New Hampshire, moving in with a staffer in Oregon, finally announcing himself as campaign doctor in Chicago.

The campaign came into the house in other ways. Long before Gene's announcement I had agreed to give a December coffee for the library group from the Women's National Democratic Club and to review books written by Senate wives. Mrs. Philip Desmarais, whose husband was a former Minnesotan, was chairman that year and had thought having the coffee might bring more than the usual fifteen or so to the library meeting. Isabelle Shelton wrote of what happened in her nationally syndicated column:

> Abigail McCarthy, mother of four and former college teacher, knew her life would change after her husband announced that he was a candidate for Democratic presidential nomination.
> But she didn't quite expect the campaign would gallop into her own living room and overflow out into the hallway and library. . . .
> "They said about twenty of us would sit around the fireplace and chat," Abigail later said plaintively. . . .
> As the day of the meeting approached, the club office was inundated with phone calls from members and and also from the national press, all wanting to attend. . . . The McCarthys have a fairly roomy house—having recently rented the house in northwest Washington, where columnist Walter Lippmann lived. . . . But it isn't that roomy. Not much is, except a hotel ballroom or a football stadium.
> The library committee did its best. It banned the press, and cut off member's reservations at 120 (20 more than Mrs. McCarthy thought she could comfortably accommodate). Furniture was shoved back against the walls, and rows of folding chairs were set up there and in the entrance hallway. But there were still standees.

The press, of course, did not stay banned. I had admitted Isabelle early, thinking that she was the pool reporter who usually covered club functions. Her presence angered other reporters, who were held at bay at the door by library committee members. Marie Smith, then of the Washington *Post*, a tall, handsome woman, stood in the doorway and said she would not move until she was admitted, since it was a matter of her job. It was not my intention, naturally, to alienate the press and we finally invited everyone in. Isabelle Shelton went on to say that the committee should not have worried.

> First taking note of the crowded room Abigail said with a twinkle in her eye: "But then I should have known people would like to see what we did with Walter Lippmann's house."
>
> In passing she recalled Eric Sevareid's reference to "those great cold states from North Dakota to Michigan that produce maverick political leaders," then commented deadpan that this was "very instructive reading now."
>
> . . . She selected for quotation a comment by Mrs. Proxmire that had clear and obvious meaning for her own present situation, "If your husband is controversial (and most of the men who have been successful in historical terms are controversial during their careers), you have to develop and survive a new emotional state of being. There is pride mixed with concern for consequences, there is the need for a relaxed, self-assured outward appearance despite churning inner discomfort . . . there is some hesitation in your relationship with others. Because most senator's wives follow the news closely, you wonder whether or not you will be accepted in the same warm way as before."

In thinking about it afterward, I was conscious of something Isabelle had not noted. Of all the members there that day only one was a Senate wife. And I felt it was as poignant as she did when she called attention to a photograph in our library. "The photograph shows Mrs. McCarthy seated at a state dinner in the White House, and the inscription reads 'to Abigail McCarthy with warm affection, Lady Bird Johnson.'"

The campaign followed us everywhere—I found that we could not escape from it any place. We had looked forward to a dinner which Carolyn Kizer, a poet and member of the National Arts Council, was giving for her father; James Dickey and his wife were to be there. Dickey, at the time, was the poet in residence at the Library of Congress and Gene was very fond of him. It was a pleasant informal dinner but among the guests were the Michalowskis, the Polish ambassador and his wife. The ambassador came to sit beside me after dinner and told me that both he and his wife were very much interested in what Gene was doing—that they, too, wanted nothing so much as an end to the war in Vietnam—but that he was concerned that negotiations which at that time were being maneuvered through Polish contacts, would be harmed if Hanoi had the idea that we in the United States had nothing to trade. (There is a reference to these negotiations in Lyndon Johnson's *Vantage Point*.) The ambassador had been the Polish ambassador to North Vietnam and knew the people there very well. He suggested that Hanoi would have less interest in the negotiations if the prevailing opinion there was that public opinion in the United States would force an end to the war. His concern on this particular night was stirred by something that Gene had said on a television interview program the Sunday before. Gene had not, I was sure, suggested unilateral withdrawal. His position was that peace should be negotiated with a coalition government in the South. He also had given some support to the enclave theory proposed by General James Gavin. The ambassador said that he would very much like to discuss this with Gene privately, on a very unofficial basis. And Mira Michalowska suggested that we might get together as families when our young people were home for the holidays. I agreed and we set a date for when their son would be home from Carleton.

I was deeply troubled by what the ambassador said. It seemed a great burden for Gene to bear. Soon after that, our friend of our farm days, Marie Bonne de Viel-Castel, now Mrs. Eugene Roberts, called to plead in her lovely fluting voice the cause of her stepson. He was completing graduate school of business in New York and had a plan for recruiting young businessmen for the New Hampshire campaign, both in New Hampshire and in the neighboring states. He was desperate, she said, because he could not seem to get in touch with anyone in charge of the campaign or interest anyone. Would I do something about it? I suggested that he come to the same young people's gathering and promised to have somebody there from the campaign office. And so the campaign invaded our holidays.

New Year's Day came and with it 1968—a year of great personal loss and gain. It was a year in which old associations were irrevocably sundered and a way of life disrupted forever. It was a year of abrupt introduction to kinds of people who heretofore had been only abstractions to me. It was a year in which I was thrown into a kind of unsolicited intimacy with people whom I would never have sought out but from whom I learned much about the times in which we lived. It was a year of momentary but intense communication with people who, to all intents and purposes, seemed to appear out of nowhere as witnesses to an unseen America and then to disappear again. It was a year in which the voices of strangers quickly grew as familiar on the phone as those of my own family. It was a year of trips shared cosily with men and women whom I remember now only for a driving habit, a regional turn of phrase, or a penchant for certain foods. It was a year of education.

Wives of candidates are always in an anomalous position. Protocol decrees that a wife takes her husband's rank, but campaign cohorts are not so sure that is a good thing. Campaign aides, local chairmen, campaign correspondents—especially female correspondents—find wives something in the nature of excess baggage. Yet the American campaign image demands a wife and family, ever faithful, ever admiring, ever at the side of the ideal husband and father. This poses something of a problem in any campaign.

In 1968 I was caught between two traditions: that of the eastern Establishment whose point of view dominated the press and is covertly anti-feminist ("Mercifully, she makes no speeches," wrote *Time* of Ethel Kennedy) and the midwestern in which I was expected to support my husband's cause by giving it another dimension and reaching support not otherwise available to him in the tradition pioneered by Martha Taft and Belle La Follette.

Twice in the first month and a half of the campaign I was cajoled and coerced into the latter role by old supporters of Gene who expected, almost demanded, that I appear at events they had planned. Each time I learned a little about the New Constituency. Under the stress of Gene's frequent absences—and Jerry's—office communication with the house about schedules often broke down completely. I had an anguished call from Kay Nee in Minnesota just before Gene was to appear at the Conference for Concerned Democrats there. The invitation to the women's luncheon of the conference had gone out with my name on the invitation and all prior publicity had been built around my presence there. No one had told me. I did not see how I could get ready and make all the necessary adjustments at home in such a short time. Kay was disappointed but professed to understand.

Her call was immediately followed by one from Alpha Smaby, the representative in the Minnesota legislature who was the first elected official in the country to announce her allegiance to the Conference of Concerned Democrats. Alpha was adamant. I had to come. I could not let them down when they were risking everything to prove that there was strong and responsible opposition to the war among the people in the Vice President's own state. It was to be Gene's first appearance there after his announcement and I should be with him. I went.

We arrived at a time when Gene was almost swallowed up in the pre-dinner press conference, interviews, requests from the television reporters, and the press of people wanting just a word with him here or a moment there. There was great network interest in the meeting because it seemed to be a confrontation between the forces of the Administration and the forces of dissent. Vice President Humphrey was in the state to speak the next morning to the Democratic Central State Committee.

In our suite, old friends and some of Gene's early supporters gathered before the dinner, among them the Gablers, the Carlsons, and the Nees. Sometime during the course of the pre-dinner hour, I discovered that I was the main speaker at the luncheon the next day. I had thought that I was just an honor guest at the head table. Since the rest of the evening was taken up by the rally downstairs— we walked together for the first time blindly into the glare of television lights, between rows of cheering people whom we could not see—Gene's speech and the follow-up time of meeting and greeting people there, I had no time to prepare the speech that evening and I tried to put it together hurriedly the next morning.

Although we could spot old friends, independents, and some old Democratic stand-bys among the people at the rally, most of the people were new to me and new to Gene. This was true of the luncheon also. I rose to face them with no very clear idea of what they expected of me. It was a patchwork speech, full of quotations from a recent article of Eric Fromm's which had impressed me on what the Vietnam war was doing to our national values and ending with testimony to what women could do and had done and how women, in many cases, had turned politics from the consideration of personalities to the consideration of issues.

In passing, I paid tribute to Myrtle Cain who was present at the head table, one of the first women in the country to have been elected to office—to the Minnesota State Legislature—after women achieved the vote. I gave tribute also to Mrs. Smaby, presently serving in the legislature. I pointed out that the transition from the militant feminism which was necessary for Miss Cain's success and the acceptance of Alpha as a person who had originally exercised her talents as a volunteer and graduated to politics from volunteerism, with the support of her husband and children, was a phenomenon peculiar to recent years.

Just before I left for the airport, I received a call from another of the women who had been at the head table, Mary Heffernan, a young mother very active in the peace movement, who had done more than anyone else to organize the forces of dissent in St. Paul. She wanted to tell me, she said, that although my speech was very nice and she didn't want to upset me, she thought my emphasis on the work of women in a campaign such as we were facing was "counterproductive." She said: "It may be all right for women of your generation and Mrs. Smaby's, but we younger women want to work shoulder to shoulder with the men."

It was from women like Mary that the thrust was to come in the women's liberation movement in the year of great disillusionment after the campaign. I said that I was sorry that had I not made it clear that many women would naturally work in the main drive of the campaign, but that there were many other women who by reason of the circumstances of their lives could not work that way; they had to work within the context of their own lives. And I thought to myself of how often working "shoulder to shoulder" with men left women carrying coffee and taking notes.

Gene was to speak at a state conference in Florida in January. Although I did not wish to attend the conference, my resistance to the trip was worn down—little by little—by calls from Bea Baxter Mayer, a former Minnesota television personality, who had worked hard in Gene's first Senate campaign when her name meant a great deal to us. She and her husband were now in public relations work in Florida and dedicated to the anti-war movement there. At that conference I had a startled realization of how much the people coming together in Gene's campaign were a floating population of like-minded people not well-rooted in the states in which they lived. This was of course more apparent in a state like Florida.

Up to that time, too, I had thought of the venture as Gene's campaign. In Florida I had a sense of how hard a struggle it was going to be to make it that. So many of these people looked on a candidate as the instrument of their will to bring about change, rather than as someone to follow. But I also had a happy discovery in Florida. I had dreaded the interviews Bea had insisted on arranging for me. The hostility to Gene's move which had been so thinly veiled with courtesy in Atlanta had made me wary. In Florida I experienced for the first time, even in the seasoned and savvy reporter from *Women's Wear Daily*, the disposition among press women to give me a little more than an even break, because of their own underlying concern—as wives and mothers and concerned women—about what the war was doing to the country. So, even though what I thought of as a fairly chic French twist came out in *Women's Wear Daily* as a "schoolteacher's bun," I did not fare too badly, and the cause didn't suffer.

Then came New Hampshire and every effort to keep the campaign a low-keyed, rational effort to discuss the issues foundered. Everything changed.

There had been increasing concern in the latter part of December about the credibility of the campaign. It seemed to be stalled, people said, not getting off the ground. Gene was not inclined to file in New Hampshire. His first idea was to wage a limited campaign focused on four primaries: Massachusetts, Wisconsin, Oregon, and California. He looked on the New Hampshire primary as a publicity generator, not a true test of strength. However, the pressures were great. On January 3, 1968, he announced that he would file.

His schedule was jammed with appointments in California, Wisconsin, and even Georgia, so that just getting to New Hampshire to start working on the primary was difficult. The New Hampshire workers, naturally completely absorbed by their own problems, became increasingly vocal and restive about their inability to produce the candidate. The young people, who by this time were coming to the campaign in great numbers, were especially upset.

In retrospect, I think this was because the communications media, especially the national commentators and columnists, were fixated on New Hampshire and could not seem to see the campaign elsewhere. In Wisconsin in early December when two local people opened a McCarthy campaign office in Madison, according to Mrs. Ed Miller, the manager,

> All of a sudden there was an avalanche of people just begging for a chance to do anything. People would walk in off the street and pick up paintbrushes, without ever introducing themselves. They

would walk in off the street, give us money. There was practically nothing that you could ask that wasn't given. . . . It was a sort of dammed up frustration which had been released by the removal of the hopelessness. And the desire to make this succeed was so strong that people just literally came on their own.

Two and one half months later on February 15, when Ben Stavis and his wife Roseann set to work to help open the New Hampshire state headquarters on a full-time basis, he noted that "the campaign existed in the national press and on television, but had barely begun in New Hampshire."

Does this mean that Gene was right in his original plan—to raise the issue in Wisconsin, Oregon, Massachusetts, and California? To let people come to his banner? I don't know, but it is true that the most solid primary wins in Oregon and in Wisconsin were based on local people exercising their initiative with the help of large groups of local volunteers. The national staff, when they appeared in these states, were more or less frosting on the cake.

The decision to enter New Hampshire changed all that. The people of New Hampshire are politically different from the people of Wisconsin and Oregon. They are, according to Sylvia Chaplain in whose living room the first organizing meeting took place, "spoiled. Because in any little town, all of the candidates for the presidency come through it at one time or another; and everybody gets a chance to look him in the eye." The tendency in New Hampshire is to put the whole burden on the candidate. And the people are a bit crotchety. The Republican senator from New Hampshire, Norris Cotton, blamed Senator Kefauver's campaigns for making them think too highly of themselves: "The average voter in New Hampshire feels ten feet high. He is thinking how his vote will have this terrific meaning for the whole country. He gets too thoughtful and too self-conscious."

It is interesting that the New Hampshire primary was twice won on the Republican side by the people who weren't there at all, nor were they the choice of the local political structure—General Eisenhower and Ambassador Henry Cabot Lodge. This would seem on the face of it to belie the necessity for voters to look the candidates in the eye. But in 1968 New Hampshire was made to seem a vital test, not only of the reality of Gene's campaign, but of his will to win.

Our daughter Mary called me during this period saying that she was going to quit school and campaign in New Hampshire if "you guys," as she referred to her father and me, were not going to do something about it. Gene told an interviewer in that period that only Mary's increasing disillusionment worried him.

Mary's concern was understandable. She was in Cambridge, in daily contact with the students of the New Left. Many of them, including the more militant members of the Students for a Democratic Society, looked askance at the idea of a political solution to the problems of America. They had been bred in the civil rights movement and blooded on demonstrations and confrontations. They wanted to change American institutions. They were unwilling to settle, as Ben Stavis was, for the "introduction of flexibility and unknowns into the political situation." Mary heard their arguments in the student dining rooms. And in listening to the more moderate students reject her father's style (he refused to stigmatize the President personally as either tyrant or war criminal), she must have scented approaching repudiation and what seemed to her potential disaster.

Because of her distress I decided that perhaps I should do something about New Hampshire, at the very least look into the possibility of extending the volunteer effort there and seeing how the volunteers in Washington might help. Gene agreed. Jenny Moore and I had planned to take our younger children somewhere for a ski weekend. We decided to take them to New Hampshire.

By this time Barbara Haviland had taken on direction of the Attic Group as a full time project. Barbara was the Quaker member of our prayer group. She had the Quaker commitment to peace as well as the emotional concern of a mother of boys about the war. Furthermore she was a capable professional woman with a history of experience in community action. She and her husband had a summer place in New Hampshire, and Barbara asked her friends there about a good family place to go. They recommended the Dexter Lodge at Sunapee. It had the advantage of being in the southern part of the state, accessible from Boston. It was close enough so that I could visit Manchester if it seemed possible to do so.

Meanwhile Patricia McGerr, an old friend of ours who had affiliated herself with the Attic Group, set about studying New Hampshire. Pat is a professional writer of distinction in the mystery story field, having in the past won an Edgar Allan Poe award and its French equivalent. She also writes religious biography. She researched New Hampshire as she would the locale for one of her detective novels. As she said, to write about Monte Carlo meant that she had to make a study of the population—the nature of the population, the education of the people, the history of the origins of the people, and so on, if her book was to ring true. Since she had been a good working Democrat in her native Nebraska, and one-time candidate for city council in Washington, she included very practical information about the number of votes cast in the last elections, the number of registered Democrats in each town, and the vagaries of the primary law.

All this was compiled into a little mimeographed booklet. On the final page there were some rather pathetic notes gleaned from conversations with almost everyone. The section was entitled "People Who Know People." There were notations that "Dick Fryklund (Washington *Star* reporter) has a friend in N.H. He's enthusiastic about McCarthy campaign"; "Paul Niven has brother with newspaper in Maine just over border. Substantial N.H. circulation"; "Riley Hughes's college roommate is baseball great Birdie (George R.) Tebbetts whose home base is in Nashua, N. H. Riley also suggested Dr. Adrian J. Levesque—Georgetown U. alumnus who received distinguished alumnus award. Very active in civic and French groups but may be Republican"; "Check May Sarton and Dean Sayre"; "Pat McGerr knows Sister Mary Walter, editor of *Magnificat* in Manchester. Sister of Mercy order which runs Mount St. Mary College in Hooksett and many parish schools"; "Letters of support were signed by Alice Pollard of Women for Peace in Hanover and Alexander Laney of Voters Betrayed by Johnson."

After Pat gathered her material, she visited the newly opened campaign office in the Transportation Building in Washington to see if she might co-ordinate her research with whatever had been done there. This office was opened shortly after the first of the year by Meyer Samuel Frucher, called Sandy, a young man who had become assistant to Blair Clark by dint of repeated phone calls offering himself and citing his credentials. It was only after he became deputy campaign director that we discovered he was only twenty-two. Also working there by that time were young Peter Barnes who had taken leave of absence from *Newsweek* and Seymour Hersh, a young AP reporter who had written a book on chemical warfare. It was Sy Hersh who talked to Pat—they had Mary McGrory as a mutual friend. He gave her a pamphlet, saying grandly, "Yes, we do have research on the primary states." It was her own.

Except for Blair, Peter Barnes, whom I had met during the Christmas holidays, and Sam Brown, the newly arrived co-ordinator of student effort whom I thought of as a friend of our Mary's, the gathering national staff were unknown to me. I heard names from time to time, but had only the haziest ideas as to their responsibilities. From time to time Curtis Gans would call to ask me how well I knew this or that contributor. I know it seems incredible, but I didn't even know who Curtis was.

It did not occur to me at the time that what seemed to be confusion at the center of the campaign might reflect a disparity of aims. After the campaign, I read that Blair had recruited Sy Hersh with the assurance, "All we want to do is get Kennedy in." He also had told an interviewer, "I never knew the McCarthys really except for an occasional meeting." This last was true, and the first made sense in retrospect; Blair was a long-time Kennedy friend. At the time I write of, he was being given credit for persuading Gene to enter New Hampshire, and, of course, any success for Gene there would be meaningful for Bobby Kennedy. Such an aim would also explain Blair's preoccupation with California. Complaints were loud at the time that he was neglecting the central organization and New Hampshire to concentrate there. He was, it seems, trying to broaden the McCarthy organization, which Gene had entrusted to the California Democratic Council and Gerald Hill, to include some other state political personalities. This provoked almost disastrous controversy at the time, but also made sense in terms of his long-term objective, since California was the projected plum of primaries. But I did not think of these things then, nor did Gene.

In looking back, one can see that the others in the national office had mixed aims as well, having to do with their commitments and their personal ambitions. My own aim was rather primitive and simple. My husband was in a campaign and wanted to win. My children wanted him to win. Therefore we would help him win in the ways we knew. To someone who lives in complexity and who, by academic habit of mind, tends to see all sides of a question, there is something marvelously energizing, even exhilarating, about a simple, well-defined goal.

So Jenny Moore and I and the children, Michael and Margaret, Michael's classmate Roberto Suro, and two of the Moore children, went off to New Hampshire in a burst of good spirits. They to ski, I to politic. Arleen Hynes, who had moved into the new national headquarters, had made some preparation for me. ("I don't know what Mrs. Hynes is doing," Blair phoned once to say accusingly. "Neither do I, Blair," I had answered. What Arleen was doing was filling vacuums. One of them was communication with people in the states.) Arleen, worried like everyone else about New Hampshire, had visited there the week before and she tried to set up contacts for me. I myself had tried to think of everyone I knew in New Hampshire.

Among these were Bishop Primeau, the bishop of all New Hampshire, whom we had seen in Rome several times during Vatican II. We knew him as a Midwesterner who was relatively liberal. There was also Mary Perkins Ryan, a pioneer and scholar in the liturgical movement, whose husband was a professor at St. Anselm's College in Manchester. And there was a Colonel Diekmann, the retired army officer brother of the theologians Father Godfrey and Father Conrad at St. John's.

It was a slim list, but at least they were people to whom I could talk and find out something about New Hampshire. I had called Bishop Primeau prior to leaving Washington and he had been most gracious, emphasizing, however, as he was bound to do, that he was interested in seeing me as an old friend, not as a political figure, and I had been equally insistent that it was only friendship which interested me in seeing him while I was in New Hampshire.

When I arrived at Bishop Primeau's residence in Manchester on Sunday afternoon, we sat down for coffee and a casual chat. I was soon lost in admiration at the bishop's astuteness. He kept saying, "We, of course, cannot be political. We are neutral." I agreed that this must be the case, but that perhaps he knew some people I could be in touch with. Perhaps there were some prominent Democrats he could introduce me to, so that I could explore the possibility for volunteers? Once assured of my prudence, he got up briskly and went into his desk where he gathered up a collection of literature which had come out from the peace groups in New Hampshire and was now being issued as McCarthy campaign literature. He also "just happened" to have a map of New Hampshire on which he indicated to me the most heavily Democratic areas. It was clear that the heaviest concentrations were in Manchester, Nashua, and Berlin. I had not heard of Berlin—the memo sent to Gene by David Hoeh, chairman of the New Hampshire committee, had stressed the downstate area.

The bishop told me that the people in Berlin were largely all Roman Catholics of Canadian origin who preferred to speak French, that they were more or less cut off from the rest of the state because the mountains interfered with radio and television transmission, and that very few of them subscribed to out-of-state papers. In fact, they listened to radio and television programs from Canada and Maine more than they did to any from the rest of New England. As bishop, he was aware of these things because they complicated the administration of the diocese. He also adverted to the one fact everyone did seem to know about New Hampshire, that the Manchester paper with its hostile conservatism blanketed the area.

He showed me the campaign literature and indicated obliquely that, with his knowledge of the candidate and his "splendid record," this literature was doing Gene a disservice, since it was not really representative of him. He also felt that the kind of campaign rallies held so far were more inflammatory and divisive than persuasive. He gave me the names of two or three Democrats I might call, but said he thought it a courtesy gesture since they were administration stalwarts. I left with the impression that this was a bishop who knew his diocese. To me this small sensible exchange made the trip worthwhile. I came away with some practical information and the confirmation of my intuitive feeling that the campaign was not yet geared to the candidate, in that it was still primarily a peace demonstration campaign.

The New Hampshire campaign organization sent a student driver to the lodge. He was a Yale graduate student who had been coming to New Hampshire weekends since it was announced that Gene would run there. He was deeply disappointed in what he had been asked to do up to that time and spent the time on the road plying me with questions about campaigning. We talked about such practical things as how to make up a mailing list and what groups in communities one might get in touch with to broaden the campaign base.

What I did not realize at the time was that the two young men who ran the office, David Hoeh and Gerry Studds, both teachers, were then able to give only spare time to the campaign. They had young people to work with, but no very clear plan for using them. They were rather at a loss as to how to proceed in any area outside Concord, where David Hoeh was planning to run for Congress in the fall.

When I got back to Washington I received a memo from Arleen which underlined their difficulties. "Need for a full-time person for next five weeks desperate," she had written. "Hoeh and Studds cannot even do small essentials for adequate coverage without permanent paid secretary at Concord office. They say they have no money. They hope to get brochures for state-wide mailing ready but no mailings have been made." She also underlined what I learned from Bishop Primeau—the greatest need was for a more general knowledge of Gene and his stands on issues other than peace. "Among those I met," she said, "the only supporters he appears to have gained in the Manchester area are the peace-oriented people."

I came away from this little exploration feeling that, given the size of the population—less than that of a Minnesota city—and the possibility of reaching them through personal campaigning, the chances were much brighter in New Hampshire than anyone could believe. (Pollsters of the time were giving Gene 5 and 10 per cent of the Democratic vote.) Gene and I talked about the similarities to his first congressional district and his first campaign. During the 1948 campaign, too, the people he wanted to reach were in a fairly concentrated area so that his record and connections could be made known to people in a relatively short time. There were also troops of students in that first campaign, most of them veterans who had come back from World War II with an entirely different view of their home communities. There had been the challenge of attacking an entrenched organization. There had been a hostile newspaper which shut Gene out of the news. In the experimentation of that first campaign, we had come up with happy ways of circumventing our disadvantages—like the campaign newspaper, personal mail, and the blanketing of the district by volunteer distribution of literature.

There were also obvious differences between 1948 and 1968. In the first campaign Gene had had time to build personal contact with many people, and he had known the student leaders well for a year or more. Now, he had little more than a month. He had commitments in other states as well. We knew very few people in New Hampshire, and the people in New Hampshire did not know Gene. Above all, there was no money—no money for literature, no money for offices, no money for radio and television.

Clearly the thing the Washington volunteers might do was to start letting people know about Gene as a person and a senator with a distinguished record on many issues. We women had been financing our volunteer effort by a simple expedient: a certain amount of the letters pouring in with small contributions came to the house. We appropriated that money for the volunteer committee. It wasn't much, but it kept us in stationery and stamps.

We might not know people in New Hampshire, but people who knew Gene, who knew of his record, who approved of his stand, did. They had connections—old school ties, Church ties, professional ties. So we set about the backbreaking work of extracting the New Hampshire names from the alumni lists of the eastern schools: Harvard, Yale, Cornell, Princeton, Bowdoin, the University of New Hampshire, and so on.

We also set about trying to get the lists of alumni from the smaller schools. For some reason this is always more difficult to do. The great Ivy League colleges have alumni lists readily available in any library. Smaller schools are jealous of their lists or seem to have some desire to keep them secret. Perhaps their graduates are less used to solicitation and perhaps they are more responsive to complaints from irate graduates who do not want to get letters from controversial sources.

The writing of personal letters was a comparatively new idea for reaching people when we first used it in Gene's 1948 campaign, and I truly think it has never been used in any campaign with the degree of personal devotion the volunteers had given to it in Gene's succeeding campaigns. In the Senate campaigns, it had been used by the Women for McCarthy in Washington, writing to people in Minnesota to let them know what people in Washington thought of their senator.

Squads of women appeared in the third-floor headquarters every day. Coffee was kept perking on a stand and little snacks were brought in. (One day Eric, our dog, made away with five pounds of chocolate-covered cherries.) A really professional operation began to take shape. Certain women took certain days. Worksheets were worked out. Envelopes were addressed, zip-coded, and stacked in boxes, awaiting the letters to be inserted and the brochures and the fact sheets which were to accompany the letters.

Campaign stories and old clippings of Gene's record were secured for quotations and information about him which would be especially interesting to the people receiving the letters. The difference between a normal campaign and the 1968 campaign was immediately apparent. Again and again I had to reassure one or the other that we were not asking anyone to vote for Gene as a favor to another Harvard graduate, just asking another Harvard graduate to consider

My tea for International Group II in the 1950s. Left to right: Mrs. Sidney Herlong of Florida, Mrs. John Courtney, Abigail McCarthy, Lady Harcourt of Great Britain, then our president.

Gene delivering nominating speech for Adlai Stevenson in 1960.

Far right, Mrs. McCarthy being interviewed by the *Washington Post* on ecumenism, 1963.

Right, With President Kennedy at the White House.

Below, Abigail McCarthy and other friends helping Lady Bird Johnson with the mail in a third-floor room at the Elms, the Johnsons' residence while Lyndon Johnson was Vice President. Left to right: Wendy Marcus (now Mrs. Henry Raymont), Mrs. Oscar Chapman, Mrs. Johnson, Abigail McCarthy, Mrs. Stafford Hutchinson, Mrs. Hale Boggs, Mrs. Frank Church.

Below, Meeting of International Group II—c. 1964—in the Vandenberg Room of the Capitol. Seated left to right: Señora Gomez-Enarruriz of Argentina, Mrs. McCarthy, Mrs. Caranicas of Greece, Mrs. Gerald Ford, Señora de San Roman of Spain, Mrs. William Springer. Standing: Mrs. Don Edwards, Mrs. George Bush, Mrs. John Tower, Mrs. Allen Frear, Mrs. Frank Church, Mrs. Ross Adair, Mrs. Shepherd of New Zealand, Mrs. John Williams, Mrs. Raza of Pakistan, Mrs. Malinen of Finland, Mme. Müller of Switzerland, Mme. Gaussen of France.

Abigail McCarthy and President Kennedy attend Mass in St. Paul.

Senator McCarthy and President Johnson on the White House lawn, 1964.

The McCarthy family on the boardwalk in Atlantic City during the Democratic convention, August 1964. Senator McCarthy was known to be a serious candidate for the vice presidency on LBJ's ticket.

"Nineteen-sixty-six was a happy year." Mrs. McCarthy during an interview on Senate life.

Right, greeting Hubert Humphrey at a coming-out party for Ellen, 1966.

Far right, Gene and Abigail discuss press reports on the eve of the New Hampshire campaign, 1968.

Below, Mrs. McCarthy at White House dinner for King Hassan II of Morocco in 1967. Left to right: The Moroccan Foreign Minister, Mrs. McCarthy, unidentified member of Moroccan party, Mrs. Rusk, the King, Mrs. Johnson. Mrs. McNamara is seated between two others from Morocco.

UPI Photo

Abigail, after her illness during the Wisconsin primary, shares a press conference with Mary in Indiana.

The McCarthys look on with pride as Senator McCarthy addresses the fund-raising rally at Madison Square Garden, August 15, 1968. From left to right: Margaret, Abigail, Michael, Ellen, Mary.

Gene's qualifications; that we were not asking any Catholic graduate to vote for Gene because he was a Catholic but to consider Gene's qualifications on issues of special interest to them.

"It is the principle of like to like," I explained over and over again. "A person is more apt to listen to you if he has something in common with you. For example, Gene is a teacher, he's done a lot for education. I was a teacher. If we can meet teachers on common professional grounds, they may consider Gene's candidacy."

A search for signers to the letters went on. Often the signers were husbands of the women working. Other times they were people just sought over the phone until we found a willing person. The signers were to be, if possible, people who would mean some-thing to their fellow alumni, people who had been prominent for one reason or another in their college careers. Often they might be prominent enough, but the alumni group was so great that the name went unrecognized. And sometimes, the letters were met with frank disbelief.

Even the most devoted and admiring of Gene's campaign workers of New England background were apt to become very wary at the mention of things Catholic, so it was just as well that Church lists were very hard to come by and Catholic signers few and far between.

Studies of Gene's campaigns in Minnesota have shown that he drew less than 1 per cent more of the so-called Catholic vote than any of his Protestant opponents or Protestant predecessors had. We have always firmly believed that religion should not be used as a campaign issue, but in the years following World War II, the years of the Cold War, to establish that a person was a Catholic in good standing was a sort of Sanskrit for denying that he was a Com-munist, and of course, the Communist charge was being made against Gene in New Hampshire, too.

No study was ever made of the effect of the mailings, but I had a leap of recognition in the aftermath of 1970, when Dale Bumpers of Arkansas attributed his win as governor to mail like this. It had been, he said, more important in his campaign than television.

While all this behind-the-scenes work was going on, I had been acting in my usual role as campaign wife. But I was having to do it without any of the help I had had in previous campaigns. This was also true of Gene. Richard Stout has written in *The People* that Gene did not measure up to what his primarily novice constituency thought of as a presidential candidate, a man with a well-organized hierarchical staff, who traveled with a retinue and had expertly handled press relations. Gene, of course, had none of these things. And neither the constituency nor the staff he had were moving to provide them. It is hard for people new to politics to realize that preserving and protecting the candidate is not a concession to his sense of importance, but a necessity if he is to give a good performance. Politics is to some extent theater. It is a waste of effort to gather a crowd if a speaker's energies are too depleted to sway them.

As I moved about New Hampshire on those first trips with Mary, I was without transportation except what was provided by local people. Several of them often piled in with me and sometimes visiting media people traveled with us, too. I would arrive at the next stop, clothes crushed, spirits dampened by the local campaign woes retailed to me en route, and tired from dealing with the questions of the accompanying newswomen.

At a meeting at the courthouse in Peterborough one day, Mary and I were to meet Gene for a joint appearance and reception with the townspeople and the students from a college nearby. There was no advance work and no one to think of little details like providing time to go to the rest rooms. It was a pleasant, homey setting, but when we arrived no one seemed to know what to do with us. The students were assembling gradually, the townspeople were there. Shortly after my arrival, former Congressman Perkins Bass, the New Hampshire Republican national committeeman came up to recall himself to me and to say that he simply came by to say hello to Gene as a former colleague. He surveyed my situation and decided to do something about it. He found the chairman and suggested that a receiving line be formed. Joy Miller, Associated Press correspondent, found a rest room, led me to it, and took charge of my coat. Then, with the Republican committeeman performing the introductions and a reporter standing at my side as campaign aide, I met the people of Peterborough and Mary earnestly chatted with the students.

By that time there was a large and increasingly restless audience in the auditorium and it was suggested that I speak because it was necessary for the students to go back to the college. I was sure that Gene would be there, so I launched into a random and rather halting account of who we were, introducing Mary, talking of the other children, and of our delight at being in New Hampshire. Fortunately, I was rescued by Gene's arrival.

Joy Miller had that meeting in mind, I think, when she wrote, "Her lanky husband is a low-key campaigner and Mrs. McCarthy often comes across more warmly. Although she speaks incisively on major issues, her quiet voice is very soft and she makes it very clear that she is only saying what her Gene would say if he were there. . . . She rarely tackles these major issues until she has softened up the crowd with homey little discussions of how her four children and even Eric, the dog, are doing their bit to help Dad with the Democratic nomination for President."

Later in the campaign, I used to go back to those New Hampshire clips to reassure myself that whatever unsought and strange roles were thrust upon me in the campaign of '68, that at least in my traditional role I had done Gene no harm.

In between trips to New Hampshire, I tried to keep a reasonable routine going at home, but it was not easy. Gene was gone most of the time on trips to other states and I couldn't consult him. I tried to keep the hours until ten or ten-thirty free each morning to see Michael, Margaret, and Ellen off, order groceries, and put my clothes in order. To my distress I found that the volunteer helpers and Grace Bassett, former *Star* reporter who took a small fling at managing press relations for me, were explaining to early morning callers that I was not a morning person.

I found in my own way, as Gene had in his, that working with so many strangers who knew nothing of our backgrounds and experience and little of conventional campaigning led to multiple misunderstandings and misinterpretations. This was especially true because of the inexperience of the campaign office staff. They were bright, capable, and ingenious, but novices. Most of them were too young to remember with any clarity even the press reports of former presidential campaigns. Only Curtis Gans seemed to think that something could be learned from our personal past experience. As it became clear that help from Washington would have to be sent to New Hampshire, he called frequently to ask me what the senator had done about this or that in other campaigns. I told him everything I could remember. In the struggle going on for control of the campaign (about which I knew nothing), this communication was interpreted to mean that I was pro-Curtis.

Perhaps the most consistent misinterpretation in the days to come was from Sandy Frucher, at that time a frequent caller at the house. He was an appealing newlywed at the time and was anxious to have his pretty wife Floss, a Stanford graduate, find a place in the campaign. (Many of the workers were husband–wife teams.) Floss did travel with me on one organizing trip and later became an organizer for Women for McCarthy in Los Angeles, when Sandy took over the campaign headquarters there. It was through Sandy that Ellen, our oldest daughter, began to take an active part in the campaign, appearing and speaking at rallies and representing us at headquarters.

Sandy was a knowledgeable, hard-working, impressive organizer, but he never gave his full confidence to anyone over thirty. The distrust was mutual as far as Eller and the rest of the Senate staff were concerned. Eller was convinced that Sandy was disloyal when he discovered him lunching with Frank Mankiewicz, Robert Kennedy's aide and recruiter, on the day of the New Hampshire primary. But Sandy went on loyally to the California campaign—the most divisive of all in relation to the Kennedy forces.

Because of the children, I was in close touch with him and, at the end of the campaign, I was dismayed to learn that he assumed that my offer of file space for the historical early correspondence meant that I wanted to read Blair's correspondence—and his. I could never keep up with my own! This story and others turned up later in books about the campaign by journalists like Richard Stout, who should have had better judgment and experience.

But Curtis and Sandy and occasionally Arleen were my only contacts with the national office and conversations with them were few. At night I was harassed by calls from old friends with advice they wanted relayed to Gene. Among the most frequent callers was Eliot Janeway, the economist and columnist. Eliot had acquired from Larry Merthan, I think, a touching faith in my organizing ability. He also had the outsider's low esteem for political activity and was convinced that the proper use of money would ensure victory in New Hampshire. "You can buy it," he would say, "buy it the way Kennedy bought West Virginia." The rhetoric was alarming although I knew he was not actually suggesting bribery. He also kept referring to potential contributors as if I knew who they were. Finally one name rang a bell. According to Eliot, someone named Howard Stein was being treated very badly.

After Gene's first trip to New Hampshire, I had heard references from Jerry Eller and Mary McGrory and Blair to a person who, they said, wanted to take over the New Hampshire campaign and was willing to finance it completely if he could control it. According to these accounts, he had arrived in New Hampshire with a huge car, a black chauffeur, and a television crew. Gene had been offended by the implied supervision. The television crew, strange and exotic in the New Hampshire scene, had come between Gene and the people he was trying to talk with on Main Street. To me this Howard Stein was a mythical figure. But I was told he was president of the Dreyfus Fund, a large and successful mutual fund. Jerry and Mary and Blair seemed to think that collaboration with him might be worse than losing.

Now Eliot was talking about Howard Stein. And John Cogley, an old friend and former editor of *Commonweal*, New York *Times* religion editor, now putting out the *Center* magazine, kept urging his cause. Finally Gene received in the mail at home a passionate, denunciatory letter from Janet Stein whom he had met several times in New York. The burden of her letter was that he did not care about peace if he would not let those who wanted to help him achieve peace for the country. Gene fingered it for a while, then gave it to me to read and said that perhaps I should talk to the Steins. Perhaps something could be worked out. He was troubled, I knew, because Mary and Blair would not approve, but he was deeply worried about finances. He had tried to keep campaign expenses under control by asking first Grace Bassett and then my brother, Stephen Quigley, who had been state comptroller in Minnesota, to go to the national office to keep expenditures and hiring at a minimum.

That night I had my first telephone call from Howard Stein. The conversation was cautious and noncommittal on my part and half-humorous and half-bitter on his. He was reading a book, he said, to find out why he was so undesirable when his only desire was to help. He asked a few questions, too, about how I thought money could be usefully spent in New Hampshire.

When I told Gene about the conversation, he said he thought that it wouldn't hurt for me to meet and to talk with Howard. Gene himself was on his way to a meeting in Minneapolis. When Howard called again in the next day or two, I told him that Gene and I would meet him in Kennedy Airport on our way to New Hampshire that weekend and that perhaps we could discuss some useful ways to spend money. I told him that Women for McCarthy needed money to function and that what they were doing was really worthwhile.

By that time, it did not seem at all strange to me that the president of one of the largest mutual funds in the country would be arranging a meeting with the wife of a presidential candidate in the Eastern Airlines lounge at Kennedy Airport, nor did it seem strange that I was trying to combine fourteen-year-old Margaret's semester break vacation with our second campaign trip to New Hampshire.

On Thursday, February 22, less than three weeks before the New Hampshire primary date of March 12, Grace Bassett, enlisted by Mary McGrory to help me, Charlie Callanan, and Margaret and her friend Ann Bierbower set off from Dulles Airport complete with skis, hand luggage full of press releases, speech materials, and changes of wardrobe supposedly adaptable to life at a ski lodge and at campaign receptions.

When we arrived at Kennedy, we went to the Eastern lounge. When I saw the Howard Steins for the first time, I was astounded. Janet Stein is a beautiful slender woman, with long dark hair casually arranged, with a beautiful small head on a long swanlike neck. She was dressed in an understated country-casual ensemble. Howard was tall and fair, blue-eyed, rather New Yorkish in clothes, and seemed quiet and shy.

Later I was not at all surprised to discover that the black chauffeur who had been described to me was really Ernest—gray-haired, rather distinguished, business-suited—a driver who was more of a family friend than a servant. The large car which I had envisioned as a huge limousine rolling about the New Hampshire roads, knocking aside the natives, turned out to be a brown Mercedes—luxurious, it is true, but not conspicuous.

We made small talk. Janet was enchanting to Margaret and Ann and suggested that she spend some time with them while Howard and I talked.

Because the lounge was also occupied by a bustling Texas business-man, making loud conversation with the official in charge and showing every indication of curiosity about us, Howard and I strolled up and down the balcony corridor outside the lounge.

He was concerned about what we might do with the money he was prepared to hand over to Women for McCarthy and I did my best to explain it to him. I've since come to realize that Howard Stein operates largely on his measure of the person in-volved rather than on facts and figures and that his judgments often are highly intuitive. It could have been a compliment of sorts that he gave me that day a check of $7000 from funds he had collected for Women for McCarthy and suggested that I get in touch with him when they needed more. Or it could have been a measure of his desperate and sincere desire to find a place in the campaign in which he could be effective.

Soon Gene's plane came in from Minneapolis and he joined

us in the lounge. His meeting with Janet and Howard was very cordial and they left after having a brief conversation and drink with him.

From that moment, Howard Stein was in the McCarthy campaign and was there until the very end.

Some time in 1969 when I was having dinner with the Steins, I said to Howard, "I can never forget how surprised I was that day. I had heard that you were such a horrible person." And he said, surprisingly, "Perhaps I was horrible then. I thought it was so important to make a great showing in New Hampshire. Perhaps if I hadn't come in and insisted on the television and advertising, the senator's percentage would not have been so big and then Kennedy would not have entered. It might have gone as the senator originally planned, a showing in New Hampshire, a showing in Minnesota, a larger percentage in Wisconsin, a win in Oregon, and a win in California. Everything might have been different and Bobby Kennedy might be alive today and Gene in the White House."

It is always easy to look back and to second-guess a situation, but I think this statement of Howard's shows his unique detachment, his willingness to admit what he considers mistakes and to acknowledge them. People often said to me during the campaign, "Janet is so lovely but Howard is so cold and withdrawn—how do you communicate with him?" I never found him so. He was always willing to discuss a problem or an issue not only in its practical aspects but also in a speculative way. He liked to think about possibilities and people's potentialities. I found him very easy to talk to, but perhaps this was because in the early stages ours was a telephone acquaintanceship and Howard was the sort of person who can use the telephone for communication when he is very reluctant in a face-to-face encounter. He became one of the personalities of the New Hampshire campaign. As did Dick Goodwin.

There is no denying that Dick Goodwin with his ugly, compelling face, his direct, black eyes, and his cheerful, permanent half-grin brought a lift to the campaign. To Gene it meant that a man of real talent and reputation was willing to certify the validity of Gene's effort by his presence and help. To the young people he meant the same thing. He brought a sense of reality, immediacy, and continuity with his reminiscences and stories about John Kennedy and Lyndon Johnson.

He talked interestingly about the dominating effect Lyndon Johnson could have on his closest associates. "It is very strange," he said one night at the Wayfarer Motor Inn in Manchester, New Hampshire. "You are mesmerized by the personality of the man. There is a hidden menace in what he says and in the way he looms over you, and quite frankly you are afraid. When you leave the room, when you get outside, you shake it off. You say, 'What can he do?'"

On the same night in the half-lit living room of the suite, he ruminated about the appointment of Dean Rusk as Secretary of State in 1961 and the way in which history was affected by the motivations behind the appointment.

"We knew very little about him," he said, speaking of the advisers putting together the Kennedy administration. "It was clear that we couldn't take Fulbright because of his stand on race, or at least the way the blacks looked at his supposed stand on race; and Kennedy was not about to take Stevenson who would, by reason of his following and his own brilliance, take some of the spotlight away from the Administration. So he settled for someone we knew nothing about; and Vietnam and our involvement in Vietnam comes directly from that choice."

Goodwin's utter frankness about things like this were part of his charm. Dick was good to have around. There never was any doubt in my mind, however, that he came to New Hampshire in the first place to prove to Bobby Kennedy that he should run. Mary McGrory kept warning that he should not be trusted. One night, before he knew the extent of her commitment to the campaign, he had asked her idly if she thought Gene would accept a Cabinet post in a Kennedy administration. "He's a Trojan horse," she said darkly. Dick said revealing things to me, too. He did not like the statements that some of the young people like Ann Hart and Sam Brown had made to the press saying that they were not interested in the Kennedy candidacy, that Gene McCarthy had risen to their need and they would never desert him. "Kennedy staffers aren't allowed to make statements to the press," Dick told me. It was a hint that he was thinking of a transition. But I saw no point in bothering with these things.

Dick is a man of great talent and restless energy, and in order to achieve his ends with his talent, he needs a vehicle of power. He tried the Johnson vehicle, but I suppose he was never really quite trusted there; and he did have an honest aversion to higher escalation in Vietnam.

He had tasted power with the Kennedys. He had given his affection there, and he could not quite shake it off even if he had wanted to.

The speeches he wrote for Gene in New Hampshire were Kennedy speeches. The phrases were the sort of phrases that came happily from the lips of John Kennedy but strangely from Gene McCarthy. Yet Dick was honestly fascinated with Gene's mind and with his great capacity to use television effectively. "Bobby's old-fashioned on television," he told me once. "Gene is perfect for it. He can use it better than anyone I have ever seen; if he only knew what he could do with it, he's the original, cool personality that McLuhan talks about."

Gene developed a real fondness for Dick and said later that Dick had been perfectly honest with him, which was not quite true. He knew that Dick could probably not be part of a campaign against Bobby Kennedy. But Gene was genuinely hurt when he discovered that Dick was willing to be part of the campaign against him in Indiana. "I remember what he said in New Hampshire," he told me bitterly. "I asked him how long he was signing on for and he said, 'I'm going all the way.'"

In Berlin, New Hampshire, everything that was positive about the campaign came together and was effective: the way in which it provided a channel through which average Americans could express their rejection of the war; the way in which Gene's style of candidacy began to appeal to people; the way in which the new and old, young and adult could work together, the way in which it offered, through Gene, a new kind of candidate; the way in which it became a symbol to the nation of reconciliation between the generations. **Marc Kasky,** the student organizer there, could work well with local people, as a catalyst to help them organize. He was the key. He was, to me, a symbol of all that was good in the student involvement in the campaign, all that was good in the new politics, all that was good in the campaign itself.

It was of Berlin, New Hampshire, that Bernie Boutin, President Johnson's organizer, kept talking on the night of the primary. "Wait," he said to the reporter from *Time*, "until the returns from Berlin are in." It was of Berlin I thought when Bill Dunfey, the Kennedy analyst and owner of the Wayfarer, said on that same night, "Twenty-two per cent is all you'll get." And it was Berlin which delivered 52 per cent—the magic 52 for which the students had clamored in the days just before the primary.

I knew that it would, because I had been there and I had seen what Marc Kasky was doing. I went to Berlin, I think, in response to the pity Mrs. Dunn, who was scheduling me, felt for Marc Kasky who was up there alone. It was significant that she did not go with me—it seemed to be axiomatic that people did not go to Berlin. It is not a typically picturesque New England town. In winter a constant fall of snow and smell of burning rubber hangs over it. The main street is dark and narrow.

Marc Kasky went to Berlin by accident. When he went, he had never participated in a political campaign before. He thought of himself as a liberal Democrat, very much opposed to the war. He was a Yale graduate student in urban planning when the campaign began. He went to New Hampshire, intending to spend three or four days, as a result of a casual conversation with a friend who suggested that they needed help in headquarters at Concord. When he arrived in Concord they assumed that he was one of the Yale students who had come up to try to set up headquarters in various towns and asked him if he would go to Berlin and set up headquarters there. He was rather intrigued by the idea and went more out of curiosity and a sense of challenge than for any other reason.

Marc has an open curious attitude toward life. I always think of his response to my suggestion that there must be parochial schools in the Berlin area on which he could draw for help. He called me later and said, "What do you call those head ladies in convents?" I said, "You call them Mother Superior." When I came back to Berlin, Marc was a good friend of every mother superior in the radius of Berlin and in Berlin itself. It is not an easy relationship to achieve with nuns of the rather austere French-Canadian tradition.

By some happy chance of innate character and upbringing, Marc was at home wherever he went. He liked people and he accepted them totally as they were. He wanted to be in the places where he was one of them. After he left Berlin, he worked in the Connecticut campaign. When he went to Nebraska, he asked for a small town and was given Grand Island. When he left Grand Island they wrote an editorial about him in the town paper. He worked in Eugene, Oregon. And on his way to California, he sent me a message saying, "Look for me in Death Valley."

Marc arrived alone in Berlin and found and rented an empty store on Main Street on the very first day. Then he spent several days just drifting around town, in and out of the coffee shops, chatting with the patrons and waitresses, getting to know the feel of the town. He didn't tell people that he had come to campaign. As he said, he didn't think of himself as a campaigner yet, just as somebody visiting the town.

After a few days, as he said later, he knew the names of about thirty or forty key people in the town. He realized that in a town like Berlin, people have overlapping identities. The radio announcer may also be the most influential person in some club as well as a member of the town committee. It was better, he thought, to meet them as people rather than as town committee member or editor or chairman of the Democratic Club. In a short time he had established a friendly "hello, how are you?" relationship with the people on the Main Street. When he opened a headquarters, he was able to borrow some chairs from the church and some tables from a restaurant and find someone to paint a sign saying MCCARTHY FOR PRESIDENT. He was also able to arrange an appointment to attend the town Democratic Committee meeting. The very innocence and freshness of his approach, I suppose, was what made them agree to announce that he was there and let him speak.

He appeared that night at the same time as an organizer sent out by the Johnson people, who came with stacks of pledge cards to be sent to the White House. In his campaign report, Marc described the sheepish way in which the members of the committee went up to this man, got their pledge cards, then after the meeting, dropped them in waste baskets and said to him, "Don't worry."

His report is interesting because of his ideas about what brought campaign success in Berlin. First of all, the campaign was continuous, in that he stayed there from beginning to end for a full five weeks. This made the people look on the campaign as part of the town life for a while.

As Marc sensed, in a small town the importance of establishing relationships is really very great. He insisted on staying in Berlin because he didn't want it to become a typical campaign, which he characterized as one in which the approach to people was "We're not interested in you, yourself, we're just interested in whether you can deliver votes."

He also presented the headquarters as a source of information so that they could make up their own minds. It was this he stressed when he went up to meet the teachers at the school and talked at the school. In that way, a number of local high school students began working regularly in the headquarters.

On my first visit to Berlin, when I arrived cold, hungry, and disheveled, I was met by a group of these high school students with a bouquet of roses and rushed immediately to the radio station for an interview with the very friendly local radio announcer, by then an admirer of Marc's.

Before the canvassers arrived, Marc in effect, asked the town for permission for the canvass. He let people know that young people would go from house to house asking questions, and he made it clear that if they had objections to the canvass, they had veto power over it. "If they had said 'no canvassers,' I was fairly confident that there was a reasonable and rational enough case in favor of it that they would listen to, and for that reason I was sure there would be a canvass, but I let them make the decision that there would be a canvass instead of my making the decision.

"In this respect too, they had almost all the planning for Senator McCarthy's visit and Mrs. McCarthy's visits and Paul Newman's visit. All I did was go around to people who had been in Berlin a long time—and almost everybody was a native of the town—and ask them what they thought McCarthy should do when he's in the town, and quite often, they felt that these ideas, well, they didn't really feel that they were their own, but in reality they were their own. I wasn't snowing these people. I had no idea what he should do and who knows better than the people living there? Quite often they'd suggest things and I'd sift out things that just didn't fit in or didn't seem as productive as others."

Marc even had help from Johnson supporters because they liked him and because they felt that he was alone in his effort. He also thought it was important that he had never denounced Johnson: "Although I didn't like him, I always felt more sorrow for him than hate toward him. What was important was the fact that even if he was a victim of circumstance, he was unable to govern because of the way his reputation had been painted; and for that reason I wasn't attempting to pass judgment on his decisions or on how he arrived at them, but simply that what had happened had made him the wrong person to lead the country."

It was striking that at that point in the campaign, this was more or less Gene's own approach. He had announced his candidacy as a challenge to the Administration's policy, and he was consistent in advancing that point of view in all his New Hampshire speeches. This was disappointing to reporters and to many of the students in the beginning.

Perhaps all three of us, the candidate and his wife and this lone student campaigner, had an instinctive feeling for the fact that this was the best approach to take with New Hampshire people. After all, these were people who had supported Johnson; a vicious attack on him was in a sense an attack on them.

When we first came to Berlin we took rooms in a little motel near the Costello Hotel where Marc had arranged events. It was bleak, but modern and warm.

My initial impression of Marc, whom I had just met, was a good one. He was unruffled by changes in schedule and uninsistent about adhering to his arrangements. He was amiable and open, convinced that things were going well during Gene's visit. I spent a little time having coffee with him and talking with him. Gene was making an appearance somewhere and it was characteristic of Marc that he didn't feel the need to be with the candidate at all times. In a campaign, sometimes the only reward for lots of hard work and long days spent in detail is the chance to bask for a little while in the aura of the man of the hour. The only point Marc made that evening was that the people in town were very appreciative of the fact that we were staying in the town itself, despite the comparative lack of comfort. No other candidate, Republican or Democrat, had stayed in town.

Fifty or more local high school students had become Marc's regular volunteers in the headquarters and they were happily at work on the reception in the hotel's combination lobby-reception-meeting room. I remember them happily stretching crepe paper to make huge wheels, cheerfully wearing the McCarthy hats and buttons. It only gradually dawned on us that they were not the imported campaign workers from the Concord headquarters but actual citizens of Berlin and that the people who solemnly filed through the receiving line that night at the reception were their fathers and mothers.

The next morning we had breakfast with Marc and a student couple who had come to help him from Yale for a few days. He was euphoric about Gene's effect on the community. It was his belief that the people in Berlin were not concerned about the war as an issue but principally because boys from their town or friends of theirs were in Vietnam and some were being killed. We talked about getting women interested in the campaign. Marc had talked to several during the reception the night before, those he noted as being especially impressed. It is difficult, of course, to mobilize women volunteers in a town in which both women and men work six days in a factory—

a fact to consider about Berlin and about Manchester, too. The percentage of working wives is very, very high and the women do not have the time and energy that women who stay home can give to a campaign. The traditional campaign volunteer is upper middle-class.

Marc telephoned me later when I was back in Washington to say that he had worked out a way, he thought, that he could build a corps of women in whom other women in the town would have confidence, if we could compensate some of these women for their time, pay for their expenses. I wasn't quite sure whether the money I had turned over to Barbara Haviland for Women for McCarthy could be used in this fashion, but I did ask Barbara to send Marc a small amount of money.

By the time the canvassers had covered Berlin the first time, Marc had a corps of women visitors who went to houses the canvassers had visited in which the response was favorable, reinforcing the favorable attitude in that household by their own expressed interest in Gene. I have always been amused by Marc's comments, "I never knew why these ladies were interested in the senator. They weren't very issue oriented."

The people who had expressed interest in this way thus found out that they were not isolated, that there were other people in the community who felt strongly about the candidate, and they perhaps became more vocal proselytizers for him as a result of this.

At our breakfast meeting, Marc had also suggested that if I came back he might be able to find a way to mobilize some women around my visit. We thought of two groups. The public school teachers in a town like Berlin are always opinion leaders in the community, and even if they would not and could not properly take part in a campaign, their expressed interest in it could have a very good effect.

I suggested the nuns. The nuns in a small community are often surprisingly aware of things in a way that perhaps other teachers in a community are not, because nuns belong to large worldwide communities, often communities with missions abroad and, thus, they often have a surprising fund of information about life in countries affected by our foreign policy. Some of our most effective peace workers elsewhere in the country were nuns, and I thought it just possible that in some of the communities in Berlin there might be nuns like that. Nuns also, although many people forget it, are human beings with relatives. A given convent of say twelve or fifteen nuns will have an outreach into twelve or fifteen communities or extended families where people are often interested to hear what Sister has to say on a subject. They also have ex-students.

The surprising interest I had noted earlier in doctors and hospital workers I thought might also be true of hospital nuns. Many of the full-habited, old-fashioned nuns were often world travelers in disguise. Many of them had a very shrewd appraisal of the way things were going in world affairs. In my hometown, the hospital was run by a group of nuns known as the Sisters of the Sorrowful Mother. They were primarily German in origin and drew their vocation from German families in this country. There was a tendency in Wabasha to discount them as ignorant although we knew they had nursing degrees, because we were put off by the fact that they usually spoke very broken English. Yet one of those nuns could be stationed in Wabasha one year and in their hostel overlooking St. Peter's Square in Rome the next. She might very well have knowledge of the great and near great that no one in Wabasha had.

Marc had no difficulty in grasping the point of view that Gene expressed throughout the New Hampshire campaign—Gene refused to enlist Catholics as Catholics. We both resisted what seemed to be a standard New Hampshire tactic, going to Mass to meet people. Marc understood that finding the common bond with teachers and nuns was just one way of forging a link so that they could come to an understanding of the candidate and what he stood for.

It was in connection with my second trip to Berlin that another technique, developed by Women for McCarthy, sprang into being, the technique we later called "Operation Penetration."

Marc knew that some of the religious leaders of the town, ministers and priests, were probably peace-oriented, but he was not quite sure how to approach them and he felt that they would not know what to do about approaching their congregations who would resent political exhortation from the pulpit. Another problem in Berlin, of course, was that such a large part of the population was French-speaking and took much of its information about news events from the French radio and television programs.

I thought of Mariette Wickes, a remarkable young woman whom I had known for years. Mariette had perfected her French in French Canada years ago when the Grail was thinking of expanding its activities into French Canada. She had worked in Africa establishing an African-run high school for girls, and as a result of her experience there—the only person from one culture in the midst of another— she had come back to the United States determined to devote herself to the problems of the black and poor in this country. She resigned from the inner circle of the Grail but was still considered a part of the Grail movement. Currently at the Institute for Policy Studies in Washington, Mariette went to Berlin the same weekend that I returned there. She went as a returned missionary, a French-speaking one, billed by Marc to the radio stations and to the newspapers as a minor celebrity of sorts. She had several interviews on the French-speaking stations. She also visited every clergyman in town to familiarize him with the material of the Clergy and Laity Concerned About Vietnam and with Gene's background on the issues. She also got their permission to pass out literature at the church doors.

Operation Penetration, which developed from Mariette's work, never became a very big operation. It always took so much explanation. Based on Mariette's experience in Berlin, the Women for McCarthy tried to use it across the country in difficult neighborhoods and places hard to reach otherwise. The idea was always the same —to visit the opinion leaders of the community, the teachers, the clergymen, social workers perhaps, and to arrange distribution of material in hard-to-reach areas. We tried to keep the distribution politically neutral to some extent. It was material which was informative about Gene's history and family, but not directly aimed at the election.

Sometimes the distributions were in schoolyards or in schools, the children being asked to take the material home. This might seem a waste of literature, but in working areas often the material brought home by the children is of great interest to the parents and the children are the working parents' contact with the larger world.

As Marc Kasky said, "I'm convinced the kids did as much, just by wearing a button home or bringing literature home to make them aware of Senator McCarthy, as the canvassers or Senator McCarthy himself did. I think the high school kids were very important, not only in Berlin but in other cities and towns I worked in."

The first canvassing demonstrated the problem in Berlin which was the problem in working neighborhoods across the country: the fact that people were not at home during the day, the mothers worked and many households went untouched. Although some of these people could be reached in the evening, the canvass was not really set up that way, and people were not particularly cordial to this kind of visitor in the evening. Many of the men frequented clubs, women did their housework or had their favorite television programs which they did not want interrupted.

The church door distribution was, as I have said, something we discovered in Gene's first campaign as a practical way of reaching the whole family. Parts of the family could be reached by plant gate distribution and this was done too.

One of the canvassers working the last weekend told of the distaste the imported canvassers felt about a piece of literature about my ecumenical work and our family life. He said that he really couldn't see the connection but added that it turned out to be surprisingly successful. By evening, headquarters was swamped with calls from the various Catholic parishes asking if the same kind of distribution couldn't be made at the evening Masses.

Michael and Margaret and Mary had been with us during our first appearance in Berlin and Ellen came back with me for the second visit. "It almost became a family thing," said Marc Kasky. "She brought Ellen back with her and that was the child Berlin hadn't met and the townspeople were suddenly taking an interest in the family—"

On my second visit I was terrified to find out that Marc had scheduled a television appearance for me. I had always avoided television in Gene's previous campaigns, feeling very strongly that I was not photogenic and feeling too that the camera made me stiff and stilted in my response to questions. But it seemed too cruel to refuse not to do it when Marc was so pleased and proud of having arranged for the interview.

Ellen and Janet Stein helped me with makeup. We decided that my lipstick was too red and I adopted Ellen's, put on my new pink suit, and went off, frightened but determined to do Marc and the campaign credit if I could. The television announcer turned out to be a homely and homey Irishman, not particularly photogenic himself and amiable as could be about rehearsing the questions with me beforehand. And the camera setup there was so simple that he had to ask all the questions first, then the camera turned to me and I gave all the answers. I don't know how they managed to splice it together but very soon reports came in from various parts of Berlin that people were stopping their shopping in the supermarkets to watch the program.

I didn't see the show but it did break the barrier for me as far as television was concerned. I decided right then and there that television was part of campaigning, that the essential thing was to be as true to one's self as possible, to do the very best you could to transmit the message of the campaign, to do Gene credit and interpret him for the television watchers and let the other chips fall where they might.

I think my fear of television came from what was really a desire to hide whenever I had to appear in public; although the years of teaching and speaking had given me freedom behind a lectern or a desk, the person-to-person exposure on television was as frightening as the eighth-grade oral book report had been, when I had trembled and blushed furiously, ages ago.

The ward women who had been working as Women for McCarthy had arranged a reception in the town hall and I remember one incident vividly. A young high school girl came up with her mother in tow and said, "Mrs. McCarthy, Mama wants to meet you. I told her about you when I came home from school this afternoon and she said she'd like to talk to you." I turned to the mother, I think with the public manner one acquires after years of receptions, and said, "I'm so happy to meet you, is there anything I can do?" Her answer stunned me. She said, "Yes, ma'am, my son was killed a month ago in Vietnam and I've been wondering and wondering what I could do so that other boys wouldn't have to die like that. When my daughter came home this afternoon, I thought maybe there's something I can do to help Senator McCarthy win, maybe Mrs. McCarthy can tell me, maybe if he wins, other sons won't die."

I was to meet many parents like this in the campaign and I never ceased to marvel at them. The professional, patriotic mother who has given up her son for her country and lives in the pride of that is all too familiar to people in political life—these others were new to us.

In my talks at the convent school, at the large Catholic high school, I sensed that the Catholics of Berlin were hearing for the first time of the Pope's anguished cries for peace and of the cry of the Vietnamese bishops, "For God's sake, let this killing stop!" One French priest who heard me quote these things was polite but disbelieving and demanded that I send him copies of the statement.

His attitude reflected one of the unfortunate results of the Know-Nothing attack on the early Catholics in this country and the consequent re-Europeanization of American Catholicism. This has been the emphasis Catholics have placed on showing their patriotism by the support of our country's wars.

The negative elements in the campaign certainly existed in Berlin. There was a hostile newspaper which refused to send a photographer to the reception, for example. There were the Catholic "hawks." There was a strong Administration machine and there were the aloof Republicans. Berlin, in a smaller way, had everything that Manchester had. What made the difference in the campaign?

First of all, there was Marc who drifted in and was an interested and earnest observer rather than a political organizer who counted only on votes. He sought for and found the positive; then the negative elements were neutralized by the candidate's character and the candidate's approach. Finally, every technique by which one could expose voters to the candidate, to the candidate's ideas, was used without cynicism, without manipulation, and with a deep respect for people. The true new politics is this—a politics of liberation.

By the time we got to Berlin the first time, I had begun to understand what it was that Gene was evoking from people all over the country. I had read enough of the letters and seen enough of the response in dedicated people like those working in the attic and the young scattered across the country to have a dim understanding of what might be possible, and that is why I went back to Berlin. It seemed so clear to me that Marc Kasky could make it possible there.

When we say the true new politics is liberating, I think we mean that it is based on the assumption that people can make free choices and affect their lives by doing so. In the ideal new politics, people are provided with information, they are not sold on image, and it is assumed that they will make their own decision on the basis of the information provided them. It takes great faith in people and in the democratic process. Marc Kasky said, "I never saw my job as trying to win any votes for him but just as making information available and being there to answer questions and furnish whatever else people wanted, so that the people could decide who they wanted to vote for. For this reason, I never asked anybody who they were voting for, never even cared who they were voting for."

The effect of this approach, he felt, was shown in the fact that in the last few days of the campaign, people began dropping by the headquarters, saying that they had reached a decision to vote for Gene McCarthy. Or they phoned in to say this. "They were actually proud that they had reached this decision because they knew they hadn't been talked into it, that it had been entirely their own decision."

Marc did not accept the idea that the ethnic vote could be delivered and he rejected the opinion of people in Concord that if you could swing the French-Catholic vote, which is 90 per cent of the vote in Berlin, you had the city of Berlin. "Doing what I was doing was the direct opposite of looking for the people who could deliver the ethnic vote or deliver any groups." He was a realist, however, and did not object to a direct mailing to the ethnic groups in Berlin because it was directly connected to his idea of getting information into people's hands so that they could make their own decisions.

Disgruntled Johnsonians were later to attribute the victory in

Berlin to Paul Newman's visit. Since Paul Newman had visited Manchester, Nashua, and all the other places as well, the logic of this argument was hard to see. It is interesting to note, though, that Marc Kasky opposed this visit when it was first suggested to him by the Concord headquarters and only allowed it in the last few days so that people could make up their own minds uninfluenced by local boss or celebrity from afar. They would say, according to Marc, "Who do you listen to, the mayor or the labor union counsel or the movie star?" And they wouldn't be making up their own minds.

New Hampshire people, like Canadians, are very enthusiastic about hockey, and since Berlin had had championship hockey teams, the town was especially enthusiastic about the sport. The last weekend before the election, the championship hockey game was being played there; the local radio announcer wanted Paul to drop the puck at the hockey game. Marc also arranged a visit to a shopping center and a radio broadcast. Paul's presence served as a climax to the campaign, created a great deal of excitement, and since even the mill hands who had been impossible to reach in the canvass were all either at the hockey game or listening to it, it meant that everyone in Berlin had been reached in the last push of the campaign, and even the most indifferent must have had some positive response to Paul Newman's appearance.

The last days of the New Hampshire campaign were euphoric. Gene had felt the continued reassurance of personal response from the voters he met, and estimates were that he had met between fifteen and twenty thousand. The same style, his own, which had been convincing on Minnesota main streets was convincing in New Hampshire. It was what Gene had seen on his first campaign swing when he had expansively said that he might get 55 per cent of the vote, having discerned "something that no one else saw that day," as reporter Richard Stout noted sourly. His followers were beginning to believe in him. And the media had discovered the students. Besides providing energy and manpower, they were picturesque and newsworthy. They became the topic of the hour. And they were truly remarkable in dedication and effort. A nation of parents, worried to death about student radicalism and disillusionment, took heart from the students willing to be "Neat and Clean for Gene," willing to work sixteen hours a day within the system. Senator Philip Hart of Michigan said it for all of them four years later: "Gene McCarthy turned my children around. He gave them hope."

It was a mistake to think of these students as eighteen-year-olds faced with the difficult choices of accepting the draft for a war in which they could not believe, going to prison, or leaving the country. They were led by graduate students and some young professionals— men and women who if they had lived, as I said in speeches that year, in the first era of our nation's history would have been among those who shaped our destiny. They were not much younger than George Washington at the time of his first service, than Patrick Henry making his impassioned speech, than Thomas Jefferson writing the Declaration of Independence. Without realizing it, we were a nation which idealized youthfulness, but rejected youth and kept it from meaningful participation in our lives. For almost a decade some of them had been part of what was loosely called "the movement" which had grown out of the civil rights struggle of the early 1960s and espoused other goals: civil rights for Chicanos, Puerto Ricans, poor whites, Indians; war on poverty; peace.

Curtis Gans and Sam Brown were of the movement and they used the organizing techniques they had learned to marshal the student forces. Curtis came to New Hampshire as national staff director and Sam as youth co-ordinator. Together with the help of brilliant graduate students like Ben Stavis, John Barbieri, Dianne Dumonofsky, Tony Podesta, Jack Martin, many others young but past college age, they welded a working organization.

Another harbinger of good things to come was the presence in increasing numbers of celebrities. There was, of course, Robert Lowell whose presence meant so much to Gene. And Paul Newman and Dustin Hoffman, not just attending rallies but slogging away at street-corner campaigning.

On election night Gene went before the television cameras alone. Our children were part of the chanting, singing crowd waiting to hear him; I was in the suite with our election night guests. "Chicago, Chicago," the young people chanted.

"People have remarked that the campaign has brought young people back into the system," Gene said. "But it's the other way around: the young people have brought the country back into the system." But, perhaps it happened too late.

*B*y this time Women for McCarthy had grown into something quite different from what we had planned in the beginning—a national campaign effort modeled on the volunteer groups of Gene's Senate campaigns. The group was originally formed to deal with the great outpouring of letters just after Gene's announcement. There was no one to answer them. Some volunteers had come to the Senate office, but Jerry Eller had deemed a form letter a sufficient answer—a note briefly expressing thanks for support and saying that the letter was being referred to the campaign office for answer. The only trouble was that there was no campaign office at the time. The volunteers were troubled when they noted that they were stuffing letters with such a vague answer into envelopes addressed to such potentially important helpers as congressmen from New York and former Congressman Jerry Voorhis in Chicago, to say nothing of numerous scientists, army officers, and scholars offering to write position papers. Complaints about unanswered letters came in by word of mouth from all over the country.

In this period of vacuum the ladies on the third floor started working on the letters. The effort was to code the letters, and to give some sort of indication of the writer's interests and possible helpfulness and arrange them according to state so that there could be some way of putting together committees in those states and discovering just what kind of support was there. It was a cumbersome way to proceed, but since the Senate office insisted that the letters themselves be saved for historical purposes, and since we could not answer them directly, it was all we could do.

The direction of the volunteers was, of course, a problem. There was nobody in the group who had very much background in political campaigning. In this period, Senator Philip Hart dropped in one Sunday after church, and mentioned that his daughter Ann was very much interested in the campaign and was contributing some of the money she made as a photographer's assistant. He implied that this was a very positive development in Ann's life. Ann was, in some ways, symbolic of the drop-out student who came back into the system during the campaign. She was a classmate of Ellen's in high school, had dropped out of college, and had become temporarily alienated from her family and former friends. Senator Hart felt that her interest in the campaign was perhaps the beginning of her re-entry into the main stream.

Ann came to dinner one evening and I asked her if she wanted to work with the volunteers. I said there was nobody there with previous political experience such as hers. She said that she was willing to work, wanted to do something for the effort, but that she couldn't talk to people. It was rather amazing to see what happened, because in one week Ann had improved the coding system we had developed for the mail and had become expert at explaining it to volunteers as they came in to the third floor. By the end of the week I said to her, "Ann, you are talking to people." She said, "I don't mind talking to them in this context." From then on Ann went from task to task and was one of the student executives in New Hampshire. By the time the Alban Towers volunteer office opened and the women moved there, Ann was the unacknowledged director of volunteers, at least of the younger volunteers, and I asked her if she wanted to go over to the Towers to continue directing things. By this time she had a very solid relationship with the students who had come on the scene shortly after Christmas, and they worked out a good liaison between Alban Towers and the national office.

"If the original children's crusade had had Sam Brown and Ann

Hart," said Gene on election night in New Hampshire, "it would have succeeded."

From this beginning two separate but co-operating ventures developed. Arleen Hynes's office in the Transportation Building became a center of communications for volunteers from around the country. Women for McCarthy at the Alban Towers took on some of the more practical aspects of the ongoing and ever-moving campaign from primary to primary, such as the direct mail effort. Women for McCarthy operated in the realm of new politics, reacting to each situation as it developed and providing services as they were demanded. The other office acted as a national over-all directive service.

Women for McCarthy operated at a breathless pace. Dick Stout described it rather flamboyantly, "My gosh, now these women are addressing the whole Berlin telephone book, ripping out pages and sending some of them to the McCarthy group in Baltimore to address. A shuttle system is developing. They're also going through the Nashua and Manchester phone books, identifying nationality groups by name and sending them personalized letters. Now they've run out of money for stamps again and so they send out the teenagers who are hanging around, like Kathy Grogan and Steve Klein, to Georgetown to sell McCarthy buttons and bumper stickers to get money to keep the mail going—more than a million hand-addressed pieces out of Alban Towers before the campaign ends." Actually, teenagers did much more than hang around. They took over when the women went home to make dinner for their families. I speculated once as to why they were so much faster at coding and sorting. "Mother," said Ellen, "this generation has been filling out blanks since they were born!"

A New Hampshire Women for McCarthy had formed in the last weeks of the campaign there. A newsletter was now going out to other state groups (finally twenty-one in all) and the Wisconsin group was a very going concern before we started campaigning regularly there because of the organizing work of Elsa Chaney, who later became field director of Women for McCarthy.

During the campaign I became aware of a very surprising thing.

Ever since the pioneer days, women have been the glue and mortar of American communities—or, as a social historian at Harvard said in a lecture I heard with Mary, the communicators. But I found in 1968 that most men do not know what women *do*. This was true of the working press too—male and female. It was as if the whole interconnecting world of women's organizations and volunteer groups which have undergirded everything from hospitals to high school bands, from international relief to symphony orchestras, did not exist. It has occurred to me since that the flight to the suburbs which happened in the last generation may have contributed to this lack of knowledge and, perhaps, to the obsolescence of the network. Or it may be because, as Vance Packard said in his study in the 1950s, the separation of men and women is greatest at each end of the social scale. Many of those who made up the huge new college generation after World War II had made the leap in one generation from enclaves of working people and ethnic groups.

Women have acquired certain techniques of organization and facilitation of projects and some practical and useful knowledge which enables them to throw big fund-raising events together in a hurry, or to manage such unnecessary but complicated affairs as the network of inaugural balls drawing thousands from all over the country. One trivial example will do: in New Hampshire one of the campaign contributors, a manufacturer, came to me with a campaign hotel bill. He wanted to know what I thought of it. I thought it very large, and suggested he ask the management to itemize it further. "How many courtesy rooms did they give you?" I asked. He looked blank. I told him what every woman who has managed a luncheon knows, that it was the custom for hotel managers to give a certain number of meeting rooms and official suites in exchange for the business brought to the hotel. "All the newsmen are here, and all the restaurant business has increased because of the campaign," I pointed out, drawing on the knowledge of years of listening to Washington experts like Mrs. Hale Boggs and Mrs. Clifford Davis in committee meetings.

Elsa Chaney drew on the knowledge of women's organizations to put together Women for McCarthy in Wisconsin. She was a former Grail member who had worked briefly in Gene's office and then in Senator Proxmire's office as a press aide. She had a degree in journalism and in 1968 was a candidate for a doctoral degree in political science, teaching at the state college in Eau Claire until she finished her thesis. We met once in February in the Minneapolis airport, and, as she laughingly said, she got the rest of her on-the-job indoctrination over the telephone. When I came to Wisconsin on March 16, she had scheduled large luncheons in Madison, Green Bay, Superior, La Crosse, Beloit, Wausau, Eau Claire, and Milwaukee. In addition she had put together daily schedules for me like the following:

10:15 A.M.	Lake Edge Congregational Church. Discussion of *First Steps in Christian Renewal* [a collection of essays on ecumenism which I had edited]
12:00 A.M.	Press conference
12:30 P.M.	Luncheon and speech
6:30 P.M.	Interfaith dinner, reception, and speech St. John's Lutheran Church

The objective of Women for McCarthy was to reach women as yet uncommitted. The technique was to get together a committee of women "prominent enough," as Elsa said, "and well thought of enough" in the community so that other women would not feel strange in turning out for the affair. Elsa also relied on what she called "Church and world" events, as the schedule shows, at which I could talk about what she called my "very legitimate and real concerns—ecumenism and Church unity."

Her own account is interesting as a glimpse into the workings of the women's effort:

". . . to begin with, the setting was always rather deceptive. It looked like any woman's affair. There would be the hotel ballroom or the special affairs luncheon room at the country club. And there would be the inevitable long tables and the head table on a raised dais. And the women would turn out in their absolute best.

". . . But this was really the outside impression. Actually these groups were not very typical. Our women committee heads would make us aware of this afterwards with comments like: 'It's absolutely amazing that this particular group of women ever got together in the same room, because of the great diversity of interests, the great diversity of civic concerns, the great diversity of backgrounds, the differences among social classes and among occupations of husbands.' And diversity of party also, because Mrs. McCarthy's events often drew the independent woman voter and Republicans who would not cross the threshold of the regular headquarters but would come to hear about Senator McCarthy on neutral ground.

"Mrs. McCarthy always made an impact. I really never did see her flop . . . Sometimes she would be obviously tired; and sometimes she would not project as much as others. But I really, honestly, have to say that I never saw her fail to get across and to really speak to the women.

"I was reminded often of a famous saying from Newman, *Cor ad cor loquitur* (heart speaks to heart). Mrs. McCarthy does not have a flashy, oratorical style. But she has a way of looking out into the audience, catching individual eyes of women here and there, and making them feel that she is really talking to them, woman to woman, in a conversational tone.

"And also, because of her very evident concern about the things women had on their minds in the spring of 1968, the need for involvement, the need for the people to register disapproval of the war in Vietnam, the need to make some kind of impact on the policy of the country. And I remember that her talk often revolved around the idea that women, and the citizens in general, were not helpless (as we sometimes feel before this great, impersonal machine, all-powerful and incommunicado, that government has become) but that we could all do something; that we could affect policy *if* we would get to work, if we would be active, and if we would take a stand at what Mrs. McCarthy called 'the choice level' out in the grass roots where policy really starts.

". . . afterwards the women would not go away until they had spoken to Mrs. McCarthy personally. And this is not typical of a women's luncheon or brunch group. Usually these things clear out in about ten seconds flat."

Naturally, I would like to accept Elsa's evaluation of my effect. The press in general upheld it. My press was kind, except for an occasional slashing swipe—"She's as uninteresting as her husband" (in Chicago), and "She's given to tear-jerking accounts of bereaved mothers" (a jaded New Yorker in the hinterland). But if this was the effect, it did have its roots in my sincerity. It stemmed from my increasingly serious thought about how woman power and energy were being wasted and how they could be channeled into solving the problems of our country. Everywhere I went I met women of such capability and depth and courage. It seemed to me that they were being held out of the mainstream of American life. Or allowing themselves to be held out. I often thought of something Mother Stuart wrote before World War I, that it was our fault if we were not taken seriously. And yet it was increasingly clear that we were not taken seriously at all as partners in the affairs of the nation.

It has been said by a modern sociologist that the 1970s will be the decade of women and youth as the 1960s had been the decade of civil rights. If that is so—and statistics seem to indicate social changes of the first magnitude—the McCarthy campaign of 1968 will again have proved to be prophetic of the years to come. The story of youth involvement is well known, but concentration on it has obscured the story of the women. As Gene has said, it is a story which remains to be told, and I can only tell what I saw myself.

I know that in 1968 women entered politics and had political effect in an entirely new way. A very good example was the involvement of the women of the press. Never before in my experience have women correspondents and women columnists taken such a decided stand on a candidate and a candidacy, and never before have they had precisely the same influence.

Mary McGrory's influence within the campaign was substantial, as I have said, but her writing was much more so. It was Mary who discovered the young and sounded the note which set the press to telling their story to the nation; it was Mary who developed the theme of reconciliation which became the theme of the campaign from New Hampshire to Wisconsin, replacing the Don Quixote theme of the pre-primary months.

Shana Alexander, at that time *Life*'s connoisseur of the off-beat in her column "The Feminine Eye," was the columnist who discovered the unique character of the candidate and communicated it to the country. It was also Shana who discovered that he was a poet and who shared his poetry for the first time with his followers and detractors.

Neither Mary McGrory or Shana Alexander is a feminist. They are not interested in politics in the sense earlier feminist columnists like Dorothy Thompson and Doris Fleeson were. The first dean of Barnard College, Emily Putnam, elucidated one aspect of the problem in her book, *Lady*. Throughout history, she maintained, the lady—that is, the woman whose fortunes rise and fall with men's—was unconcerned with the exploitation of other women and was, in a sense, a hostage in the conflict between the sexes. One could say that Mary and Shana belonged to a modern career hostage class. They accepted the fact that they were making their way in a man's world and were quite willing to make it on men's terms. They both possessed peculiar gifts which made it possible for them to advance without in any way fighting men for that advancement.

Mary McGrory always rejected any identification with the women's press corps as such. She refused to join either the Women's Press Club or the American Newspaper Women's Club. Her good friend Doris Fleeson often pointed out that the benefits they both enjoyed had been won for them by feminist groups, but it was not a view congenial to Mary's mind.

Yet she had no illusions about men. "On their best days, the best of them are eight years old," she often said; but she was perfectly willing to give them the attention, the comforting, and the teasing to which an eight-year-old boy would respond. When she redecorated her apartment, she bought a man-sized red damask chair which was always assigned to the man most in need of comfort and attention at her parties or "little evenings." She was perfectly willing to listen endlessly to the stories of copy boys, paper boys, janitors, publishers, hip leaders, as long as they were interesting, and she had a corps of devoted followers and helpers for this reason. On campaign planes Mary had fellow reporters to carry her typewriter and help with her bags—something more feminist reporters lacked.

Mary was ever beguiled and sidetracked by the amusing, the charming, and the eccentric. Despite her early support of Stevenson, once she started following Jack Kennedy's campaign she could not resist his style and charm. Once he was elected, her column became a great chronicle of the human side of the Kennedy administration. She became a power in Washington because she was an Administration favorite. Her columns decided whether people existed as persons or not. In 1967 and 1968 what she said mattered because her column was read by so many influential people.

Shana Alexander's "The Feminine Eye" was a hard column to classify. It was even harder to satirize, as one can demonstrate by citing the *Harvard Lampoon* parody of *Life* in 1968. In a column with the by-line Sauna Avocado, the Harvard writer characterizes the column as filled with "rambling real-life anecdotes . . . picked up hanging around the A & P checkout boy," and its style as an effort to prove "that us females can write as tersely and gutsy as you men." The purpose, according to the Harvard writer, was to make the American public see that "life is not that simple." The first two descriptions may be canards but the last, perhaps by sheer luck, is a very accurate, capsulized description of Shana's column. It was her very ability to question the commonly held assumptions of the public and of other writers in a pleasant and catchy way that made her the first to realize that Gene McCarthy, by his background, was perhaps a unique candidate. In February of 1968, when, as Peter Barnes of *Newsweek* said, it was not at all the fashion to take McCarthy seriously, Shana's column did just that.

It is impossible to overestimate the importance of Shana's personalization of the candidate for a mass audience. There were others who were attracted by his gifts and his differences. But they did not have the audience which *Life* afforded. Shana's presence, like Mary McGrory's, on the campaign planes and press buses did a great deal to assure local supporters and the traveling young campaigners of the seriousness and importance of the effort they were engaged in.

Male reporters, I learned later, annoyed at Mary and Shana's easy access to the candidate, were sometimes acid about them, referring to them as the "Little Sisters of the Press." Their role evolved from their original commitment to the issues, however. Neither of them in the beginning would, I am sure, have thought of playing such an active role in a campaign. This campaign was different. It really belonged to them as much as to the candidate.

As the campaign went on into Wisconsin and Indiana, I began to feel this, too, partly because I was in a campaign for the first time as much the mother of children as the wife of a candidate, partly because I was beginning to feel that, just as a woman interested in the cause of women, I had a large personal stake in it, and partly because of the way Women for McCarthy was growing into an independent organization, rather than just an auxiliary.

It was clear from early interviews in New Hampshire that I tried hard to say only what I thought Gene would say. "She prefaces her remarks with 'Gene has said' or 'I think Gene would say,'" wrote one reporter. I was disturbed that so many of the first nationally distributed interviews from Washington stressed the problems of women, although I had been speaking about them for years to women's groups when I was on my own and I was the proud possessor of the first mayoral award to a woman in St. Paul, given to me at the request of the Business and Professional Women's Club for this reason. I actually shuddered when I read the report in the New York *Times* of a wide-ranging interview and found that the interviewer had only included quotations about women and work.

As a housewife and mother, with a heavy program of outside work, Mrs. McCarthy is bound to have strong ideas about the so-called conflict between home and the outside world. She does. She calls it "a false dichotomy."

The basic conflict is not "Should mothers be outside the home?" she said firmly. "They are outside the home. The basic conflict is adjusting the emphasis to the rhythm of women's lives."

Just because she can't work on a 9-to-5 basis every day of her life doesn't mean that a woman's professional skills, once she becomes a housewife, should be lost to the community, Mrs. McCarthy insisted.

"If all the women qualified to do so were working on the city's problems I think they could be solved very soon," she noted.

"Today the welfare and future of their children is all bound up with the welfare of the city," Mrs. McCarthy said. "Therefore the care of one's children is involved in seeing that community facilities are the best possible—schools, libraries, health, and recreational facilities —and it means a good deal of volunteer and professional work. Our housekeeping extends beyond our doors."

Oh *no*, I thought, that sounds too strong-minded. I believed it, of course, and it was rather mild talk from the point of view of historical feminism. But I was keenly aware that it was not traditional talk from a candidate's wife—all right for the New York *Times*, perhaps, but Coös County, New Hampshire?

What I did not know and what no one knew was that the latent women's revolution was lurking just beneath the surface everywhere. The very mindlessness of our adherence to the Vietnam war, the masculine addiction to process which seemed to make it impossible to reverse ourselves, were moving women to question and to act more independently than ever before. I found that women were increasingly responsive when I talked about their role in politics and that they themselves were thinking deeply about the need to—as I put it again and again—"stop this rush toward death and make an affirmation of life." I was most affected, I think, by a woman whose name I never knew. She was part of a group I met in a poverty housing project in New Hampshire. After she heard what I had to say—and I had scaled it down carefully for what I thought my audience could accept—she rose. She said that she had six sons, that she saw no way of keeping them from the war. What troubled her most was that when they returned they seemed to have become unthinkingly militaristic. "Don't you think, Mrs. McCarthy," she asked, "that Lord Russell is right—that war feeds on people like us, the poor who do not know how to escape it?"

I was suddenly ashamed. I felt I owed a woman like that all the truth that was in me. I needed to share with her the best of my thinking, the questions in my mind, and my true hopes. It did not really matter whether my image as a campaign wife was right or not.

It was not only congressional wives like Mrs. Philip Hart and Mrs. Henry Reuss who dared to take a stand against the Administration and the war and what it was doing to American life. In Green Bay, Wisconsin, a reporter canvassed an unexpectedly large crowd of two hundred and fifty or more women who had come to a luncheon for me. He was astonished at the number of Republicans. "I'm for McCarthy because of the dilemma we're in," said one forthrightly. Another said, "We need a peace candidate. We need a solution." Another, "Why am I for McCarthy? Because of everything he stands for, particularly the Vietnam issue." Most of them echoed the woman who said, "I'm not speaking for my husband, you understand, but I'm glad to see McCarthy challenge Johnson." To one with years of experience in trying to lead women gently into positive political action, it was almost stunning to find them with the courage to say such things publicly, and to a reporter who would cite them by name.

Since 1968 I have become increasingly skeptical of history and the way in which it is written. The historian is necessarily dependent on contemporary documents and the records of the time of which he is writing. If there are enough documents, a truly sensitive and conscientious historian might be able to balance one record off against another until he arrives at an approximation of the truth. But even then he will unintentionally alter what he finds in the most complete documentation by the very fact that he will have his own point of departure for research and his own thesis to support. It is a matter not only of perspective but of cultural norms as well. (The classicist will see a horrid wilderness where the romantic will see sylvan glades.)

In at least two books, *An American Melodrama*, and Theodore White's *The Making of the President: 1968*, it has been reported that Senator Edward Kennedy returned from Green Bay, Wisconsin, on the night before his brother's announcement in 1968, to wake him and report, "Abigail killed it." What did I kill? How did I kill it? Did Teddy Kennedy actually say this? Or was the quotation imputed to him by Blair Clark who was interviewed for both books? Or by Richard Goodwin?

I asked Dick Goodwin about it one night in 1969 when we were both guests at Martin Peretz' house in Cambridge, and he said rather shamefacedly, "Well, Teddy thought that your being there—and Mary's—meant that Gene had decided against the deal." But he never told me what the deal might have been.

The truth was that I had no idea that Senator Kennedy was coming that night in Green Bay. Nor did I know what he was coming for, or what we were supposed to do about it. Susan Perry and I returned to the Northland Hotel that evening after a long day of campaigning. One would have had to have campaigned in places in Minnesota like Marshall, Hibbing, and Albert Lea, as we had, to know why we felt we were coming home to the Northland. It was like so many old hotels in small towns, dimly haunted with the ghosts of traveling men and their stories, their sample rooms, their spittoons, and lonely nights. It was a hotel once grand in its region, full of large unnecessary spaces, modernized now with a veneer of commercial-grade carpeting, of plastic, and Grand Rapids versions of Danish furniture and lamps.

Our suite was probably its best. There was a large living room in a truncated L-shape with banquettes and sofas which opened into beds, and a bedroom from which there was no escape except through the living room. There was also an odd arrangement of dressing room and bath off the living room. Magdalen Downey, the extraordinary local organizer of Women for McCarthy in Green Bay had provided us with instant coffee, some lovely old cups from her antique collection, and fresh daffodils.

Our daughter Mary joined us there, still filled with outrage at Bobby Kennedy's press conference about his "reassessment" of his position. Now his announcement that he would be a candidate the next day had been authoritatively predicted by Walter Cronkite on the evening TV news. It was upsetting but surely not unexpected, I thought. There had always been the hint that, if Gene did unexpectedly well in New Hampshire, Robert Kennedy would take over. There had been the more decisive statements about our foreign policy in his recent speeches and the careful separation from the President's position.

Susan went out to her own room and was soon back with word that Gene was on his way to join us. We were delighted and decided to wait until he came before ordering dinner. When Gene and Jerry Eller arrived alone, unannounced and unaccompanied by advance men, press men, and speechwriters, Gene seemed preoccupied and depressed. Mary and I both assumed that this was because of the general concern in the campaign about the effect of Kennedy's impending announcement and we did our best to cheer him up with a recounting of Mary's campaign experiences which usually diverted and pleased him.

Mary had been somewhat annoyed that the Wisconsin women in this eastern part of the state had tended to schedule her with me. At the Green Bay University Center the day before, she had settled the mother-daughter roles once and for all when I was answering questions from a mixed audience of students and professors. She decided that one question was unreasonably hostile and with a sweeping gesture motioned me to my seat, saying grandly, "I'll handle that one, Mother." And she had—with a flood of facts and statistics about Vietnam which reduced the questioner to helpless mumbling.

Gene listened, talked a little in an aimless fashion, then pleaded exhaustion and went to bed almost immediately.

Mary wandered away to her own room and was back in a state of suppressed excitement almost at once. She had heard that Senator Edward Kennedy was flying in to see Gene. We had heard earlier from Jerry Eller that there was supposed to be a meeting with Teddy Kennedy, but that it was either delayed or that it had been canceled because of Gene's reluctance. Now it seemed that Kennedy was on the way!

They were all coming from Washington in a chartered campaign plane, Mary told us. "All?" I queried. "Yes, all—Blair Clark, Dick Goodwin, Curt Gans, Jessica Tuchman." "But why, why are they with Teddy?" I asked blankly. Could they have all gone over to Bobby so soon? (Ned Kenworthy of the New York *Times* was to reflect my puzzlement in his question the next day, "Senator, what were all your staff doing escorting Teddy Kennedy?") I thought of Dick Goodwin's pledge in New Hampshire, "I'm with you all the way." I thought of Blair, trench-coated, bag in each hand, arriving precipitately in our front hall on the night of our return from New Hampshire. "Gene, we mustn't give up. You can beat him because he just doesn't have what it takes. He showed that when he wouldn't come into it in the first place."

Eller was of the opinion they had probably gone over. Like most of the Senate staff he disliked and mistrusted the new people. One thing he was sure of was that Dick Goodwin had spent most of the previous day at Hickory Hill, the Kennedy home in Virginia. The CBS stake-out man had seen him come and go. And Dick and Blair had breakfasted with Teddy that very morning.

Well, I thought, Gene will not have to meet them alone. Mary and I are here. And Jerry and Susan. We can look like a staff, if there are newsmen around. Jerry became a look-out man. Word came that the senator from Massachusetts had arrived at the Holiday Inn. Word was sent back that the senator from Minnesota was at the Northland Hotel and had retired. I have a confused memory of Curt Gans and Jessica Tuchman and Sam Brown in Mary's room, of Curt saying that it was the movement that mattered.

I appealed openly to Sam Brown who headed the youth movement, "Sam, are you going? If you do, the youth movement will fall apart."

Sam looked miserable, but was honest. "I don't know—I've spent the last two years of my life in the peace movement . . . I don't know." I could not imagine what the meeting was to be about. Was it a courtesy call, confirming Bobby's decision, already announced on the evening news? Then why were we trying to keep it from the press? Was it more? How could it possibly be more?

On the way back to Susan's room I saw Dick Stout, the *Newsweek* man. "I was certain something was up," he said later. "I began lurking in the sixth-floor corridor outside McCarthy's room, and wandered into an unlocked adjacent room to listen at the wall. There was only the sound of radio music." I had caught him in the act of eavesdropping and knew very well what he was doing, but I pretended shock and confusion at finding him in Susan's room. He muttered that he thought it was Jerry's. With mock seriousness I directed him to Jerry's room and watched him out of sight down the hall.

There had always been the hope among us, I think, that somehow our interests must converge—that perhaps Robert Kennedy was truly putting the issues first, that somehow the McCarthy and Kennedy interests could flow together. Gene had honestly thought that, I know, in the beginning when he said to Mary McGrory—to my own and to her frankly expressed amazement, "Well, tell him if I run, I will only want one term. He can have a free run in 1972." That had seemed an incredible position two months before. Now, after New Hampshire it was not quite incredible. Bobby's entry was ignoble in manner, but politically sound. There had already been an erosion in the belief in the inevitability of Robert Kennedy. He could not afford to wait. Even now, though, it still seemed possible to the young people, including our Mary, and I think it seemed possible to Gene, that something might work out.

Mary and I went in to ask Gene what to do. He did not want to see Teddy Kennedy, he said. He had decided that. Mary argued, but he was adamant. "I'm going to sleep," he said. And, incredibly enough, he did.

There followed a bitter interlude when Blair and Dick Goodwin arrived. Mary and I met them in the living room of the suite. Blair was blustering and arrogant. "What's all this, Abigail? I thought this was all arranged." "I don't know, Blair," I said. "Gene has gone to bed and says he doesn't want to see Senator Kennedy. I don't know what all this is about. What *is* it about?"

Dick took over smoothly. They had breakfasted with Senator Kennedy that morning and he had suggested that something could be worked out. The real enemy was Lyndon Johnson. Our real aim was to stop the war. Perhaps Gene and Bobby could help each other.

"Is that what you talked about at Hickory Hill yesterday?" I couldn't help asking and I was pleased at his surprise and Blair's. He focused on the tip of his cigar and mumbled that we couldn't expect him to stay away from friends of twenty years' standing. I experienced one of those changes of feeling that Dick brings about in people. Maybe he is sincere—he is a friend of the Kennedys after all, I thought. And he has been a help. "But what can be worked out, Dick? I don't see—" But Blair had had enough of dealing with women and underlings. He sprang up, the omni-present coat in hand. "Abigail, either you wake Gene up or I will," and he advanced on the door.

This Mary thought too much and she went into the bedroom and was successful in persuading Gene to come out to see them. When he emerged the conversation was inconclusive. Blair and Dick urged that he hear Kennedy out. They were sure something could be arranged.

As always Gene responded to Goodwin, albeit grudgingly, and turned his attention to the mechanics of bringing Senator Kennedy into the hotel. By this time of course, the press was alerted to the impending meeting, so it was decided to ask the hotel manager to arrange for Senator Kennedy's entrance into the rear of the hotel and that he come up in the freight elevator, the door of which was very near our suite. I still do not know why the meeting was supposed to be secret from the press. It is one of the unexplained mysteries of the campaign. By that time in 1968 I blindly accepted things as they came along. I had little or no way of seeing an over-all pattern and was seldom briefed for any occasion. Everything was ad hoc and ad lib. We set about making the suite presentable for the forthcoming meeting.

Gene went back to dress and I went down the hall to find Susan and tell her that she was welcome to be in the suite when the senator arrived. In the course of that trip, I ran into David Schoumacher of CBS. With this further evidence of the interest of the newsmen, I decided that the best thing I could do was to stay behind the doors of the suite myself.

It had been an exceedingly long day. The plane with Senator Kennedy had evidently not arrived in Green Bay until eleven or so and the trips back and forth from the hotel to the motel took forty minutes each way, so it was well after two in the morning when he finally appeared with Blair and Dick Goodwin. However, he came in radiating good grooming, charm, and bonhomie.

Gene introduced the occupants of the suite. Senator Kennedy started out by saying that he wished that they were there to discuss and see the Packers—that it would be a more pleasant occasion if they were—and Gene agreed. Susan offered coffee to everyone and Senator Kennedy launched into a discussion of the great good spirit of the St. Patrick's Day celebration in Boston, assuring Gene that he would surely enjoy it, that it was really a great occasion. "Political divisions just seem to melt away that day," he said. This disquisition was met by a rather general silence. He looked about and ended it rather lamely, "It's like that on St. Patrick's Day everywhere, I guess."

At about this point in the discussion, Susan and Jerry excused themselves and went out. Then Senator Kennedy got down to what we thought was probably the nub of the discussion. He started by saying that he had come because Bob wanted the senator to know that he had waged a fine campaign so far.

The scene is etched very vividly in my mind. Senator Kennedy sat on the sofa along the wall, Gene in an armchair facing him with his back to the rest of us because of the strange shape of the room. Gene wore a fresh shirt. I remember the French cuffs and the cuff links and the opened gesture of his hands. He stopped Teddy with a gesture. Senator Kennedy sat holding a brief case on his knees as if he were about to open it like a lawyer or an insurance man, about to give documents to his client. (That brief case became a byword in the campaign after that. "What was in that brief case?" insiders would ask and laugh.) I remember thinking of the determined, precise way in which he referred to the other Senator Kennedy as "Bob," never as "Bobby," as he was so generally known to both his detractors and his admirers.

Gene said quietly that he appreciated the senator's coming but, of course, that it wasn't necessary if he had come to talk about the impending announcement since it had been detailed or discussed in the six o'clock news. (The rumor is strong among the communications people that Cronkite flew to Washington to discuss Bobby's coming into the race and to persuade him to do so. He was supposedly in favor of it.) Teddy had the grace to look a little uncomfortable at this juncture, but he went on to say that Bob had instructed him to offer what help he could in Wisconsin and to say that, of course, their objective was the same.

Gene said, "From all the indications we have, we are doing very well in Wisconsin. We need no help, and I think it is better to have the primary here clear cut." He added that he could not, of course, promise anything. He had nothing to offer Kennedy, nothing to deal with, that the people for him were not people committed in such a way that he could turn them over, that he was committed in Nebraska in any case by the law. That this was also true in Oregon and that he would not withdraw in California unless the people there asked him to. He said he had responded to the desire of the people there to have a candidate and if they asked him to withdraw, of course, he would, but not until then. Then I remember his saying thoughtfully and coolly—I remember being very proud:

"Of course, if we really want to challenge the President, there are primaries which have not been entered, and which it would serve a real purpose to enter."

He mentioned West Virginia and Louisiana, perhaps Florida.

In retrospect, it seems to me that even in that conference in the wee hours of the morning in Green Bay, he still entertained an irrational hope for a rational solution to the nation's problem, that there might be some way in which the Kennedy forces and the McCarthy forces could truly work together and become a majority in the nation. At this moment in March, he was still true to his thought of October and November, that a clear run for him might mean victory in November and of course in August. It was always his thought that Robert Kennedy could not be a unifying force, that by his very nature he was divisive, that he aroused fears in the suburbanite and the middle class. Teddy made no answer to the suggestion about primaries. He made polite conversation for a little bit about the South. Blair and Dick moved into the conversation. There was discussion of how to get Teddy out without facing the cameras. Jerry came in smiling slyly to say that escape was impossible; CBS cameras were set up outside the door. I rose to see him out like a hostess at a normal gathering. While the others were trying to clear the way and to argue with the cameramen and reporters outside the door, I talked with Senator Kennedy about Fanny Lou Hamer, the civil rights leader, who was at that time speaking in

Wisconsin. I said how much I wished that I had been able to appear with her, that I had such admiration for her courage and her strength. He talked about people in Mississippi and Alabama who had been beaten and abused because they sought to register to vote or to put their children into schools. My impression was of someone very well informed and of someone in touch with the overriding problems of our day. There is probably in many people's minds a conflict like mine about Teddy Kennedy—the awareness of a certain insensitivity, an inability to quite assess the temper of the people he is dealing with, and yet the impression of a man who has done his homework, a man who knows what he should know. In a moment he was out the door, smiling, handling the reporters deftly, "It's too late to talk, we just had a pleasant visit. It's three o'clock in the morning. There isn't much we really can say, we all need to get a few hours sleep," and he was gone.

For a minute, Gene, Mary, and I were alone in the room, and Gene said to us bitterly, "That's the way they are. When it comes down to it, they never offer anything real." Whatever may have been his feeling about Robert Kennedy, to the very last his hope for a reasonable and realistic *rapprochement* was there.

In the morning Mary left very early for a tour of her own through the Fox River Valley. She left behind her a note for her father. I have searched for that note without success. But I remember some phrases: "Dear Dad, I apologize for insisting that you deal with them . . . I just want you to know how cool you were . . ." It was at this point, I believe, that Mary became identified with her father's cause, no longer simply as a member of the younger generation seized with ideas and ideals which the older generation must be made to share and for the attainment of which the older generation could be used.

What was the "deal" which I was supposed to have stopped? I'm not sure that we will ever know.

I have wondered, of course, whether Dick Goodwin's explanation was the right one—that Senator Kennedy thought that because Mary and I were present that Gene had decided against any serious discussion. That could only mean that in the Kennedy camp, women did not participate in important councils and I did not think that completely true. I thought of another meeting in 1960 when, after the primaries, John Kennedy came to Minnesota seeking delegates. The vice presidency was being dangled as a lure and the famous Minnesota team spirit was crumbling a little in the face of the temptation. Orville Freeman, then governor, asked Gene and me to come to his suite to meet with Kennedy after the official dinner. It was a small group. Dorothy Jacobson, former state chairwoman and the governor's executive assistant, was there. And Jane Freeman, of course. The case for Orville as vice-presidential candidate was obliquely discussed, and everyone present made some comment about what he could contribute to the ticket: a young image, administrative experience, representation of an agricultural state, balance of religion because of his Lutheran deaconhood. Did John Kennedy discount what he learned that evening because of the participation of the women there?

On March 31 President Johnson announced that he would not be a candidate for re-election. On April 2 Gene won the Wisconsin primary with 57 per cent of the votes. All indications were that if there had not been some last-minute sympathy vote for the retiring President and if the urgency for the Republican crossover had not been lessened by the President's announcement, the victory would have been by at least 62 per cent.

This was an even more stunning result than New Hampshire, but the press and other media, lost as they were in speculation about Robert Kennedy's plans, almost completely missed its significance. It was not only historically astonishing—an incumbent President defeated by such an overwhelming majority in his own party was unprecedented and Gene also outpolled the Republican winner in what was to be a Republican year in Wisconsin—but it was done in a new way. The Wisconsin people had done it almost alone without any of the traditional organizational help, with only last minute help from the young national staff, with not one single important political figure from Wisconsin on their side until the very end. It was the real new politics.

"By the New Hampshire primary, the Wisconsin organization numbered nearly three thousand adults," wrote Stout. "This army had raised close to $200,000 and created their own radio and television commercials, newspaper advertising, billboards, campaign literature. A force of some four thousand students from state colleges was building under the direction of George Wilbur, a senior at the University of Wisconsin. Some four hundred women banded together as concerned Women for McCarthy under Mrs. Jeanne Galazan and would prove as effective in their largely unseen roles as groups of women in other states." And Minnesota students, fresh from the precinct caucus victory there on March 5, poured into the western part of the state.

The campaign around Milwaukee was more conventional and it was here that the national staff set up headquarters and directed canvassing. (Other parts of the state had already been canvassed—sometimes twice—by Wisconsin-directed students.) It was because of this geographical fact that they did not understand how much of the victory was owing to the Wisconsin people themselves (the only two districts we lost were in the Milwaukee area and national staff was needed badly there). For example, the people of Green Bay produced two large audiences for me, a secondary campaign figure, and the women and the college people had been working for weeks before the staff people from New Hampshire arrived. Yet in discussing the campaign, staff sources always cited the 70 per cent majority in Green Bay as the achievement of Rick Grandjean, a young lawyer from St. Louis, who arrived that week without even the New Hampshire experience behind him. Press figures had come to know the national staff in New Hampshire and tended to get their information from them, an additional reason for missing the unusual and grass roots nature of the Wisconsin story.

The Wisconsin adult effort was governed by a committee with loose lines of authority. Almost first among equals was the Madison office manager (for lack of a better title), a remarkable woman named Midge Miller. Mrs. Miller is a handsome, fresh-faced woman with pleasant ways and incredible energy. She tackles every task with a minimum of fuss and with non-compulsive efficiency. At the time the campaign began, she was working as co-ordinator of religious activities at the university, taking care of a twenty-two-room house and the combined family of nine children—and two farms! She and her first husband had been missionaries in Japan. When widowed she had decided to interest herself in politics because she felt that the good will the missionaries tried to build up was often dissipated by executive decisions on foreign policy. She had been a Stevensonian, a delegate to the 1960 Democratic convention and politically active as a Democrat in Wisconsin's liberal Dane County for almost ten years. She was also involved in Clergy and Laymen Concerned about Vietnam.

It may seem absurd to say to those who think of liberation in terms of freedom from family that she seemed to be a truly liberated woman. She worked with ease and no sense of inequality with the men and with the same ease with the women when she went on, after Wisconsin, to be a field worker for Women for McCarthy. Her children and her husband seemed to feel neither threatened nor neglected because of her work. "The children did all of the meals and all of the housework," she said. "Ed took wonderful care of them. It was a family project." This was the sort of thing one heard often from the people of the new politics. They had found a satisfactory way of working together without bothering much about marital or parental roles.

In Sheboygan that week Gene talked about the people who had responded when he took the step to challenge Johnson, not the politicians, he said, who should have had the courage but "first the academicians, then the women . . ." He had often said that among the few free people left in the country were the college people, students and professors both, and the women.

It seems strange to those observing a campaign, but the candidate and his family are so pressed by their rush from one place to another and are assaulted by so many new names and faces that they have difficulty piecing the whole picture together. When, after the campaign, the *Atlantic Monthly* asked me to review the books written about it, I read them with real fascination. "Oh, so that's who that was," I would say to myself, and "No wonder that happened."

As I read I thought increasingly of the New Constituency about which I had been asked to speak when I talked to college groups that April and May. I had felt confident then in saying that there really was a New Constituency—groups of people actively engaged in politics for the first time; students who, with serious participation in the new politics, entered the mainstream of society. I used to quote from an article which appeared in the *National Observer* at that time:

> Senator McCarthy's campaign is singular. Unlike Senator Kennedy, he has no political agents with either the reputation, muscle, or inclination to peel off support from Indiana's power structure. He is exclusively the product of participation or citizen's politics. It would be premature to write off Mr. McCarthy or his brand of politics.

I said that the article quoted Gene as calling the new politics "a new kind of politics," a politics of conscience and a "politics of participation." "In another speech here in Indiana," I went on, "Gene pointed out that, in a way, to call it a New Politics was to call it a new politics in the context of our post-World War II world; but it was not new in the American idea; participation politics was the original American idea. And we have, of course, the residue of the old kind of participation politics in the New England town meeting which is a total kind of citizen participation that has come to us from our earliest history. But the new politics we have today is the adaptation of our original ideal to the technological age in which we live."

I cited other segments of the New Constituency—the numbers of professional people, scientists, Republicans, and—a surprising group, too—the new citizens. "Three people have come up to me in the past few days and said, "I finished taking out my papers [one from England, one from Norway, one from Denmark]—I finished because I believe in America again and I want to be able to vote for your husband." Others spoke of the need to find ways, practical ways, of making our choice of program and candidate real and effective.

I talked of the way people of the New Constituency in Connecticut had discovered an old primary law and made it effective again, petitioning for the primary, village by village, town by town, collecting thousands of signatures for the petition, fighting the petition through the court for the primary, getting the people out to vote in the primary, and finally winning a quarter of the votes to the state convention. I talked of the people in California who collected thirty thousand signatures in one night to secure the preferential first place on the primary ballot; I talked of the precinct caucuses in Minnesota —all the preliminary triumphs of hard work grass roots politics.

There was a new politics in 1968. There was a New Constituency. It was bigger than the so-called "movement" which unites the New Left and the civil rights and peace activities, although they were part of it. It was bigger than the reformers of politics, although they were part of it. It was more than academia united with the mobile society of scientists, educators, technologists, and the new post-World War II college class. It was more than the coalition of these and the liberals of the suburbs. The factory people of Berlin, New Hampshire, voted McCarthy. Rural Wisconsin voted McCarthy. And the people of Oregon who voted McCarthy were people whose occupations made them very different from the voters of Scarsdale. The McCarthy vote was 40 per cent of the ghettos of Milwaukee and surprisingly high in Watts and among the Chicanos of California.

I think it was the best of Middle America and most of Middle America. It was an educated vote in the most profound sense in that it was the constituency of thoughtful America and troubled America. It was the America liberated enough by the good things democracy should provide all citizens to have time to wonder and to question.

A miasma of distrust and emotion hung over the entry into Indiana. Robert Kennedy was now in the campaign and where he went the crowds seemed stirred to a fever pitch. "There was the adulation, but as always there was also the hate," wrote Jules Witcover. There was also the murky water of Indiana politics, not the most savory in the nation. Officeholders in Indiana pay a check-off percentage of their salaries to the state party; representatives of minority groups make straightforward offers to campaign managers of so many votes for so much money. All in all, it was not a very good atmosphere for discussing the role of the presidency as Gene had said in Wisconsin he wished to do: "The role of the presidency at all times, but especially in 1960, I felt, must be one of uniting this nation, not one of adding it up in some way, not of putting it together of bits and pieces, and not even one of organizing it. The need of America is not a need for organization, but a need to develop a sense of national character, with common purposes and shared ideals."

In many ways the campaign seemed to come apart in Indiana. It was no longer a campaign against the Administration and its policies, but, as Gene said, a campaign between personalities. Gene had treated this half-humorously in Wisconsin, but it was an uncomfortable kind of humor, reflecting his feeling about the calculation in the manner of Senator Kennedy's announcement and the kind of campaign it heralded. If you do not differ on an issue, he asked, what do you differ about? "If you can't do that, the campaign becomes a question of personality, of competence and qualification. I don't know what else you argue about. If he wants to pick on us over our size, I'm willing to use that as a determinant. Or age. I don't think those should be standards, however. He plays touch football; I play football. He plays softball; I play baseball. He skates in Rockefeller Center; I play hockey. . . . If these are the bases on which you are going to make a decision, why, I mean, it'll become abrasive, I suppose."

After Wisconsin there was a sense of alienation from the New Hampshire veterans who were called national staff, a lack of communication with them. This stemmed, I think, from the night at Green Bay when it seemed that Curtis Gans and Sam Brown had joined Dick Goodwin and Blair Clark in what was essentially an essay in old politics—the working out of a deal. The manipulative spirit of Green Bay seemed to hang on.

Even though only one of the veterans defected to the Kennedy campaign after the announcement, Gene probably felt that some of the others stayed less out of loyalty to him than out of the feeling that the campaign was theirs and that they were not likely to have the same status in another campaign. And the eight-thousand-member organization of Hoosiers for a Democratic Alternative, which chairman Jim Bogle had offered as the core of a McCarthy campaign, did not seem to exist, at least in the tangible form of lists of names and local headquarters. Everything seemed to depend on help from the outside—on the McCarthy campaign organization which, as Gene had said in a happier time, was "least organized at the top."

The last days in Wisconsin, campaign organization relations had been clouded. Quite unreasonably in view of Gene's record and his strong civil rights speeches, some of the young people began to question Gene's concern for minorities, especially for the blacks in the ghettos. Their concern was based in part on Gene's refusal to compete emotionally with Robert Kennedy. In part the dissatisfaction stemmed from the decision of Curtis Gans as campaign director to hold the campaign aloof from Father Groppi's confrontations, which were going in Milwaukee at the time. Gene had nothing to do with this strategy. Curtis had arrived at the position of making such decisions almost by default. He had gone to New Hampshire (ostensibly at Blair Clark's decision) to manage the campaign there. At the time, Blair told us that it was a choice between Curtis and Harold

M. Ickes of New York. I think the chaotic state of things in the Washington campaign office and the inconclusive relations with the Senate office disposed Curtis to go. In New Hampshire he saw something manageable and comprehensible, where planning and the execution of plans were possible.

Murray Kempton, writing in *The New York Review of Books* about the Moratorium the next year, has this description of Curtis:

> Leaving, you came upon Curtis Gans, once coordinator of the McCarthy campaign, talking on the telephone in a low voice to some one whose confidential information, you understood at once, could be of no use to him at all. It must have been a long while ago, say Nebraska perhaps, that Curtis Gans commenced to act from the certainty that something, at any moment, was about to pass out of his control and to go at random, whether for good or bad was not the point, but just wildly out of his hands.

I had to smile at that description because it touched so aptly on Curtis' Achilles' heel. He did not easily let himself go with the tide or co-operate loosely or in some kind of loose liaison with other people. New Hampshire had been ideal for him. It was probably his finest hour in the campaign. It was the place in which he built up a close community of subordinates to whom he was the leader and the only leader, and it was on these subordinates that he tried to place the burden of the whole campaign as it widened out all over the country in the months after New Hampshire. He had very positive strengths for directing a closely knit and unified organization; he made decisions and took responsibility. He presented them with a clear plan of action. He was, from my point of view, a point of contact with the main campaign since he was at least willing to give Women for McCarthy and its emerging staff office space and some co-operation. He was a superb political theorist, but New Hampshire had provided no experience in working with large groups of local people. In Wisconsin, with its well-developed campaign and its experienced issue-oriented campaigners, "national staff" became something of a separate and closed organization, and remained so until the end of the primaries.

At the same time two of the young press staff, disgruntled be-

cause of difficulties with an older New York *Times* reporter, resigned dramatically. The resignations coincided with a debate within
the staff on tactics in the ghetto—a debate initiated by Curtis, who
called a large-scale meeting in his hotel room. The debate leaked,
of course. Inevitably, the resignations were equated with staff dis-
satisfaction with Gene on the problems of the ghetto.

"I couldn't say anything that would do the damage that story has
done," Gene told a reporter. Gene also felt that a deliberate effort
was being made to discredit his civil rights and labor record and little
done to defend it. "Negro papers were being provided with charges
from some unidentified source that I was against civil rights. The first
report in a Negro paper claimed that I had not voted for civil rights sixteen or seventeen times."

The campaign had just moved to Indiana when Dr. Martin Luther
King, Jr., was assassinated. If the Berlin experience had exemplified
all that was good and positive in the 1968 campaign, the experiences surrounding the Martin Luther King funeral drew together all
the things which were bad and disturbing.

Among the very few people Gene had consulted about his candidacy, aside from the senators he felt bound to advise of his intention, was Martin Luther King. He had called him in response to the
urging of his new supporters, Martin and Ann Peretz of the Massachusetts Pax group, who were contributors to the Southern Christian Leadership Conference, and also because he saw in Martin
Luther King the only black leader who realized how much Vietnam
was involved in the plight of his people. When I had lunch with
Coretta King at the Church Women's meeting in Atlanta in November, I realized that she did not know of the telephone conversation in
which her husband had expressed support for Gene's effort, although
he could say nothing publicly at the moment, a fact which did not
surprise me, being the wife of another public man. Our lengthy conversation that day gave me some poignant insights into her life.

She was a woman who had lived under great strain, a mother
of children still small, yet she was an educated woman with great
issue commitment, probably every bit as great as her husband's.
She was a woman who had for years been able to spend less and less

time at her husband's side because of the projects and the people who had claim on him. This is a very real dilemma for the committed woman, who is also the wife of a public man and a mother. She is expected to speak for him and to represent him, but her moment-to-moment contact with him is poor because of the people who come between—who are at her husband's side as aides, whom he meets in places she cannot go—and because her role is mixed when he is at home.

At the very moment we were at the Church Women's meeting in Atlanta, King and his Southern Christian Leadership Conference advisers had withdrawn to a place of retreat to discuss the coming Poor People's Campaign. Coretta's imagination was fired by the prospect of the Poor People's Campaign and she was very eager to take full part in it. She confided quite openly, however, that her husband felt that being with the children was more important. I jestingly told her about Saint Felicitas, a great name in the early Christian martyrology. Felicitas was a young wife with child when she was thrown into prison by the Roman persecutors and had borne her child in prison. Taunted by the guards even when she was in labor, she had given her new-born child to her relatives and refused to recant, even in the face of separation from that child and her other children.

"I don't think it's always true that mothers should leave their children but it is certainly in the tradition of the early Christians to do so when it's a matter of a great and terrible moment," I said. She was charmed by the story and I promised to send her a clipping of it later.

In the early stages of the campaign, various contributors and members of the campaign hierarchy had urged me to get in touch with Coretta directly to ask her to serve on Gene's volunteer committee or to sign a letter to black organizations. I was reluctant to do this because I felt that her husband had made the commitment and he had made it more or less conditional at the time. I also felt that there were more orthodox ways of communication than that of wife to wife. Then, too, all of us at the meeting in Atlanta had felt that Coretta was not well. I had learned later that in January she had undergone major surgery which left her in great need of rest and quiet.

The entry of Robert Kennedy into the race made their position difficult, I was sure, because the Kennedys were contributers to the SCLC and the Kings must surely feel a debt of gratitude to the Kennedys for their help in effecting Martin Luther King's release from prison in 1960. The memory was fresh of the well-publicized telephone call on the part of President-elect Kennedy. Finally, I had a rather deep reluctance to use my ecumenical and Church contacts in such a direct way. My feeling was that if people wanted to rally to Gene's cause because they knew him through me, or were reassured or convinced by their personal contact with me, that was good and I was glad of it, but I didn't feel that I should exploit such relationships or demand a loyalty there was no reason for their giving.

After my hospitalization in Wisconsin, Dr. Madison in Milwaukee had been very insistent that I go South for a rest. He had phoned Gene and recommended it very strongly, so it was agreed that I should go for a week or ten days. Susan Perry and I made reservations at the Palm Beach Spa, a pleasant health resort in Palm Beach where I had been earlier in the year with Dorothy Marks. I was anxious to slip away as quietly as possible and the management of the Spa was very co-operative about assuring me privacy.

The Women for McCarthy in Washington were already involved in co-operating with the planning for the Poor People's March. Barbara Haviland, the director, was most eager that I get in touch with Coretta about their co-operation. This seemed to me a thing that we really could do. I did want to see her on my way through Atlanta, anyway, so I arranged to stop for a visit between planes. The morning before I was to leave, I woke with the uneasy feeling that I should call her and talk to her, but there seemed no real reason for doing so, since everything was in order. I know it's the kind of thing one always thinks afterwards, but I confided this feeling to several people that day. It was with no surprise that I heard the cathedral bells begin to toll that afternoon. I knew that Martin Luther King was dead.

For Coretta it was certainly a blow she had been expecting for years. It was hard to know whether Martin King had a real premonition of his own death or not. His last sermon to his people, in his own church, certainly seemed to suggest that, but his choice of life and leadership of his people made him the target of such hatred that he must have lived with a sure knowledge of a fateful end for a long time.

I was uncertain about whether I should go to see Coretta. Although Gene and I had been in public life for twenty years, I don't think we had ever learned to make the public gesture in times of grief and joy. We had remained private persons.

While I was wrestling with the problem now posed by my visit to Coretta—would it not seem I was using her husband's death to political advantage?—Robert Kennedy's offer of his plane was already being broadcast. His representatives were already on their way to Atlanta. Coretta, also a public person and fully aware of her role as a symbol, had already accepted these offers graciously. The struggle for leadership in the Southern Christian Leadership Conference, the struggle to be Martin Luther King's successor, was already engaging the energies of his former friends and aides. I solved my own dilemma by sitting down and saying to myself, "What would you do if you were not a public person and she was not a public person? What is the normal thing to do under the circumstances?" I decided that the normal thing to do in the case of a bereaved friend is to go to see her. So I continued with my original plans.

As our plane touched down in Atlanta, the Eastern Airlines passenger agent came aboard to welcome me and to say that there was a car waiting for Susan and me at the bottom of the ramp. She said, "The King plane is just coming in from Memphis and we will take you over there to meet it." Susan and I looked on the coincidence as a sign of sorts. We had been debating whether or not we would go out to the King home, once in Atlanta, and had decided more or less to leave it to fate.

The airline people thought I should join Mayor Ivan Allen at the foot of the ramp as the coffin was lowered and Coretta followed down the steps, but I, mistakenly perhaps, felt that I should greet her as a private person, not as part of an official delegation. So I stayed back and waited until she approached her car. We embraced wordlessly. She asked me to join her in the car on the ride to the funeral home. For some reason it seemed to me that it would not be correct on my part to join her in this public way, thus getting publicity for myself. So I said that I didn't think I would do that, that I would go to the house and wait for her to return and see what I could do for her.

The King house is a spacious but modest rambler in the heart of Atlanta's black community. Neighbors were coming and going in the perfectly normal pattern of a house of grief in any middle-class neighborhood. When I came in, I was greeted by the King's baby-sitter, a white college girl who had been with them from time to time and had come now in the emergency, and by some of the friends who were sitting in the living room waiting for Coretta's return. They seemed very glad that I had come because the Israeli consul had arrived with a formal message of condolence from Premier David Ben-Gurion and there seemed to be nobody official to accept the message.

No one seemed really in charge. There were women in the kitchen, taking care of the food which had been brought in and preparing coffee. The bedroom wing stretched to the back of the house and one of the bedrooms had been turned into an office by the SCLC and the Kennedy staffers who had arrived. After fifteen minutes or so of being treated as a VIP, sitting in the parlor, making polite conversation with the other women there, I noticed that the people came and went in a sort of haphazard way, wanting to leave some mark of their having been there. I decided that one way in which I might be useful would be to set up a guest book and I occupied myself with doing that with the help of the local president of the Woman's Strike for Peace and Freedom.

The most beautiful part of that day to me was the fact that despite the horror of the assassination, there was no effort to screen the people who came to the house, and it seemed that all of black Atlanta and a great many white people came and went in a quiet, subdued way, murmuring their condolences, holding little conversations with whoever happened to be present and departing. I especially remember one very haggard and shabby man who came and said that he had been going through town on a train and heard the news. "I just had to get off and come up here," he said. I wondered if he had been on a freight train in the manner of the traveling poor of the Great Depression. He signed the guest book and joined in the general conversation with great dignity and departed when he felt that he had been there for the appropriate length of time for a call at a house of mourning.

When Coretta returned, she had begun to show signs of strain. She stood for a few moments with her arms around me and one of her other friends with her head bowed. I explained to her about the Israeli consul and presented him to her. She accepted his formal reading of the message from Ben-Gurion with great dignity and in slow, hesitant, widely spaced words, she replied to him with equal formality. Everyone urged her to lie down and rest and she agreed that she would do so. I told her after she had rested a bit that I would come back to see her.

Shortly after Coretta retired to her bedroom, it was decided that the time had come to feed the helpers who were working. Susan went off with the people from the airlines to get lunch and to get some flowers for me to leave behind when it was necessary for us to go to our plane. I declined lunch and moved the guest book to the kitchen where there were two large breakfast tables, because I was anxious to complete the book before I had to leave. I was working quietly at one of the tables. The other table was occupied by some officials of the SCLC whom I didn't recognize and by the Kennedy men who had been working in a makeshift office in one of the bedrooms. I could not help but overhear the conversation, which was a very frank discussion of the political implications of the assassination and the way in which the funeral should be arranged. To my distress, they veered into talk about how to stop the McCarthy campaign. One man, later identified to me as a union official, kept saying, "You've got to mess up this 'Clean for Gene' bit. You've got to stop his identification with the students. Kennedy has the blacks, but he's got to get the students back." Just at that moment, some one, perhaps Burke Marshall, whom we knew socially, looked up and recognized me. I had kept my eyes steadfastly on my work but I could feel the sudden hush fall on the other side of the room. In a moment Burke came over himself. I asked about his wife, a fellow Minnesotan, and reminisced a bit about the town in Minnesota from which she came. I don't know whether or not I read a certain pointedness into his offer to have me driven wherever I wanted to go, but I thanked him, saying that the people who brought me would take me away and that in any case I wanted to have another talk with Coretta before I left. Everyone disappeared from the kitchen and I heard a heated discussion in the hall leading to the office. I was acutely uncomfortable.

After a while Susan came back with the flowers and a touching account about the neighborhood florist who had been so pleased to have the request from us; he had gone to great lengths to make the flowers especially beautiful. We decided that the card should read very simply, "With our deepest sympathy and prayers, Gene and Abigail McCarthy." Our conduct had been private so far and I thought it should stay that way.

Plane time was drawing near and I approached the black clergyman who was stationed as a sort of guard to the bedroom wing and asked him if he would see if Coretta was awake now because I had wanted to see her before I left. He said, "Are you really Mrs. Eugene McCarthy?" and I said I was. He said, "Well, they told me that back there but I just didn't believe them."

Once beside Coretta's bed, I felt human and natural again. Whatever tensions, whatever strains, whatever extraneous is going on, in times of birth and death women have a community with each other.

While we were talking quietly, one of the children ran in shouting, "Mama, Uncle Harry's here," and Harry Belafonte came into the room. Harry Belafonte's very real closeness to the King family and his dedication in setting up trust funds for the King children so that Dr. King could feel free for his work is well known. For the first time, I felt that Coretta's calm which was partly induced by sedatives, of course, was really broken and after that greeting, I rose to go.

Earlier I had said, "You know Gene and I want to pay our respects and our tribute, but we don't want to make things difficult in any way for you and we don't want to do anything political. If you'd rather I would come to the funeral as one of the Church Women's delegation, I'd be glad to do that."

Now, in Harry Belafonte's presence, her quiet reserve seemed to disappear and she said to me, "Oh, Abigail, we want you and Gene to come to the funeral, we want you to come as one of our friends. We want all our friends there." There was a little tray table beside the bed with the remains of her untouched lunch and Harry Belafonte sprang to take it away as I leaned over to kiss her good-by. I was shaken at the moment and protested nervously, "Oh, don't take it, she hasn't had a thing to eat," and he said half-humorously, "Mrs. McCarthy, I'm going to put it back, I wouldn't take her food away," and we parted on a half-humorous, half-sad note.

The kind agents from the airline took us to our plane and said that they would arrange for us to be met in Miami and would arrange transportation for us to West Palm Beach. By that time, the first news of the rioting in cities began to come over the radio. When Susan and I arrived in Miami, my first concern was to find out what was happening in Washington. The Eastern agent in Miami—perhaps he was a Wallaceite—was not very happy to see us nor very eager to help us, but he did arrange for us to get the late news in the Eastern lounge. We found that the Washington airports were going to be sealed. The TV news was terrifying, from one city after another. There were scenes of looting and burning. The news from Washington seemed especially alarming. Mary and Ellen and Michael and Margaret were alone at the house with Niki Ainsworth, a former teacher of Margaret's who used to stay with her when I was out of town. I used all the authority and pull I could command with the telephone company in order to get it to put a call through to Washington, and I talked to Mary. Mary rather scoffed at my concern, but admitted that they knew very little of what was going on in Washington and that probably the news reports in Miami were more complete.

Susan and I decided that we really should go back to Washington because of the children, but no commercial airlines were going into Washington. We explored the idea of trying to get a private plane to fly us in. I thought of calling, among other people, Bill

Baggs of the Miami *Herald*, a Stevensonian liberal who was a friend of Gene's but not openly a supporter. He was out of town; I was to find out later that he was in North Vietnam on a shadowy and never quite verified mission for the State Department.

The Eastern agent got more and more impatient with his charges. We decided we might as well go on to Palm Beach as originally planned. There seemed nothing else to do. There seemed no way of getting in touch with anyone. We couldn't reach Gene in California and we couldn't reach anyone else in Washington, so we rented a car and Susan drove to Palm Beach.

The next day and a half my orders to rest were completely forgotten. Gene called to find out what had happened on my visit to Atlanta and I relayed Coretta's invitation. Curt Gans had called to say that Dr. Herbert Reid of Howard University, who was one of the McCarthy supporters and staff and also a member of the SCLC governing board, had gone to Atlanta as our representative. When I talked to the children the next day, my fears of the night before seemed groundless. I was touched by Mary's saying, "You know, I never felt that any place was home really, not St. Paul, not Bethesda, not Boston, I never felt any city belonged to me, but when I saw Washington burning last night, I felt that it was my city and that it was terrible that it was going." Mrs. Kathryn Dodson, who frequently helps in our house, echoed this reaction in another way. "Fourteenth Street was our town, Mrs. McCarthy. You don't know how it feels to have it gone."

The riots had altered the mood of the country about the death of Martin Luther King, but the general feeling of people all over the country was still one of enormous concern and horror at the assassination of a great man. I had told Coretta that I would talk to her before returning for the funeral to find out what her wishes were, but it became impossible for me to get through to her. Dora Jackson, Dr. King's secretary, told Susan, very firmly, that all affairs connected with the funeral were in the hands of "a protocol chief." "After all," she said, "we have to think of the heads of state who are coming and this is going to take a great deal of arranging."

Margaret Shannon of the Church Women called to ask if I

would be part of their delegation, but she confessed that they were unable to get in touch with anyone to know how their delegation should proceed. I told her that I was happy to go with them if there was no arrangement for Gene and me to go officially. Gene, who had consistently refused to make a special appeal to the blacks of the nation for support, was repelled by all the maneuvering and finally decided that he would go to Atlanta on the official Senate plane. There seemed nothing left for Susan or me to do but to return to Atlanta and await developments. The office had made reservations for a suite for Gene and me in a downtown hotel and for accommodations for Susan.

In the end the situation was saved, if one can call it saved, by a sort of balance of forces. The President decided to send the Vice President in the official delegation which included Archbishop Terence Cooke of New York. Governor Nelson Rockefeller, a patron of many black institutions and a substantial contributor to the SCLC, sent a black clergyman as his personal representative to help with the funeral arrangements. The other Republican presidential candidates were also coming. Governors of the various states were coming. Dr. Reid told me later that it was the influence of Governor Rockefeller's envoy which finally brought about an agreement to have the arrangements strictly according to a kind of protocol with all presidential candidates in some sort of order, the governors behind them, and so on. Even with this arrangement, it became clear that there were still strong forces contending that the funeral should be made a showcase of the Kennedy-King relationship—I think it became apparent the next day that the Reverend Ralph David Abernathy was one of these forces—and, of course, there were the militant blacks who felt that this funeral was strictly a black affair, a black tragedy, and that no whites should be present at all. Dr. Reid was at the meeting of the SCLC until two that morning and even then, he was not sure how the arrangements would work out. But he and Curtis Gans and Susan worked out a plan for us. Dr. Reid and I were to go the the church. Our friends at Eastern Airlines were to take Gene from the Senate plane and rush him to the church so that he would meet me there and arrive approximately at the same time as the other dignitaries.

Margaret Shannon came to see what we thought the Church Women should do. It was decided that if for some reason the arrangements had been changed again, something Herb thought very possible, I should meet her and the rest of the Church Women's delegation on the church steps and go with them. Margaret had brought me one of the buttons the Church Women had hastily made, reading "Church Women United for Peace and Justice" with the black and white hands clasped.

A car came for Dr. Reid and me and we set off. Two blocks from the church we were stopped by a policeman who said that we could not get any closer to the church. I did not mind walking, but I was not quite prepared for the surging, seething crowd which pressed upon us from that point on. An Atlanta policeman preceded us. He was courteous enough in his request that the crowd open up and make a path for us and at intervals he kept announcing who I was but he became increasingly distressed at the rather understandable reaction of the crowd. People kept calling out, "Why are the whites going in? This is our man, this is our funeral." Occasionally, women would catch my arm and say, "We belong to the congregation." I kept saying right and left, "I agree with you. It is your funeral. I think you should come with me. Come right behind me." The policeman kept saying, "This is a disgrace, this is a shame on Atlanta!" Finally, we were on the church steps and inside the church door. Until that time, I had had no idea of the potential danger in the situation, but when I looked at Herb who had been behind me I saw that he was covered with perspiration and trembling. He was determined not to leave me, and after some colloquy with the clergyman in charge, he accompanied me to the seat which had been reserved for me.

At that time there were very few people in the church, only Governor and Mrs. George Romney of Michigan in the sections set aside for distinguished visitors. Herb took his place beside me partly because he didn't want to leave me, partly because he wanted to be certain that Gene was saved a place on the aisle. In a short time, a man came to tell him that he had to leave, and despite his protest he was literally taken away. He kept assuring me that he would be in the back of the church and if for some reason Gene did not get there he would be there to take me out. I could see that he was really worried and that he considered the day potentially explosive. He had been seated with me long enough so that when former Vice President Nixon came into the church, he was ushered into the pew beside me from the inside aisle. So it came about that Richard Nixon and I had about twenty minutes alone for low-voiced conversation about campaigning in New Hampshire and the problems posed by the situation in the cities and by the grievances of the blacks. It soon was apparent that the pew immediately in front of us was the Kennedy pew because Senator Edward Kennedy was ushered up the side aisle and into the place at the extreme left. Shortly after his arrival, Gene came in. He was in disarray, having made his way as best he could alone through the crowd in front of the church and had lost a button from his coat. People told me later that they had seen this on television. Then the other dignitaries began to come in—the Vice President's party, the governors, Bobby and Ethel Kennedy, who took their places immediately in front of us, and, last of all, Jackie Kennedy and her friend Mrs. Paul Mellon were escorted to the Kennedy pew and placed in the center between Senator Robert Kennedy and Senator Edward Kennedy. We all greeted each other and shook hands.

The main body of the church had been filled up with people —the true mourners, members of the congregation to whom both Martin Luther King and his father ministered. The King family filled the first pew, Coretta, serene and dignified, in her widow's black, the children with her.

Despite the television lights and the press in the front of the church, the funeral was truly impressive. It seemed like a church far away. The noise of the crowd outside, when the windows were thrown open, seemed like the noise of a storm and we inside seemed passengers in a frail boat. No one who was there could ever forget Mary Gurley singing Martin Luther King's favorite hymn, "My

Private Faces/Public Places

Heavenly Father Watches Over Me," and the tape recording of his last sermon in that church.

> If any of you are around when I have to meet my day, I don't want a long funeral. And if you get somebody to deliver the eulogy, tell him not to talk too long . . . Tell them not to mention that I have a Nobel peace prize. That isn't important. Tell them not to mention that I have three or four hundred awards. That's not important. Tell them not to mention where I went to school. I'd like somebody to mention that day, that "Martin Luther King, Jr., tried to love somebody." I want you to say that day that I tried to be right on the war question. I want you to be able to say that day that I did try in my life to clothe those who were naked. I want you to say on that day that I did try, in my life, to visit those who were in prison. I want you to say that I tried to love and serve humanity.

We sang hymns together, "When I Survey the Wondrous Cross" and "In Christ There Is No East or West." The funeral was less than satisfactory to some of his friends however. I remember the high, startled cry of a woman on the extreme right side saying, "Oh, what is the matter with us all? Why, what is the matter? Martin's dead, Martin's dead." And I understood that if we had not all been there, there would have been much more frank, open mourning. The Eastern Airlines driver had commented that the black people of the South would not think this funeral unduly drawn out since the South puts great emphasis on the celebration of death. It was always a time of coming together and for a great sharing of singing and speaking and calling on the Lord in the bonds of affection and relationship.

(Even the funeral had its moments of the absurd madness of 1968. While the church filled, I had noticed the busy comings and goings of men who seemed to be part of the Georgia security force. When the Vice President's party had arrived, a larger party than was expected, I gather, especially because of the accompanying secret service, some of the distinguished guests had been displaced and had taken their places along the wall near the open window, among them Governor Rockefeller. A man had importantly called out to another plainclothes man, "Cover Rockefeller, there, cover Rockefeller there. That's dangerous against the windows!" Then he had come up and shaken Gene's hands and said, "We are going to take care of you, Senator," and reached over and took Mr. Nixon's hands and said the same thing. "We know how to take care of you in Georgia," he said. During most of the funeral, he squatted in the aisle beside us, joining lustily in the hymns. At the end of the funeral, as the mourners' procession was to start down the aisle beside us, he squeezed himself into the pew behind us. Just as Coretta King neared our pews, Ethel Kennedy turned to me and said, "I've dropped my gloves. Will you look under the pew for me?" I complied automatically and was invisible as Coretta passed by. Once the mourners' procession was passed, we waited in some uncertainty for Dr. Reid to find us and take us to the car which was waiting for us. People milled about in the aisles. Mr. Nixon greeted the black athletes there, making a special point, I remember, to say to Floyd Patterson, "You keep trying—that's great—you keep trying." At that moment, the man who had made himself so responsible for our security, said, "Follow me, Gene, follow me, Richard." That seemed excessively familiar but I thought it was perhaps just his way. He shook aside the people in the door of the church, tried to lead us out, and then said, "That's really not safe that way—we'll go down through the basement." He took us down through the basement and disappeared. We waited for him thinking that he had gone to connect us with our car but he did not reappear. We finally went out the side door and found we were in the churchyard near no exit, so we retraced our steps and went out the front door after all. The next day in Washington, I read in the Washington *Post* that a perennial imposter had been discovered at the funeral, a man who liked to appear at important occasions posing as a security guard. I had no trouble recognizing our unwanted friend.)

The plan for the day of the funeral called for a long walk, a march with the coffin on the Poor People's wagon drawn by mules through the center of Atlanta to Morehouse College. Bobby Kennedy had plunged immediately into the march in shirt sleeves. There was a long delay the reason for which was not clear to me since we were not close to the head of the procession and there was much milling about. I was astounded at the numbers of people who had come from all over the country to the funeral who recognized Gene and who came up to him and said, "We are for you, Senator, we are supporting you in our state." We finally got into the car and started following the line of mourners. Gene was adamantly opposed to the idea of walking. He felt that it was not the kind of thing he would enter into any competition about. As the car inched forward I was watching the crowds along the way waiting to fall in behind the coffin. They carried signs from almost every state of the union. There were many people who had come from as far as California and Oregon, with their children beside them. I was saddened as we went through the main part of Atlanta where there was only a straggle of people on the streets. Most of the business people seemed to be going about their daily roles as if Martin Luther King, Jr., had never lived or died. I know that Atlanta is a progressive southern city, I know that Mayor Ivan Allen had offered the new auditorium for the funeral; still, it was clear that day that the white people of Atlanta were still far away from looking on Martin Luther King or any black as a hero.

As we came into the street near Morehouse College, Gene began to feel the simple emotion of the situation and he and Dr. Reid decided to get out of the car and walk the rest of the way. By that time we were truly in the black community and the people at the side of the road were simply glad and open in their acceptance of those who had come to pay tribute. At Morehouse, the car caught up to them and Gene had to leave to go to the plane. He couldn't stay for the ceremonies at Morehouse because he had interrupted a speaking schedule in California and had to return to it. He and Herb were to take the car and go on. Herb Reid entrusted me to one of the SCLC officials who solemnly promised to see that I was sent in a SCLC car to the airport for my own plane back to Washington. The campus at Morehouse was lovely with magnolias and camellias in bloom. People were seated everywhere under the trees; in the center before the stage chairs were arranged in regular rows. The SCLC official took me up to the family and friend section and said, "I think this is where you are supposed to be." There was no one else there yet and I was tired. Gene was gone and I thought no one would notice what I was doing. I looked around, saw that there was a congressional section over to the right and I asked one of the ushers to take me over there. I found a place among Gene's old House colleagues in a seat beside Sidney Yates of Illinois, an old friend, and I felt very relieved and at peace to be there. Various congressmen and senators left their seats to come and greet me and I felt that perhaps we hadn't become completely estranged from all our old friends after all. The ceremony at Morehouse was interesting, but it did not have the moving, simple quality of the service in Martin Luther King's own church.

Even then the political drama of the day was not all played out. Suddenly the Reverend Ralph Abernathy announced an unscheduled event. He said, "Senator Robert Kennedy will now come to the stage to address us." There was a spattering of applause from the black college students in the front of the assembly and immediate pandemonium on the stage. While the next hymn was being sung, it was apparent that a violent altercation was taking place up there. Governor Rockefeller's representative was arguing with Mr. Abernathy and various other people were gesticulating and expostulating with him. As the last strains of the hymn faded away, Mr. Abernathy stepped to the rostrum again and announced, "As I said, Senator Robert Kennedy will come to the stage as well as many other distinguished visitors who are here today. Governor Rockefeller, Senator Eugene McCarthy," he went on with a long list. "Please come to the stage." People began to call out from the congressional section. "Senator Morse is here, Senator Gruening is here!" It was all in vain because although a few of these people pressed forward—I saw Governor Rockefeller trying to make his way—it became clear that they could not get to the stage because of the crowd in front. People had come pressing from the sides, pressing around the arranged seats, and by now there was a very big crowd on each side of the stage.

It was time for me to leave. I began to worry about how I would make my way through the tremendous crowd between me and the gateway. Sidney Yates suggested that I stay and go back on the congressional plane, but just then the SCLC official arrived

Private Faces/Public Places

nd said, "The car is waiting to take you to the airport, Mrs. Mc-Carthy." It was with relief that I followed him through the crowd o the gateway. It had been a long day.

However disordered the funeral arrangements at the center had een, the handling of the large crowd and the feeding and bed-ling down of great numbers of people who arrived overnight from lmost all over the country had been beautifully arranged. As I reared the car the driver asked if I would mind sharing the car vith a family from New York also going to the airport. I was glad to do that and it was one of the most beautiful things about he day. They were a father and mother and two children. When hey had heard of the death, the parents had suddenly decided hat they would bring their children. They had taken their savings nd taken the first plane to Atlanta. The SCLC had found them lormitory space in one of the colleges and they had eaten in the lining rooms hastily set up by the SCLC volunteers. They had aken the long march from the church to Morehouse and now they vere going back to New York feeling that they had given their hildren a moment to remember. They had paid tribute and had lone what was good in the face of a national calamity.

At the airport, I went to the Eastern Airlines lounge. It was illed with Atlanta businessmen and businessmen from Florida chang-ng planes in Atlanta, drinking, talking, playing cards. The color elevision was on and the ceremonies at Morehouse were visible ut no one was watching except one black man in a Roman collar. t seemed a place of final testimony. I was still wearing my black mantilla and I sat beside him on the settee facing the television set. We introduced ourselves to each other—he was a clergyman rom Chicago—exchanged information about the funeral and the lay, and sat silently watching the little figures on the Morehouse stage until it was time for me to go to my plane. I felt very alone nd very much in the minority once again, just as I had felt in he car going through downtown Atlanta.

It was in the campaign in Indiana that I finally carried out my esolution to overcome self-consciousness and laid aside any reluctance to be photographed or to face television. I had early come to the conclusion that the campaign meant more than Gene's personal victory, much as I hoped for that for him; that the important thing was, as he had said, that America be united again, a symbol to the world of shared goals and shared ideals. Therefore I had refused no interviews or press conferences. During the Indiana primary I traveled for a week with a team from *Life* and for three days with Pulitzer prize winner Haynes Johnson, who was writing an article about me. I did interviews with the "Today Show," with Dick Cavett, and with Aline Saarinen for the "Huntley-Brinkley Report," and with one local Indiana station after another. I found that it was not such a horrible experience after all. Sometimes I found myself putting the interviewer at ease. Dick Cavett, who wore a McCarthy button under his lapel (as did Senator Hatfield), was worried when he inadvertently called Gene the senator from Wisconsin, and I said that he *was* in a way from Wisconsin after the primary win there. A flustered Indiana interviewer called me "Mrs. Kennedy" by mistake and went into an agony of apology until I said I would have been enormously complimented if it had been an honest mix-up instead of a slip of the tongue, because Ethel Kennedy was such an attractive young woman.

(I had *some* viewers. A friend and I were in an Indianapolis elevator when the doors flew open to admit Ethel Kennedy and a friend.

"Mrs. McCarthy."

"Mrs. Kennedy! How are you?"

Quick mutual introductions of our companions.

"I've been watching your interviews. They're marvelous."

"Thank you, but I'll never be the campaigner you are."

The doors flew open again and we were out going our separate ways. I hoped she had seen the interview of the day before, and thought sadly of the chasms between people created by politics.)

What was really the problem in Indiana was that the campaign seemed to have fallen into three sharp divisions. Gene and his aides and traveling companions formed one part; the national staff, who had opened seventy storefront headquarters around the state, formed nother part; and the Women for McCarthy, who worked with he national headquarters wherever they could, but planned and executed their own events, formed the third part. Also, in Washington and New York and Boston there were fiercely feuding campaign financiers and finance staffs.

The women's effort by which I was scheduled seemed almost as organized as it had been in Wisconsin. "When I went to Indiana," said Midge Miller, the Wisconsin organizer, "I fell into a nest of women so similar to the workers in Wisconsin and so deeply committed; and it was satisfying to find that there was nothing for me to do but to go on working with them." Other women came to the aid of the Indiana women faced with the emergency of a short time for planning and organizing. Maria Kavanagh, my close friend and member of my prayer group, came from Washington with her friend Bernice Maloy for Operation Penetration and they gave talks in schools and convents and to professional groups, as they had in Milwaukee; Mary Alice Lewis of Eau Claire and Maggie Downey of Green Bay, who, as Elsa Chaney said, had had "their baptism by fire" in Wisconsin, went to Kokomo and Evansville respectively; Mary Anne Gabler and Mary Anne Hamilton, old friends, came from Minnesota. And there were others, some drawn by the excitement of the experience, some—and this was natural enough—by hope of office for their husbands. A schedule of events took form that blanketed the state: Indianapolis, Fort Wayne, South Bend, Gary, Schererville, Michigan City, Lafayette, Terre Haute, Seymour, Evansville.

During those weeks I also had full-day schedules of interviews, speeches, and receptions in Massachusetts, New York, Lincoln and Omaha, and Kansas City—all to which I had been committed before the decision to go into Indiana was final.

It helps to feel that one is working effectively, but no matter how committed one may be to the issue, for a wife and mother there is a sort of persistent personal anguish of concern for one's husband and children as they strive and suffer through such periods of intense strain.

During this first confrontation with Senator Kennedy in Indiana,

Gene was angered and depressed by an organized effort to smear and distort his record of twenty years in congress; the smear effort was traced to Senator Kennedy's campaign office (and ultimately after the campaign, it was attributed to Pierre Salinger). Gene has described this attack in detail in *The Year of the People* and refuted it, but, as he said, the harm still lingered on. The charges are repeated today in articles about him.

I could understand Gene's preoccupation with the attack on his record and the sense of outrage behind his biting response. But I hoped that he would find heart to resume the leadership which had called forth the New Constituency, a constituency which grew every day despite the Kennedy and later the Humphrey challenges. I shared his frustration that no one seemed to be interested in helping him defend his record, and I tried my best to find someone to put together a properly researched refutation of the complicated and misleading charges. For us it evoked memories of the ordeal in 1952. But to most people, the effort to blot and blur Gene's record hardly mattered. To the rank and file of the people who had rallied to his banner, the legislative record hardly seemed important. He was their symbol of a new day ahead. And, in his focus on his defense, they felt him sidetracked in the past.

People thought he was drawing away from them—especially because his scheduling became chaotic in the hands of whomever was doing it at that time. "There was a real breakdown," said one of his most loyal supporters later. "There were times when the schedule was changed days—and sometimes hours—before he was expected to be there. This meant it was very difficult to get sufficient crowds, also local people had put in great effort and put their status on the line. To have appointments swept away, often for unexplained reasons, was damaging to morale and left resentment. I think people are humorous about it now, but at the time it was very hard."

I didn't know all this at the time. What I did know was that my time at home became a nightmare of fending off desperately unhappy and critical supporters, some of whom had been mainstays only short weeks ago. Mary McGrory, still deeply committed, came one night, distraught and upset. Gene was being petty, she thought. I must tell him to return to his original high plane. I asked her to talk to Gene herself, but she said her way of giving advice was to write a column.

The thought of the effect of such a critical column at this juncture was terrifying to me. I persuaded Mary to write a letter which I promised that I would see was hand-delivered to Gene. What we would like to hear, she wrote, was Gene talking again about his concept of the presidency, about our foreign policy. Other critics were more demanding. Mr. Jack Dreyfus, one of the biggest contributors to the campaign, called to talk to me and to urge me to persuade Gene to take Dilantin. Dilantin is the drug in which Mr. Dreyfus had so much confidence and which he was so sure promoted calm and efficiency that he had established a foundation to promote its use. He sent me some by special messenger. Dr. Davidson called at all hours with suggestions, analyses, complaints. I must see to it, he said, that people like Erich Fromm were properly scheduled to help Gene. A New York writer called to say that I must do something to improve relations with the Indiana senators. "Don't you know that Gene is the most hated man in the Senate?" he shouted. This was too much. I hung up on him.

What worried me more was the children's concern. Both Michael and Margaret attended schools where their classmates were divided and there was much Kennedy sentiment. I was glad for spring vacation when they could go to Indiana. Michael, earnestly trying to help, agreed to be the speaker at the opening ceremonies at seventeen of the store fronts. Not wanting to bother his father he brought the speech that had been written for him to me, and we rewrote it to conform to Michael's own idealistic thoughts about the campaign. I felt the universal helplessness of all mothers as I watched him go, nervous but eager, to I knew not what kind of reception.

I tried to convey people's worries and fears, and my own, to Gene by every wifely recourse known, but I could not really reach him. It was as if he was temporarily unable to gather the import of C. Day Lewis' lines to a political worker he quoted later in his own account of this period:

> Do you not see that history's high tension
> Must so be broken down to each man's need
> And his frail filaments, that it may feed
> Not blast all patience, love and warm invention?

It was meant for him, for me, for all who wanted to help.

I became ill again in Indiana and Dr. Corcoran, one of the campaign committee members in Evansville, reluctantly broke my schedule and sent me to the hospital there. After that, except for a few previously scheduled speeches in Oregon and California, I did not campaign so actively.

*A*t the end of the summer I went to Chicago, as I had gone to Atlantic City four years earlier, knowing that I had to play out a part in what was largely a charade of custom. On the basis of any reasonable political estimate, the outcome of the convention was a foregone conclusion. My part was laid out for me. Like the other candidates' wives, I would accompany my husband to the mayor's reception; I would sit in our box at the convention hall; I would attend the various women's activities—the luncheons, the style shows—and sit at the head table. I would meet the press, be smiling, noncommittal, and optimistic. I would be constantly under the observation of the women's press corps as the drama played out to its finish. It was not an inviting prospect.

However, I had spent the summer getting ready, trying to recover from the strains of the previous year and fortifying myself for this final glare of publicity for Gene and me and for the children. I don't remember coming back from California, except that I remember the children were with me and that the Secret Service had joined us. Gene had instructed us to leave Washington at once for the Greenbrier, a resort hotel in West Virginia where we had often spent family vacations. Susan Perry had already made the arrangements. But once in Washington, safe in the familiar rooms of our house and secure in the familiar network of the streets in Cleveland Park, none of us wanted to leave. It seemed so good to be home, at least superficially united as a family, once again under the same roof, that I called off the Greenbrier plan. Gene scolded about the change when he arrived but I think he, too, fell under the spell of everydayness—Petra banging about the kitchen, Eric sliding along the hall rug in pursuit of his ball, Margaret tending her neglected gerbil, Ellen and Mary and their friends sprawled on the rug in the upstairs study before the television. So, after the first complaint, he said nothing more.

I was so exhausted and so glad to be home where things seemed solid and real after the still unbelievable events in California, the murder of Bobby Kennedy, that I took little note of the strange things going on around me. The Secret Service took up residence in the basement and installed telephones and an air conditioner there. (The children reported that the men had a Hubert Humphrey dart board down there; I went down to see if that were so, and sure enough, it was.)

Decisions were made that I did not understand. Tom Finney, who had become campaign manager in the last two weeks of the primaries, and Gene were adamant: I should not go with Gene to the Robert Kennedy funeral. Philip Murphy, Gene's press secretary, since the Indiana primary and a Bostonian to the bone, and I argued that this was against all Catholic and Irish tradition, but they could not see our point. And secretly I was glad to be relieved of the ordeal. I did not think that I could really stand it.

"Then," I said, in one last try, because I did not like to think of Gene going alone, "at least take Michael. He was young Joe's schoolmate and I'm sure he'd like to be there."

Tom Finney agreed that it would be proper to take Michael. But in the end, the Senate plane on which Gene was going was restricted to wives and senators only.

So I was a television onlooker at the funeral of Robert Kennedy, with its great massing of resources, its use of the funeral train, its use of advance men to get out the crowds, the crowds of the blacks and the poor along the route of the train, the shocking irony of the people being killed by the train. I could not shake off the sense of the terrible irrelevancy of such an end to a bright life—death in a kitchen corridor.

Those who had known him and loved him had their grief to

sustain and their memories to cherish, a man to mourn. We who had not known him had the burden of terrible questions. Some people talked of guilt, but there was no guilt. If anything, there was a malaise and a paralysis born of horror at the society which bred this hate and violence which mocked the effort of rational order.

In the days after the funeral, Gene seemed deeply depressed and almost unreachable. Night after night he lay beside me sleepless, staring at the ceiling.

One morning he dressed to leave the house earlier than usual. When I asked about his breakfast, he said he was going to have breakfast with Vice President Humphrey. Vaguely alarmed, as I had been by the Humphrey emissaries like Judge Miles Lord, who appeared and disappeared during the various primaries, I asked why, but he impatiently refused to discuss it. That day I decided that things were beyond my understanding and beyond my ability to help. The one thing I was sure of was that we would have to get through the summer and the convention and that my first obligation was to get as well as I could myself, do something about my troublesome gallstones, and help the children through the summer. But before I could enter the hospital there were things to arrange. The press clamor for information and interviews was still insistent and, although the staff of Women for McCarthy were patient, they were at loose ends and looking for direction and decisions. I had already talked to Ann Alanson, the California national committeewoman who had supported Gene's campaign, about taking over Women for McCarthy. She was ideally suited to the delegate work, which was to occupy the Women for McCarthy in the summer, and to setting up some kind of relations with the national committee and with the convention planners.

Gene had agreed that Ann's coming was a good idea and she was due to arrive in a few days. As to the press, I thought it would be a good idea to divert them to Ann as soon as possible so that they would be distracted from my physical ills. It had seemed to me that the press reports of previous hospital stays had been unattractively anatomical—I particularly remember one headline which read ABIGAIL'S GALL BLADDER. Now it seemed to me that if I made a quiet announcement that I was no longer campaigning, it would show, like Gene's recess from the campaigning, a sense of decent restraint in the wake of the Kennedy tragedy and it would buy me time before I would have to face the reporters again. After all, I reasoned, I could not possibly go on to teas and coffees as if nothing had happened. And nothing I could say in an interview would seem anything but unfeeling in face of the Kennedys' bereavement.

I discussed this with Blair Clark and he seemed to think that my instinct was sound. Then I talked to our long-time friend Ymelda Dixon about including in her next regular column in the *Star* (so that not too much stress would be put on it) a statement about my plans and a quotation, so that it could be picked up easily by other newswomen if they wished to do so. Ymelda was eager to do it and willing to accept my stipulation that she print verbatim the statement I gave her. She came out to the house with our mutual friend, Edith Bralove, and we worked the wording out together. This is how the beginning paragraph of her story originally read: "When interviewed by the *Star* about her future plans, Mrs. Eugene McCarthy said she could no longer campaign personally because of her health but she added, 'In his last speeches Senator Robert Kennedy stated again and again that the combined support for his candidacy and *that of my husband* in the primaries made it clear that a majority of Democrats sought new direction and new leadership. Despite the tragedy, I know this holds true. Although I cannot find the heart and strength to continue the campaign personally, I hope women will not turn aside from their new involvement in the political process.'"

The next day Blair called in great agitation saying, "Abigail, I didn't know when you said that you felt it was unseemly to keep on campaigning in the usual way that you meant to make a public statement."

"Oh," I answered, "but Blair, that was the point of the whole thing. So that I wouldn't have to go on giving interviews and statements. I thought this was the best solution."

"But it's got to be more explicit. It's got to say something about your illnesses," said Blair.

"Well, I don't see why," I countered. I argued that it was very bad taste to discuss the mechanics of my various illnesses and that, although this medical frankness had been started by President Eisenhower in the detailed reports issued about his illnesses, I did not feel the same obligation. Since I wasn't the President, nothing depended on whether I was well or not.

Blair was so obviously upset, however, that I finally relented on that point.

"Oh, go ahead, Blair, I really don't care," I said. "Rewrite it or say whatever you think is best."

It did not occur to me to question how he happened to have a copy of the text of Ymelda's column. I think I had some vague idea that it had appeared already in the early edition and that he wished to issue some further statement about it. By the time Ymelda called to say that Newbold Noyes, the publisher of the *Star*, had insisted on the story's being rewritten, I had changed my mind again and decided that my critics were being unreasonable.

"I think it's all right the way it is," I said stubbornly. But Ymelda kept talking about her publishers' orders, she kept saying that she could understand Mary McGrory's point of view—that, after all, it was a national story and that she, Ymelda, was just a local writer.

"But if it was McGrory's kind of thing," I said, "I would have given it to her. It's a woman's page story." Only after Ymelda hung up did I realize it must have been Mary McGrory who had raised the hue and cry about the story. Later I heard that this was indeed what had happened. Someone had called Mary's attention to the story as it came across the copy desk, Mary had alerted Gene and Blair and had stormed into Newbold Noyes's office to say that the *Star* could not do that to a presidential candidate.

I never understood, and Mary McGrory never explained.

The story finally appeared in the *Star* with a black headline and many irrelevant details including a picture of me campaigning in Harlem in April of that year. The story was not picked up elsewhere to any extent and the whole thing seemed to have been a tempest in a teapot.

Yet, within the campaign itself, everyone seemed to continue to take an undue interest in my insides. My brother-in-law Austin, a surgeon, in consultation with our family doctor, insisted that I should have an operation.

"It's the conservative treatment for gallstones, Abbie," he repeated over and over. He scheduled the operation for July 8 in St. Paul with an old friend, a prominent surgeon there. I was to fly out with Gene on the campaign plane. After the operation, while I was recuperating, Gene planned to rest at St. John's, where the newly built ecumenical center, somewhat apart from the college and monastery buildings, could be set aside for his use and for the staff accompanying him.

Still, as I began to feel better, I became more and more loath to undergo further major surgery. My reluctance brought on a storm of advice and pressure. Dr. Davidson called Jenny Moore and Maria Kavanagh to exert their influence on me. Austin called from Minnesota.

Finally, with great good sense, my friend, Sue Safer arranged for me to go to Johns Hopkins to get a third opinion. And at about the same time, I received a letter from our friend the surgeon in Minnesota, saying that he was perfectly willing to operate if I wanted him to, but if I was reluctant he saw no urgency about the operation at all and added cheerfully that his mother had managed to get to the age of eighty-four before she had it.

By that time, however, the Minnesota trip was built into Gene's schedule for the summer and it was decided that it would cause less trouble for him to go ahead with his plan than to change it suddenly. This was a source of the much-repeated report that he had taken off abruptly, mid-campaign to pray and meditate in a monastery. To anyone who knew St. John's and the spirit of *Gemütlichkeit* for alumni there, the story seemed absurd in any case, but it was added to the growing legend about Gene McCarthy.

Gene, still alarmed at the ugly spirit which seemed to permeate the political life that spring and summer of 1968, wanted the children safe away. Michael agreed to go to Ecuador for two weeks with his friend Roberto Suro. Hopeful as always, Michael thought that the trip might call attention to his father's interest in Latin America. He planned to call on officeholders there and to visit as many as he could of the self-help projects instituted with American aid. He was solemn and serious about the trip and made a very good impression in Ecuador where he had an excellent press.

Margaret got off to Minnesota to camp. Mary stayed on with her friends in the campaign who were now working on Operation Grass Roots, a desperate last minute effort to influence the delegates. Ellen and a friend preceded me to Cape Cod where Katie and Walter Louchheim had offered us the use of a house they had rented that summer.

Gay Friedman came to Chatham to be with me because, rest or no, the campaign chores went on. There was a press kit to be prepared for the convention and we kept in touch with the women in Washington on that. There were mounds of letters to answer and bills to cope with and sort out. Nevertheless, the stay in Chatham was a delight. After the clashing emotions and raw confrontations of the campaign, it was like a return to civility to lunch with Katie and Walter Louchheim, to picnic with Jim and Libby Rowe. Jim, one of those behind-the-scenes advisers to Presidents who flourish in dignified Washington law firms, was a devoted supporter of Humphrey, but there on the sands of Nauset Beach, we were able to discuss the political future in purely analytical terms, and to tease each other a little. Gay and I exercised and swam and lay on the beach in the sun and I tried to walk a mile or so in salt water each day. Gay was good and devoted company and unaffectedly delighted as she saw me looking better.

In the meantime, no matter how foreordained the outcome, the campaign went on like a machine without a driver. Gene was being rushed from city to city for the huge and successful rallies which were supposed to demonstrate to the press and to the delegates the great constituency for his candidacy. He had called before and after the great Fenway Park rally in Boston—the rally which filled that huge area and the surrounding parking lots with people who had paid to be there, an unheard of occurrence in the history of Boston politics—and I had urged him to break the cycle and spend a few days with us at the Cape. He sounded tired and disconsolate, but he wouldn't come.

The young staff, loyal to the movement and to Curt Gans, were intent on their effort to take over or to influence delegations, if not for the candidate, at least for the platform he represented. And, of course, always for the end of the war. The so-called "New York group," largely a euphemism for Howard Stein and for those political leaders who had coalesced around him, had pinned their faith on M-Day, August 15, on which there were planned simultaneous fund-raising rallies in thirty cities at which the great corps of McCarthy entertainers and personalities would appear, all to reach and influence public opinion through television.

Gay and I decided to drive home from the Cape because we had accumulated so much gear of our own and the children had left things with us. We stopped overnight at the Steins' country house at Cross River, New York. Janet and her five girls and a ferociously, defensive poodle were waiting to meet us as we drove into the courtyard of their idyllic place. The French house overlooks a pool on one side and a long weirlike pond on the other. We had cocktails on the graveled terrace overlooking the pond where willows trailed the surface, black and white swans floated, and a flock of ducks swam busily about. We talked amusedly of how the campaign had affected even the life there.

"I could hardly wait to get back to my kitchen," Janet said. (It's a marvelous French cook's kitchen.) "I thought of it all the time. I thought of what I would cook, but when I got back and stood in the middle and looked at everything, do you know what? I didn't want to, I didn't want to!"

The Steins were to play hosts at a fund-raising luncheon for the New York Democrats for Gene in a week or so and we talked about where the tables should go in the garden and on the terrace. And Howard talked hopefully of how we might still be able to influence the convention. He still thought it must be possible to

412   *Private Faces/Public Places*

translate the people's demonstrated aversion to the war into delegate votes. He clung to his faith in direct communication through television and rallies, a faith he had certainly seen justified in the business world. Sitting there in the dusk, I found his arguments persuasive.

The children came out one by one from their supper, and at a call from them, kittens and cats came scrambling from the stables and the far reaches of the yard, bounding lightly through the twilight. It was hard to believe that a climate for reason could not be established and that—all men wanting to feel good about themselves, as Howard reasoned—feuds could not be healed and agreements negotiated, torn friendships mended and the good of all considered. I told Howard of a plan that Ruth Kodani of California, a member of the national board of Women for McCarthy, had suggested. She thought that a coalition of women who had been prominent in all the large women's organizations might be put together for Gene's candidacy and for peace. She had said that of course current officers could not involve their organizations, but past presidents and other past officers have an equally impressive network of communication and their names mean just as much. It was a technique which had been used successfully in the effort to motivate public opinion to solve our transportation problems by adding a cabinet department. Their work, I said, could be coordinated with the M-Day effort, and perhaps with a pre-convention platform conference.

The Steins thought this was a good idea and, rather to my surprise and quite out of step with my plans, I found that when I got back to Washington, I was helping to organize such an effort literally from my bedroom. Ruth Kodani came from California to set up New York headquarters in the Gotham Hotel near the St. Regis where the M-Day headquarters were, and Alban Towers in Washington became active again with Betty Key in charge. There was a gradual gathering at the Gotham of women volunteers who had not found their way into the summer effort of Women for McCarthy.

I heard echoes that summer of a fierce struggle about the convention arrangements going on at Gene's headquarters between the Finney and Clark forces, but I had no direct contact with it. I remember Blair calling once during that period ostensibly to inquire about my health but really, I think, to fine out how I felt about the young staff going to the convention.

"Oh, Blair," I said half playfully, "I think everybody should go to the convention. Let's all go down together in one big boat."

"Bless you, Abigail," he said. "Bless you," he said fervently, "bless you."

And I realized too late that I was probably to be cited to some one or other as supporter of full staff at the convention. It was probably to my brother who, unknown to me, was fighting a single-minded and far too dogmatic battle in support of Gene's supposed order that no one should go to Chicago except the Senate staff and a few others. Gene was far too pressed and distracted and harried by one group, then the other, to be steadfast about any such executive decision, but Steve was inclined to take him at his word.

Ben Stavis wrote that many of the young McCarthy staff members became cynical toward Gene during this period. He wrote that the multiplicity of leaders in the Washington headquarters caused a paralysis; were it not for this, he wrote, "How many committees could have been organized, how many letters could have been sent, how many delegate contacts could have been made, how many delegates could have been swung cannot be guessed." And Shana Alexander wrote of traveling with Gene during that time: "The candidate's sense of aimlessness and drift was shared by everyone aboard the plane." But she reasoned that part of the letdown was due to the inevitable change-over from the tempo and tactics of primary fighting to the quieter sport of delegate hunting.

It seemed to Gene all that summer that we were simply going through the motions. Going through the motions is easier for a woman than for a man since so much of a woman's life is spent in largely meaningless ritual, in support of causes and people she never really can question.

Antoinette Hatfield, wife of Senator Mark Hatfield of Oregon,

ho had been unfailingly kind to me throughout the year and who
as soon to face a somewhat similar ordeal at the Republican
ational convention, arranged for me to go to New York with her.
he set up appointments with sympathetic dress manufacturers so
aat we could be suitably dressed for the conventions, and for the
ll campaign if need be. Antoinette is a truly beautiful woman,
xtremely well organized and frugal in her management of the family
sources. She taught me a good deal that day about buying
othes all at one time and about the opportunities on Seventh
venue to buy dresses in different fabrics from those the manu-
acturer intends to use for the main line. We lunched with Adele
impson and her husband and were entertained by Sydney Wragge
ad by the chief designers at several other establishments. And
ae thing I learned all over again: if Seventh Avenue was any
riterion, business was against the war. We ended the day with
hat was, for me at least, a hilarious make-up session at Saks
ifth Avenue, where the make-up buyer knew Antoinette well.
bought shading rouge which I had learned to use when I was
aade up for the Dick Cavett show, and brush-on eye shadow, and
: Antoinette's insistence, artificial eye lashes. No matter how I
ied and no matter how patient the coaching, I could not seem
o put them on myself. The fact that I always cry when I laugh
aade the problem even more difficult. But Antoinette was adamant.
"You need them for television, Abigail, you really do," she said.
Finally, the make-up attendant glued them on for me.
I was leaving New York by plane that night to join Jenny and
aul Moore at the Moore family summer camp in the Adirondacks,
• I donned dark glasses to hide my unaccustomed glamour until
would see them. I knew they would find my false eye lashes as
anny as I did. The flight was short, but the drive to Camp Otter-
cook was much longer than I expected. I was met by two of the
uides, short muscular men in plaid hunting shirts and billed caps.
was quite surprised by what they told me of Camp Otterbrook.
was ten thousand acres of Adirondack Mountain forest and
ontained two lakes within its boundaries. At one time it had had
s own railroad station and hunting parties invited by Paul's father

and his brother had been met there by the staff with breakfa
and hot coffee before they continued on their way to the camp
The camp itself proved to be a small village of lodges on the shor
of one of the lakes, with a communal kitchen, dining room, an
great lodge.

It was heavenly to be there. The talk with Jenny, Paul, an
the children was good. The days were clear and sunny and th
stove in my small cabin was lit for the cool nights. I devoure
mystery stories and *The Good Soldier* by Ford Madox Ford, talke
mysticism with Paul and a little politics with the guides. I dis
covered that northern New York state was quite solidly Republican
but had been quite open to Gene's candidacy, more because h
challenged the Establishment, I gathered, than for any other reason
But this in itself was a small indication of the yearning fo
change in the country. When I was taken in to Sunday Mass—I fel
almost discourteous to want to go with a perfectly good Episcopa
bishop in the house about to perform his own Mass—I made
courtesy call on the priest of the parish. He was taken back,
thought, by the fact that I was visiting an Episcopalian bisho
within the very boundaries of his domain, and although he wa
kindly, his one remark to me was, "You know your husband doesn'
have a chance, don't you?" I don't know why this should hav
made me inwardly furious, but it did.

"You never know, Father," I countered coldly. And I left think
ing that while Father might be right about the situation as it was
he knew very little of the political motivations of his own parish
ioners.

There was one last trip to New York before the convention
for the final Madison Square Garden rally. Late in the year as i
was, this was my first experience of the New York fund-raisin
technique, an art in itself. Gene was rushed away from us to
reception for the really big givers held before the pre-rally dinne
Through some mistake in timing, the children and I arrived fo
dinner after most of the people had already eaten and the rall
preparation was in progress.

For the first time I heard a rehearsal of fund raising. This was

416

technique which had been perfected over the years by some of the large Jewish charities, particularly the United Jewish Appeal, and is now generally used in political efforts. The master of ceremonies described the procedure to be followed in the Garden and said that it would be led off by certain very generous donations. He introduced Stewart Mott who said he was willing to give $50,000. There was another donation of $25,000. Then there was prodding, cajoling, appealing to other people present, calling on them by name to say what they would give, sometimes bullying one or the other with "Oh, you can do better than that" or "Come, now, we know you've had a good year." It worked. And later in the Garden, it set up a contagion of giving so infectious that young Mrs. Bruce Gimbel saw her husband write a check for what she thought was $5,000—and then saw him add another zero as the fever of enthusiasm mounted.

It was the second time that summer that the Garden had been filled with thronging, pressing McCarthy supporters. I was content with the gathering in of the summer as I stood there with the children and Gene's sister Mildred and her husband, knowing that we all shared a family pride. I knew we would have that memory of Gene—his arms lifted high in greeting, pinioned by the spotlights, smiling, having drawn these people together, having become their symbol—a thing for the children to remember come what may.

I had two chores left before the convention. One was to fulfill a request of Martin and Ann Peretz that I hold a press conference in New York. To the very end, Marty tended to piggyback one of his causes on the other. That summer his energies were caught up in the cause of Biafra and he had been eager to have Gene take a strong stand for the embattled secessionists. "There has to be some McCarthy stand," he insisted. Now, he thought if I would say something before leaving New York it would be helpful. I had thought that I could combine such a statement with an announcement of the platform conference which the Women's Coalition for McCarthy had been planning all summer.

All through the campaign I had been frightened of facing the cynical and hardened New York press. But now, toughened perhaps by the foreknowledge of personal and political defeat, I found it no problem at all. My reception was surprisingly warm. The usually astringent women's page of the New York *Times* was especially nice: "Her intelligence outshone the television floodlights and melted the usual inanity of a news conference . . . Unlike most other current candidates' wives, Mrs. McCarthy is not buttressed by press bodyguards charged with keeping her from putting her foot in her mouth or marring her husband's freshly painted façade. An eminently huggable woman of 52 who simultaneously personifies mother and favorite college professor, Abigail McCarthy can think for herself."

The press had asked, of course, about the children and whether they would go to the convention. And I was happy to report what I was relieved about myself, that each one of them, of course, was going and that each had found a job to do there. Ellen had taken a course in operating a teleprinter; Mary was involved with the young staff as usual; Michael was to work at the switchboard as he had at headquarters most of the summer; Margaret would do whatever she could.

A few days before Chicago, I went to join Gene for a night and day of rest at the second home of some friends of ours. It is on Maryland's Eastern Shore, only an hour's drive from Washington but in a completely different world, in an area where for three hundred years people have lived close to the sea, the sky, and the land, content with fishing and hunting, good eating, and sociability. The low, spreading house was on the edge of a farm on Cox Neck Creek, a spreading estuary of Chesapeake Bay. We were alone there except for the Secret Service men who slept in a motel nearby and watched through the night inconspicuously at the edge of the grounds. It was a quiet hot night and the moon cast long strange shadows across the lawn.

As I lay beside Gene, my mind was gripped with a bizarre, fantastic idea: the President might be going to declare martial law. He had each of the candidates under surveillance. They could be seized at will. All over the country troops were available at Army amps, at Air Force bases, at Navy installations with no recourse out to obey if he ordered their moving out. In the dark and weirdly quiet hours of early morning, this seemed perfectly possible. What would we do if this happened? I indulged in a Walter Mitty-like fantasy of disguise and escape which involved a flight up the New Jersey Turnpike—to Chatham? Or perhaps to Tupper Lake where we could hide out in the Adirondacks until we could slip across the border into Canada? I remembered what a newswoman had said to me about the time the President had called her in the late hours of the night to complain about a news story. All of a sudden I was paralyzed," she had said. "Here's the man who controls the Army, the Secret Service, the FBI. What if he wanted to spirit me away, eliminate me?"

It was unreal and ridiculous, of course. But fantasies, like dreams, bring to the surface anxieties rooted in some perception of the real. This one was built, I think now, on my growing consciousness throughout that year of the repressive powers inherent in the presidency and of the danger when President and people were no longer responsive to each other, and the normal means of communication and change were aborted or stultified. Long ago, Dr. Rommen had written

> Democracy presupposes, instead of loyalties to persons, loyalties to moral ideas common to all. The collective moral will to live together in mutual solidarity must be so strong in all groups that their antagonistic interests, their dissatisfaction with the social and economic distribution of power, with apparent social injustices, will always be controlled by the stronger moral will to live together and thus use only the legal means of social and political reform and abstain from appeal to violence; where the antagonism of groups or classes outbalances the will to live together, democracy becomes impossible, and its institutions are directly contributing factors to its destruction.

I woke Gene to tell him of my fears. I knew he would dismiss them as nonsense but I wanted to hear him do just that.

The next day was almost as surrealistic, as we sat in our bathing suits in the bright sunlight beside the pool. The Secret Service fended off all but the most serious telephone calls, but these punctuated Gene's rambling ruminations over the past and the time to come. "We're not tough enough for this," he said at one point. And at another, "I'm going to call Ed Muskie and ask him to wait, to make a run for it at the convention. I can throw him my votes, my delegates." He spoke of his conversations about theology and liturgy during his last visit to St. John's. "It's all different now," he said. "They're not sure what the sacraments are, what really were the sacraments in the beginning. Father Aelred says marriage was probably never a sacrament."

Gene told me that during his visit to St. John's, one of the community had been disarmed of a revolver by the Secret Service when he was on his way to see Gene. What had brought about this grisly and horrible thing? Drinking, I thought privately, and a man's pride bruised once too often in the rough ragging which went on there, all enlarged and distorted by the wide screen of national attention—of press and Secret Service—on that serene isolated campus. It seemed terrible to me that in that summer of all summers Gene's spiritual home at St. John's should have been wrested from him—as it surely had been—by this incident. We know the terrible effect of actual assassinations. But what of the assassinations which are only attempted or planned? To live with the knowledge that there are men who desire you dead for whatever reason—hate, personal or impersonal—is shattering.

My final chore was the convention itself.

Gene had to stay in Washington for a Sunday television talk show. I went ahead to Chicago to provide a focus for the events and activities planned for the McCarthy delegates during the convention week.

I was, in that week, like Alice at the Mad Hatter's tea party, moving through a nightmare in my white gloves, murmuring the conventional and correct things while the world I knew lost all shape, form, and sense. There had been a valiant effort on the part of the women's committee to plan for my activities and to see to it that I would not be stranded alone as I often had been in Los Angeles, where staff work had broken down.

Stanlee (Cissie) Coy, who had volunteered as my press secretary for the summer, was waiting for me in Chicago. Margaret and I— Ellen, Mary and Michael were already there—were accompanied to Chicago by Gay Friedman and a few of my friends from that group which Gay designated as "The Ladies"—Jenny Moore (always eager to be at the center of action), Maria Kavanagh, Sue Safer, and Betty Key. My sisters were there, too. They would all take turns being with me. We knew, of course, that Chicago was an armed camp. *The McCarthy Advance,* the little newspaper put out by the campaign staff, told us that security forces, including Army troops on stand-by alert, totaled twenty-five thousand or more. And as we moved into the Conrad Hilton Hotel, we passed demonstrators massed in the lobby, on the steps, and packed into the mezzanine, chanting alternately and monotonously "We want Gene" and "Dump the Hump." I was distressed by the ugly sound of the latter chant. Yet on the fifteenth floor where the staff operations were centered, and on the twenty-third floor where our rooms were, the outward appearance of normal convention operations had been achieved despite incredible difficulty. The McCarthy press room, for example, was really a cloak room, open to the hall. The hospitality room off the lobby run by the Chicago Women for McCarthy (and named "Abigail's" in my honor) was really just a raised part of the lobby which had been partitioned off as well as the McCarthy staff could with potted palms and screens. Once again the McCarthy people, especially the Chicagoans, had coped with the situation, undeterred, and with great ingenuity. They had provided a fleet of cars and home hospitality for McCarthy delegates and workers.

I have often wondered whether it was one of our Chicago women drivers who was seen in that horrifying television vignette: A woman frantically backing and turning a station wagon only to be blocked at each turn by police cars and guardsmen in jeeps. "But I've only come to take them away," she expostulated. "That's what you want, isn't it?" I still hear the frightened gasps of the viewers in the living room of our suite as a guard suddenly thrust a tear-gas gun in her face—that was his only answer. The scene broke off. Probably the cameraman had been driven away. What happened? Where did she go? And what happened to the scene itself? I saw it once more that week and never again in the documentaries of Chicago.

The children went with me to a press breakfast and conference on Sunday morning where I began to live out the role for which I had been preparing the last month. This was what I had been trained to do, not only by the demands of political life but by my heritage—from those daughters of the pioneers, my grandmother, my aunts, my mother—to face disaster with as much dignity as possible, to affirm whatever was positive. Although I suppose I felt there might be some slim hope for Gene's nomination, the political realities seemed all too clear. Yet nothing is a total defeat; in a struggle something always has been gained on the way. At that press conference I spoke of "the freedom and courage of issue-minded women" and the dedication of the young. I think I was trying to say in effect to the delegates who might listen: "You cannot afford to lose these—you cannot afford to forget that these are the future of the party."

Women, I said as I had said so often, worked hard to support Gene, "not only because he has been a defender over the years of the rights of women, but also because he recognizes that our problems at home require peace abroad." And I quoted Gene for the last time on this subject: "The last free people in this country are women—they are the source of our hope."

I hedged when asked if I would support Senator Humphrey should he receive the nomination (what conventional political wife would make such a decision independently!) and said that I thought a family should stay united in those matters. I took note, too, of "the difficulties we were all having in communications and getting together"—a reference to the telephone and taxi strikes which seemed all too fortuitously to be helping Mayor Richard Daley control the city. I predicted that the convention would be one of those happenings "we'll talk about years later and say we were there." It was already impossible to ignore fully the repressive atmosphere surrounding the Conrad Hilton.

I went with Pat Lucey, now governor of Wisconsin and then

acting director of our convention forces, and Congressman and Mrs. Don Edwards of California to Midway Airport to meet Gene's plane when he flew in on Sunday afternoon. Our big car inched its way through Sunday traffic slowed almost to a halt by city construction workers who, strangely enough, had chosen Sunday afternoon to work on the road to the airport at just the time announced for Gene's arrival. For the last few miles the car was almost paced by hundreds of people who had abandoned their cars and were walking toward the rallying point, many of them carrying their children, all of them wearing McCarthy buttons, carrying purses and knapsacks plastered with the McCarthy daisy, waving the familiar banners, "He walked alone" and "We want McCarthy." And two new ones: "Welcome to Chicago" and "It's more than a dream with Gene."

I had told Pat Lucey that I was worried because Gene seemed depressed in his television appearance and I asked Pat when he went aboard the plane to tell Gene of some of the hopeful things happening among the delegations. There *were* hopeful things—the California delegation had not yet decided; Illinois was still to be heard from; illegally elected delegations were still to be challenged.

Once we had surmounted the final harassment—when Senator Ralph Yarborough of Texas tried to introduce Gene on our improvised platform on the back of a flatbed truck, the sound system suddenly gave out, so we were transferred to the media truck. Gene's words were hopeful. He was glad, he said, to be in Chicago for the final test. "Till now, every test of the soundness of this country's political judgment has been sustained." He had confidence in the outcome of the convention. It was only necessary to persuade the delegates that he had reached the American people and would be the best candidate for the Democrats in the fall.

This was true. Right up to the last, polls showed that Gene would beat Nixon by a much wider margin than Humphrey could hope for in most states and would certainly beat Nixon in others which Humphrey would lose.

We went from the airport to do what Pat Lucey had arranged, to call on Mayor Daley in his office. Pat was insistent that I go along. The Chicago papers had described me as "warm and motherly," exactly what he thought Mayor Daley wanted in a candidate's wife. It was a strange meeting. There were men there in the office who were known as political party powers around the country. I remember Joe Barr of Pennsylvania. I remember the Daley sons, stout like their father but dark, conservatively clad in business suits with short-cropped hair. I felt a pang of nostalgia for the stern family values the mayor undoubtedly held, and had a moment of understanding of his inability to feel or to know what the young people converging on Chicago meant and what a different world it was that they saw. The mayor emerged from a caucus a little later to say that the Illinois delegation was still uncommitted. He said it was "in the interest of friendliness and hospitality, and in the interest of keeping an open convention." All strategists thought that it was in the interest of keeping things open for Senator Edward Kennedy, but the important thing was that the mayor was not completely happy with Humphrey's candidacy. If Mayor Daley, a political realist, doubted the choice, surely others did too, so they reasoned. When did this slight and rational hope vanish? I don't know. I think it died in the violence.

We occupied two large suites thrown together across the front of the Hilton. My bedroom behind the living room in the suite was so situated that by a strange trick of acoustics I could hear what went on in Grant Park below almost as clearly as if I were there. The people in the park were not, I think everyone knows, the McCarthy people. Gene had asked his supporters across the country not to come to Chicago. And the campaign staff had diligently discouraged volunteers except those they really needed. The central core of the people in the park were the young people who had never believed that you could effect change through the system. They believed that only confrontation, only protest, would work. It was too late for the political process. Militancy was required. Revolution was possible. Out there in the park were the people of the Mobilization to End the War, and SDS activists, and the remnants of the Yippies whose nonsensical mock convention had ended in blood and death the week before. From our windows we could see the menacing blue lines of police and the massing of the National Guard, the constant passing of the weird jeeps armed with front screens of flesh-tearing barbed wire. The insistent chant rang from the park through the night, the obscenities against Johnson, Humphrey, and the police. And the chant: "Stop the war, stop the war now!" The orders had been to clear the park at dark. Obviously the demonstrators were dug in, refusing to move. I listened in dread as the announcements from the police bullhorns bounced against the hotel walls and the refusals echoed back. I sat up in bed as the tension mounted, wondering what to do, whom to call. I could hear the shouts from the park: "You McCarthy people, you there in the Hilton, are you with us? Flick your lights if you are with us." And then the approving roar as hundreds of lights in the hotel flicked. With each police incident, with each person stopped and questioned, with each one shoved aside at the hotel entrances, the demonstrators in the park had more and more sympathizers in the hotel. Finally I heard a welcoming roar: people had crossed over from the hotel. And then I heard the strong clear voice of Mary Travers singing, "Where have all the flowers gone?" And soon they were all singing—one protest song after the other, it is true, but rage went out of the voices and quiet gradually came to the park. I slept a little.

The following days became a strange confused jumble of incidents and planned events. Gene went the round of state caucuses, I the round of women's activities.

Patty Crowley of the Chicago committee made it possible for me to entertain the McCarthy women delegates and the wives of McCarthy delegates so that they could meet Paul Newman and other stars, and there was a rally in my honor to which Paul had invited the delegates. I went out on the stage to receive his hug of welcome and a bouquet of roses, to hear his warm speech for Gene, to thank the delegates. All the while I was wondering what to do about the children of Truong Dinh Dzu, the Vietnamese opposition leader who had been imprisoned for advocating a coalition government. They were behind stage, seeking help.

I made the conventional visit to the Amphitheater to sit in our box with Gene's sisters and Ellen and Margaret. I was stopped at the door by beefy guards, barely civil in their speech, demanding to search my purse. The Secret Service with me protested. "But you can't do that. This is Mrs. McCarthy. She's the wife of a candidate."

"Don't make no difference," they said and turned the contents of my purse out, seizing with curiosity the small case at the bottom.

"Those are opera glasses," I said with mock politeness. "Would you like to try them?"

They shoved the things back without response. The Secret Service men were sick with apology. "What can we say, Mrs. McCarthy? We're learning that we have no authority here." They had had the same trouble having our car moved up to the entrance of the hotel to pick me up.

My sisters and Maria Kavanagh told me later that one of the guards tried to force them back physically, pushing my fashionable and respectable-looking sister Ellen in the stomach. It was more than Ellen could bear. She advanced upon them, brandishing her finger and backed the guards down step by step, scolding them every inch of the way. She accomplished what the Secret Service men were unable to do; she aroused a faint spark of shame. It was a strange and isolated place to be. The security regulations within the hall were designed to keep the McCarthy people from communicating with each other. Wisconsin and Connecticut delegates, who tried to move toward me, were pushed back. One network man escaped through the security to interview me, but other press people were held back. A message was slipped to me that a newspaper woman from North Dakota who had known me in Mandan wanted to greet me but she was not allowed out of the press section. The atmosphere was sullen. There was none of the happy milling about, the going and coming that I remembered from other conventions. But I had done what I was supposed to do and it would be noted on television that I was there, loyal and hopeful as I was supposed to be.

I went to the luncheon arranged by the women's division of the Democratic National Committee and sat at the head table between pretty Eleanor McGovern and Mrs. Richard Hughes of New Jersey. Muriel Humphrey and I posed together, smiling for the photographers. We kept up the amiable in-group chitchat of political wives. "That Eleanor McGovern," said Mrs. Hughes whose recent dieting had been headline news, "I remember her at Atlantic City. She came to rehearse for the style show and kept saying that the size fives were slipping right off her. I said to my secretary, 'Let's drown her in the punch bowl.'" Yes, we all knew each other from other conventions, other times, and the supposition was that we would meet again in similar circumstances. I went from that luncheon to hear Jenny Moore and Maria Kavanagh tell of the brutality of the police moving through the lobby of the Hilton on the pretext of clearing it for some dignitary or other, knocking one of the young demonstrators down the stairs and then dragging him by his feet and clubbing him in the stomach.

And then to argue with the Secret Service. "Someone down there in the park is signaling to someone on the roof," I kept saying. "Come, look, you can see him." "Don't worry, Mrs. McCarthy," they answered reassuringly, "we're taking care of the senator, nothing will happen to the senator."

"But you don't understand," I said, "It isn't only the senator I'm worried about. What are they doing down there? What are they planning?"

They were smooth and discreet, but they never gave me an answer. Later, I was certain that there had been police on the roof or on the top floor and that they were signaling to plain clothesmen in the park. When objects supposedly thrown from the fifteenth floor were displayed later by the police as reason for invading our headquarters I remembered that signaling.

We had a family dinner in the main suite and it was interrupted by friends fleeing from the latest violent sweep of the police who drove the crowd back into the plate glass window of the Hilton coffee shop. The window broke under the pressure and bleeding fugitives were catapulted through shattered glass. Walter Ridder came in, shaken and white, and Gilbert Harrison of the *New Republic*, saying, "It's like the Nazis all over again. The man beside me was clubbed to the ground."

Austin, Gene's brother, came in. He had gone to help the battered refugees from the park who had been taken into our staff rooms for first aid. Austin was pale, too, dabbing at blood spots on his suit. "There was a medic there," he said, "a girl medic. Abbie, you wouldn't believe it. They clubbed her across the breasts. She was wearing her hospital coat and a red cross."

"I hate you," said Mary. "I hate all of you. You wouldn't pay attention to what was happening until it started happening to you and your friends." In a way she was right. It had taken us longer. It was much harder for us to believe what was happening. For the first time we knew what it was to be victims of government rather than to be protected by it. As one of the young staff girls said when the headquarters were raided, "I thought I must tell the police. But then I realized that these *are* the police."

I became frantic with worry. All one night I looked for Margaret. She and her friend, Janine Safer, also only thirteen, were nowhere to be found. The Secret Service were no longer taking any responsibility for the children, it seemed, but Gay kept repeating to me soothingly when I sent her repeatedly to see what she could find, "The Secret Service says they are sure she is in the hotel," and then, "They say she is with Michael."

"Gay," I said, at last frantically, almost hysterically, "why can't you understand? I don't want to know what they say, I want to know where Margaret is. Something terrible may have happened to her. Where is she? Where can I look for her?"

At four in the morning, Margaret and Janine came back. They had been in the park and had had difficulty getting back into the hotel. By that time the police were openly harassing the known McCarthy people. Gradually, but surely, we were being forced into the streets, figuratively if not literally.

On the night of the nominating speeches, when the children and I were dressed to go to the Amphitheater to hear Gene nominated by Governor Harold Hughes of Iowa, Julian Bond of Georgia, and John Kenneth Galbraith, the Secret Service came to our wing to tell us that they could not be responsible for our safety, that we could not go. "But why?" I asked. "The demonstrators won't hurt us. Look at all the people already there," I gestured toward the television screen. "Probably not the demonstrators," they said shamefacedly, "but they might provoke an incident—we just can't be responsible." They were saying, I thought in consternation, that they could not protect us from the Chicago police. We stayed then and watched on the screen. The galleries which had been kept sparsely filled all week by the security regulations now seemed open to all comers. They were crowded with men and women, wearing Daley buttons, carrying WE LOVE DALEY signs. Michael, who had been working on the teleprinter, went to the box to wait for us. He stood lost and confused when the box filled up with strangers bearing passes from Mayor Daley. (We heard later that one of them was Roy Cohn, famous as an aide of the "other" McCarthy.) Only the McCarthy workers inside the Amphitheater and a handful of other supporters had been able to squeeze into the galleries. The signs and the banners they had hoped to use in the demonstration were confiscated. But to the very end they did their best. They had a demonstration. They made chains of the daisy stickers and banners of the print-outs from the press machines and held them aloft and chanted and sang to the very last, creating the illusion of hope as they had learned to do along the way in the "children's crusade."

It was over at last, but not quite over. Hubert Humphrey called Gene in the morning to say, I think, that they would surely go on working together in the future as they had in the past. He asked Gene's advice about the vice presidency and Gene told him that Senator Edmund Muskie of Maine would be a good candidate. And Muriel Humphrey called to ask if she might come to visit me. We arranged to have coffee at eleven o'clock. Because I was fond of Muriel Humphrey and because I knew she was doing what she thought a wife must do, I did not want to be in a position of refusing to campaign with her, something I was sure she would ask me to do.

I gathered everyone together in the big living room—Janet Stein, Jenny Moore, Maria Kavanagh, Sue Safer, women from Gene's staff, my sisters, my sisters-in-law, Ellen and Margaret, Gene's sisters and sister-in-law, our nieces, some old friends from Minnesota. We were exhausted, nervous, and perversely giddy. "I just can't sit here," said Janet Stein. "I have to do something." I gave her the crewel work I had been working on sporadically all summer and she began to stab at it with the large gestures of the inexperienced needle-woman. Then Muriel arrived and I was introducing everyone, serving coffee, and keeping the conversation light. Inevitably, our talk turned to campaigning but we were able to keep it impersonal and reminiscent, for Muriel and I shared many memories.

"Do you remember the time we were two hours behind schedule in a coffee caravan," I asked, "and the highway policeman caught you for speeding just on the edge of town when everybody was waiting for us in the hotel?" She remembered and told the others how we used to stop to freshen and change dresses in the minuscule rest rooms of wayside gas stations before we entered the small towns as visiting VIPs. We all relaxed and the others began to discuss bits of campaigning. There was only one awkward moment when our daughter Mary came in unexpectedly, looked at the assemblage in surprise, said, "Oh my God," and left abruptly.

When at last Muriel said, "I'm going to need your help," I was able to accept it as a general statement and to answer brightly, "Oh, all these people here are wonderful campaigners." And to add sincerely, for it was true, "You won't need help, Muriel, you are a wonderful campaigner."

When she rose to go I followed her into the narrow hallway of the suite and, pulling her out of earshot of the Secret Service men, asked, "Muriel, can't you get Hubert to talk to Daley about calling off the police? This is a terrible situation—it's dividing the nation."

"Who tells Daley anything?" she answered ruefully, and then added, "But, anyway, these young people have to learn to accept majority rule. That's the democratic way."

We looked at each other across an unbridgeable gulf. What had democratic or majority rule to do with a locked convention, packed galleries, legitimate delegations gaveled into silence, delegates rushed off to police stations—what did it have to do with mayhem in the streets? I knew that the Humphreys did not understand what had happened.

That afternoon I went with Gene when he made his farewell speech to the McCarthy delegates in the Florentine Room of the Hilton. It was packed with weeping and cheering people. I sat on the platform with Harold Hughes, Julian Bond, and others as Gene made his speech, one of the finest he made that year. He reviewed the campaign briefly: "I think the country has passed a judgment on the war. Our failure here was not with the people, not with reference to our not having accomplished our purpose—because we did accomplish that. It was only that the judgment of the people could somehow not be put through the procedures of politics in 1968."

He continued: "We have not lost the fight on the issue. We have not lost in terms of the potential of the American system to respond in a time of need such as this. We have had a great victory to this point, one which should reassure us about the system itself."

But more importantly, he said, we have tested the people of the country. "I think that we can say we were willing to open the box and to see what America was. We have that kind of trust and that kind of confidence. And when we opened it, we found that the people of this nation were not wanting."

We were led out of the room through the hand-shaking, reaching, touching crowd, led by Jerry Eller and some of the young campaign staff. Suddenly, we found that they had led us to a smaller packed meeting room where people sat quietly, looking at us expectantly. "I didn't know that we were coming here," said Gene to me, half angrily, ready to believe that I had connived in this arrangement. We were facing the Minnesota delegation, most of whom were pledged to Humphrey, and who looked at us now, truculent and unhappy. I smiled at old familiar faces, one here, one there, drawing reluctant smiles in return; and I tried to reach across the intervening months to remember who was that? and that? On what side had they stood? Had the meeting been arranged by Eller and Miles Lord in the hope that Gene, stirred by old sympathies and old memories, would endorse Humphrey there? If so, they did not know their man. He spoke half bitterly, half jestingly of things that still rankled. Of the fact that he was held to be a man without compassion and without tears. "I still think you might have given me that half a delegate," he said, referring to some heavy-handed maneuver at the state convention. He ended with a paraphrase of his review of the campaign in the other room. We had tested the system, he said, and we have not found the people wanting. And then in the tepid applause the chairman was saying, "And now we will hear from that lady we all love so much, Abigail McCarthy." It was only political politeness on his part, but I tried to reach them, to tell them how they fitted into what had happened. One of the painful things about the year, I said—which *had* been a year of great adventure and widened experience—was the fact that we had not been able to get home to Minnesota as often as we would have wished; but we had taken Minnesota with us wherever we went. In New Hampshire, I said, we heard a great deal about issue politics and participatory democracy. But I had told them there that that was what we had learned in Minnesota twenty years ago. What Gene brought to the country this year, I said, was the best of what had become part of us in Minnesota and I was proud to be with him. As we left the room, Robert Lowell stopped me. "That was a good speech," he said, and I felt he was really seeing me for the first time. "That was a very good speech. Did you know you were going to give it?"

"No," I said, "but it was in my heart."

Gene went out then to the park over the protests of the Secret Service. They would not let me go with him, so from our floor I watched as he crossed Michigan Avenue; with a pang I saw his head with its thinning, silver-gray hair parting the crowd. We could hear his voice saluting the "government in exile" in the park and we could hear the derisive heckling fade as he went on. He said again what he had said so often, "So let us be prepared to make mistakes, if we must make them, on the side of trust rather than on the side of mistrust in our fellow men or in other peoples around the world. Let us be prepared to make mistakes on the side of hope instead of on the side of despair and fear, whether we look to the present or whether we look to the future . . . so let us go from here to do the thing we can do, and not worry about what we cannot do; here this afternoon to make the kind of commitment, as I made it to you and as you have made it to me." He was laying claim to the people in the park and leaving the campaign and the convention behind him.

That night the Chicago police took off their badges and raided the fifteenth floor, pulling sleeping young people out of their hotel rooms, beating them and brutally pushing them into elevators, taking them to the lobby in a travesty of arrest. There Richard Goodwin held the police at bay until Gene came and rescued them. The Humphrey suite was called for help, but the caller, Steve Cohen, was told that the Vice President could not be disturbed. It puzzles me to this day that so little was ever made—even in the Walker report—of this gross and unprecedented suspension of civil liberties. What presidential candidate in our history has had his staff submitted to such indignities?

Our idea had been to get everyone out of Chicago as soon as possible and the chartered Boeing 727 was scheduled to make two trips to Washington the next day. Gene and I were to go on the first trip and in the morning we started out planning to stop only for a short press conference in the hotel ballroom. We were a small group under the big chandeliers, and the press conference was soon over. I waited while Gene talked to the television people and then he came over to me to say that the television reporters had told him that his remaining staff was to be arrested as soon as he left the city. He thought he should wait until the plane came back but that I should go on with the children. I protested that I would like to stay with him, but he was adamant.

"After last night," he said, "anything could happen. You all must get out of here." When our dispirited little group reached the plane, we had to wait for the bus from the Hilton. They had had difficulty getting away. We were not sure why. I was sick because Michael was on the bus and I feared they might make him a special target if they knew who he was. The bus came finally and there was only one casualty among the group. Young Tom Saltonstall arrived looking faint and sick, his hand wrapped in his handkerchief. He had been in charge during the campaign of the taping of all of Gene's interviews and speeches and now, at the very last, he had run back into the hotel to pick up the tape of the press conference. As he came out, the policeman at the door had stopped him and said, "Are you one of the McCarthy staff?" and Tom had innocently said "Yes." The policeman quite deliberately held Tom's arm and slammed the door on

his hand. Tom kept telling me this over and over, obviously un-
believing, and in a slight state of shock.

"Welcome back to America," said the American Airlines pilot as
we touched down in Washington. A loyal band, a few hundred people with the familiar signs, was waiting. They were disappointed that
Gene was not with us. But they were still there a few hours later
when the plane returned the second time from Chicago, carrying the
last remnants of the staff and the news people who had traveled a
good deal with the campaign and could not bear to stay behind in
Chicago now. The last to come aboard in Chicago was Marya Mc-
Laughlin of CBS, and a great cheer went up as the pilot said, "We
are now leaving Prague."

At the house we waited for Gene, a little group drawn together
by the desire to make his homecoming with its inevitable let-down less
traumatic. Mary McGrory was there and Gertrude Cleary from Gene's
office. Michael and his friend Roberto Suro and our friend Pastor
John Schramm, the Lutheran minister who had campaigned Nebraska and Oregon. He just happened to drop by and I pressed him
to stay. We drank and we ate, saying the same things over and over
as tired and dispirited people do. The Secret Service men came to
say good-by. The one assigned to me was to go to the Muskies and
I told him that he would like them very much. Gene's agent, Ernie
Olsen, Charlie Callanan had told us, had asked not to be reassigned
to another candidate. I don't know if that was true. I had never
felt close to the Secret Service men but I kissed Ernie good-by.

Epilogue

Gene left our home in August of 1969. He had long since come to the conclusion that the concept of life-long fidelity and shared life come what may—"for richer, for poorer; for better, for worse, in sickness and in health until death do us part" to which we agreed in the church—was no longer valid. And many people today do find this —or any permanent commitment—an impossible ideal.

I do not regret that for thirty years, in the words of Simone de Beauvoir, "I spontaneously preferred another existence to my own." I think I am a much richer person for having shared that existence and because of the sharing that my own existence developed dimensions otherwise outside its scope. Nor do I see any sense in putting it all behind me as if it had not been, because, quite obviously, it is part of me.

Despite the fact that the campaign brought almost unbearable emotional strain and disaster to our family, I cannot wish that the campaign did not happen. Through it I crossed the barrier into the world of my children and of all the young people to whom this world really belongs. I see the world now as they see it. I feel a sense of surprise that it is so easy to lay aside what once were rocklike basic assumptions as I look at injustice in the fierce light of their outrage. But I do not wish to have crossed this barrier having brought nothing from the other side, as have so many older people in a kind of headlong rush to join the young. What I would like to bring with me is a sense of the past, its continuity in the present, and a sense of identity stemming from the past which enables each one of us to withstand the assault of change. I can only do that by examining my own past as I have begun to do in this book.

Index

RECOMMENDED BY THE NEW YORK TIMES. . .

KATHLEEN AND FRANK
by Christopher Isherwood   (01041, $1.25)

KATHLEEN AND FRANK is a love story—of a certain period and a certain place.

Their story is told through letters and Kathleen's diary with a connecting and elucidating—even revealing—commentary by Christopher Isherwood. And although he writes as a detached historian and appears (as he did in reality appear during the course of the story) as a minor third-person character, Christopher Isherwood believes that, perhaps, on closer examination, KATHLEEN AND FRANK will prove to be "chiefly about Christopher."

"A MASTERPIECE OF THE HEAD AND THE HEART."

—Glenway Westcott